Hermann Cohen

Hermann Cohen

Edited by
Samuel Moyn and
Robert S. Schine

WRITINGS ON

NEO-KANTIANISM AND

JEWISH PHILOSOPHY

Brandeis University Press

Waltham, Massachusetts

BRANDEIS UNIVERSITY PRESS

© 2021 by Samuel Moyn and Robert S. Schine

All rights reserved

Manufactured in the United States of America

Designed by Eric M. Brooks

Typeset in Albertina and Verlag by Passumpsic Publishing

For permission to reproduce any of the material in this book,
contact Brandeis University Press, 415 South Street, Waltham MA 02453;
or visit brandeis.edu/press

Library of Congress Cataloging-in-publishing Data

NAMES: Moyn, Samuel, editor. | Schine, Robert S., editor. | Cohen,
Hermann, 1842–1918. Works. Selections. English.

TITLE: Hermann Cohen: writings on neo-Kantianism and Jewish
philosophy / edited by Samuel Moyn and Robert S. Schine.

OTHER TITLES: Writings on neo-Kantianism and Jewish philosophy

DESCRIPTION: Waltham, Massachusetts: Brandeis University Press,
2021.

SERIES: The Brandeis Library of modern Jewish thought |
Includes index.

SUMMARY: "Hermann Cohen (1842–1918) was among the most
accomplished Jewish philosophers of modern times. This newly
translated collection of his writings illuminates his achievements
for student readers and rectifies lapses in his intellectual reception
by prior generations"—Provided by publisher.

IDENTIFIERS: LCCN 2021004461 (print) | LCCN 2021004462
(ebook) | ISBN 9781684580422 (cloth) | ISBN 9781684580439
(paperback) | ISBN 9781684580446 (ebook)

SUBJECTS: LCSH: Cohen, Hermann, 1842–1918. | Neo-Kantianism. |
Jewish philosophy.

CLASSIFICATION: LCC B3216.C74 H4825 2021 (print) | LCC B3216.C74
(ebook) | DDC 193—dc23

LC record available at https://lccn.loc.gov/2021004461

LC ebook record available at https://lccn.loc.gov/2021004462

5 4 3 2 1

Contents

Foreword

Hermann Cohen (1842–1918) was among the most accomplished Jewish philosophers in modern times, yet his work has not yet received the attention it deserves. Just as Moses Maimonides sought to recast medieval Jewish thought through the Islamic reception of Platonic and Aristotelian philosophy, Cohen leveraged his understanding of Immanuel Kant as the beacon of a modern philosophy of individual freedom, an idea that therefore should serve as the basis for a philosophy of Judaism. Moreover, Cohen asserted that Kantian ethics drew from the wellspring of Judaism, especially its prophetic sources. This volume presents three elements of Cohen's thought as entailing one another: the philosophy of Judaism, neo-Kantianism, and prophetically inspired commitments to social democracy and the dignity of all.

This new collection of Hermann Cohen's writings, most of which are appearing in English for the first time, illuminates his achievements for student readers and rectifies lapses in his intellectual reception by prior generations. It presents chapters from Cohen's earlier *Ethics of Pure Will* and essays connecting politics, Judaism, and philosophy. The volume also presents conflicting interpretations of Cohen by Franz Rosenzweig and Alexander Altmann. Ernst Cassirer's eulogy for Cohen delivered at his graveside also appears here for the first time in English. Containing full annotations and selections that concentrate on both the philosophical core of Cohen's neo-Kantian ethical writings and the politics of interpretation of his work at the time of his death and afterward, this anthology allows the reader to register anew the force of Cohen's achievement.

Eugene Sheppard and Samuel Moyn
Series Editors

Acknowledgments

Translating an anthology of texts by and about Hermann Cohen and presenting them to an English readership proved to be a task of special complexity, involving many people. We would like to acknowledge them here: Elias Sacks and Paul Nahme, who furnished preliminary drafts of several selections at the start of the project; Avi Bernstein-Nahar, who also helpfully participated at an early stage; and Michael Zank, one of today's leading Cohen scholars, who translated and annotated "Autonomy and Freedom." (Unless otherwise indicated, the selections were translated and annotated by Robert Schine, whose notes to the texts are bracketed. Notes without brackets are from the original.)

Robert would like to thank his research assistant Charles Cacciatore as well as several colleagues who offered counsel at various stages of the translation: Frederick Beiser, Dana Hollander, Marjorie Lamberti, Michael Zank, and in particular George Yaakov Kohler and Hartwig Wiedebach. George Kohler's invaluable critical comments led to numerous and substantive improvements in the translations and annotations. Much in this volume also draws on Hartwig Wiedebach's richly informative notes in the German critical edition of Cohen's writings and on his expertise, which he has generously shared. Robert and Sam would both like to thank our copyeditor, Jeanne Ferris, for her skillful and meticulous work, and both Sylvia Fried and Eugene Sheppard for having faith that this project would someday come to fruition.

Finally, Robert dedicates his share of this anthology to Rivi Handler-Spitz. Sam dedicates his contributions to this volume to Dina R. Berger and Paul S. Berger, his parents-in-law.

Samuel Moyn

Introduction

No thinker strove more mightily than Hermann Cohen (1842–1918) did to seek the compatibility of Judaism with the teachings of modern philosophy. Writing voluminously as a university professor in Germany (he was the first Jew to hold a chair in philosophy there), Cohen won justifiable fame for working throughout his career to reground and update the system of his philosophical inspiration, Immanuel Kant, while concerning himself with its relationship to Jewish thought.

Cohen's sometimes forbidding prose advanced an extraordinary intellectual project that made secular and Jewish thought indissociable. As Moses Maimonides had done for the Aristotelianism of the Middle Ages, Cohen saw Judaism as harmonious with the philosophy of his time—in Cohen's case, with Kant's call to bring philosophy beyond metaphysics in an age of human freedom. Yet Cohen also managed to interpret Judaism as one of the sources for Kant's venture. And Cohen believed that Kant's theory of human spontaneity as the foundation of ethics fulfilled the social vision of the Jewish prophets, leading to a moving program of ethical socialism for modern times.

In spite of its extraordinary significance, several events consigned Cohen's enterprise to near oblivion soon after his death shortly before the end of World War I. Existentialism, ascendant in secular and Jewish philosophy after that war, eclipsed Cohen's neo-Kantian vocation. And the reactionary victory of the Nazis shattered the "German-Jewish synthesis" that Cohen had once both defended and epitomized, even as it took Germany down a very different path than the humane socialist one of which Cohen had dreamed. Among Jews, Cohen's principled rejection of Zionist politics also marginalized him for much of the century following his death.

Yet at no time since the 1920s has interest among philosophers in Cohen's undertaking been greater than it is today. For students, this volume attempts to get closer to the core of his philosophical enterprise than the prior English-language collection of Cohen's writings, which dates from 1971. Cohen's monumental final work, *Religion of Reason out of the Sources of Judaism* (1919) first appeared in English in 1972, but until now no translations of the neo-Kantian philosophy from the height of his career have been available in English, making it difficult to appreciate Cohen's core project in conjunction with his Jewish philosophy.[1] And in part by placing the two side by side, our selections attempt to rescue Cohen from his dissident existentialist successors—above all, the famed German-Jewish thinker Franz Rosenzweig (1886–1929)—who have controlled his legacy for too long.

Cohen's texts are difficult, if not—as Ernst Cassirer (1874–1945), Cohen's leading student, described them in a lecture before the Oxford Jewish Society in 1935 —entirely "closed to a general understanding." Cohen's works, Cassirer added, "never could get any real popularity—and even the professional philosophers very often failed to overcome [their] difficulties."[2] Yet to assess Cohen without his neo-Kantian texts, or to read his Jewish writings without keeping in view aspects of the philosophical core of his enterprise, is to neglect one of the most impressive episodes of Jewish thought in modern times.

* * *

Cohen was born in Coswig, a small town on the Elbe River in the Duchy of Anhalt. His father was cantor at the small synagogue there and religious teacher for the town's handful of Jewish families. Cohen always returned home for holidays and to visit his parents, but at age eleven he moved ten miles to Dessau (the birthplace of Moses Mendelssohn, Cohen's predecessor in modernizing Jewish thought), where he spent four years in German high school.[3] At age fifteen, Cohen traveled to Breslau, a Silesian city in what is now Poland, where he studied at its renowned Jewish seminary. Under still unclear circumstances, however, Cohen interrupted his path to rabbinic ordination after four years and transferred to the town's German university, where he continued to focus on the classical philology that had already been his main interest in seminary. After a year in Berlin, Cohen finished his philosophical training in Halle, where he earned his doctorate in 1865. At that time, however, there was little sign of the commitment to Kant's philosophy that would mark Cohen's later life.

After five years in Berlin as a tutor and an associate of the founder of an early form of anthropology and sociology called *Völkerpsychologie* (folk psychology), Cohen published the book that made his early reputation, *Kant's Theory of Experience* (1871). It was because of the enthusiasm for this book from one of the era's leading philosophers, Friedrich Albert Lange, that Cohen won the position at the University of Marburg, where Lange taught, that defined his long career. *Kant's Theory of Experience* was epoch-making in the history of the rise of the broader neo-Kantian movement in German philosophy, of which Cohen was the leading exponent for decades. He became Lange's formal successor in 1876, teaching for forty years in the Hessian university town.

Kant's memory had fallen on hard times in German lands in the mid-nineteenth century, not least because of his apparent supersession by G. W. F. Hegel (1770–1831), whose philosophical legacy dominated the era (though Cohen resisted it from the first). The point is not that Cohen rediscovered Kant. The beginnings of neo-Kantianism are traditionally dated to the publication of Otto Liebmann's *Kant and the Epigones* (1865), and Cohen's initial interventions tried to resolve a heated dispute between Kuno Fischer and Adolf Trendelenburg, who proposed different readings of the epistemology of the Enlightenment thinker.[4] But Cohen's *Kant's Theory of Experience* argued not only for a general reclamation of its title thinker but also for a "critical idealism," with which Cohen and his students were associated ever afterward.[5]

Kant's transcendental idealism, especially in his *Critique of Pure Reason* (1781), is an account of the necessary conditions for the possibility of human knowledge. Cohen reclaimed Kant not as a protopsychologist (as he had frequently been read earlier in the nineteenth century), but as a philosopher of the validity of knowledge. Like other neo-Kantians, Cohen did so in an age of the ascendancy of natural science. And with other neo-Kantians, Cohen's intent was to attack a reigning materialism to insist that only an idealism in Kant's lineage could furnish the epistemological foundation that natural science, like all knowledge, requires.

Kant proposed that human beings do not just passively receive sense impressions of a world that is really out there. We can know that world of things-in-themselves only as appearances, and therefore by means of what we bring to them—that is, as we represent them. This focus on representation is what made Kant's epistemology idealistic, but it was a transcendental idealism because it focused on the conditions for the possibility of knowing anything empirically. This was anthropocentric—Kant called his move a "Copernican revolution" in thought—but neither relativistic nor subjectivist, for the transcendental conditions of knowing are universal for human beings. Furthermore, Kant's transcendental idealism even allowed for justifying scientific laws as necessarily true claims about the world as we know it.

Cohen's restoration of Kant's transcendental project was important, but even more so was his interpretation of that project. In some of the most famous sections in the *Critique of Pure Reason*, Kant proposed that space and time are among the a priori and necessary conditions of the possibility of knowing. In turn,

Fischer and Trendelenburg almost came to blows over whether Kant meant to rule out the possibility that things-in-themselves were also spatial and temporal, given that the appearances are necessarily represented in space and time. Cohen's masterstroke was to propose that the question was badly framed.

The entire purpose of Kant's philosophy, according to Cohen, was to restrict the theory of knowledge to what we can know, rather than pursuing "dogmatic" or metaphysical claims about things we cannot. Indeed, the radicalism of Cohen's approach was to suggest that the very concept of things-in-themselves was illegitimate. Its function was not ontological but methodological, aimed not at better grasping the nonhuman world but at improving human knowledge and allowing for its further progress. It was not as if modern philosophy could suppose that knowledge matches some reality beyond the bounds of sense to which the human mind regrettably does not have unmediated access. Rather, Kant's revolutionary outlook was that epistemology must be a theory of human knowledge and nothing else.

*　　*　　*

This approach, especially if it unmoored philosophy from what humans cannot know, put in question what traditional religious commitments could justifiably look like in general—and Cohen's commitment to Judaism in particular. Kant had famously claimed that he had "limited reason to make room for faith," but the question of how the resulting faith would resemble religious traditions of the past haunted his project. Cohen was never troubled by this question, living his whole life as an observant Jew and always confident that he could reconcile Judaism and Kant's philosophy—and he even saw his Judaism as the source of that confidence. At the same time, he was aware from an early age that Kantianism ruled out most traditional understandings of religion, starting with the idea that the Bible is God's word, and it is equally possible to interpret Cohen's career as an apologetic quest to refashion Judaism in the name of fidelity to it. And as Cohen put it at the end of his career, "It is a question whether such reshaping is not the best form of annihilation."[6]

While a young professor in 1875, Cohen was shocked by the birth of modern political antisemitism, and he participated in the Berlin controversy around antisemitism kicked off by the historian Heinrich von Treitschke's public worry that the Jews were bad for the German people. It was not for nothing that a youthful Leo Strauss could call Cohen in 1925 "the greatest German Jew of his generation from within German Judaism and in the interest of German Judaism."[7] Across Cohen's long career, notably in his famous (or notorious) World War I essays and pamphlet on "Germanism and Judaism" (*Deutschtum und Judentum*), he assumed that Jews were Germans and that the latter owed Judaism a great deal for the remarkable civilization they were achieving. Indeed, Cohen argued throughout his career not against German nationalism but for a cosmopolitan form of it in which Jews could participate with pride, out of loyalty to universal principles. (Cohen opposed Zionism for the same reason: it localized in one homeland what Jews brought to world politics in their different lands.) Then, in 1888, Cohen participated in the libel trial against a local antisemite who had alleged that the Talmud commanded Jews to be duplicitous toward their neighbors. Cohen contended that love of strangers is central to Jewish monotheism, with weighty consequences for the history of Western life.

For Kant, a move from epistemology to ethics had led to his most direct reconsideration of what role the idea of God played in philosophy as well as to the elaboration of his version of an Enlightenment rational religion. It was the same for Cohen, who published his second study of his predecessor, *Kant's Grounding of Ethics*, in 1877. In his introduction, Cohen announced his hope to be more Kantian when it came to ethics than Kant himself had been. This would remain true when, in 1904, Cohen published his own system of ethics, *Ethics of Pure Will* —important excerpts of which (from the second edition of 1907) this volume presents in English for the first time.

In his *Groundwork of the Metaphysics of Morals* (1785) and *Critique of Practical Reason* (1788), Kant had been concerned with justifying morality. After proving its basis in autonomous self-legislation and outlining its content as conforming to a universalization test and respect for the dignity of humanity, Kant struggled with what to say about the fact that human freedom—if it existed—was not knowable in the realm of appearances, though it was a necessary premise for action. In the spirit of his critical idealism, Cohen's goal was an ethics that did not need such a struggle. He hoped instead to derive the validity of ethics in just the way Kant had shown that space and time were necessary conditions of experience. Cohen applied the transcendental method of Kant's *Critique of Pure Reason* to ethics, which Kant had treated in another way. This was the reason why Cohen's study of ethics bore a title that matched Kant's original classic, promising an ethics of "pure will."

But there was one point on which Cohen followed Kant's ethics carefully and attempted to redeem it. In both his 1877 and 1904 ethical works, Cohen devoted special care to reconstructing and rehabilitating one of Kant's most contentious arguments, reclaiming the idea of God for modern philosophy. Cohen agreed with Kant that the premodern attempt to prove God's existence had run aground. But both thinkers argued that the idea of God was a way of filling what Cohen called a gap that threatened not only his ethics but his entire system of thinking. Even in a system that bases ethics on good intentions, I am practically committed to the possibility of the practical success of my actions, in the same way that when I send a message, I trust that it can arrive. For Cohen, that commitment to the realizability of ethics in practice is what the idea of God guarantees, ensuring a connection between nature and ethics. To the objection that the God of Abraham, Isaac, and Jacob is very different for believers than the God of the philosophers, who is less encountered or experienced than inferred or postulated, Cohen is said to have responded unrepentantly. To the question of how one can love God as an idea, Cohen replied with a disarming rhetorical question of his own: "How is it possible to love anything besides an idea?"[8]

In *Ethics of Pure Will*, Cohen offered a reductionist account of religion as ethics. In his own time, Kant had boldly affirmed that "even the Holy One of the Bible must first be compared with our ideal of moral perfection before he is cognized as such."[9] Similarly, as late as his 1904 study Cohen equated religion and ethics, as if the first were nothing more than an inadequately justified version of the second. There were even signs that Cohen hoped that ethics would displace religion entirely, leading to "the end of religion."[10] Religion did not necessarily conflict with ethics, though it could—especially in its sectarian and violent forms. Religion could even provide a beautiful anticipation of ethical relations without the justification for them that philosophy alone could supply. But it was reasonable to wonder how Judaism could survive such statements, especially since Cohen made almost no reference to it in *Ethics of Pure Will* even while reassuring the Frankfurt Lodge of the B'nai B'rith that the book demonstrated "the meaning of Judaism within a philosophical system."[11]

There is agreement that Cohen's views shifted substantially in the final decade of his life, though controversy has raged about precisely how much and in what ways. Because of his reduction of religion to ethics in this phase, Cohen has been dogged by the suggestion that he refashioned Judaism in the image of progressive Protestantism.[12] But in his interim study, *The Concept of Religion in the System of Philosophy* (1915), Cohen gestured toward a limit in philosophy to be overcome by religion. It might make the latter indispensable, or at least useful, in a way that Cohen had not acknowledged before. And in his posthumous *Religion of Reason*, Cohen indicated religion's importance in the individuation of people.

It is clear that—rhetorically, at least—Cohen granted religion far more than the status of a kind of redundancy once a full-fledged philosophical ethics existed. And he also shifted his views about the relations of Judaism and Christianity to one another. Throughout his career, furthermore, Cohen spent far more time reinterpreting the traditional doctrines of Judaism than his prediction of the obsolescence of religion could explain.

* * *

After beginning with *Ethics of Pure Will*, this volume turns to some of Cohen's engagements with Jewish tradition. For whether as a propaedeutic for ethics or as a supplement to them, there is no doubt that Cohen found interest and solace in interpreting those sources. These engagements with Jewish tradition occurred alongside his intermittent encounters with some of its greatest thinkers, such as Maimonides and Benedict Spinoza (whose pantheism Cohen ultimately rejected). The essays reach the heart of Cohen's characteristic integration of Judaism into Western civilization, in associating the Jewish past with the trajectory of philosophical idealism from its Platonic origins to Kant's modern rendition.

Throughout his career, including in his touchstone essay on Plato and the prophets, Cohen credited the founder of Western philosophy with the impulse to certify and secure knowledge (*Wissenschaft*) that Kant made modern in his discovery of a transcendental form of idealism. But Plato lacked the idea of universal humanity, especially the notion of its perfectibility in history. What was equally significant for Cohen, therefore, was that the Jewish prophets—while by no means philosophers and thus unable to validate ethics—made an indispensable contribution to the social good that ethics demands. In a sense, the prophets recognized love as its own form of knowledge, and—unlike Plato's fellow Greeks—oriented ethics not to heroism and valor but to the elimination of the suffering that can occur in human history. In this way, the prophetic sources of Judaism made it a precious resource in the history of Western civilization and—as Cohen eventually acknowledged—for any secular ethics. To play on a Kantian saying, without idealism, ethics is blind, but without the prophetic call for social justice, it is empty. Athens needed Jerusalem, and vice versa.

Gershom Scholem, a German Jew who became perhaps the greatest scholar of Jewish mystical traditions, referred to Cohen in an obituary as one of the "great men" given to the Jews who "carry with them the essence of the ancient prophets."[13] Daringly, Cohen not only insisted that prophetic social ideals needed Platonism (and vice versa), but that those ideals also helped pave the way for Kant's theoretical and ethical project. Ironically, Kant had been acerbic about Judaism, repeating the Christian accusation that it amounted to no more than a superannuated dry legalism (equally ironically, such charges were also later made against Kant's thought). Unfortunately, Cohen remarked, Kant had been ignorant of the significance of the Jewish prophetic tradition; and in any event, Kant's desire to reinvent his Protestant legacy could not mask the concordance of his thought with the universal Jewish contribution to civilization. Furthermore, after the prophets, Jews insisted that their ethics were rationally defensible, just as Kant did in bringing about modern philosophy. Not only did Kant call for an ethical theory that recapitulated Judaism's original defense of obligation as grounded in freedom—and its approach to the divine—but his vision of a cosmopolitan plan for humanity also matched Judaism's messianism oriented toward suffering.[14] Cohen struggled passionately to establish that his neo-Kantianism and his Judaism overlapped so substantially in their teachings.

Though he wrote no freestanding works of political theory, Cohen's politics were in the vein of ethical and parliamentary socialism. Notwithstanding his patriotic allegiance to the German side in World War I, for which he propagandized, Cohen repudiated romantic nationalism. He lived through the economic tumult of the late nineteenth century and warned against ethnonationalism as a scapegoating response to it. Instead, Cohen argued for high taxation and worker representation, as well as supporting reforms to make schools religiously neutral and class-blind.[15] He had a significant impact on the development of a non-Marxist socialism, including on the "evolutionary socialism" of the social democratic theoretician Eduard Bernstein (1850–1932), who followed Cohen in proposing to base a parliamentary movement on Kantian principles.

Cohen may not have been representative of German Jewry in his socialism, but he voiced an exemplary confidence among German Jews in a universalistic understanding of both German nationalism and the Jewish faith, which made him skeptical of the Zionist politics that emerged in Europe during his lifetime. In 1916, two years before his death, Cohen was embroiled in a controversy with the charismatic Zionist theoretician Martin Buber (1878–1965), who equally claimed the authority of the prophets but whom (among other errors) Cohen accused of disregarding the fact that Jews had done more than any people to contribute to world affairs.[16]

*　*　*

Cohen passed away in April 1918, before World War I was formally concluded. After retiring, he had moved to Berlin, where he taught at a Jewish institute called the Lehranstalt für die Wissenschaft des Judentums. Almost immediately after his death, a dispute broke out about his legacy, centered on the meaning of his final writings. And in part because the philosophical fortunes of Cohen's project were so disastrous in the following decades, the wrong side may well have won. The intent of the third part of the selections in this book is to allow an assessment of whether it is time, as a number of contemporary scholars have argued, to reconsider the marginalization of Cohen's neo-Kantianism in the way in which his work is read. In particular, whether or not Cohen's project deserves to be surpassed in philosophical or political terms, it is common to believe that Cohen himself had overthrown it out of an aspiration to give way to a new form of thinking. The final texts in this volume suggest that this assumption is partisan and troubling.

"Don't you think that today we have seen a prophet die?" So Ernst Cassirer's wife, Toni, asked him, after Cohen's final hours.[17] Cohen had hoped that Cassirer would succeed him in his Marburg philosophical chair, but Cassirer's appointment was blocked—much to Cohen's consternation. At Cohen's funeral, three days after his death, Cassirer delivered an absorbing eulogy that celebrated his teacher and friend. While Cassirer reported that he had just begun to digest Cohen's posthumous work on religion, he strikingly affirmed the continuity of Cohen's career—and, indeed, the unity of the project of Marburg neo-Kantianism that Cassirer attempted to take forward. As the title and much of the substance of Cohen's last book implied, his allegiance to a religion of reason never wavered, while his personal compassion and piety were merely the embodied and individual side of his abstract commitments to rationalism.

If this view did not fare well in the following years, in general or Jewish philosophy, it was in part because of the coming of existentialism. In that movement, Rosenzweig—who knew Cohen intimately in his final years—was the most notable Jewish participant. Serving the German Empire as a soldier at the front in April 1918, Rosenzweig reflected right away on the very different Cohen he had come to know, who seemed—Rosenzweig claimed—to depart surreptitiously from the premises of the system he had laboriously constructed.[18] In a classic and enormously influential introduction to the compilation of Cohen's Jewish writings in 1924, Rosenzweig pursued this interpretation at length. Extrapolating clear innovations in Cohen's thought into full-fledged transformations and citing personal communications, Rosenzweig made the provocative case that the neo-Kantian system collapsed of itself to give rise to the Jewish existentialism that Rosenzweig advocated.[19] In question is not just the legitimacy of the teleological reading according to which, as Strauss commented in 1925, "Rosenzweig understands Cohen's development from its end."[20] Also in question is whether its end strayed very far from its beginning and middle.

Though this volume does not provide all the materials needed to decide these questions, it provides Rosenzweig's interpretation in English for the first time, to be read in relation to the neo-Kantian core of Cohen's ethics and to Alexander Altmann's 1962 counterargument, likewise presented in English for the first time. Regardless, there is no doubt that after World War I, Cohen quickly came to be seen as a figure of the past. The appeal of his project waned, not only in Rosenzweig's filial appropriation but also in the siege that other existentialist philosophers such as Martin Heidegger brought to the neo-Kantian citadel. The same reversal of fortune that existentialism wrought philosophically occurred even more drastically in politics, which saw Germany and Europe stray so far from Cohen's ethical vision in practice that many later took that vision to be irretrievable—even before the Nazis put Martha Lewandowski Cohen, whom the philosopher had married in 1878, to death in 1942. (She died of severe malnutrition in Theresienstadt, the Nazi camp.)

Of course, a philosophical idealist in the tradition of Plato and Kant would be the first to insist that history provides no final verdict on morality. And contemporary philosophers—both in their reading of Kant and in their return to his thought—testify to the viability of a kind of project much like Cohen's. It is our hope that this volume will assist in the contemporary reassessment of Cohen, who may be not just a historic master thinker of forgotten secular and Jewish traditions, but a model for future endeavors in both.

Notes

1. The prior English-language collection, restricted to Jewish writings, is Hermann Cohen, *Reason and Hope: Selections from the Jewish Writings of Hermann Cohen*, trans. Eva Jospe (New York: W. W. Norton, 1971). The last book is Cohen, *Religion of Reason out of the Sources of Judaism*, trans. Simon Kaplan, 2nd ed. with new introductions by Steven S. Schwarzschild and Kenneth Seeskin (New York: Atlanta, GA: Scholars Press, 1995). For translations of individual books and pamphlets (mostly oriented to Cohen's place in Jewish philosophy), see the Suggestions for Further Reading, which also lists the English-language secondary literature.

2. Ernst Cassirer, "Cohen's Philosophy of Religion," *Internationale Zeitschrift für Philosophie* 1996, no. 1 (1996): 91.

3. I follow Frederick C. Beiser's magnificent *Hermann Cohen: An Intellectual Biography* (Oxford: Oxford University Press, 2018).

4. A classic statement is Ernst Cassirer, "Hermann Cohen and the Renewal of Kantian Philosophy," trans. Lydia Patton, *Angelaki* 10, no. 1 (April 2005): 95–108. The standard literature in English on neo-Kantianism includes Thomas C. Willey, *Back to Kant: The Revival of Kantianism in German Social and Historical Thought, 1860–1914* (Detroit, MI: Wayne State University Press, 1978); Klaus Christian Köhnke, *The Rise of Neo-Kantianism: German Academic Philosophy between Idealism and Positivism*, trans. R. J. Hollingdale (Cambridge: Cambridge University Press, 1991); Frederick C. Beiser, *The Genesis of Neo-Kantianism* (Oxford: Oxford University Press, 2014). See also Manfred Kühn, "Interpreting Kant Correctly: On the Kant of the Neo-Kantians," in *Neo-Kantianism in Contemporary Philosophy*, ed. Rudolf Makkreel and Sebastian Luft (Bloomington: Indiana University Press, 2010).

5. For a brief excerpt from *Kant's Theory of Experience* in English, see Hermann Cohen, "The Synthetic Principles," in *The Neo-Kantian Reader*, ed. Sebastian Luft (New York: Routledge, 2015), 107–16.

6. Cited in Leo Strauss, preface to Leo Strauss, *Spinoza's Critique of Religion*, trans. E. M. Sinclair (New York: Schocken, 1965), 24–25.

7. Leo Strauss, review of Hermann Cohen, *Jüdische Schriften*, in *Jüdische Wochenzeitung für Cassel, Hessen, und Waldeck* 2, no. 18 (May 8, 1925), in Leo Strauss, "More Early Writings," *Interpretation* 39, no. 2 (Spring 2012): 118. See also Steven S. Schwarzschild, "'Germanism and Judaism': Hermann Cohen's Normative Paradigm of the German-Jewish Symbiosis (1979)," in Steven S. Schwarzschild, *The Tragedy of Optimism: Writings on Hermann Cohen*, ed. George Y. Kohler (Albany: SUNY Press, 2018), 93–118; Jacques Derrida, "Interpretations at War: Kant, the Jew, the German," trans. Moshe Ron, *New Literary History* 22, no. 1 (Winter 1991): 39–95.

8. Cohen, *Religion of Reason*, 160.

9. Immanuel Kant, *Groundwork of the Metaphysics of Morals*, trans. Mary Gregor (Cambridge: Cambridge University Press, 1997), 21.

10. Hermann Cohen, *Ethik des reinen Willens*, in *Werke*, 7:586.

11. Hermann Cohen to the Frankfurt Lodge, December 11, 1904, in Hermann Cohen, *Briefe*, ed. Bruno Strauss and Bertha Badt-Strauss (Berlin: Schocken, 1939), 71.

12. See, for example, Leora Batnitzky, *How Judaism Became a Religion* (Princeton, NJ: Princeton University Press, 2011), 53; David N. Myers, "Hermann Cohen and the Quest for Protestant Judaism," *Leo Baeck Institute Year Book* 46 (2001): 195–212.

13. Gershom Scholem, "In Memory of Hermann Cohen," trans. Sander Gilman, *Modern Judaism* 5, no. 1 (February 1985): 1.

14. For more on this theme, see Andrea Poma, "Suffering and Non-Eschatological Messianism in Hermann Cohen's Ethics," in Andrea Poma, *Yearning for Form and Other Essays on Hermann Cohen's Thought* (Dordrecht, the Netherlands: Springer, 2006), 243–60.

15. This topic, neglected in Anglophone scholarship, has best been surveyed in Hermann Lübbe, *Politische Philosophie in Deutschland: Studien zu ihrer Geschichte* (Basel, Switzerland: Benno Schwabe, 1963), part 2. On school reform, see selection 3.

16. The main texts of the debate are translated in Martin Buber and Hermann Cohen, "Martin Buber and Hermann Cohen: A Debate on Zionism and Messianism," in *The Jew in the Modern World: A Documentary History*, ed. Paul Mendes-Flohr and Jehuda Reinharz, 2nd ed. (New York: Oxford University Press, 1995), 571–77.

17. Cited in Pierre Bouretz, *Witnesses for the Future: Philosophy and Messianism*, trans. Michael B. Smith (Baltimore, MD: Johns Hopkins University Press, 2010), 722n5.

18. Franz Rosenzweig, "Der Dozent: Eine persönliche Erinnerung," *Neue jüdische Monatshefte*, May 10, 1918, 376–78.

19. On the personal communications, see Steven S. Schwarzschild, "Franz Rosenzweig's Anecdotes about Hermann Cohen (1970)," in Schwarzschild, *The Tragedy of Optimism*, 35–42. For excellent examples of the more proleptic reading, see Bouretz, *Witnesses for the Future*; Peter Eli Gordon, *Rosenzweig and Heidegger: Between Judaism and German Philosophy* (Berkeley: University of California Press, 2003).

20. Strauss, review, 125.

Robert S. Schine

A Note on Terms

These translations seek to render a selection of terminologically difficult texts accessible to contemporary students of German-Jewish history and philosophy of religion. The brief guide to philosophical terms presented here is arranged not alphabetically but topically and is intended to smooth the reader's path into the texts.

Wissenschaft

The closest English equivalent of the term *Wissenschaft* (pl.: *Wissenschaften*) is "science," but in English "science" and "scientific" refer only to the natural and social sciences. The German term has a much more capacious semantic field, encompassing not only the natural and social sciences (*Naturwissenschaften* and *Sozialwissenschaften*) but also the humanities (*Geisteswissenschaften*). In a general sense, then, *Wissenschaft* is the systematic pursuit of knowledge (*Wissen*), a way of seeking knowledge with methodological rigor. It can thus apply to any discipline and to the collective of all disciplines. Cohen's Marburg School was concerned with the methodological grounding of all divisions of knowledge (*Wissenschaften*) within a system of knowledge in general (*Wissenschaft* and even *Gesamtwissenschaft*). In this volume, the term *Wissenschaft* is rendered variously as "science," "discipline," "systematic knowledge," "academic study," or "methodological, systematic, or philosophical discipline." Its adjectival form, *wissenschaftlich*, is translated "scientific" or "systematic." All of these terms point toward the idea and ideal of systematic knowledge, or *Wissenschaft*.

Wissen and *Erkenntnis*

Whereas *Wissen*—the noun form of the verb *wissen*, meaning "to know"—is unambiguous and means "knowledge," German also has a more equivocal noun: *Erkenntnis*, formed from the verb *erkennen*. The simple verb *kennen* also means "to know," whereas *erkennen* has a reflexive element: "to make oneself know" and then "to recognize." The noun *Erkenntnis*, accordingly, can refer not just to the product of knowing (knowledge) but also to the process of knowing. In such cases it is translated as "cognition," as in the title of Cohen's *Logik der reinen Erkenntnis* (*Logic of Pure Cognition*) or paraphrased in a way that hints at the process of knowing or acquiring knowledge. The reader should be aware that "cognition" always refers to *Erkenntnis*, whereas "knowledge" may represent either *Wissen* or *Erkenntnis*.

Geist and *geistig*

Geist and its adjectival derivative *geistig* also sparkle with ambiguity. *Geist* may mean "spirit," "mind," or "intellect" (which explains the two English titles under which Hegel's main work circulates in English, *The Phenomenology of Spirit* and *The Phenomenology of Mind*). As we saw above, the humanities, in German, are conceived of as the sciences of the spirit or mind—that is, the sciences of the *Geist*, or the *Geisteswissenschaften*.

Ethik and *Sittlichkeit*

Following Kant's critiques, Cohen delineates three divisions of consciousness: logic, ethics, and aesthetics. Instead of divisions, Cohen uses the more dynamic term *Richtungen des Bewusstseins*—translated here as either "directions" or "trajectories of consciousness." The term "ethics" in English indicates its cognate *Ethik* in the original, a philosophical discipline (a *Wissenschaft*). German, however, also has the term *Sittlichkeit*, an abstract form based on the noun *Sitte* (meaning "usage," "custom," or "moral"). Although other interpreters of Cohen have rendered the term with the more concrete "ethical life," it is rendered here as "morality." The reader should not be misled: "morality," though also an abstract noun, is not identical to "ethics" as the philosophical discipline whose subject matter is moral (or ethical) life. Just as the laws of nature are the subject matter of the natural sciences, the laws of lived morality are the stuff of ethics—which is thus, in turn, a kind of knowledge. (This theme is one of the main topics of the introduction to *Ethics of Pure Will* [selection 1] and returns in selection 4. To be sure, the reader should be aware that occasionally—for example, in Cohen's discussion of the Ethical Culture movement—*sittlich* and *ethisch* are virtually synonymous and thus might be translated "moral" or "ethical.")

The *Eigenart* of religion

The question of the place of religion in his system preoccupies Cohen, as is evident in the essay on "Autonomy and Freedom" (selection 6) and emerges as a focal point in *The Concept of Religion in the System of Philosophy* (1915). Religion is not a distinct trajectory of consciousness. Cohen gives it special status:

it has its *Eigenart*, a term that signals religion's resistance to easy alignment in Cohen's system and that I translate variously as religion's own "particular character," "particular characteristic" or "particular form."

Individual, plurality, and totality

This trio of concepts was introduced by Cohen in his *Logic of Pure Cognition* and has a pivotal role in his moral vision, the individual (*der Einzelne* or *Individuum*), plurality (*Mehrheit*), and totality (*Allheit*).[1] These concepts denote a progression of stages of moral involvement, from the individual to an association or collection of individuals (a plurality) and then to a unity of individuals, the *Allheit* or totality, which culminates ultimately in the highest form of totality, the unity of humanity altogether. The progression is essential to understanding what, according to Cohen, it means to be human. The concept of the individual means not the individual in isolation, but the individual who can be realized only as a member of a group that is directed toward a moral purpose. Examples are associations; cooperatives (*Genossenschaften*); trade unions; and, most significantly, the state. Any such association of human beings is what Cohen calls a plurality (*Mehrheit*). It sounds as peculiar in German as it does in English, for the term *Mehrheit* connotes either plurality or majority and is usually associated with the mathematics of elections. In Cohen's ethical thought, however, when a plurality as a union of individuals contributes toward the realization of the social good, it is an *Allheit*, or totality. These terms thus bring mathematical and logical abstraction to his conception of the expanding horizons of moral concern, from I (the individual), to more (*mehr*) than one individual united in a plurality, and finally to the all (*All*) in which the human being is fulfilled. Admittedly, however, "totality" is not an adequate translation of *Allheit*, for *Allheit* does not signify a mathematical sum, and certainly not a total or sum of individuals. Cohen cautions explicitly against such a misunderstanding in his *Logic*.[2] It is a logical term that points toward an ideal whole. The confusion is amplified by the fact that Kant also deploys the term "totality" (*Totalität*) in connection with the ideals of pure reason. In addition, Hegel uses *Allheit*, and English translators of both Hegel and Cohen (in the case of the latter, starting with Simon Kaplan's 1972 translation of *Religion of Reason*) render *Allheit* as "totality." We have, then, a terminological tangle, but can say this much: in Cohen's *Ethics*, "totality" points toward an ideal unity. All possible moral acts are pointed toward "the whole" and turned toward the one unified goal, for which reason Cohen also uses the Latin *universitas* in his *Ethics* ("*Universität*," which in this case does not mean "university"). *Allheit* or "totality" is thus, as Cohen's use of the Latin term demonstrates, a turning toward unity, signifying an ideal that can be thought but is neither an abstraction nor an object that can be known. The reader is forewarned: "totality" is a misleading translation, but is the best available. The concept is the key by which Cohen, in his magnum opus,[3] expands the moral horizon from the "next man (*Nebenmensch*), or the human being in a plurality, to the fellow man (*Mitmensch*), integrated finally into the unity, or the whole of humankind—in Cohen's religious language, into the unity and peace of the messianic age.

Notes

1. For a helpful discussion of these terms, see Frederick C Beiser, *Hermann Cohen: An Intellectual Biography* (Oxford: Oxford University Press, 2018), 229. A summary explanation of the terms "plurality" and "totality," is also found in Andrea Poma, *The Critical Philosophy of Hermann Cohen*, trans. John Denton (Albany: SUNY Press, 1997), 121–24. Note that for "totality," Poma's translator uses the misleading abstraction "universality." In Cohen's *Ethics of Pure Will*, the terms come into play in the introduction (selection 1, 5–6).

2. On totality, see *LrE*, 205–6.

3. *RR*, 113–15. See also ibid., 15n.

Abbreviations

BR   *Der Begriff der Religion im System der Philosophie*. Giessen, Germany: Töpelmann, 1915. *Werke*, vol. 10.

ErW   *Ethik des reinen Willens*. 2nd ed. Berlin: Bruno Cassirer, 1907. *Werke*, vol. 7.

JS   *Jüdische Schriften*. 3 vols. Edited by Bruno Strauss. Berlin: C. A. Schwetschke und Sohn, 1924.

LrE   *Logik der reinen Erkenntnis*. 2nd ed. Berlin: Bruno Cassirer, 1914. *Werke*, vol. 6.

RR   *Religion of Reason out of the Sources of Judaism*. Translated by Simon Kaplan. 2nd ed. with new introductions by Steven S. Schwarzschild and Kenneth Seeskin. Atlanta, GA: Scholars Press, 1995.

RV   *Religion der Vernunft aus den Quellen des Judentums*. 2nd ed. Frankfurt am Main: Kauffmann, 1929.

Werke   Cohen, Hermann. *Werke*. Edited by Helmut Holzhey. Hildesheim, Germany: Georg Olms, 1977– . (This is the critical edition of the works of Hermann Cohen, under the general editorship of Helmut Holzhey. As of this writing, fourteen of the planned seventeen regular volumes have been published, along with two supplemental volumes.)

1 | Ethics of Pure Will (1907)

Prefatory Note to Selections 1 and 2

After writing a trilogy that commented at book length on each of Immanuel Kant's three critiques, Hermann Cohen embarked on his own version of each. This section presents the introduction and one chapter of his *Ethics of Pure Will* (2nd ed., 1907). Though demanding, the selection is an indispensable text for coming to grips with Cohen's neo-Kantian and neo-Platonic philosophical project and connecting it with modern Jewish thought—even if Cohen did not do so in the text.

Cohen's introduction, selection 1 in this book, is nothing if not methodically organized. After demarcating the subject matter, which implicates not only individual choice and conduct but also—from the beginning—a plurality of individuals and indeed the totality of human beings, Cohen rescues ethics from reductive anthropological and psychological approaches. Because these two understandings of human beings reduce ethics to the behavior of nonhuman animals, neither reckons with the soul that Plato discovered. Nor does either reach the necessity of obligation that Kant rightly insisted must make ethics a matter not of the contingent facts of the human constitution, but of the necessity of rational justification. Cohen's critique of philosophical naturalism (which he applies to Darwinism, as in selection 2) remains relevant in our time. It outlines a theory of ethics centered on human beings as normative creatures who can govern themselves in political states.

In the remainder of the introduction, Cohen goes to great length to insist on the importance of defining ethics as a matter of pure practical reason. Ethics presupposes logic (to which Cohen had devoted the first volume of his trilogy, the *Logic of Pure Cognition* [1902]). And Cohen's ethics differs from materialism—including the historical materialism of some political socialists —as well as sociology. Equally important, Cohen insists that ethics sets the terms of religion and theology, arguing that the latter cannot be concerned with the otherworldly but instead must recapitulate our ethical obligations. Finally, in a controversial argument, Cohen claims that jurisprudence, which is concerned with action, is of special value to ethics, serving as a method-ological analogy. It plays approximately the same role in relation to ethics that mathematics plays in relation to logic.

Selection 2 presents the chapter from the *Ethics* on the idea of God. Cohen reaches the topic by considering the frightening prospect that human ethics could have no forum of application—for example, if nature simply ceased to exist. Cohen says that in this regard, ethics is like Prometheus: desiring to be free of nature, but enduringly chained to it. The function of the idea of God in Cohen's system of ethics is to guarantee that nature will last as long as ethics applies: for all time. As for the thing-in-itself in Kantian epistemology, God in Cohen's ethics has a methodological character. Nothing is predicated of God, as if He were an entity. Instead, the idea of God is presupposed to unite logic and ethics and gives the good that ethics pursues a kind of anticipatory victory in the midst of history, which is full of reversals.

The implications of Cohen's idealist religion are startling. He denies that God is a person and that faith is distinct from knowledge. (In a rerun of the German theologian Friedrich Schleiermacher's critique of Kant, Cohen was to be challenged by Wilhelm Herrmann, a colleague of his at the University of Marburg who argued that Cohen had neglected the experiential content of religion.) But because the concept of God is by definition outside the domain of nature, guaranteeing its concordance with ethics, Cohen could affirm the traditional notion of divine transcendence and sternly condemn any pan-theism that equated God and nature.

SOURCES

Selection 1: *Werke* 7:1–82

Selection 2: *Werke* 7:428–66

Of all the problems that make up the content of philosophy, ethics may be regarded as the one that belongs to philosophy more than all others. There is, therefore, no discipline nor any division of philosophy that may dispute its special status. This relationship between ethics and philosophy as a whole has obtained since the very beginning of ethics itself. When *Socrates* conceived of ethics, he made it the focus of philosophy as a whole. Until then, philosophers had been just as much mathematicians and natural scientists as philosophers, no matter how much they also thought about human affairs. Socrates, however, spoke of nature as a Nazarene would: not the trees, but the human beings in the city can teach me.[1] Only when the road begins with the human being can it then lead back to nature. *Ethics, as the doctrine of the human being, thus emerges as the center of philosophy.*[2] Only in this center does philosophy attain autonomy, its particular character, and its unity.

The central significance of ethics in philosophy has asserted itself throughout the latter's history. Not only are all great philosophical movements reflected in their ethics, but more than that, their deepest origin and ground are located in ethics. Therefore, controversies about ethics are just as varied and involved as controversies about logic. After all, interest in ethics is more widespread; and as a result, its value is more readily evident. Thus, no matter how diverse the angles of approach or the connections that, throughout the ages, have linked questions of culture to ethics, one idea has endured, the idea through which Socrates created philosophical ethics. It may well be that not all of these movements were fully conscious of this idea, not in all their variety and not at all

1. [Socrates's famous statement is from Plato's *Phaedrus* (230d): "You must forgive me, dear friend; I'm a lover of learning, and trees and open country won't teach me anything, whereas men in the town do" (Plato, *The Collected Dialogues of Plato, Including the Letters,* ed. Edith Hamilton and Huntington Cairns [New York: Pantheon Books, 1961], 479). Cohen compares Socrates to the Nazarenes, a romantic school of painting at the beginning of the nineteenth century that was founded by German artists living in Rome and Vienna. In their works, the portrayal of human life eclipses nature.]

2. [Here and elsewhere, italics indicate Cohen's emphasis in the original.]

times. Nevertheless, the force and truth of the idea proved itself even then: *the object of ethics is the human being*. Whatever else one might want to include within the scope of ethics, any such accretions can find their place in ethics only in their connection to and relationship to the human being.

Since ethics is thus the focal point of philosophy, the human being becomes the focal point of all of philosophy's content and values. Through ethics, philosophy takes the human being as its center of gravity, the basis of its existence, and the source of its legitimacy—the eternal source of its eternal legitimacy. What discipline and what type of discipline would wish to relieve philosophy of the problem of the human being and take on this problem itself? Is there a theory capable of taking upon itself the uniform treatment of this problem: a problem that, as a central—indeed, as *the* central problem of philosophy, requires uniform treatment? Although the value of philosophy has been disputed from every angle and in every age, no other discipline has ever challenged philosophy's claim to ethics.

More than any other factor, it is the relationship between theology and ethics that allows *theology* to distinguish itself from naïve religion, a move that is both advantageous and consequential. Religion lulls itself in the illusion that it can dispense with ethics. Theology, however, never commits this error, except in the heat of battle, in polemics. Theology can claim to improve and complement ethics, but it will always be dependent on ethics. No matter how strong—or ineffectual—may be the objections that theology levels against ethics, it never wanders so far astray as to eliminate entirely all wisdom concerning the essence of the human being, to eliminate the human doctrine of the human being. Even if theology were to acknowledge ethics, and even if only as a potential task, what other discipline could have a well-grounded interest in contesting the relationship of ethics to philosophy?

It could thus appear as if ethics were granted a secure, clearly demarcated zone within the field of philosophy as a whole, and as if ethics therefore were also recognized as a [philosophical] problem with a rational basis and a precise definition. What subject matter appears to be *clearer and more precise* than "the human being"?

This view, however, is based on a thoroughgoing illusion. No one wants to dispense with ethics; nowhere is ethics regarded as superfluous. But it does not follow that there is a shared understanding of the task of ethics or even of its concerns. One might think that the concept of the human being, or even just a shared perception of the human being, would necessarily result in a common concern and would direct all human beings toward a common task. However, this view is likewise based on a fundamental error. For if indeed only ethics is able to sketch out the *doctrine* of the human being, then only ethics will be able to disclose the concept of the human being. Yet how can a perception of the human being attain such a level of universality and certainty without presupposing its grounding in the concept of the human being? It is way off the mark, then, to argue that ethics begins from a unified perception of the human being. Rather, a unified perception of the human being is its purpose and true content.

As the doctrine of the human being, ethics is thus the doctrine of the concept of the human being. Socrates, by envisioning ethics through the human being, discovered the *concept*. In the concept of the human being he discovered the concept.[3] Prior to and apart from ethics, there was no concept of the human being, just as, prior to ethics, there was no concept at all. This important line of reasoning arises from the nexus of these three discoveries: of the concept per se, of the human being, and of ethics. Just as these three concepts require one another, or at least have emerged in mutual dependence, so too the concept of the human being is linked to the concept of ethics.

However, although this line of reasoning rests on such logical precision, it is understandable that it gave rise to disagreements about the domain of ethics and spread ambiguity about the contents and the problem of ethics. As long as the topic seems to be "the human being," without further definition, ethics remains unchallenged. However, if the content of ethics per se claims to make the concept of the human being into the exclusive domain of ethics, then competitors come calling from all sides. In fact, even the term "the human being" is apparently ambiguous: *does it signify the singular or the plural?* Even if it signifies the plural, our questions are still not at an end—including the question of the meaning of the plural, of a plurality.[4] The question arises whether a plurality, in turn, is able to yield a new type of unity.

This is the twofold ambiguity with which the term "the human being" has been burdened from the very start: first the question concerns the individual human being, but the meaning of the term then passes over to a plurality of human beings. Yet the plurality is not the end of the matter; instead, this plurality is itself to become a new unity. This is the general process that takes place

3. [That is, the concept per se.]

4. [On Cohen's technical terms *Mehrheit*, or plurality, and *Allheit*, or totality, see the Note on Terms.]

in judgment—only with the qualification that unity, as a discrete category, is absent, as we saw in *Logic of Pure Cognition*.[5]

Plurality, however, evolves into totality, giving rise to a new kind of ambiguity that is attached to the term "human being." Expressed logically, the first such ambiguity lies not so much in the opposition between unity and plurality as in the apparent opposition between the individual and plurality. In thought this opposition does not exist; it stems only from an illusion of popular consciousness. The individual is, in himself, an individual member of the plurality; in no way does he constitute an independent unity, however much common illusion may support such a view.

However, the second ambiguity does, in fact, possess a basis in logic. We said that plurality evolves into totality. This does not have to mean that the plurality must transform into totality and be subsumed by it. Instead, just as the plurality constitutes its own category in logic, it also constitutes a category for the human being. The plurality of human beings is still a valuable, necessary concept. However, it is now accompanied by the totality of human beings, as a concept with a value of its own. This is the great progression through which the ambiguity of the term "human being" passes. Compared to the plurality and totality of human beings, the distinction between the individual and a plurality seems unimportant. One should certainly not believe that the difference lies in number! After all, a totality cannot be calculated; the distinction, therefore, cannot consist of "more" or "less." Totality signifies, according to the *Logic of Pure Cognition*, an infinite union that itself allows for varying degrees. The totality of human beings signifies at one moment merely the *universitas* of a class or of a city, at another moment the *universitas* of a state, and finally the *universitas* of humankind.

Thus, we are able to understand the result of this line of reasoning—and it is certainly more than merely interesting—that the concept [per se] is discovered in the concept of the human being. The unity achieved by the concept always points beyond itself. To limit oneself to the individual would amount to incorrigible shortsightedness. Although individuals may coalesce into a plurality and be preserved by the plurality, the plurality too only constitutes an intermediate stage in the development of the concept. The development of the concept, in turn, culminates in totality and only then, in totality, does it complete its formation into a unity.

Moreover, it is instructive for our historical understanding to see how Socrates,

5. [See *LrE*, 144.]

as if he were a novice, gives only a partial explanation of the diverse meanings of the concept of the human being, and thus of the concept in general. To be sure, he seeks out human beings in the city to question and challenge them concerning their desires and their doings. Socrates is not a hermit, nor does he seek out hermits. Moreover, he does not address himself only to the noble and the educated; nor, for that matter, only to the uneducated. All the occupations of his fellow citizens interest him in equal measure—not only because they are of equal logical interest, but also because, as human beings, they are all equally near to his heart. However varied his interest in human beings, however broad his range and horizon, for Socrates a plurality of human beings is always an *image of individuals.* To be sure, such an image is a concept, but only the beginning of the concept.

The image of the human being, the plurality that Socrates, in turn, assembles into a unity in his concept of the human being—this image presents the human being only as an individual being. Whether he is a helmsman or a commander, a physician or a tanner, he is still a human being engaged in a trade, a human being of the active life, a human being who is still just an individual. However much the human being may relate to the whole that is the object of his striving, he remains, within that whole, an individual. He has to take care of himself, so that his life may fulfill its purpose. That whole to which he is subordinate is not more valuable, in every respect, than the individual being. Rather, it is merely the signpost that, in the end, always leads only the individual along the proper path. Socrates drinks the cup of hemlock not to sacrifice himself for the state, but because he believes that he sees, in the law of the state, the rule of conduct for his actions—another *daimonion,*[6] so to speak, with expanded authority. For Socrates it is always the *individual* that provides the content of his concept of the human being.

With *Plato* it is different from the very start. It is well known that in the *Republic*, which contains his ethics, he deliberately takes as his point of departure not the soul of the individual, but the human soul as represented by the state, the human soul that conducts its life within the state. *The concept of the soul is now joined to the concept of the human being.* Whereas up to this point—especially, for instance, according to the Pythagorean view—it was only the world soul that was joined to the human soul, Plato conceives of the *soul of the state* as a new type of world soul; and it now appears as a new type of human soul as well.

6. [*Daimonion* is a diminutive form of the Greek *daimon,* a spirit or genius that dwells in the individual.]

In this new type of human soul, the human being exits the limits of a plurality and enters into the domain of *totality*. For the soul of the state is conceivable only as an abstraction of an infinite connected whole. Only through such an act of abstraction does the concept of the human being attain completion and fulfillment. The human being is then no longer an individual, neither a unique individual nor an individual belonging to a plurality. Instead he now belongs to totality. Only in this totality does he acquire a soul. To be sure, Plato says only that one can know the soul of the human being better in the state than in the individual. However, Plato's statement also implies, after all, that the concept of the soul attains its more precise and solid articulation in the totality than in an isolated being.

Thus, we see that, in the emergence of ethics, ambiguities appear in the concept of the human being that later come to be recognized not as ambiguities, but as changes and *stages in the development of the concept of the human being*. From the beginning, we see the individual appearing. Then, in what seems like an expansion, the individual is joined by a neighbor and by an assembly of neighbors. The assembly grows and coheres, always, however, remaining the collective of a plurality. When the plurality emerges, the individual that is part of it is not somehow just submerged. After all, the individual, despite his autonomy, has his place only in this plurality. Instead, the individual endures, even if it is his connection to the plurality that remains the measure of his value. On the other hand, however much the plurality may assert its own value, it too is necessarily limited by totality. *Therefore, without the totality, and indeed without beginning with the totality, the concept of the human being not only remains incomplete; it cannot develop or form at all.* Totality is not only the happy ending; it is also the proper beginning.

This, then, is the complicated picture presented by the concept of the human being: individuality and plurality, that is, particularity, and—totality. It is all of these simultaneously, all in one. That is, after all, the meaning of the method that Plato introduces into ethics, by means of the concept of the state soul of the human being: that the end is actually the beginning. End and beginning are neither methodologically nor objectively separate from one another. There are three trajectories for which the concept of the human being is the guide—the individual, the particular plurality, and the totality. They are not crossroads. Instead, at every step of the way they must proceed together; the path of the human being consists only in their unification.

Earlier we said that the special status of ethics is not disputed by any other discipline.[7] Now a reason for this claim emerges. To be sure, insofar as the human being is the object of any of the disciplines, they must study the human being along these three trajectories. For it is through these three trajectories that the concept of the human being attains fulfillment. However, we may surmise, and we will have to show, that the significance of the unity of these three trajectories —the unity that they not only require, but also attain—is achieved in ethics with greater clarity, force, and precision than in any other discipline. Only ethics reveals the *essence* of the human being—to substitute this term, just for a moment, for the arid logical *concept* of the human being—ethics alone reveals this essence, in the interaction and merging of individuality, particularity, and totality.

Is the human being then an individual? He certainly is not only an individual. Rather, he is a member of a plurality, indeed of any number of pluralities. Yet he is also not only that. Rather, he completes the orbits of his existence only in totality. Even this totality in turn has a number of gradations and levels, until it reaches its conclusion in a true unity, that is, in humanity—a completion, however, that is an eternally new beginning.

This understanding will be the guiding principle for our construction of an ethics. It does not take on the same significance for all ethical systems. It is certainly not common to all ideas of the meaning of the human being. With this in mind, we can understand the distinctions and differences in the development of ethics, and in the relationship of systematic disciplines to ethics. Likewise, we can also understand why accounts of ethics reflect the belief that they stand in closer affinity to individual disciplines.

* * *

First of all, the focus on the *individual* leads to *anthropology*, and from there to psychology. Anthropology is, in the first place, biological. Biology, in turn, is the legitimate field in which the concept describes its induction. Who could hope to discover the concept of the human being while believing that its biological nature could be ignored? If ethics is supposed to be the doctrine of the human being, then it cannot afford to neglect or give insufficient attention to the problems and the results that biological anthropology is able to produce as it progresses through the stages of its development. However, that certainly does not mean that the biological concept of the human being should serve as the

---

7. [Stated at the beginning of this selection.]

point of departure for determining the concept of the human being. That determination is the task of ethics. Just because biological anthropology should not be ignored and should always receive attention, this does not in any way mean that it should also serve as the methodological guide. Just as the concept of the human being is not identical to its biological concept, likewise the biological concept should not be given the role of providing methodological guidance for the inquiry. Totality itself cautions against such a move.

And if such caution applies to biology, then it applies no less to *psychology*. We saw that it was the concept of the soul that Plato used to define the crossroads of ethics. At these crossroads he created not only ethics, but, at the same time, psychology too, and chiefly through ethics. We should mention here only that prior to Plato, psychology did not exist as a coherent field with its own method. *Plato is the real founder of psychology.* Although the fundamental investigations in which Plato created [the field of] logic—his discussions of thinking, in particular his discussions of thought in cognition, as opposed to thought in perception and representation—were an important (and necessary) basis for the origin of psychology. Nevertheless, one can probably say that in Plato the relationship between ethics and psychology was still more direct and more far-reaching.

For desire is intermeshed with perception. As a result, the interest of logic is implicated in the interest of ethics. And so it [logic] goes, farther and deeper. Likewise, the soul of the human being is located not in the web of its individual activity, but rather—so to speak—beyond itself, in an expansion and extension of the self. Just as this macrocosmic concept of the soul originated in ethics, psychology was likewise able to receive direction from ethics, and the macroscopic presentation of its object as well. However, psychology was not able, conversely, to lay claim to being the guide for ethics. For it is ethics alone that discovers the true concept of the soul.

Nevertheless, even today uncertainty and controversy prevail about the natural *relationship between ethics and psychology*. The conflict would be serious enough if the dispute concerned only the method of ethics. However, psychology too, as if by fate, is affected by this controversy. For the point in question is not only the method of psychology, but the entire content and object of the discipline. The skeleton that, in our day, is called "psychology" presents an alarming picture of the discipline. Animal psychology is no longer explicitly studied as a field in its own right, although it would be very useful and important. And yet, most of what is studied as psychology in our day is really and primarily animal psychology at best. If psychology is supposed to be human psychology—and it should be human psychology, in keeping with the eminent significance of the concept of the human being—then it must accept the ethical concept of the soul as its prerequisite, a concept of soul that follows Plato's direction and his fruitful paradigm. Our deliberations will demonstrate that this proposition is correct. For now we will just offer a brief preliminary observation.

In spite of psychology's conceit that it is a foundational discipline of philosophical thought, its systematic value still consists of its connection to physiology. The insights that have emerged from this connection are now indispensable. Incidentally, serious philosophers, to say nothing of classical authors, never failed to pursue this connection and advance these insights. Insufficient attention is given to the fact that *Malebranche* and *Berkeley*[8] are the founders of physiological optics and that *Descartes* was also very influential in this field. It is therefore beyond any reasonable doubt that the interstice of the fields of physiology and psychology yield insights that are indispensable for psychology as well. The only objection to this form of modern psychology is this: that it claims to be psychology both in itself and on the basis of its physiological method. Moreover, it claims to constitute the basis of philosophy. It thus attributes to its subject matter, its important subject matter, the status of a methodological foundation. Therein lies the confusion. By contrast, the questions and interests of psychology extend, in principle, beyond this subject matter, no matter how much it has been expanded and refined. Therefore, psychology must have its own, independent principles—and not principles that just make it an appendix to physiology.

However, as a consequence, just as was the case with the problem we considered from various angles in *Logic of Pure Cognition*, ethics should not accept its guiding principles from psychology. For then its instructions would simply derive from physiology, as would be necessary to secure a body of material. Thus, despite all its efforts to extend its reach, psychology is not able take the human concept of the soul beyond the concept of the individual. Whatever can be accomplished under the banner of "ethnopsychology"[9]—in research that is

8. [Nicolas Malebranche (1638–1715) is known primarily for his Cartesian philosophy. George Berkeley (1685–1753), noteworthy for his defense of idealism, also wrote on the psychology of vision. Spinoza's interest in optics also corroborates Cohen's point.]

9. [Ethnopsychology (*Völkerpsychologie*), a field invented by Wilhelm Wundt (1832–1920) and distinct from philosophy, developed its own methodology for investigating the psychology of the nation (*Volk* or *ethnos*) and is the forerunner of modern sociology and anthropology. For its significance in Cohen's development, see Frederick C. Beiser, *Hermann Cohen: An Intellectual Biography* (Oxford: Oxford University Press, 2018), 22–29.]

methodologically questionable—it does not go much beyond some more or less astute suggestions and is limited to language, myth, and custom.

In their actual *cultural* trajectories, nations follow the common paths of humanity and—despite their distinct articulations in poetry, art, and law—these trajectories represent general human individuality with a uniformity similar to the uniformity that is taken for granted in science. *In psychology the individual is and shall remain the core concept of the human being.* That is the obstacle that psychology would present for ethics, if psychology were permitted to determine the latter's method.

The aim of ethics, as we envision it, is that the individual be infused with both particularity and totality. If psychology were able, at best, to describe the particularity in the individuality of nations, totality still lies entirely beyond its reach. For example, it is able to speak of the state only in metaphors derived from organisms; it is helpless when confronted with the unity of humanity, where craniometry is of no avail.[10] Thus, the concept of the individual that psychology produces using its own tools is incomplete and, for ethics, inadequate and misleading.

Because of its essential methodological connection to physiology, psychology has also inherited its *naturalism*, the mortal foe of ethics. For ethics, the individual as understood in psychology would constitute the foundation of individualism, egoism, and solipsism. And no matter how eagerly we sought to remedy the narrowness of these concepts, to broaden [the concept of] the individual and free it from its natural limits so that it might seem to absorb other aspects—no matter how eagerly we tried, naturalism would still hold the ego in its thrall. Thus, naturalism itself would remain firmly entrenched. And naturalism in itself, quite aside from its concept of the individual, represents a fundamental *methodological danger for ethics.*

It would be entirely incorrect to think that by taking up the issue of naturalism here we intend to deliver the customary sort of diatribe against *materialism.* In defending the foundation for ethics against all forms of naturalism what is at stake is not just some edifying ornament, but the frame and foundation. That is the profound and far-reaching meaning of the Kantian distinction between *Is and Ought.* The *Is* that Kant thus distinguishes from ethics is by no means merely what is customarily called sensible being, which finds its adequate expression in

10. [Craniometry (*Schädelmessung*), a popular field in the nineteenth century, claimed that a person's psychological characteristics could be derived from measurements of the skull. It has since been discredited as pseudoscience, especially since its use in the twentieth century for nefarious racist purposes.]

eudaimonism. Rather, it is the *being of nature in general,* even in its most spiritual interpretation. This is the reason for the irreconcilable difference between eudaimonism [and ethics]. For eudaimonism is inextricably joined to naturalism, and not just to some ambiguous version of it. Nature itself is the adversary. Nature, even in all its purity and sublimity, should not be regarded as the refuge toward which the moral spirit steers. Thus, Kant was able to overcome the thoroughly Rousseauian mood of his times, for there breathed in him a more active, lively, zealous, and authentic spirit of creative morality. It reined in the Rousseauian yearning for solitude. The contemplative innocence of nature may be fitting for art, but ethics seeks, first and foremost, to learn not from the trees, but from the people of the city. And meanwhile, the horizon had broadened, encompassing the people of the entire world.

For this reason, the Romantics could neither understand nor tolerate this principle. It redounds to Fichte's credit that he set himself apart from all the Romantics with respect to this basic idea. It was not just his sense of history, nor his sympathy for the German fatherland. To him, that fatherland, because of its spiritual world, was like a real possession. For that reason he was unable to believe that it could be in decline. Nor was it his sympathy for the poor among his people, who had not yet had the benefit of German national culture or education. It was just as much his philosophical capacity that was captivated and illuminated by this new term, this shibboleth of a new doctrine and new worldview. Not only psychology, but all philosophy was occupied with the *Is,* with being—with the being of nature and with its laws. Only ethics posed as its problem a different kind of being; only ethics was searching for laws other than the laws of nature.

At the moment, we are not considering the meaning of the *Ought* itself. For now what is under discussion is only the difference between the *Ought* and nature. That is what is meant by the distinction between the *Ought* and the *Is.* And although the *Ought* must also culminate in a kind of being, this being is nevertheless fundamentally different in kind, so different that, because of the distinction between the *being* of nature and the *being* of the *Ought,* this new "being" should be termed the *"being" of the Ought.*

It should be mentioned at this point that this formulation is not without flaws. In fact, it is related to the terminological foundations which it is our task to emend.[11] However, we honor, as Kant's eternal legacy, the intellectual

---

11. [That is, the task of the present work, *Ethics of Pure Will,* in which Cohen offers his revision of Kant's ethics.]

orientation and the world-historical significance of the distinction between *Is* and *Ought*.

On this dictum Kant is in agreement with Plato. It is the path taken by idealism: to free itself from the reins of nature and the tyranny of experience. Late antiquity had no patience for this kind of idealism. Thus, it is extraordinarily instructive that *the Stoics*, like *Epicurus*, always speak only of the individual and believe that the task of ethics is to be found in the *ideal of the wise man*. Full of anticipation, they dream of totality. Just as the idea of cosmopolitanism runs in the very blood of the Greek philosophers, the Stoics venture to formulate the idea of humanity. But such ideas constitute only ornaments or, at most, consequences of their thought; the focal point still remains the individual. These Greek philosophers are incapable of establishing a relationship or interaction between their type of totality and the individual. They do not even succeed in positing types of particularity. That is also not their goal—and certainly not the merging of the individual with the totality of humanity, even if in the long, historical view, this is their goal after all.

This Stoic inclination to locate the ideal in the individual has been adopted in every subsequent age for the reason that Christianity—which arose in the same time period—also adopted it as its own. Although Christianity then freed itself from the legacy of naturalism, it still preserved this basic Stoic inclination, combining God and a human individual into a unity. This inner connection between Christianity and Stoicism made it easier for the modern world to regenerate itself through Stoicism as it sought to liberate itself from the omnipotence of Christianity. However, since it was the general tendency of the *Renaissance* to return to nature, Stoicism also provided useful vocabulary. Nature and the individual thus combine in the Renaissance in yearning for a new morality. But could a new ethics—an ethics that would follow in the footsteps of Platonic idealism—emerge in this way, through nature and the individual?

Spinoza gave the title "Ethics" to his main philosophical work and thus to his philosophy itself. There is probably no other ethical system in the modern period before Kant that was so successful in thoroughly imposing its underlying spirit on an entire age, especially on its most influential thinkers. Even so, Spinoza was unable to surmount the consequences of his relationship to Stoicism. What is repellent in Spinoza is not actually his naturalism—the naturalism that Herbart,[12] not without a trace of hostility, is eager to expose. For this naturalism

12. [Johann Friedrich Herbart (1776–1841).]

frequently consists only in his excesses of terminology. However, Kant's obvious aversion to Spinoza, more than any other philosopher, is due to a difference in substance and principle. Spinoza enchants the reader by his serene air of superiority to prejudices and prevailing opinions. By placing human passions and actions on the same plane as mathematical figures, he assumes the appearance of a classical nude sculpture. This mode of thinking is honorable when we are dealing with prejudices in a battle among opinions and factions; however, it is incompatible with the possibility of ethics as conceived by Plato.

If the actions of human beings were to be considered as if they were lines, surfaces, and bodies, as Spinoza dared to aver,[13] then not only the actions of human beings would be mathematical figures, but also human beings themselves. *These mathematical figures are the fundamental error of Spinoza's naturalism.* Human beings are not physical bodies. However, if they are construed as mathematical figures, then they remain physical bodies. Who, then, constructs these geometrical figures on the chessboard of nature?

From this question one can see that Spinoza's *Ethics* is grounded, finally, neither in these mathematical figures, nor in individual human beings. It is based on a *metaphysics*. The individual finds his place—his more than modest place —only in the metaphysical doctrine of the substance of nature. Within the *Ethics* itself, the claim that human beings are mathematical constructions cannot be justified. Kant, therefore, had good reason to direct his attack against this principle. In the case of a circle, I am not permitted to ask what it ought to be, but only what it is. Its law resides in its being. The law of the human being, by contrast, resides not in what it is, but in what it ought to be.

Nowhere perhaps can one see the inherent and necessary consequences of a foundational idea more clearly than in the dependence of philosophical Romanticism on Spinoza. *Schelling, Hegel,* and even *Schleiermacher* (despite many a divergence) all labor under a pantheistic bias.[14] However, the original danger of

13. [Spinoza wrote, "I shall consider human actions and appetites just as if it were an investigation into lines, planes, or bodies" (*Complete Works*, trans. Samuel Shirley, ed. Michael L. Morgan [Indianapolis, IN: Hackett, 2002], 278).]

14. [Friedrich Wilhelm Joseph von Schelling (1775–1854) and Georg Wilhelm Friedrich Hegel (1770–1831), constitute, along with Johann Gottlieb Fichte (1762–1814), the triumvirate of foundational thinkers of post-Kantian German Idealism. The affinity of Friedrich Schleiermacher (1768–1834) for Spinoza is apparent in his 1799 *Über die Religion: Reden an die Gebildeten unter ihren Verächtern.* For an English translation, see Friedrich Schleiermacher, *On Religion: Speeches to Its Cultured Despisers*, trans. Richard Crouter (Cambridge: Cambridge University Press, 1988).]

pantheism lies not in the threat it poses to the idea of God; that threat is only a consequence of pantheism. The error in the foundation and principle of pantheism pertains to the concept of the human being and, for that reason, to ethics. If God and nature are one and the same, then at the very least the human being and nature are the same. As a consequence, the distinction between what is (*Sein*) and what ought to be (*Sollen*) is lost. It was certainly no accident that neither Schelling nor Hegel wrote a work of their own with the specific title "ethics." Schleiermacher in particular argues against such a distinction in one of his foundational works. Any philosophy of identity[15] is a form of pantheism if it does not, in the concept of thinking itself, lay the groundwork for the distinction between what is and what ought to be. The error in the system of identity is rooted, then, in a twofold error in the concept of identity: first, that is, in a false identity in thinking, and, as a consequence, in a false identity in being. Here, however, we encounter a further error in *psychology*, in which, in general, we have found the foundation for this kind of ethics, including ethics as it is constructed in Romanticism's philosophy of identity, as metaphysics.

Psychology begins and ends with the individual. Human actions, too, are viewed from the perspective of the individual. If this is true of actions, how much more so of desires and strivings. The *relationship between thinking and willing* has thus been the subject of controversy since antiquity.

In early Christian philosophy, this controversy was complicated by the fundamental questions of Christian dogmatics. To frame the question in narrow terms for the present discussion: the will must emerge with exceptional force and power just for the sake of the evil that it must produce. However, this is equally the case for the sake of the love of God and of the human being. Thus, Socrates's point of view—that virtue is knowledge—had to be set aside. Nevertheless, the voluntarist motive in religious love came to prevent the intellectual motive in the will from being entirely eliminated. In any case, the intellectual motivation was indispensable for the freedom of the will, at least to the extent that freedom of the will was needed and acknowledged.

In *law*, too, this question has played a typical role in the early modern period. Leibniz[16] was consistent with his own principles in resisting, in matters of law, an overemphasis on the will. On the other hand, the intellectual aspect should not

15. ["Philosophy of identity" (*Identitätsphilosophie*) was a common name for Schelling's philosophical system.]
16. [Gottfried Wilhelm Leibniz (1646–1716).]

be the sole determinant of the concept of action. Otherwise, the theory of criminal law would lapse into the error of becoming a narrow ethics of conscience. Then, even in the most generous interpretation of such an ethics, the value and measure of the conscience would consist of its precision in thinking.

Now, where is the methodological criterion to be found for all these and the many similar, related questions? In psychology perchance? Is there a psychology that, when confronted with such difficulties, is able to stand on its own two feet and to answer such questions from a position of autonomy? In fact, is not psychology itself caught up in these very questions, and not only in these factual scientific problems, but also in fundamental assumptions about the animal nature of the human being? Does it not thus complicate these scientific questions still further?

In the will, more than in any other mental process, one can observe how concrete problems influence psychology. Psychology arrives at its own problems and subject matter only by way of the concrete. For Plato, the will did not yet exist; it was his ethics that gave birth to the will, but without giving it a precise psychological term. To be sure, the will was known by a verbal formulation; it was called volition or willing (βούλησις) [*boulesis*]; psychic potential was still contained in the act. But desire, the preliminary stage of the will, is known and acknowledged as a powerful and particular psychological force. Desire is also preserved in the higher stage to which the new will advances. What matters is that this aspect of striving, no matter how much the will is able to purge it, be neither extinguished nor obscured.

The *relationship between will and thought* must not be defined in such a way that the will displaces the intellect, nor the intellect the will. Both must remain. In their systematic definition neither of the two forces should be permitted to obtain even so much as predominance over the other. This requirement accounts for the inadequacy of psychology in dealing with this fundamental question [of the relationship between will and thought]. The inadequacy is exacerbated by the general fact that psychology, when its authority rests on the most solid foundation, that is, on a physiological foundation, is subject to naturalistic influence. For physiology, it is unavoidable that the drives are and remain the origin of the will. We arrive, then, at the instructive alternative offered by modern psychology. According to one view, the will is merely a drive "sicklied o'er by thought"[17]

17. [Cohen's turn of phrase, "a drive 'sicklied o'er by thought'" ("ein vom Denken angekränkelter Trieb") echoes the classic German translation of Shakespeare's *Hamlet* by

and thus hindered in its natural self-assurance. According to another, the will begins with uneasy choice, but has the chance of a career in which it can be deadened, becoming a will of mere reflex. Confronting this basic question, psychology thus seems to lack any sense of direction. How then is it conceivable that psychology could provide direction for ethics?

Moreover, it is an illusion, even if it is an illusion with a veneer of scientific respectability, that psychology itself might assume a leadership role in dealing with this problem. *On the contrary, psychology is subservient to metaphysics.* This kind of metaphysics is all too well-known: for decades it has consumed nearly all interest in philosophy. In this kind of metaphysics, the will is the *absolute*, the thing-in-itself, whereas the intellect is capable of finding only phenomena. This is the metaphysics of *Schopenhauer*.[18] It separates the two aspects of intellect and will from each other so thoroughly that it divides them into two worlds of disparate value, relegating intellect to the world of illusion, and will to the world of truth.

If a metaphysics of this kind purported to be ethics, we would have to be skeptical, and all the more so if it purported to be psychology. For we harbor an irrepressible suspicion against any truth that is based on any authority other than theoretical reason. The will, if it is juxtaposed to the intellect, cannot signify a world of truth, or even guarantee it, while the intellect assumes the role of the author of phenomena. It is a consequence, as in the "Witch's Multiplication Table,"[19] that in this kind of metaphysics, music takes the place of philosophy. If the mysteries of the world are entrusted to the will, then art will take the place of science—and, in particular, whichever of the arts arouses the most powerful emotions.

In this contemporary episode, the ultimate aim of such a metaphysics is visible only indirectly, for it has surrendered philosophy and scientific knowledge

---

August Schlegel (1767–1845). Hamlet says: "Thus conscience does make cowards of us all, / And thus the native hue of resolution / Is sicklied o'er with the pale cast of thought" (3.1.83–85).]

18. [Arthur Schopenhauer (1788–1860). Cohen is giving an epitome of his work, *Die Welt als Wille und Vorstellung*. For an English translation, see Arthur Schopenhauer, *The World as Will and Representation*, trans. Judith Norman, Alistair Welchman, and Christopher Janaway, 2 vols. (Cambridge: Cambridge University Press, 2014 and 2018).]

19. ["*Hexen-Einmal-Eins*," a reference to the "Witch's Kitchen" scene in *Faust*, where the witch (*Hexe*) recites a multiplication table ("*Einmaleins*") that rhymes like a poem but is actually mathematical nonsense. See Johann Wolfgang von Goethe, *Faust: Part One*, trans. David Luke (Oxford: Oxford University Press, 1987), 130, lines 2540–52 (hereafter, *Faust*, Luke trans.).]

to what purports to be art. That, however, is not the ultimate reason urging it on. Genuine, timeless art does not owe its origin to false, let alone falsified, products of reason. For art, there is no conflict between the intellect and the will, between theoretical and ethical reason. This kind of metaphysics produces a conception of art in which art is superior to scientific knowledge and to philosophy, but also identifies with scientific knowledge. This kind of metaphysics has another goal of its own, in relation to which art is only a distraction and a by-product. A so-called metaphysics that reveals the will at the expense of the intellect will lead to skepticism or, as it is has reappeared in our day, toward *agnosticism*. The intellect has access only to phenomena; the "In-Itself," the essence of things, remains concealed. "Scorn reason, despise learning, man's supreme powers and faculties."[20]

Human beings are easily deceived about the diabolical nature of such a revelation, feeling all the more intensely a desire for a different wellspring as their source of truth. This wellspring is the "will," located, therefore, within the human being, and thus also within reason. Therefore, philosophy and science are still in use in relation to this source, retaining their usefulness and validity. So it seems, and so it is supposed to seem. For above all one must avoid the appearance that human sovereignty and, in particular, the arbitrary power of the speculative genius who is the source of revelation have been overthrown. Nevertheless, this grand display of the spiritual power of the human being is just an illusion that, in a certain way, will dissolve of its own accord. For the will is by no means only the will of the human being; it is the will of all of nature, both living and seemingly inert. Thus, the distinction remains between the human being and the absolute will, or between the human being and the "In-Itself" of the will.

In this type of metaphysics there is always a seductive danger: it conspires with all manner of religion whose actual inner life is inimical to the autonomy of human reason. This kind of religious metaphysics is the purpose and goal, the trophy and the weapon of such a metaphysics of agnosticism. However, if human reason is unable to recognize the true concept of the human being, then there can be no ethics. Agnosticism is thus incompatible with an autonomous ethics—that is, with an ethics that is arranged and constructed on the basis of its own method.

20. [In Goethe's *Faust*, Mephistopheles is speaking in the scene "In the Study": "Verachte nur Vernunft und Wissenschaft, / Des Menschen allerhöchste Kraft, / Laß nur in Blend- und Zauberwerken / Dich von dem Lügengeist bestärken" ("Scorn reason, despise learning, man's supreme / Powers and faculties; let your vain dream / Of magic arts be fortified with sweet / Flatteries by the Spirit of Deceit" [*Faust*, Luke trans., 56, lines 1851–54]).]

However, if we have now seen, one, that the theory of an all-encompassing, absolute autonomy of the will is not psychology at all, but metaphysics, and two, that metaphysics—in the form of a metaphysics of agnosticism—leads to the elimination of ethics as an autonomous doctrine with its own method, then it has been shown that psychology is not suited to provide direction to ethics. The illusion of the will is also ruled out, for the will thus conceived conflicts with the intellect.

This is the profound, pure meaning of that formula, of the distinction between *what is and what ought to be*. To be sure, the formula is not entirely clear: the task of ethics is rendered autonomous, is distinguished from the task of theoretical reason, and yet is still acknowledged as a task of reason.

Ethics should not be ceded to religion in some sort of larval stage. Nor should religion be given precedence over ethics. Philosophy alone, in accord with its own methods, has the task of investigating, ascertaining, and defining what ethics is. What ethics is in religion—religion will have to learn the answer to that question itself, from ethics. Theology must evolve into ethical theology.

This was the great renewal of *Protestantism* that *Kant* brought about in the world of philosophical ethics. It is inconceivable that the seal of ethics should ever vanish from this Protestant renewal, if humanity marches on in the direction indicated by the history of Protestantism. If, in our day, an odious and malicious opposition has dared to rise up against the vital core of the Kantian spirit, it is clear that such opposition is enmeshed in the evil, regressive movements of our times. This connection gives this opposition its character; by this connection it should be judged.

The difference between what is and what ought to be does not mean that we must derive our definition of *what is* from science, but our definition of *what ought to be* from something other than science. Rather, it signifies, in a word, the independence of ethics in relation to logic and, consequently, to natural science.

But if ethics asserts its independence in relation to logic, then how much more so must it assert its independence with respect to psychology? This is the broader meaning of that foundational distinction. It is impossible that psychology serve as the point of departure, not only because it cannot provide methodological direction to ethics. As we have seen, psychology is in fact dependent upon ethics for its material. More than that, ethics cannot take its point of departure from psychology, because the latter does not provide the proper perspective for the concept of the human being. Psychology narrows the moral horizon. For psychology, the human being is the sensible, the physiological, and thus the animal human being; for psychology, the concept of the human being does not change, from its inception and for the duration, even if the concept of the human being comes to include the psychic organization of the human being on top of the physical. The expression *"what is and what ought to be"* transcends this beginning and goes beyond it. If ethics is to be possible at all, then the concept of the human being may not remain chained to the psychological concept of the human being.

Recently, the old Scholastic controversy concerning the will and intellect has been revived: the will has been given the role of determining the value of the truth. As a consequence, the task of determining truth-value is not vested in the intellect in itself, even though—one would think—the value of the intellect itself depends entirely on this determination. The intellect, then, possesses no self-knowledge of its value as truth; the intellect can be granted such a confirmation only by the will. To be sure, the value of the will thereby increases; but does not the intellect suffer a corresponding decline? Above all, we must take note that the entire thrust of this description, which, strictly speaking, should be the domestic affair of psychology, is driven entirely by general, systematic motives. Thus, here too we find corroboration that psychology is simply incapable of fending off such systematic concerns.

We can counter this recent view, which basically revives the idea of *amor intellectualis*,[21] by using the precision of the Kantian formula. *What is and what ought to be—that is, not what ought to be and what is.* No matter how high the priority assigned to the interest in ethics—and the Kantian adage about the primacy of practical reason[22] does in fact place that interest at the apex—the methodological sequence may not be reversed. Ethics may still be located at the apex; but ethics is not the beginning and foundation. It would, however, inevitably become the foundation if it—the will—were assigned the task of determining truth-value.

21. [Meaning "intellectual love."]

22. [Kant invokes the "primacy of practical reason" to allow for propositions that, as propositions of theoretical reason, would lead to "speculative mischief" but are admissible as postulates of practical reason—the existence of God, the immortality of the soul, and human freedom: "But one cannot require pure practical reason to be subordinate to speculative reason and so reverse the order, since all interest is ultimately practical and even that of speculative reason is only conditional and is complete in practical use alone" (Immanuel Kant, *Critique of Practical Reason*, trans. Mary Gregor [Cambridge: Cambridge University Press, 2015], 98).]

This view, too, favors metaphysics, albeit only when it is overemphasized, as in Fichte's position. Fichte also effects a reversal of method, ultimately deriving truth from ethics. Ethics thus displaces logic; however, logic ought to retain the methodological right to determine truth-value. Thus, whenever logic is circumvented and its primary authority is denied, a descent into metaphysics is the unsalvageable result—into its ambiguities, convolutions, confusion, and dishonesty.

If logic is rejected as a guarantor of truth, then one must suspect that the meaning of truth that logic is able to guarantee is also being rejected and condemned. At the very least, it is not regarded as sufficient. This judgment should not be taken as a prejudice; rather, it is based on the distinction between *what is* and *what ought to be*. It is one thing to acknowledge that logical truth is not *sufficient* for the demands of ethics; but it is something else, therefore, to forfeit the former for the latter and to sever the latter's connection to the former. However, this maneuver is characteristic of the tendency of metaphysics; by calling attention to this tendency we seek to oppose it here. If the value of the truth that logic can provide is subordinated and subjected to suspicion and contempt, then must we not ask whether there can be a truth other than the truth of logic—a truth other than the truth that is based on the foundation of logic and yet a truth that, in method and principle, does not depart from it?

What sort of truth, however, could that other truth be? After all, its content must still be the human being. If the value of truth as formulated by human beings in scientific thought has been called into doubt, then what human problem or human interest could possibly be awakened by a new question about truth? Will this not give rise to the suspicion that mythological fantasies could take the place of scientific concepts and insights? Above all, will this not give rise to the suspicion that the *types and degrees of certainty* that logic teaches us to differentiate will be blended together and eliminated?

Now we must point out a serious *shortcoming in the formula* "what is" and "what ought to be" in both the formula and its application. We said above that *Ought* must still signify an *Is*. The fact that the *Ought* is distinct from "what is" ought not rob the *Ought* of its validity as being; excluding the *Ought* from being. *What is* should signify here only the *what is* of nature, understood as the nature of natural science; this is the "being" from which the *what ought to be* should be distinguished. But what other type of Being remains, then, for the Ought? Our question here concerns not the content of this Being—the content will come later—but rather the methodological validity of this Being. What validity should be ascribed to it?

We arrive here at a most profound difficulty in *Kant's* terminology—the *relationship of the idea to the thing-in-itself*. Fichte launched his argument at precisely this point, coming to the presumptuous conclusion that it was his mission to improve upon Kant. We know from the *Logic* that the problem of the thing-in-itself was not fully resolved by Kant and could not have been resolved by Kant, since he had fully clarified neither the concept of reality nor, therefore, the difference between actuality and reality. Now we have to see how this fundamental shortcoming is connected to a similar shortcoming in the definition of "idea." However, if we are going to discuss the shortcoming in the definition of the idea, we should first call to mind its merit.

The value of the term "Idea" lies in the distinction between *what is* and *what ought to be*. Kant's penetrating insight revealed to him the secret of the Platonic Idea. He argued that in modern languages the term "Idea" came to be misused, that its meaning became unstable, and that its distinctive value was lost. The Idea should never be equated with *representation*; nor should it, for that matter, be equated with knowledge. This, Kant continues, was Plato's error: he did not distinguish between *what is* and *what ought to be*. Thus, he too suffered the same fate as metaphysics. He was like a dove that sought to fly in a vacuum, lacking appreciation for the resistance offered by air. Kant, therefore, limited the use of the Idea—apart from its regulative use in the empirical biological sciences—to the realm of practical reason, to the *what ought to be* of ethics.

Surely, there is no reason to distrust Kant's intentions in defining the value of the Idea in this way. His dithyrambic praise for the Idea suffices to counter such a charge, as well as the special place he assigns the Idea in the entire field of ethics. Indeed, Kant constructs the field of ethics by means of the Idea and on the strength of the Idea. However, even while paying homage to the scope and range of the Idea, we must still pay attention to the relationship of the Idea to the *thing-in-itself*. For ethics, this question is more ominous and treacherous than for the laws of nature and their prototype, the synthetic principle. For with respect to the latter, it can easily be seen that the thing-in-itself, in relation to the laws of nature, is merely a product of unscientific, dogmatic superstition. Natural law is in one's hands; the power of nature is posited in natural law, and then the being and activity of nature is posited in the power of nature in turn. And still the thing-in-itself remains elusive. One arrives at the critical insight that the things of nature are objects of science, and thus are *appearances*, to use the old Platonic term. And then one ventures to adopt the seemingly critical, skeptical view that they are only appearances. This is how bread is transformed into stone.

How did the term "appearance" arise in Plato's thought? To Plato, it signified the thing insofar as it had not yet been verified by the true being of the Idea. Because of the scope of such verifications, Plato was still entangled in errors. It appeared that only the *Idea of the Good* was able to guarantee the true and full validity of being. By contrast, however, other Ideas, the mathematical Ideas, still concealed things behind the veil of the appearance. Now, however, such cause for distrust of appearances has been completely dispelled; now, through the law of nature, appearances have acquired true being, far removed from any hint of illusion. How, then, can one still doubt that the thing-in-itself has simply dissolved into a methodological formula, and that it is only through this formula that the value of the thing-in-itself is determined and described as a regulative and heuristic maxim?

Thus, there is no question that, in the realm of theoretical reason, it was Kant's clear intention to do away with this antiquated metaphysical term — the thing-in-itself. Metaphysics was in the habit of using this term to disrupt reason's domestic tranquility and to intrude deeply into its domain. Nevertheless, Kant did not conclude his analysis with a specific, clear statement that, in the realm of theoretical reason, the significance of the thing-in-itself is only to fulfill the function of a regulative idea.

It is otherwise, however, in ethics. If the relationship of the idea to the thing-in-itself is not fully clarified, then the status of the Ought, as a kind of being, will somehow be called into question. For the suspicion will then arise that the idea is in fact only an idea, in relation to which and behind which an actual and genuine reserve of being would present itself as the thing-in-itself, or rather would conceal itself and close itself off. This suspicion also affects the Kantian formula, insinuating that it thus separates the Ought from the Is — as if the Ought, even if it does not signify a catechism of commandments, still signifies an imaginary realm of pious hopes.

That is the grave and constant danger to human morality, the gravest danger that systematic ethics must overcome. This point of view, which in itself is cause enough for concern, is then taken up by those who share in the superstition and the popular resentment of reason. They expand this point of view, abetted by so-called metaphysics, until it has become a yawning gap, and, on account of the fragmentary character of all systematic human inquiry, the gap is just left exposed. And yet this gap, so they believe, must be filled in — with truths, but not with scientific truths. Here, then, every trace of a gap, every possible refuge must be eliminated, lest the powers of darkness sully the honesty and integrity of the human zeal for truth.

Therefore, the idea must merge entirely, without remainder, into the Ought. The thing-in-itself may not be allowed to linger in the background. The idea is the Ought. Ideas signify nothing other than precepts for the use of practical reason, aggregated in the Ought. *The value of ethics as being lies in this Ought.* The Ought describes and defines the acts of willing that constitute the content of ethics. It signifies nothing other than the will in accordance with law, or willing in accordance with the precepts, with the laws of ethics. These are the laws that make ethics into ethics and also constitute the condition for the possibility of willing itself. For willing consists only in the Ought. Without the Ought, there would be no will, only desire. Through the Ought, however, the will effects and conquers true Being.

Securing such true Being for the content of moral willing will be a main focus of the ethics presented here. That is the most urgent interest of ethics; ethics seeks to base its autonomy and special character on this true Being. There should be no doubt that ethics is not concerned with some transcendent, bucolic pastoral world, while reality remains merely the [reality] of sensible nature. We have to achieve incisive clarity, precision, and certainty on the value of the kind of being that inheres in the creations of ethics.

Therefore, to the extent that psychology claims to be the foundation of ethics, ethics must be categorically separated from psychology. For when psychology stakes that claim, then inevitably either naturalism or supernaturalism benefit —and, not coincidentally, often both of them at once. Neither, however, can do justice to the particular value of moral Being. Therefore, they usually form an alliance to compensate for their mutual deficiencies. Faced with the urges of the moral, the naturalistic human being appears to be subhuman. Then it is not beyond them to elevate such a one to the realm of the supernatural, so that he becomes a kind of overman (*Übermensch*).

Mythology, with its transcendence and its phantom-like human beings, is not extinct; it lives on in religion. Metaphysics is supposed to protect this kind of purported moral Being from the charge that it represents nothing more than mythological illusion. For metaphysics withholds truth-value from the intellect altogether, to entrust it, apparently innocently, to the will. A view of the will, however, that elevates it at the expense of the intellect should be regarded with deep mistrust. Since this misguided conception has again become the fashion, we are justified in voicing this methodological suspicion with a clarity suited for the general public: psychology is an inadequate foundation for ethics.

Our ethics is defined as ethics of pure will. Ethics does not concern itself simply with the will: there is no such will. Only ethics is capable of deciding whether or not there is a will. Only from ethics can psychology learn whether it is possible and permissible for the will to exist. But since ethics recognizes only the pure will as the will, then ethics too, in that respect, depends upon logic. For only logic can define the concept of purity. Purity is the Platonic term that describes the basic methodological character of knowledge. If ethics is to be a doctrine of the pure will at all, then it must, as a doctrine and because it is related to purity, be a *kind of knowledge.* The determination of the kind of knowledge depends on the use to which the concept of purity is being put with relation to the will. *Thus, the second rank in the system of philosophy is assigned to ethics.* Ethics takes the second rank, after the first, which rightly belongs to logic—to logic, but not to psychology.

However, the illusion that ethics must be grounded in psychology might gain new strength from a consideration of the problem of the pure will. We must examine this illusion before we can draw on logic for the concept of purity as logic defines it, to deploy it in dealing with the problem of the will. As logic defines it, the pure is juxtaposed to what is impure, to a mixture. Every variety of the empirical contains a mixture of elements. Logic and, consequently, ethics must disaggregate these elements in turn, in order to separate the foundation—as the pure—from secondary elements. It is therefore unavoidable that an experience must be given and must be found that can be examined for purity. It turns out that the experience in question can only be an experience of human psychic life and thus belongs necessarily to the domain of psychology. Now we need not repeat our earlier deliberations, but we can apply them to a new arena of psychic life; in this new arena the prejudice of psychology will confront ethics with a new danger.

* * *

This new arena is *history.* Now is it true that in history we face a new form of the prejudice of psychology? We have already considered the prejudice of psychology in two powerful, basic forms: in the correlation of the individual, plurality, and totality, and then in the problem of the will. In history, both of these aspects are in play. In all of the controversies concerning the value of history as a scientific discipline, the first and second considerations constitute the real core of the controversy, for in it they both converge.

Ultimately, all questions about the value of a scientific discipline concern *the concept of law.* Only where there is law is there power, for power is nothing other than objectified law. Of what does the motivational power of history consist? One cannot ask "of which law," for law is already anticipated in power. The question refers directly to psychic power, to *consciousness* and its like, if indeed both the power of nature and mythological powers, which impinge from without, are ruled out. Are we concerned, therefore, only with the human being? And with which powers and tendencies of human consciousness?

Let us consider, first, the controversy among differing views on the concepts of the individual and particularity. Hero cults have influenced and promoted not only religion, but also politics. According to one modern view, the polis is based principally on the hero cult. Quite aside from mythology, the hero still functions, through the individual, as the driving power of history. All history is just the spirit of those men in whom their times are reflected.[23] History is merely the mirror, the reflection; the source of the light is located solely in the individual. That is the basic idea of the Stoics—an idea that is itself only a consequence of their naturalism. If nature contains the ultimate law of ethics, then that claim implies the correction: that nature represents what is right, that nature is the right nature. However, nature as right can be represented in human beings only in rare cases. Thus arises the concept of the *ideal of the wise man.*

The wise man represents nature. However, he does not remain just an ideal; he becomes nature. He is nature. But nature becomes reality, in turn, only in such an exquisite individual. The rest of reality is not only distinct from nature, but also stands in opposition to it. It is the meaning and the goal of the reality of the ideal to be a paradigm for the actual reality that is distinct from it. Why, however, is the wise man, in this worldview, still called "nature"?

There is a profound contradiction at work here, and it pervades the entire system of Stoicism. *Ideal and nature:* both supposedly coexist, yet both limit and infringe upon each other. This aspect of Stoicism entered into *Christianity.* God became an individual. Here we will disregard the problem of monotheism entirely and focus only on the significance of Christ the individual as an ideal for humanity. We conceive of his significance as God, exclusively from the perspective of his significance as a human being. Thus, our sole purpose is to constitute

23. [Another allusion to Goethe's *Faust:* "My friend, the spirit of an earlier time, / To us it is a seven-sealed mystery; / And what you learned gentlemen would call / Its spirit, is its image, that is all, / Reflected in your own mind's history (Was ihr den Geist der Zeiten heißt, / Das ist im Grund der Herren eigner Geist, / In dem die Zeiten sich bespiegeln)" (*Faust*, Luke trans., 21, lines 575–79).]

ethics by human means. Fundamentally, however, this is also the strongest basis of the argument for the divinity of Christ. To be sure, it is not in Paul, and perhaps not yet in John, but it is quite unmistakable in the Greek Fathers. Thus, it continues to influence the history of philosophy. For the pious *Malebranche* as for *Leibniz*, Christ is the ideal of humankind. We must understand the God-man as an individual, doing so from this undogmatic, most ideal perspective.

One should not raise the objection that, if we eliminate the individual, we destroy the concept of the ideal. For that is precisely the question that we are considering here—whether the ideal, whether ethics, can be represented in an individual. It would be wrong to say that, for just that reason, Christ is God. For what is at issue here is not God, but the human being—not holiness, but ethics.

Nor should one say that history, for its development and progress, presupposes the ideal of the individual. For the resolution of this question should not be prejudged, whether the individual is the exclusive or even the genuine moving force in history. With Christ the preoccupation with this question only becomes all the more confused and problematic, since he is at once God and human being. That is, he is not just a human being; but when conceived in the most ideal form, he is supposed to signify the ideal human being.

This is the grand notion of free moral critique by means of which *Lessing* achieved emancipation from historical religion: he recognized that the imitation of Christ constituted a great harm, caused by Christian ethics. Furthermore, such harm will not be ameliorated, at least not as it concerns the interests of philosophical ethics, by appending the consolation "O well for them that he was a good man."[24] Whether this fact had a decisive influence on the progress of history—that question too should not be prejudged. Rather, the enduring question is whether the concept of history is adequately served by the concept of the individual.

---

24. ["Wohl ihnen, dass er so ein guter Mensch / Noch war!" Cohen is quoting from act 2, scene 1, of *Nathan der Weise* ("Nathan the Wise"), the drama by Gotthold Ephraim Lessing (1729–81) set in Crusader-era Jerusalem. Sittah, the sister of Saladin, delivers a sardonic critique of Christianity: "Their pride is to be Christians, and not men. / For even that which from their Founder's day / With human nature spices superstition / They don't love for its human worth: because / Their Jesus taught it, by him alone it was done.— / O well for them that he was a good man!" (Gotthold Ephraim Lessing, *Nathan the Wise*, trans. Bayard Quincy Morgan, 13th printing (New York: Continuum, 1989), 35. Lessing's drama has endured as an iconic statement of the German Enlightenment's critique of revealed religion and as a plea for religious toleration.]

There is one more difficulty in the concept of Christ's individuality worthy of attention: it exacerbates the difficulty in the Stoic ideal of the wise man. This ideal is supposed to be realized not just in one individual; and yet Christ, as the God-man, is *unique*. In the case of Christ, the individual not only contrasts with particularity; it contradicts it. For that reason, the heresy that envisioned the eternal gospel and the eternal Christ, the analogy between Christ and Adam, remained, for the most part, esoteric. There is a close connection between this view of the philosophy of history and the socialist theory of the forces motivating history. Once this view was implicated in its kinship with politics, the heresy was exposed and stamped out.[25]

However, the serious obstacle presented by the view that Christ is an individual is this: he must be conceived of as the *only* individual. Furthermore, this obstacle applies to all intellectual culture, for the realm of reason is the realm of the intellect. A plurality of individuals is required for the outpouring of the Holy Spirit. Just as the individual is inexhaustible, so too the Spirit cannot be exhausted by a single individual. And just as the content of ethics is inexhaustible, no individual is capable of doing it complete justice.

The Stoic-Christian idea of the ideal power of the individual, which, at least in Stoicism, is rooted in naturalism, has been the dominant influence on our entire view of the principal sources of history. Its influence has not been limited to an idealism of suffering and renunciation. It has manifested itself often enough in the materialistic veneration of power, even in our own day. For in history, it is not the poor and the wretched, but the powerful who become heroes. One's view of history thus becomes one's formative view of *politics*.

The moral value of a historical idea thus recedes behind the question with which individual the idea is associated. Now the party stands behind the individual. Thus, the individual is associated with a particular group. Is the question of the basic force of history, then, a question of the opposition between the individual and the particular? Or is the individual himself only one link in the chain of a particular group? Is it not, in fact, implicit in the concept of the individual

25. [The "Eternal Gospel" is a heresy that invokes a verse in Revelation (14:6) and was purportedly disseminated by followers of Joachim of Fiore (c. 1135–1202). In suggesting a connection between the Joachite conception of "three stages" of history and the "socialist" (that is, Marxist) theory of history, Cohen anticipates a connection drawn later by others as well. See Warwick Gould and Marjorie Reeves, *Joachim of Fiore and the Myth of the Eternal Evangel in the Nineteenth and Twentieth Centuries*, rev. ed. (Oxford: Oxford University Press, 2001), 2–3.]

that he does not split into a plurality of such individuals, but rather develops in their midst? For the concept of history, the true opposite of the individual is not particularity, but totality.

For that reason, we also cannot say that ultimately the *people* (Volk) is the opposite of the individual. For the people constitutes, at least for anthropology, a concept based on unity—on a physical basis—and is thus a totality. By contrast, in the political understanding of history, it is the *state* that takes on a moral mission. In a fateful ambiguity, that moral mission is commonly attributed to the people. The people breaks down into classes; hereditary nobility is an enduring example of this phenomenon that is still insufficient as a deterrent. In its social classes, the people is an aggregate of particularities, and consequently is itself a particularity. It falls to the concept of the state to juxtapose this aggregate to the concept of totality. Totality is the compelling unity to which all these particularities must be subordinated.

The degree to which the concept of a people in itself constitutes a particularity is evident when we consider the conflicts among peoples as individualities, without even considering the relationship of the people to the concept of the state. Of course, the political substance of world history should not be examined solely as a matter of the opposition between these particularities on the one hand and the concept of the totality of humanity on the other. That would be both absurd and incorrect. It is an error to think that peoples, as individualities, in and of themselves constitute the ultimate content and object of history. This error is in no way based on the claim that it would be prejudiced to regard the concept of a people, in and of itself, as an ideal unity. Rather, the error comes about when the internal, objective *correlation of the concept of the people to the concept of the state* is carried out improperly.

The struggle between races and tribes is immoral, it is antimoral, and in political history, it is the moral impediment. In this struggle, a people plays itself out as a particularity. The *unity of the people*, however, is a fundamental idea of political morality, for it signifies, in fact, the unity of the state. *The state is the ethical factor in the concept of a consanguine people.*

Thus, we come to the most profound *distinction* for the individual *in the concept of history*. It is not the difference between singular and plural, or the difference in rank among individual protagonists on the world stage, or the difference between the speakers and the choir, consisting of the masses who, until this point in the course of history, had been excluded from contributing to culture autonomously. From the point of view of particularity, all these differences would, after all, still be merely relative and transitory. The individual only appears to be derived from these factors. In truth it receives its meaning from an entirely different logical consideration.

The genuine distinction is that between particularity and totality. The individual, as commonly understood and postulated, is a member of [the category of] particularity. Totality, however, can refer both to the individual and to particularity; as a result, both become something different and new. The union brought about by the totality means that individuals no longer float about in a loose structure of particularity; totality fixes, secures, and grounds them in a creative unity. They are transformed and reborn—reborn as individuals.

What then is the unifying power of the totality that we must acknowledge in the state, the state being juxtaposed, in our modern culture, to class and race? The power cannot lie in single individuals, for they belong, one and all, to a preliminary stage of particularity. Thus, we arrive at an entirely different distinction in relation to the individual: *the distinction between the person and persons in general on the one hand, and facts on the other.* What do these "facts" signify? Are they merely the conditions, institutions, and movements that, as mass phenomena, confront individuals? Even so, it would not be the movement of a mass of individuals that represents the power of the masses; rather, the facts—facts that seem to be impersonal—are the facts in which all reality of the things of this world exists. Now, what is the epistemological (*geistig*) status of these facts? Anything that has its place in the human world must have some kind of epistemological status.

At this juncture the controversies about the concept of history begin anew. Similarly, the old questions concerning the relationship between the will and the intellect are also revived, and with a significance that is more sharply focused. The question concerns the antagonism *between material power relations and ideas.*

In all branches of historiography, it is this antagonism that determines its spirit and method. Nearly everything revolves around this antagonistic distinction—not only in the history of economics, the state, and law, but no less in the history of the so-called humanities (in the narrow sense), up to and including the history of philosophy. If we are to succeed in laying the foundation of ethics, then everything depends on giving a clear and precise exposition of the antagonism between material power relations and ideas, even if this antagonism is entangled in a web of ambiguities. The task of this introduction is to outline the organization of the question, not to resolve it. The introduction must, however, prepare the way for and introduce the exposition.

We must first take into account that this antagonism must be incorrect or at least inadequate in its formulation. For its two elements are not precisely defined and therefore do not necessarily constitute a contradiction. *What is the significance of these ideas that are juxtaposed to real power relations?* Are the ideas identical to concepts? If they are universal theoretical ideas, how could they be distinct from the real things that move history? Then they would have to be the concepts of these things. But on the other hand, how could real things and relations exist apart from concepts, if these concepts are, after all, the concepts of these very things and relations? In the context of this conflict, then, "idea" cannot have the merely theoretical meaning associated with "concepts."

Thus, we arrive at the *disparity between theoretical concepts and moral ideas.* The difference between power relations and ideas is of a similar kind. Here, the controversy about the *so-called materialistic view of history*[26] becomes complicated and confused. In this distinction, moral conscience plays a dominant role, and it would be utterly absurd, in this context, to exclude the ethical perspective, replacing it with the purely theoretical perspective instead. In fact, this distinction should not even be permitted, since, ultimately, the distinction has to do only with ethical ideas. Thus, it could very well be the case that, angered and vexed by the hypocritical use of ethical ideas, one would point to unethical power relations for the purpose of revealing, in them, the driving force of all previous history. Nothing could be farther from materialism; it would, in fact, be a restrained form of idealism that guided this view of history.

On the other hand, however, it would be wrong and misleading if one were to rely only on such popular terms, seeking to conceal the fact that it is not only theoretical concepts that are embodied in real power relations. (In our day, there would be no argument on this point.) It would be wrong to seek to conceal that, in fact, ethical ideas, however obscure and however inadequately developed, manifest themselves in those real relations and institutions. It is simply not correct that natural necessity, and in particular the animal nature in the human being, has produced those institutions of culture that only a hypocrite would call "moral culture." In fact it should just be called "economic culture." It is not right to conceive of human nature as such only as a predator, while marking off some space elsewhere for spiritual and moral life. Where can one find space; where can such a space be relocated?

26. [Cohen is referring to "historical materialism," the theory of history developed by Karl Marx (1818–83).]

In this poignant account, matters intellectual and moral run the unavoidable risk of dissolving into a chimera. It is just plain spite and anger that push them into the background. The error here, as one can see clearly, is the very same error as was committed earlier, in the definition of the relationship between the will and the intellect. If the will that produces the institutions of culture were just the will of self-interest and greed, then one would have to devise another type of will to serve as the source of moral culture. It would be utterly wrong, for instance, to attribute culture to the intellect, for then the distinction between "what is" and "what ought to be" would be lost. Then the fundamental distinction on which our sense of truth is based would be obscured and undermined: the distinction between mathematical natural science and everything else in the intellectual and moral realm that has the potential to become a field of systematic inquiry.

We are thus permitted, as a methodological step, to annul the sharp distinction made in the socialist conception of history between real power relations and moral ideas, and we can do so without spreading misperceptions or suspicions, or casting aspersions on the socialist conception of history. At the same time, in no way does this mean that the objective difference between real power relations and ethical ideas would cease to be, only because the ideas were congruent with the things and merged with them without remainder. This would contradict the concept of the Ought, which itself, according to our maxim, is the significance of the moral ideas. But it is false realism and false nominalism to present things as products of economic drives on the one hand, but to depict moral tasks as phantoms and as posthistorical forces, as if they were flashes of heat lightning illuminating the darkness of history.

Instead, ethics has to reach a logical understanding with history: it has to be able to recognize its own ideas, however undeveloped and stunted they may be, in the objects of the economic world. For there is an inescapable choice between two alternatives: In the first alternative, all culture in its institutions is the work of the devil, and the will itself is therefore also just a force of evil; in this case, however, it is no longer possible that the intellect could be a psychic power sufficiently heterogeneous that it alone could constitute a force for the good. In the second alternative, the goal of the intellect is not evil, and the will, which is related to the intellect, is directed toward the good. Then its creations—partial and inadequate though they be—are still representations of ethical, and not just theoretical, ideas.

For that is the basic idea, and we ought not lose sight of it: *ethics presupposes logic, but logic is not, in itself, ethics.*

Thus, ethics presupposes natural science too, in all its varieties, but ethics is not absorbed by natural science. As a consequence, moral ideas must be distinguished, now and always, from theoretical concepts. This distinction, however, must not be allowed to sunder the relationship between them. That would be the case, however, if the distinction between real things, in which theoretical concepts are realized, and ethical ideas were irreconcilable.

This is the fundamental error in every materialistic slogan: if the possibility of any relationship or correlation between the ethical and the intellectual is annulled, then the basis of *pure, generating consciousness* is also erased and destroyed. In fact, ethical ideas are not exclusively ethical; they are also theoretical, despite the distinction that must be made between these two types. For both are types of pure consciousness: the one of thought, the other of the will. If, on the other hand, ethical ideas are not taken as causes of culture and history, then consciousness and *spirit are denied altogether*. Only then does materialism inevitably enter into this way of thinking. Then it will be claimed—uncritically—that nature, in concert with human beings, has produced, from its own soil and climate, all these objects that are the playthings of the human world. Then this materialistic and naturalistic view of history is exposed for what it is: the *annulment of history*, for history—as the history of human beings and their works and deeds—is the history of the spirit and of ideas. Otherwise there would be no world history, only natural history.

The result of all these considerations is this: history, by its own definition, cannot be the precondition of ethics; history in fact presupposes ethics for its own foundational concepts and its own problems. It cannot carry out the ongoing labor of defining the content of these concepts without the guidance of ethics. We have seen, for example, that the emendation of the concept of the will depends on the concept of ethical ideas, considered in relation to theoretical concepts.

Now, from this angle, the *concept of the individual* can appear in its proper light. The individual person is not an individual of a particular plurality. This remains the case even if the individual is conceived of as unique. For the overman must, after all, be returned forthwith to the confines of his milieu. Despite all *hero worship*, the clash of opinions and ideas will see to that. The perspective that is based on social milieu represents a mild reaction to the notion that a man of such power should enjoy special status.[27]

27. [In a number of places in his *Ethics of Pure Will*, Cohen refers to the notion that the social and economic "milieu" constitute the determinant of the moral character of the individual, as opposed to a conception of the individual derived from the idea of freedom.]

But we now see that the opposition between the individual and institutions, material as well as ideal, is entirely erroneous and false. Individuals do not merge into institutions and ideas. For ideas, and similarly institutions themselves, exceed in their universality even the greatest individuality. Still, just as ideas must be actualized in institutions, so too must they be represented and generated in individuals. In the end, then, it turns out *that the individual can only be the individual of the idea.*

*   *   *

Nor can sociology be posited as the precondition of ethics. As for the concept of society, we will deal with it later in greater detail. For now we will give our attention only to the method that guides the science of society. The meaning of the term "society" emerged in distinction to the firm and seemingly finished formations of history, as they coalesce, for instance, in the formation of the state. This distinction endures. The dynamic perspective of movement has now taken the place of stasis, against which state and law in particular appear to be a kind of perfected form of nature. But the helpful perspective afforded by the concept of "movement" leads to confusion, which we just observed, with a change in terminology, in the case of history. The confusion concerns the concept of *development*.

Since the perspective of movement is now being applied to the human being, "movement" should be narrowed to mean "development." The significance of movement for a material point is analogous to the significance of development for the biological individual. The social individual too is conceived of, first and foremost, as a biological individual. Just as organic evolutionary history traces the development of the organism from the cell, so too sociology aspires to the function of evolutionary history, for the study of what it therefore likes to call *social organisms*. It strives to trace the development of the compact, powerful, and complex institutions of culture from their most primitive, simple elements. Now this is not a conclusive discussion of the methodological value of sociology; we are far from disputing its utility. At issue is only its relationship to ethics, and we are deliberating on the principle that sociology may not serve as the precondition of ethics. Such a possibility is incompatible with the fundamental concept of sociology, the concept of development.

In biology, evolutionary history presupposes precise knowledge of the finished organism. Embryology does not have in mind a general, unstable image of the normal organism. Rather, the whole organism and each organ in its normal physiological state is the precise model. *However, does this precise organism have its analogy in the social organism and its social organs?* Is not the use of the term "organism," in fact, a metaphor, and, in the end, an imperfect one?

Even the relationship of organs to the organism does not apply here. It may be possible to regard discrete social institutions as social organs, but it is questionable to call them social organisms. *For an organism is a unity of organs.* Where, however, would such a unity exist for individual social institutions, even if in a condition that was only an approximation of normalcy? Moreover, where is the unity that applies to all of them and would make it possible to transfer the name "organism" to the unity of the whole? Might not the state be this unity? Unity is certainly the task of the state, but does the state fulfill its task? Is it not, in fact, precisely because the state does not fulfill its task, that the sociological perspective intervenes with a corrective, to prevent—say—skepticism and nihilistic anarchism from gaining ground?

Thus, there appears to be *a contradiction in the task of sociology* that can be eliminated by correctly defining the relationship of sociology to ethics. Absent such a definition, this contradiction renders the subject matter of sociology uncertain and imprecise. Sociology is driven by the idea that the objects of culture are not, so to speak, finished substances of absolute value. Sociology uses the developmental perspective to reveal the bare seeds from which the objects of culture grow. In general, of course, this may seem feasible: the most wild forms and rules of *mating*, if they are only rules of copulation, may be regarded as elementary structures of monogamy, and one may make analogous assumptions with respect to the elementary stipulations of the laws of *inheritance* and *property*. But this line of thinking will not take us beyond general analogies that, because they are general, are often not a precise match. One will always have to consider the *ideas and ideal feelings* that distinguish the higher orders from the lower ones, subtly to be sure, but all the more precisely. The elementary structure inevitably becomes more complicated as a result.

The contradiction thus becomes twofold. One begins with the assumption that one should refuse to regard the finished structure as perfected. This is contradicted, however, by the scientific concept of development, which in fact takes, as its methodological presupposition, the normal, final form of the organism. Yet it is precisely this notion of "normal" that is being questioned and challenged here, indeed *in both senses of the term*: "norm" as correct functioning, "norm" as a standard and paradigm. Rather, the aim here is to show that the social structures of our culture, which to us, in our arrogance, seem to be in a perfected state, are still in their infancy. However, if this is the charitable understanding of the meaning of such an approach in research, then this approach must now realize that it lacks the norm that the scientific developmental method clearly presupposes.

Despite these fundamental weaknesses, however, since sociology, operating according to general historical points of view, produces illuminating results and discoveries, a *twofold contradiction* appears, in that the second contradiction seeks to correct the first. More specifically, the thoughts and feelings that—in marriage and property, for example—influence the higher, later forms of these institutions are inevitably also taken into account in their lower forms. As a result, a *type of normal form* is presupposed nevertheless, and taken as a plan for development.

However, by means of such anticipation, the methodology of sociology is corrected, understood as the methodology of development. More than that: the entire direction of the discipline is changed. It can no longer proceed against *individuals*, letting them be absorbed and vanish in the masses. For sociology needs such individuals and uses them for ethical thoughts and feelings. Or could there be thoughts and feelings without individuals? Thus, sociology also cannot proceed against *ideas*, replacing them, say, with institutions. For in institutions too sociology must anticipate ideas. Sociology cannot sustain a distinction, let alone a contradiction, between the two. It is incorrect to say that ideas are institutions reduced to vapor; rather, institutions are ideas congealed into solids.

It turns out, then, that the contradiction that ails sociology can be cured by correcting its relationship to ethics. *Sociology is not the precondition of ethics; rather, ethics serves silently as the precondition of sociology and of social development.* Ethics constitutes this precondition, however, not as a part of the system of philosophy, but rather as a fictitious combination of ethical ideas. The present task, then, is to replace this well-intentioned fiction and allow ethics to take its place as constituted in a system: presupposing logic, but still as ethics of the pure will, with its own content and its own method. Ethics must take its place in accordance with but apart from, and apart from but in accordance with, the logic of pure cognition. The logic of pure cognition remains the precondition, but it points beyond itself to ethics. It is true that history of any kind presupposes first and foremost logic. However, aside from this universal, formal foundation, the content of its concepts is provided not by psychology, but solely by ethics. Ethics is foundational.

*   *   *

This examination of the concept of development is incomplete, however, without considering another central philosophical question. To do so, we return to metaphysics, but now to metaphysics in the history of philosophical thought in its classical forms. The developmental perspective dominates *Hegel's* way of thinking. *Dialectical movement* is nothing other than *development*, and it is only too clear, everywhere in Hegel's thought, that the final result is always presupposed. Even *Schelling* was defined by the concept of development: his "potencies"[28] are nothing other than stages of development. This thoroughgoing perspective may have contributed more than a little to the fact that the philosophy of the Romantics appeared to be more sober and realistic, in the modern sense, than its abstract symbolism might otherwise have allowed. Hegel's influence, in particular on historical research, was at once so deep and comprehensive that it was permitted to regard his dialectical movement as the paradigm and model of historical research. Moreover, dialectical movement brought the developmental perspective alive for the entire system of philosophy itself. But one has to ask whether, as a result, the system of philosophy has been quickened in all its parts or, in some, been stifled. What is the status of ethics?

We already noted that Hegel, no less than Schelling, did not write a separate work on ethics. After all, just as Spinoza wrote only an "Ethics" that contained his logic or metaphysics, *Hegel's logic would contain his ethics*. The idea, as he calls the concept in its highest stage of perfection, develops as the *absolute*. And ethics, in its highest form, signifies this absolute. It is well known that, on this point, the Hegelian schools split up into extreme positions. *Religion* is one such form of the absolute. But on the problem of religion Hegelians take the most contradictory and factious positions. The state, in particular, is one such form of the absolute, but Hegelians split into political reactionaries and revolutionaries. The developmental perspective, then, has not proven to be an unambiguous guiding principle.

Now one might think that the concept of development has been applied too directly to the concrete institutions and conditions of history—to religion, law, and history in general, and no less to art. To be sure, such a direct use of the dialectical method is in itself impressive, but it is also doubtless a source of error.

28. ["*Potenz*" (meaning potency, force, or power) is the term Schelling uses to describe the fundamental powers of attraction and expansion that account, in his philosophy of nature, for the dynamic progression from inert matter to human consciousness. See Friedrich Wilhelm Joseph von Schelling, *Erster Entwurf eines Systems der Naturphilosophie* (Jena, Germany: Gabler, 1799).]

However, it does not point to the actual reason for error. The error is located in the pantheistic core of the system. That is, it is pantheism that centers the system of philosophy and all Being in nature.

In such a system, then, there may not and there cannot be an Ought distinct from the Is. In such a system the idea is not the same as the Ought, whereas the concept is the same as the Is. Instead, the idea is only a development from out of the concept. The idea thus remains the focus of the Is, which also includes the Ought. Thus, that which otherwise would be ethics becomes a product of the development of logic. *Deus sive natura.* That is the way it is. And that is and always will be the fundamental error of pantheism, including therefore the philosophy of identity.[29] It does not say "Natura necnon Deus"[30]—if, for the sake of contrast, one may use this phrase in a discussion of ethics.

The naturalism of dialectical development consists of this move. *The idea assumes the role of a power of nature,* since it is, after all, a category of being. Moreover, from the perspective of historical inquiry too the idea appears to be a power of nature. Furthermore, that perspective is also the perspective of speculative inquiry, for [the idea of] development—dialectical movement—not only unites both of these perspectives, it combines them into one. Thus, the old dogmatic metaphysics, in modern historical garb, takes the place of ethics.

The fate of humankind and of the world is thus revealed. Yet no one asks whether, in the face of fate, the human being still has a role of his own, and in fact, a twofold role: not only the role of an acting subject—because then one might still ask whether, in fact, he is not merely being pushed[31]—but the role of a knowing subject as well. However, this knowing subject must look beyond his fate, which is neither his primary nor his ultimate interest. His interest is in the type, meaning, and right of his role as an acting subject.

*   *   *

29. [See n15.]

30. [Meaning "Nature, and also God," Cohen's own Latin coinage. This is a deliberate play on Spinoza's "Deus sive natura," meaning "God, or, if you will, nature."]

31. ["Being pushed" invokes an oft-quoted passage in Goethe's *Faust* in which Mephistopheles urges Faust on, as they struggle through the crowd on Walpurgis Night. It is construed to be dismissing free will as an illusion: "Der ganze Strudel strebt nach oben / Du glaubst zu schieben, und du wirst geschoben" ("The whole mob streams and strives uphill; / One thinks one's pushing, and one's pushed against one's will.") (*Faust*, Luke trans., 130, line 4116).]

Opposition to metaphysics thus leads us to *opposition to mythology and to mythological religion.* Mythology is driven by the individual's fear—not so much of his sin, but of his fate, at most on account of his sin. However, it is always the *existence of an individual* that is at stake: whether he has an end and what then becomes of him after his end—so that the end, actually, is no end at all. His interest is not much better in the golden beyond, if his blessed end is endless and the individual can rejoice in his exalted existence for all eternity. Art contributed significantly to such a mythology of the individual. The primal mythological force of religion has thus been nourished, just as the excesses of metaphysics have been exacerbated, by the same transcendence.

It was not only that fate became the dark power that one cannot escape, as in dramatic poetry; more than that, all questions concerning the essence of the human being were reduced to this external source. *That is the unethical element in that idea of fate.* Drama itself counteracts myth by making the hero not only a suffering individual, but also an individual who acts. He acts in the midst of the very suffering in which he is subjected to fate, and yet at the same time he acts against his fate, as if out of his own volition.

To be sure, religion too draws upon the human being's capacity for action. It is the view of Christianity that the sin of the human being is not solely original sin, the sin of Adam; but human action presupposes the capacity for both good and evil. And if faith in Christ is made a condition for the propensity toward the good, then such faith in Christ can also be interpreted, as we have seen, as faith in the ideal human being. But here too the connection with myth persists, for what is ultimately at issue is still the fate of the individual, his eternal salvation or damnation.

Thus, here it is not only the concept of the individual that presents an obstacle to ethics; the concept of the individual, being one-sided and not fully developed in itself, always interferes with the autonomy of ethics. But it is also the human interest in fate that comes into conflict with ethics. Fate is an element of mythology, and fate persists in religion only insofar as religion remains enmired in mythology. *Fate is a companion of chaos.*

As a result, the distinction *between theoretical and practical reason* is annulled. Yet, it is beyond question that the distinction between these two kinds of interest is necessary; that is the meaning of the difference between Is and Ought. The one is theoretical interest in the Is of nature; the other is practical interest, interest in action and the will. However, practical interest is also a rational interest, and thus also a kind of theoretical interest. This is the point at which the distinction between the *will and the intellect* always gets slippery. Now, however, we can see what is at stake.

To be sure, the problem of ethics must also be a form of knowledge—a strict, precise act of cognition. Otherwise, the will could not be pure will, as we will later see. But the interest of practical reason is focused on the cognition of the pure will and the cognition of the action issuing from it. The concept of the human being will be defined by the pure will and by the action issuing from it. The concern of ethics is not the fate of the individual, but the concept of the human being, insofar as it is grounded in his will and his action. The fate of the individual is a theoretical question—that is, a question of mythological curiosity, which may be related to art and even to religion; that question, however, is not under discussion here, and it must not be confounded with the task of ethics. Ethics has other theoretical interests, which must always be focused, exclusively, on the will and on action. It is inevitable that these interests will ebb if they are directed to the fate of the individual.

In this light, the distinction between *faith and knowledge* becomes clearer, a distinction that has been invoked and revived in a variety of forms. We may leave aside that fundamental attitude that grounds faith on holy scripture, even if this attitude grounds the rules that govern the will on scripture as well. Faith in a book is a kind of knowledge, no matter what doctrines are drawn from the book. And even if Christ himself is substituted for the gospel, he, too, becomes a source of knowledge and its warrant, even if such knowledge may be called "lived experience (*Erleben*)."[32]

The extent to which this whole antithesis[33] is concerned with the correlation to knowledge can be discerned from the fact that it always attempts to place limitations on knowledge. Knowledge is supposed to deal only with the natural human being, in the same way it treats nature in general; knowledge, however, has no access to the ethical and is alien to it. Hence, the interest of reason in the ethical is abridged, and the theory of ethics is called into question. But if the philosophy of ethics is rejected, that is, if salt loses its savor, wherewith shall it be salted?[34]

---

32. [Cohen is alluding to the theology of his Marburg colleague Wilhelm Herrmann (1846–1922).]

33. [That is, the antithesis of faith.]

34. [Cohen's turn of phrase is an allusion to the Sermon on the Mount: "Ye are the salt of the earth: but if the salt have lost its savor, wherewith shall it be salted?" (Matt. 5:13, King James Version).]

Thus, one arrives at the unavoidable conclusion that the faith that is juxtaposed to knowledge must contradict and defy reason and its theoretical interests. Faith is now alleged to belong to a superior and entirely different category and to provide an entirely different kind of certainty than that offered by knowledge. It is true that it is an entirely different type of knowledge that constitutes the interest of faith: in faith, everything revolves around the fate of the individual. And, in this context, it should not be ignored that even if the actions of the human being are fully included in the discussion, they do not represent the main issue, and certainly not the actual or only issue that is at stake here. If that were the case, one would not insist on the distinction between faith and knowledge and continually modify it, to gain, from faith, a superior and different kind of certainty.

The argument thus remains that faith is supposed to represent a firm antithesis to ethics, as an element of a philosophical system. And this discordance is promoted by a metaphysics that purports to offer philosophical support for appealing to faith. As a consequence, the possibility of ethics is annulled.

Yet another danger has always threatened the systematic, philosophical character of ethics. Recently it has reappeared: the so-called *ethical culture* movement.[35] To be sure, one might wish to adopt a sympathetic posture toward a movement that flies the banner of ethics and seeks to gather and unite human beings of any faith and tribe, and all of this in an era beset by a confusion of humanitarian feeling and by economic greed. But this immediate feeling is not a reliable guide for politics, even less if philosophical ethics is swayed by it. Sophism, too, was not always immoral—neither in its teachers nor in its teachings. But Socrates nevertheless vanquished it by introducing the following sentence into the world: virtue is knowledge. knowledge means cognition, and cognition is philosophy.

The term *culture* is called upon to counter philosophy and philosophical ethics—as if all that mattered here were the practice and cultivation of morality, and not primarily the acquisition of knowledge. This might still appear to be an innocuous mistake, even though the Sophists declared that virtue is a matter of works and has no need of logical grounds. For that reason alone philosophy would have a justified and substantial interest in curbing the injury that, as a re-

---

35. [Cohen is describing the views of the Society for Ethical Culture, founded in New York in 1876 by Felix Adler (1851–1933). Also known as "the ethical movement," it adopted a neutral attitude on metaphysical and theological questions. Eventually a German branch was established as well.]

sult, threatens the system of philosophy. However, the weaknesses in this notion can be seen in an even more general way.

By confining the problem of ethics to culture, one encourages the prejudice that *morality is self-evident*, that there cannot really be any doubt about this claim, about which only philosophy and perhaps also religion may awaken skepticism. Then every possible vague and ambiguous stock phrase rushes at once to the aid of this claim: that the ethical is innate, that the human being (that is, the individual) is good, and that it is only the human being in the plural that makes him evil. In all of these charitable opinions of humankind, opinions that, in several variations, course through the centuries, a fundamental error recurs: the human being is conceived of in his psychological nature. For this reason, one resists philosophy or—as it is put more innocently—metaphysics. For otherwise one would have to begin with logic; but it is assumed that it is easier to work with psychology.

If, however, one takes psychology as the point of departure, for good or for ill, one will encounter the difficulties that arise from that quarter, for the individual and for the will as well. For that reason it helps little, by contrast, to raise the flag of sociology timidly, to influence the imbalance of the individual and the impulsive imperialism of his will. This will not lead to a reconciliation of the conflict. For wherever the nature of morality is presupposed and considered to be self-evident in the nature of the human being, the result is not a complete, fulfilled correlation, but only the purported correlation of the individual and the plurality or particularity. The error was committed at the very start, in not defining the problem as the task of finding the proper term of correlation in *totality*.

If this insight were to hold, it could never again be doubted that ethical culture must be grounded in the *culture of ethics*. For to survey the meanings of this totality in the history of culture and to examine its purely ethical content is an eminently theoretical task in which the value of ethics must be recognized with certainty, both in defining the task and in carrying it out. *Ethical culture diverts attention from the problem of the totality, because the self-evident status of morality, characteristic of ethical culture, inheres in the individual.*

At this juncture, however, we are confronted with an even more serious error in this notion. From the very start, the idea [of ethical culture] diverts attention from the totality, thus diverting attention from the context of problems in which morality is located and in which, therefore, it should also be discussed. *That context is the state.* Thus, in principle, morality may be subordinated to practical culture only in political movements. If morality is detached from the context of the state, then it is abandoned to the very domain it [ethical culture] was seeking to resist.

Ethical culture confronts religion for the purpose of eradicating the exclusivity to which religion falls prey. It is so consistent that it also confronts one-sidedness in politics. Nevertheless, it is also active outside the political arena. Unavoidably, then, it is marginalized as a religious sect. Whenever ethics is taken up as an issue outside the realm of politics, it inevitably lands in the confines of a cloister, no matter how hostile the attitude toward religious dogma.

Here, however, a serious wrong is inflicted on religion too, with a profound effect on the *relationship of religion to ethics*. We have observed that religion, as faith, is [a kind of] knowledge, and that this knowledge concerns the fate of the human being. Ethics, on the other hand, concerns the concept of the human being insofar as it is derived from his will and action. The distinction is far-reaching; but is the substance of this distinction enough to satisfy?

Is then the *fate of the human being* supposed to be merely a question of mythology that is prior to culture, and that will deal with the question of the *fate of the world* in the same way? Should it not rather be acknowledged that religion is a kind of knowledge, if religion were to take up these questions and make them its own, even if these same questions already engaged mythology, and even if religion were not able to resolve them? Surely it is not only blind faith that concerns itself with the *"whence" and "whither"* of the world and humankind. One is justified in saying *non liquet* [it is not proven][36] only after lengthy investigation. However, if one believes one can just dismiss the interest in these questions as vain, then that is a symptom of serious case of myopia. What is evident in such primitive questions is, after all, a sense of the interconnection of all being. It cannot be that world begins with me and comes to an end with me. Therefore, it cannot be that I myself come to an end. The only question that matters—the question that has priority—is who and what I am myself. Thus, it is still the concept of the individual that constitutes the problem.

Consequently, it cannot be the case that ethics has nothing whatsoever to do with these questions; after all, they inhere in the very problem of the individual. But ethics should not be expected to steer unassisted toward this formulation of the problem. Instead, it should, during its journey, acquire the tools needed to allow it to land safely where myth and religion would suffer shipwreck and vanish into the sands.

36. [A Latin legal term.]

Ethics asks itself the question of "whence" when it emerges from logic. We will have to consider this question. "Whither" constitutes the final question of ethics, without which it would never reach its conclusion.

Consequently, the *relationship between ethics and religion* should not be understood in such a way that ethics dismisses those ancient religious questions as the questions of a childish humankind. Rather, this relationship has to be conceived of differently: ethics must, for its part, take upon itself those questions, the solution to which eludes religion because religion lacks the necessary methodological tools. And ethics must not end in resignation, running aground in a declaration of *"non liquet." It must adopt the questions of "whence" and "whither" as its own task.* These questions are certainly relevant to the concept of the human being.

Therefore, ethics also will assume a position toward religion that is distinct from the position envisioned by ethical culture and by all contemporary movements that eschew religion. All these movements make the fundamental mistake of taking the ethical to be something natural and thus self-evident. For one, philosophy is then superfluous; but religion is even worse: unadulterated evil. We will focus only on the latter point, although the first too deserves mention in the process.

The ethical is said to be natural; that is, *innate* in the human being, like all human drives. For it is apparently not permitted to go beyond the drives. In this philosophical camp, thinking and cognition are not taken to be innate, but only sensation and perception, from which thinking and cognition, as they say, develop. In the same way, moral feeling and willing are said to develop gradually from the instincts and from the activities of the drives. This is how the innate is understood: it is that which develops gradually from the natural forces of the drives. This process of development, then, means that the ethical is the natural outcome and result. The ethical thus appears to be self-evident. An ethical justification would, therefore, be not only superfluous but also dubious and suspect, since it would claim that, in discovering the ethical, it had discovered something of its own, something new.

This claim may, in fact, seem somewhat strange. For millennia, culture has worked toward a moral goal, and all theoretical culture is involved in the development of these insights. How are we supposed to understand it, then, that ethics might implement, or just strive for, something other than the methodological definition of the concept of morality? All types of culture with a knowledge of the scope of the concept of morality must also be able to produce the characteristics that are combined and unified in that concept. To be sure, creating a unity of these characteristics requires subjecting them to certain procedures, but it is only culture that can bring them to light.

Religion, too, is part of culture. And however little it has succeeded or was able to succeed in realizing morality on earth, only bias, delusion, or militant opposition would lead one to argue that religion is just a priestly fraud and to deny that it has any value for ethical culture. The error of this judgment lies again in the view that morality is natural because it is self-evident, and that it is only religion that has so corrupted the nature of morality as to render it unrecognizable. This error can also be called an error of historical insight. Religion is also part of history inasmuch as it belongs to the history of ethical ideas as well. Ethical ideas are what, in the main, constitute the content of history.

Thus far, we have endeavored to clarify the relationship of the individual to institutions and to ideas. We recognized the individual as the individual of the idea, for the material institutions of culture, too, are representations of the idea. Now, conversely, it is our task to focus our attention on the *relationship of the idea to the individual*. Ethical ideas did not emerge on their own; rather, individuals produced them through thinking. Who were these individuals? Certainly, they were philosophers, poets, judges, and statesmen. However, perhaps it was the founders of religion who were not only chronologically prior to these others, but also superior to them in their penetrating energy and in their gravity: they conceived of ethical ideas, fought for their value, and gave their lives for them.

More recently, that type of character that is represented in the history of humanity by the *Israelite prophets* has been rediscovered. "He has told you, O man, what is good."[37] This saying constitutes the motto of prophetism. God is the one who proclaims. This is the limit. The source and sovereign medium is neither the human spirit nor scientific reason. The limit is indicated by the mythological concept of *revelation*.

However, revelation does not stop at this mythological beginning. The limit collapses of its own accord; the source that lies beyond suddenly overflows into a source of its own — into human reason, insofar as the concept of reason brings about agreement and reconciliation between the human being and God. God makes his proclamation to the human being. And what does He proclaim to

37. ["He has told you, O man, what is good, / And what the Lord requires of you: / Only to do justice / And to love goodness, / And to walk modestly with your God" (Mic. 6:8). Citations from the Hebrew Bible are from *Tanakh — The Holy Scriptures: The New JPS Translation According to the Traditional Hebrew Text* (Philadelphia: Jewish Publication Society, 1988).]

him? "What is good." Prophecy thus makes the good the content of religion. Henceforth, the subject and interest of religion shall be only morality, nothing other, that is, than the human being—or rather, human beings, insofar as they are united by the one God into One Humanity. Henceforth the name of "God" shall signify nothing other than the guarantor for this idea, for this conviction concerning the One Humanity.

Myth has an interest in the essence and nature of God and thus also requires a plurality of gods. If indeed, as the prophets teach, there is only One God, then the nature and essence of God can have no disposition of its own that is directed inward, but only a disposition that is directed outward—that is, to human beings. *Therefore, God must be transcendent.* He constitutes the foundation, not for the relationship in which the human being would be required as the other pole. He constitutes, instead, the foundation for the relationships that constitute morality among human beings, making these relationships possible. Thus, it is not the case that the human requires God for his subjective support; rather, God is required for the objective grounding of ethics.[38] He is, therefore, the transcendent precondition. The concept and the existence of God mean only that it is not a delusion to believe in, to think of, and to take cognizance of the unity of humankind. God proclaimed it. God guarantees it. Aside from this, God signifies nothing, means nothing. His attributes, through which his essence is disclosed, are not so much the attributes of his nature as they are the directions in which God's relationship to human beings radiates outward to human beings and is reflected in them.[39]

One need only reflect on the two *attributes of God*, love and justice, to see clearly the intimate share that religion has in ethics, and in the process of thinking and developing ethical insights—which must be distinguished, of course, from concepts and knowledge. It is thus ignorance and delusion to cast suspicion on religion with its moral treasures and sources or to believe that it is superfluous.

---

38. [The opinion Cohen expresses here—that the individual has no need of God—indicates the influence of Kant, yet Cohen's view would shift dramatically in his later work, where he acknowledged that religion (indeed, God) must stand in correlation to the individual human being in their suffering.]

39. [Cohen is paraphrasing Maimonides's doctrine of the attributes of action. After denying the possibility of establishing the attributes of God's essence, Maimonides allows that God reveals himself only through his actions and that the purpose of disclosing such attributes of action is to induce human beings, in their deeds, to imitate God. See Moses Maimonides, *Guide of the Perplexed*, trans. Shlomo Pines (Chicago: University of Chicago Press, 1963), part 1, chapter 54, 123–28.]

For how would one propose to replace it, especially if philosophy is dismissed as metaphysics? All that would then remain are vulgar trivialities, ambiguous and susceptible to extremes.

However, even if ethical literature were substituted for religion, the former would still not replace the latter. We will prove this later, in a different context. We will then have to delve into the genuine errors of religion. But these errors, which many feel are indeed universal, should not, however, trap us in the historical error of believing that religion has not promoted knowledge of ethics.

This error is not just a shortcoming in historical education; it is also detrimental to the position of ethics. We now know the significance of the distinction between theoretical and practical interest. We have also come to understand that practical interest is promoted by theoretical interest. *Aristotle's* formulation is both infelicitous and confusing. The problem of ethics is not "that we become good," as distinct from the problem of "what the Good is." For knowing the Good is the means by which humanity is to become good. The theoretical interest serves the practical. Yet, although this connection relates chiefly to these two types of rational interest, it is not in any way limited or bound to them.

Thus, if religion has made contributions to the knowledge of morality that are hardly trivial, then it is a waste of its practical collaboration to reject religion and exclude it from the realm of ethical culture. Furthermore, the loss of its collaboration is not the only question to consider. The damage inflicted is just as serious when religion itself, now excluded from the realm of ethical culture, is set on the wrong path. It is not just that religion's mythological interest would then be revived to excess; but the more religion is deflected from its orientation toward morality, the more it becomes entangled with other branches of culture.

Its entanglement with all the various branches of culture is the true difficulty and danger that religion presents. This is the most serious reason for calling the essence of religion into question, and it becomes confused if religion is repudiated in this way for the sake of morality. That is the great harm that has been caused by this lacuna in historical education. This idea requires more thorough discussion. Above all, it is *the relationship of religion to art* that seems to be innate to religion. Religion arises, after all, out of myth, which in turn contains within it the root of art. By means of art, religion creates its ritual worship for itself. To be sure, religion, when engaged in ritual, seems to remain entangled in myth. It is for this reason that the prophets fulminate against ritual worship.

However, ritual does not serve only to worship God, such that it could be replaced by love of humankind, in which alone the true service of God consists.

Rather, it also serves to focus the human sense of equanimity and reverence on ethical ideas. Ritual worship fosters such sentiments by using its tools to forge ideas into feelings—to release them from their conceptual context and capture them in a new web of feelings. Here, without a doubt, they gain new power. However, as a result, and again, without a doubt, their clarity, simplicity, and certainty are jeopardized.

The value of *aesthetic feelings* lies in the peculiar purity and autonomy that characterize works of genius. However, the art of a genius follows its own paths, however much it may seem to be linked to religion. True art will never be subordinate to religion; rather, it merely appropriates the subject matter of religion and of mythology in general, to shape it using its own tools, for its own purposes, and into its own content. Art is thus not dependent upon religion. Conversely, however, religion is dependent upon art. As a consequence, the danger to religion grows. For it thus becomes more firmly attached to myth, from which it appears to be liberated by the freedom of poetry. In art, however, it falls victim to a new spell that prejudices it against ethics.

Indeed, that is the great power of art—that it confers the illusion of reality upon its creations. Now, however, when religion combines with art in worship, it gives an artistic representation of the relationship between God and the human being and thus *draws the supersensible into the charmed realm of aesthetic sensibility*. It returns, as if of its own free will, to the primeval era of myth; art is its spiritual escort. The distance between religion and ethics, insofar as ethics is based on the combination of practical and theoretical interest, only increases and becomes more fraught.

Meanwhile, the close connection of religion and art means that religion poses another danger to ethics. Art has a trajectory of its own in pure, generative consciousness. Therefore, aesthetics constitutes its own part of the philosophical system. Once again, the specific character of aesthetics cannot be developed in psychology alone or by means of psychological method. From the psychological point of view, one might think that art emerges from an artistic drive, like that observed among animals too. Our German word, therefore, seems so suggestive: "art" is an ability (*Kunst ist Können*), the *capacity to create and form*.[40] It is an

---

40. [Cohen is referring to the etymological connection between the German word for art, *Kunst*, and the verb *können*, meaning to be able or capable. In contrast, the English word "art," from the Latin *ars*, originally meant a skill or handicraft and is a semantic parallel to the Greek word *techne*.]

ability to devise and shape images that compete with nature for the appearance of reality.

But is this trajectory of "ability" peculiar to art? Indeed, does not this drive to form and create follow other trajectories as well? To begin, one can say that all these creative trajectories emerge from *a drive to externalize*. Yet it is this drive to externalize that is so characteristic, in particular, of the will and of action. Now, if the drive to create and to form, in all its various trajectories and directions, is rooted in the drive to externalize, then it is rooted in the will. And if art could be said to be grounded, in the deepest sense, in the drive to create and to form, it would have no claim to a unique place in the philosophical system, for art would merge into the will and thus into ethics.

But what other trajectories does this drive to form and create follow? With this question, we confront the true powers and facts of ethical culture. Moreover, the problem of ethics depends on how these powers and facts are characterized. The psychological point of view makes it appear to be natural that all *social and political structures* have been produced by the drive to act externally, to create and to give such creative activity form and permanence. According to the psychological point of view, all human associations originate in this drive. This point of view is not averse to drawing an analogy to art: all these social and political creations are works of art; among them, the state is regarded as the work of art superior to all others.

However, this comparison between art and social and political structures should not be taken to be more than an analogy. Just as the drive to externalize takes on the specialized form of a drive toward artistic creation, it can also be diverted into another kind of ability—that is, the ability to subdue, directed against others as well as oneself. The root of the word used for this drive in many languages is related to the root of the word for ability.[41] *Power emerges as a drive of human consciousness.* Moreover, social and political structures have an effect as powers in culture. We need to recognize that these forces of political culture are objects of ethics. They are facts of culture that, in analogy to nature, should also be objects of knowledge. They should be the objects of ethical knowledge, just as the facts of nature are the objects of theoretical knowledge.

Now however, before pursuing this thought further, we must continue our discussion of religion. We have now come to know the new political creation

41. [Cohen is thinking, for instance, of the French *pouvoir*, English power, or Latin *potestas*, all of which derive from the Latin *posse* (meaning to be able).]

with which religion, from the start, seeks to forge connections. And yet these connections entail incessant clashes and conflicts for both religion and state, intense, bitter battles in which now religion, now the state, is on the brink of demise. At this point, however, we will consider only the difficulty for ethics that comes about because of *this connection of religion and politics.*

From the very start, we have seen that the concern of ethics is the concept of the human being. But we have also seen that this concept must stand in proper correlation to the concept of the individual. The plurality, as a particularity, is not the appropriate correlate. Only totality is the appropriate correlate. Thus, the question now is this: which of the competing powers, religion or the state, is able to provide the correct [concept of] totality?

To judge by its outer façade and its public claims, religion seeks to abolish all particularity and to unite all humankind in a totality. The state, by contrast, apparently resists this kind of totality, seeking stability among the multitude of peoples by granting each of them the particularity of a state. However, for better or worse, the concept of the state places limits on such particularism, both by means of international law (*Völkerrecht*) and through a federation of states (*Staatenbund*). Thus, particularity, which seems to be unavoidable, is tempered by the plan to establish a totality that is designed using the methodology of law. Imagine, by analogy, a federation of religions. The idea seems like the stuff of a satirical utopia.

But why should such a union of religions, produced by means of religion's own methodology, be an impossible idea? Why is it that all that can be offered in its stead is tolerance and similar opiates? Because religion claims to possess knowledge—because it presumes to teach, to be able to teach knowledge of the human being, of God, and of the world understood as God's creation. *However, there cannot be two sciences dealing with the same problems as their content.* If there are two such sciences, they cannot be joined as a unity; they must be mutually exclusive. *Particularism, therefore, is inherent in the concept of religion.*

Such particularism is all the more dangerous because it is misrepresented as universalism. Only when religion abandons all its other questions and tenets —that is, only when it makes ethics its sole and exclusive task—only then can the totality of humanity be its true goal. Then, however, religion will no longer have any interest in so-called faith. Then it can and must strive to formulate its teaching as a kind of knowledge. Religion must resolve itself into ethics. Without ethics, without knowledge, clear and true totality is impossible. Religion, as religion, is chained to particularity and its exclusiveness.

It is this *inherent difference between religion and the state* that makes a scandal of the alliance that religion enters into with the state. What first catches one's attention is the dependency that religion must suffer on this account. Just as art allies itself to political power, so too religion, in ritual, enters into such an alliance. In poetry, powerful ancestors become the heroes of legends, of epic, and of political verse. In the religion of ritual, these heroes become the sons of gods and gods themselves. However, in this alliance the politicization of deities that occurs on account of such alliances is the lesser evil.

The deeper, incurable problem lies in the *imitation of the state*, in the independent organization of the faith community on the model of the state; the problem lies in the *church*. In this context, theocracy is the lesser danger, for it negates the state that it, in fact, absorbs into itself. This is an idea that could be of use to ethics — that is, if religion were to dissolve without remainder into morality and thus into ethics. However, the church was neither able nor willing to put this [theocratic] claim into practice, neither in paganism, nor in Christianity. The issue was only the dependence of the state on the church. Only sects seek to bring about the absorption of the state into the church, and then, in addition, the dissolution of the church itself.

There are, then, two basic forms for the grand coexistence of human beings and peoples — a spiritual and a secular form. Which of these forms, however, is the moral one? That is the moral question posed by world history. Is it possible that only one of them is moral? Then the other will lead to moral confusion. Moreover, this confusion will not somehow be mitigated just because it happens to be a natural artistic instinct or even a drive for power that seduces peoples into secular immorality.

Or is it the case that these two, the spiritual and the secular, do not indicate only the moral path, because each of them is supposed to signify something else in addition? If, however, art is out of the question, what other something could this be besides science and morality? Religion and politics may neither offer a corrective for science and ethics nor surpass them. We repeat the question: which of the two is the basic moral form?

The question requires more precision. It should not be taken only in a historical sense, in relation to world history. For historically neither the state nor the church has followed a moral path. Furthermore, whereas the church nearly always could at least claim a connection to morality, in politics and political history morality is abandoned at precisely those moments when politics seems to wield the greatest power. Nevertheless, we must not allow ourselves to be defined by such phenomena if we wish to identify those objects of culture that will serve ethics as points of orientation. The question we have posed is methodological, and the methodological character of the question accounts for the mistrust directed toward religion as represented by the church.

If we still consider the position of the church in a general sense, from the perspective of the totality [of humanity], we can see how political existence has been captivated by the church perspective. The suspicion of political life engendered by the church extends even to the ethical conventicles.[42] Nonetheless, the state cannot and should not be rendered superfluous. Such mistrust is unproductive; it just corrupts a good conscience and spoils the joy of political life and work. However, if the state is indeed indispensable and irreplaceable in the life of peoples, then the problem can only be this: how morality, which is inseparable from the state, can be realized by the state and in the state.

Morality can become reality only through the state; it is impossible for there to be two paths to this goal. On this point we must be firm. There is no such thing as half-morality that could be complemented by the other half. From this methodological discussion, then, it is clear that the path of religion, understood as that of the church, cannot serve as the moral path of humanity. For the goal of religion must be and will always be particularity. The task of ethics, however, is to position the individual in correlation to the totality, and to bring about, in this correlation, the *unity of the human being.*

Thus, our misgivings about the alliance, in ritual, between religion and the state have led us to another fundamental question of method: the *relationship of ethics to political science.* That question brings yet another discipline into view, that of *jurisprudence,* which, in its method, is closely connected to political science.

* * *

Political science necessarily encompasses constitutional law. The method of political science derives from *jurisprudence.* It is undeniable that jurisprudence constitutes its methodological foundation, whatever role other disciplines may have had as well. If we include political economy and its ancillary fields, then we cannot avoid dealing with the "political sciences" in the plural. It is primarily *jurisprudence* that is the condition for the possibility of political science — its concept and its methodology.

Now this term, political science, tends to obscure, or better, to expose a cer-

42. [The assemblies of Puritans.]

tain indeterminacy or uncertainty. As a consequence, it does not depend on jurisprudence alone. But on what other kind of knowledge does it depend in addition? Not economics and its related disciplines; we classify them under the rubric of law. For these disciplines too cannot, in the end, disengage from jurisprudence. Values must become laws. However, the other kind of knowledge on which political science relies—we know what it is. We are seeking it here, in ethics.

Our task now is to rework this dependent relationship, if ethics is indeed to have a role as an element of a philosophical system. Within such a system, ethics must be related to culture as logic is related to nature—that is, to natural science. We have found, however, that, in all disciplines and sciences whose subject matter is culture, ethics is and must be presupposed. In the case of the problem of jurisprudence, it can be no different. However, there is a methodological difference at work here.

History operates with concepts of the human being in the various forms and modes of his existence. However, as we have seen, in so doing, history takes the human being in his psychological sense; it abstracts from the concept of the human being and presents it in plastic form. However much history may strive to present human actions as the actions of individuals, it must also consider them as conditioned by more general factors. Thus, *actions* inevitably are enmeshed in and even transformed into *passions and feelings*. However, the precise concept yields, the concept by which alone actions are guided. It must yield, unless individuals alone, in isolation, determine the course of history.

In *jurisprudence* the situation is different. It deals first and foremost with actions. It is perhaps no accident that the word for action is also the basic term of jurisprudential procedure as a whole: *actio is both "action" and "complaint."* A law or right (*Recht*) that is not actionable is not a law or right. Therefore, the concept of action, in its legal sense, is bound up with the concept of actionability. The implementation of law occurs in court. For this reason, the concept of law is also bound up with the concept of action. Action, as *actio*, signifies not so much a legal claim, as a *claim in a court of law.*

Law is thus located in action as its origin and actual content. For the form of law is not only its external form, nor only its meaning as a symbol. Rather, it is the *methodological means* of finding, discovering, and generating law. "Action," as *actio*, thus has a *twofold meaning*: it is both *action and the process of taking action* (*Handlung und Behandlung*).

Thus, we can now recognize the inherent meaning in legal procedure, and from this we come to recognize the *methodological value of jurisprudence*. Its relevance extends not only to the disciplines of political science, but also to the humanities in general, and thus also to ethics. Now one has to ask what *relationship should be posited, in the context of the humanities, between jurisprudence and ethics.* This question will be of fundamental importance for the method of ethics itself.

From the *Logic* we know how logic is related to mathematics. To be sure, for mathematics, too, there are general presuppositions that are self-sufficient and that, of course, are situated in logic. However, if logic wants to build upon and expand even these foundations, it must draw upon mathematics. We recognized this straight away with respect to the *judgment of origin*.[43] There exists, then, a clear *reciprocal relationship between logic and mathematics.* The logical conditions that are innate in mathematics increase so substantially in content that logic comes to depend upon the content of mathematics for defining its own. Logic still remains the spirit of its spirit, which has now become flesh. Logic has to absorb the spirit into its bones as new spiritual content.[44]

The situation is similar to the relationship of ethics to jurisprudence: *ethics may be regarded as the logic of the humanities.* It deals with the concepts of the individual, of totality, of the will, and of action. All philosophy is dependent on the given fact of the sciences. *For us, such dependence on the fact of the sciences is the eternal legacy of Kant's system.*

Jurisprudence constitutes the analogue to mathematics. We may call it the mathematics of the humanities, and especially the mathematics of ethics.

First, to dispel the appearance of paradox in this proposition, we shall first consider the doubts that follow from a lack of clarity and certainty about the methodological significance of *a philosophy of the a priori*. Within jurisprudence itself, one may contest the latent immanence of ethical principles, or one may concede just that they remain latent. Such an objection would not be decisive, for mathematicians and physicists take a similar position on the logical principles of their respective sciences. However, a difference persists in the methodological substructure between the conceptual elements in ethics and logic. The

---

43. [Introduced by Cohen in his *Logic of Pure Cognition*, the "judgment of origin" is a central concept in his thought, discussed by Ernst Cassirer (selection 7), Franz Rosenzweig (selection 8), and Alexander Altmann (selection 9).]

44. [Cohen's playful amalgam of biblical metaphors evokes Adam's expression of delight at the creation of woman ("flesh of my flesh," Gen. 2:23), a Christological motif ("and the Word became flesh," John 1:14), and the image of a new spirit being breathed into the dry bones of Israel (Ezek. 37).]

difference corresponds in turn to that between jurisprudence and mathematical natural science with regard to their methodological structure. However, apart from this difference, the analogy remains—only as an analogy, of course, not as a case of identity. Mathematics and physics advance by means of observation and experiment, and thus by means of experience, while the original logical grounds sustain their effect throughout these developments. In the same way, the development of law encompasses, for its part, the advance of civilization, due to its inherent foundational ethical motives. In addition, it can also be influenced by other kinds of moral experience, not unlike natural science. The decisive point is the idea that morality is not opposed to legality in an original and absolute sense, but that, in legality, morality be recognized as an immanent power. Then it is possible to draw the conclusion that morality too inheres in legality, where legality is an equal power.

One should also consider whether it is a methodological interest that cautions against making such a connection. Without it, ethics will simply lack the analogue of a fact of science. However, absent such an analogue, ethics is delivered up either to the serendipity of psychology or to the exclusive autocracy of religion. We know that the choice is in fact between these two dependencies; however, we also know that we must reject both. We may demand, then, that these doubts be withdrawn for the time being, so that we can risk an experiment that—aside from its logical advantage—brings a favorable ethical precedent to bear on the organization of world history.

If this idea proves methodologically sound, then ethics will gain a secure foundation for determining and grounding the concept of the human being; and that is the task of ethics. The human domain will then be liberated from the lack of clarity and lack of certainty that must otherwise always afflict it, if it is connected primarily to religion. In religion the relationship of the human being to another foundational concept will be constructed. Here, by contrast, we are dealing with the human being alone. For the fact that we are dealing with human beings [in the plural] constitutes no contradiction. On the contrary: the concept of the human being requires human beings [in the plural].

It is generally regarded as a weakness of ethics that it cannot rely on the support of a science. Therefore, any expression of moral certainty is treated with disdain. For that reason, those who, on principle, do not withdraw to the shelter of religion will seek refuge in psychology and the idea of a *moral sense*, or in aesthetics and the idea of *moral feeling*; they despair of using science. At best, such people are happy to be able to secure, ex post facto, the consent of science in confirming certain ethical assumptions. Even *Kant,* who sought and postulated [for ethics] the analogue of a fact corresponding to the fact of mathematics, could not find [such an analogue] in any science. He separated the study of law from the study of ethics, and established discrete metaphysical foundations for each.

Such an approach may not be inappropriate, to the extent that the *philosophy of law,* as a discipline in its own right, has the task of dealing with the full development and elaboration of legal problems and concepts. However, if the systematic context of the philosophy of law may not be limited to logic, if it in fact comes into contact with the problems and concepts of ethics wherever it goes, then it is understandable that the philosophy of law will be constructed, more or less consciously, on the basis of ethics. It is the *old connection between positive law and natural law* that reveals itself over and over again. However much one may question the existence of natural law, or even suppose that it could be replaced by some real law, by such attacks rational law, which inheres in the idea of natural law, is only confirmed all the more persuasively. (An exposition of rational law is not necessary here.) All of this opposition only strengthens and renders more evident the moral—one might say holy—value of this world-historical principle.

The idea of natural law is based on the ancient Greek notion of *unwritten laws* (ἄγραφοι νόμοι). As early as the Greeks succeeded in committing their basic laws to writing, they still felt the need to extract from the written law an original form of legality and to make it the foundation of all legality. It must be conceded that this idea is connected to Greek religion. However, it is not the religion of ritual worship, but rather the religion of ethics that, in that primitive age, acted in concert with perceptions of the state and law.

Soon this motif, a particular feature of Greek ethics, had to be put to direct practical use. Sophism burst upon the scene and made the *nomos*—which, in *Pindar,* was called "king"—into the tyrant of convention and fashion. In that context the unwritten law represented the eternal foundation of nature and of truth. It is not to Euripides's credit that he, too, had no liking for unwritten principles.

Since *Socrates,* philosophy has followed its own path, giving a more precise definition of the original meaning of the Greek concept of ethics. However, the more the classical spirit of philosophy declined, the more the Greeks clung to the magic word "nature." It served to express the antithesis to convention and freedom of choice. Thus, in *Stoicism, nature* became a term for the original, the eternal, and the true. And Stoicism became the philosophy of Roman jurisprudence.

Roman politics, too, allied with Roman law in defining the concept of nature as the ground of all validity and legal authority. The more Roman civil law extended to Roman allies, the more Roman law—civil law par excellence (*jus civile*)—had to evolve into international law (*jus gentium*). International law then spurred a further development: as it extended its reach, it deepened as well. *Natural law arose from international law* and has endured in all its permutations.

To be sure, in the *Middle Ages,* natural law was jeopardized by a serious ambiguity, for it was equated with divine law (*jus divinum*). However, the divine natural law that resulted was by no means conceived of as unwritten law; it possessed a fixed code in the Bible of the Old and New Testaments. In contrast to divine law, human, political law was considered to be unnatural. During this whole period, true natural law lay fallow.

As in other respects, here too the *Renaissance* brought the Greek spirit back to the fore. The goal of the Renaissance was, first of all, to emancipate humankind from divine, biblical law. This was the meaning of the motto "natural law" for *Hugo Grotius*[45] and his predecessors. To be sure, even Grotius did not reject the law of the Old Testament outright as a historical source. As a historical source, however, it was not to be seen henceforth as being natural or as possessing authority as the nature of reason. Reason came of age, outgrowing the medieval view that the Bible contains the ultimate ground and warrant for all human truth.

This is the sublime ethical meaning advocated by natural law. Its spirit permeates the entire modern age—even to our own day. It animated both Reformation and revolution. In its spirit, *Kant* described the French Revolution as the evolution of the spirit of natural law. Likewise, in Fichte, this nexus of natural law and ethics persisted.

Now the *historical school of jurisprudence*[46] developed from this nexus. This is especially evident in *Hugo,* in his connection between natural law and Kantian philosophy. Thus, in and of itself, the historical school in no way contradicts,

45. [Hugo Grotius (1583–1645) was an exponent of the idea of natural law, expanding it to the idea of international law that he hoped would constrain the excesses of nations at war. Cohen pays similar tribute to Grotius in *RR* (124) for recognizing the Noachide laws as the biblical source of the idea of natural law.]

46. [Gustav von Hugo (1764–1844) and Friedrich Carl von Savigny (1779–1861) were the founders of *Historische Rechtswissenschaft* (historical school of jurisprudence), which held that law develops organically from the *Volksgeist* (national spirit). The school is usually thought to stand in contrast to the concept of universal rational or natural law. Cohen deviates here from that view.]

or even opposes, the natural law school. If one does not narrow-mindedly limit the study of law to a technique for the interpretation of existing laws, and if one also recognizes the *science of legislation* as part of the study of law, then one will never deny that spirit expressed by the ancient term "natural law." It is impossible to imagine a science of jurisprudence or to trace it back to its first principles if it rejects this connection to ethics. *The justification of the law is natural law, or the ethics of law.*

However, let us recall how we came to discuss the critical question of natural law: our train of thought led to the observation that ethics seems everywhere to be abandoned by science. Even Kant severs natural law from ethics. Now, however, we want to take as our point of departure neither natural law nor the philosophy of law, but ethics. Ethics, in turn, should lead us back not to natural law, but to the positive science of law, that is, to jurisprudence.

For now, we may let rest the question whether a philosophy of law and thus a new type of natural law can arise, if we do take ethics as our point of departure. Here it is important to note that, by referring ethics to jurisprudence, its sought-after analogue to a given theoretical fact has been found. Ethics is thus liberated from its exclusive association with religion, psychology, and the inexact empirical sciences; as a result, it is now possible for ethics to attain cognitive certainty. Moral certainty acquires theoretical validity.

For any modern spirit attuned to social and ethical concerns it is beyond doubt that it is both advantageous and necessary to make this *connection between ethics and jurisprudence.* The possibility that so-called supernatural interests may suffer as a result cannot be a serious concern. Whatever serious philosophical and scientific concerns these supernatural questions may involve can be satisfactorily addressed only in concert with these problems [that is, with ethics and jurisprudence]. The only real question is whether this most necessary connection can actually be created. For it is susceptible to the same objection that reverberates from the old distinction between the Is and the Ought.

However, let us not be led astray by the shallow, secondary meaning of the Ought, according to which it is far removed from reality; instead, let us confidently confront the universal concepts and questions of jurisprudence. Is it not the case that the human being, the concept of the human being, is the presupposition that encompasses the entire field? In the concept of the human being we encounter the fundamental collision between the individual and something that is supposed to be more than the unity or, more correctly, the uniqueness of the individual. We know that the issue here is the difference between particularity and totality. Ethics requires totality as the concept that is the correlate to the individual. It seems that, in law, totality has no role. Only pluralities have the action. If this were the case, then the methodological value of jurisprudence for ethics would fall on this central point. However, this is not the case. At precisely this point jurisprudence matures into *a theory of the state*, which then, like jurisprudence, can also serve as a methodological paradigm of ethics.

First of all, however, the [concept of the] *will* is in manifest use across the board. It must be ruled out that the will, in this context, could be reduced to the intellect. That idea is inconsistent not just with criminal law, which assumes malicious intent of the will, but no less with civil law. *Contracts* and *obligations* presuppose a clarity and certainty of will. The will reaches its zenith, but does not end, when one draws up a last will and testament. *Roman inheritance law* is the law of the freedom of the will. The whole person, the human soul, is concentrated in the will. In no other legal system will ethics find the power of the will better developed than in the Roman legal system. Moreover, any system of law must deal with the question of the will. Even if the freedom of the will were in dispute, the question of the will must endure. Otherwise one would have to forgo the concept of obligation. Obligation involves will.

The will, like voluntas, *is also more than mere intention.* Intention is something interior, inwardness in general. Intention touches on a profound aspect of the will, but the actual source of the will has not yet been identified. This pious term —"intention"—does point in the direction of the will, not clearly and unambiguously to be sure, yet it points in a certain direction nevertheless. However, by being directed inward in this way, the actual force of the will is restrained. *The will involves the external*, and it can develop only by externalizing itself. The will must become action.

Action is the fundamental problem of ethics. In action, the human being is revealed. Action is the life of the ethical human being. As we already saw, action is, so to speak, the expression of law. A legal action is confirmed as such by the action of the legal proceeding. In all law, in civil law just as in criminal law, the concept of action is the general presupposition. To be sure, it presupposes the will in turn, but the two are not identical.

The real difficulty in the problem of action lies in the *possibility of conceiving of action as a composite of its discrete components*. The question is precisely whether an action is composed of discrete ingredients — or whether, instead, it disintegrates into these discrete elements. Indeed, there is no action, not even in the ordinary sense, let alone in the legal sense of the term, that is not made up of an incalculable multitude of starts and processes. There is no action that erupts and then vanishes like a flash of lightning. An action of that kind has the character of an involuntary movement, of a reflex. One can therefore say that here the entire problem of psychology comes into play.

In all *psychology*, the question is really nothing other than this: *how can unity be intelligible* in this seemingly chaotic multitude of events and elements—and in spite of it? How, in the midst of this, is the unity of human consciousness possible? This is the real problem, and thus the real problem with regard to action as well. If a movement were stuck in such atomistic beginnings, it could never expand and coalesce into action. At first, such expansion is necessary, but the action may not remain hovering in a suspended state; it must be firm and stable. Such stability and coherence can only be supplied by a concept—the old fundamental concept of unity. *Action must become unity of action.* Unity of action constitutes the concept of action.

The concept of unity, in turn, reveals to us not only the *connection of jurisprudence* to ethics, but also to *logic*. Only logic can teach the significance of unity —above all, that it must not be confused with singularity. This fundamental concept, then, makes it plain that *ethics presupposes logic*. What matters in this context is our insight that law presupposes the unity of action.

We will discuss the unity of action in detail later; here, it may only be pointed out that all the other instances of unity with which jurisprudence must operate depend upon the unity of action. A legal transaction presupposes, above all, the *unity of the legal object*. Just as with bodies that are the objects of the natural sciences, such objects occur in relation to one another and exist in these relations. It is immediately obvious that this is the case for legal objects as well. A legal object is constituted in legal transactions such as those that occur in commerce and in the making of contracts. The unity required by the concept of such an object consists of the relational character of the act of undertaking obligations. *The unity of action brings about and grounds the unity of the object.*

Likewise, the *unity of the legal subject* also emerges from the unity of action and is essentially grounded in it. Most importantly, it is beyond doubt that the legal subject, even more than the legal object, is the real problem of jurisprudence. In all legal transactions, the subject is not only the content at which all such transactions are directed, but also the source and ground from which they all flow and are derived. Action—a legal transaction—presupposes deliberate, purposeful thought. This presupposition is not limited to the problem of action; it also extends to the agent, to the author of action.

Even if only the agent, in whom all the threads of a legal transaction converged, were under discussion, the subject would be indispensable; how much more so in prominent cases, when the focus is in fact on the author of the action. The law, after all, also places particular material obstacles in the way of the concept of the legal subject. For example, it recognizes slaves as human beings, but not as persons. *And yet only a person constitutes a legal subject.* It is obvious, then, that law, in the strict and [most] precise sense, requires the concept of the legal subject. It is also apparent from this example that it is action from which the legal subject is derived and with which it is connected.

It must be *the unity of the subject that constitutes a legal subject.* Without unity a subject is inconceivable. One might imagine an object lacking unity; however, subject and unity are in complete accord with one another. Now, we have already considered how difficult it can be for psychology to establish the unity of consciousness from the enormous multitude of psychic events, and to locate, in the unity of consciousness, the unity of the subject. And yet this is the ultimate concern of ethics. In this context, would it not be a great methodological advantage if, for its ultimate concern, ethics were not dependent merely upon psychology? Would it not be an advantage at best, if it did not have to rely upon theology, as if it were an ethical version of pathology, for that abnormal condition that is the consciousness of sin? Would it not be an advantage *if, in every case, be it normal or abnormal, ethics could derive the "I" from the unity of the legal subject?*

At this point, however, we must confront a serious reservation. To be sure, the law requires the unity of the subject, and law must succeed in establishing such unity in all legal transactions; otherwise, the concept of the legal transaction would be untenable. A legal act cannot be broken down into parts; and a legal subject cannot be split, so to speak, into two owners. Now, however, a substantial, important, fundamental, and epoch-making share of legal transactions consists of *partnerships*. In associations of this kind, which can assume many legal forms, who is the unity of the subject among the several parties of which these associations consist? Does it not seem as if the unity would disintegrate, as if the "I" of the subject were transformed not just into a pathological *twofold-I*, but into the "I" of a quorum, and this as a matter of course? But can a collective "I" adequately serve in the role of the unity of the subject?

Here we can see that it is of decisive importance to acknowledge the connection between ethics and jurisprudence. From the start it was our aim to establish that the correlation of the individual and totality is the true task of ethics. The ethical subject must therefore be at once totality and the individual. The human being of ethics may not be regarded only as an individual. Religion may regard him as such, for it sets him up in relationship to an external concept. If ethics, on the other hand, in discovering the concept of the human being, is to avoid all concepts that are extraneous to its own methodology, then ethics is directed, from the start, to the pluralities in which the human being everywhere appears.

It is only an illusion that the human being is merely an individual; if he is an individual, and insofar as he is an individual, he can be such only in that and only because the individual is really individuals. It is impossible to think of him without such a plurality. The goal, however, is that the plurality not remain a plurality, not a particularity, but that the plurality becomes totality. *Now where is there an example of such a totality in the history of humankind?* Does not that question refer us to the idea of humanity? Moreover, can we not count ourselves fortunate that, although the philosophy of race[47] may succeed in making the idea of the unity of the human race despised, it is unable to render it invalid and destroy it? And yet, should we really be satisfied with the idea of humanity as the example? Should we not be satisfied with nothing less than the idea of humanity as the paradigm of totality?

Since antiquity, the concept of *community* has played a significant role in all moral and religious thought. Community (*koinonia*) is an important logical concept in *Plato's* doctrine of ideas. Before religion became the church, it was an assembly of people that evolved into a *congregation*. The congregation of those who pray and listen to the word of God was the precursor of the church of the faithful. Hence, for religion, community is inherent in the concept of the congregation. One might therefore assume that this community of the congregation of the faithful represented an example of totality appropriate for ethics. However, our previous deliberations have already made us cautious on this point. The idea of a particular covenant is inborn in a church community. Far from an appropriate example, it is an evil example, and ethics must be on guard against it. Recently,

47. [Cohen condemns the "philosophy of race" because it rejects the very idea of a unitary humanity, arguing instead that human beings are permanently divided by race and caught up in permanent conflict between the races. The most prominent proponent of these views in Europe at the time was Houston Stewart Chamberlain (1855–1927), the British-born philosopher—and son-in-law of Richard Wagner—who published his very popular book, *Die Grundlagen des 19. Jahrhunderts* in 1899. By 1942, it had gone through twenty-eight editions. For an English translation, see *The Foundations of the Nineteenth Century*, trans. John Lees, 2 vols. (London, New York: J. Lane, 1911).]

a book in the field of law has made it shockingly clear what may emerge when, guided by biblical quotations, one dissolves community into a set of ever more relative [smaller] communities. Such relative, special communities are nothing other than particularisms that can never become a totality.

Legal associations, by contrast, lead us down the correct path.[48] Historically, they have already proven their moral mission, but they are not finished with it. The *societas* is indeed, first, a firm of partners, but its title invokes the *societas* and *socialitas* of the human race. *Societas* contains fraternity *(fraternitas)*, as an old Roman legal saying puts it.[49] Thus, *societas* did not evolve into community in the modern period; significantly, this was not the term chosen. The term *communité* was reserved for the administrative structure.[50] However, in the storm of revolution, and even more in the slow course of history, *society* has taken upon itself the task of the moral education of the human race. *Under the motto of the social idea, society initiated the reformation of states.* The legal methodology and technique contained in the concept of *societas* came first, preceding the reformation of states.

We will have to elaborate on this important point in detail. For now it must suffice to be able to point out that in juridical associations of all types there can be several, many, and from time to time innumerable subjects who participate in a legal transaction and have a stake in a legal institution. Under such circumstances it might seem impossible to have a unity of the legal subject, or it might even seem that such a unity was meant to be precluded altogether—thus controverting, however, the concept of law and of legal action. Hence, it will become rather apparent that the true unity of the legal subject emerges on the basis of *just such a* plurality.

The seeming conflict is eliminated by recognizing that this plurality is not a

48. [Cohen uses the concept of a "cooperative" (*Genossenschaft*) or an "association" (*Assoziation*) as an example of a legal person (that is, not an individual), preferring *Genossenschaft* to *Gesellschaft* or *Gemeinschaft*, the social concepts popularized by Ferdinand Tönnies (1855–1936) through his 1887 book *Gemeinschaft und Gesellschaft* (for an English translation, see *Community and Civil Society*, trans. José Harris and Margaret Hollis [Cambridge: Cambridge University Press, 2001]). The basis of the discussion of what constitutes a legal person is a work by the legal thinker and historian Otto von Gierke (1841–1921), *Das deutsche Genossenschaftsrecht*, 4 vols., (Berlin: Weidmann, 1868–1913).]

49. [The Latin saying, pertaining to a *societas*, or association of partners (*socii*), is "cum societas ius quodammodo fraternitatis in se habeat (that *societas* in a certain way contains within itself the law of fraternity)."]

50. [Cohen is referring to the French usage, which entered German as *Kommune* (meaning municipality).]

plurality after all, but a totality. For *totality* does not conflict with unity; it conflicts with singularity, which is associated with plurality. Totality is itself the highest form of unity, as required by ethics. The moral individual should not remain a particular singularity. He should, by virtue of the totality of which he is a member, be elevated to the unity of the moral individual.

A *juridical person* is called a *moral person*. To be sure, this term is only supposed to express the nonnatural aspect of actual persons. Yet it is instructive that the concept of the juridical person does not appear until quite late in the development of jurisprudence. It is also generally recognized that in modern law this concept has developed beyond the innocent institutions of Roman law; it is connected to modern developments in morality and also in ethics. It is also instructive that the *family* is never defined as a juridical person, even though it is enveloped in a moral aura. Can it be that the very naturalness of the family suppressed the fiction of the juridical person?

This question will occupy us later, in connection with the concept of the *people* (*Volk*). For now we should just stress that the family is a natural body that seems to offer a strong ethical case for being elevated to the status of a person, and thus to the unity of a human being. And yet, it did not attain this juristic classification. By contrast, purely abstract relationships, *the formation of associations*, are granted this status. Of course, however much these relationships reflect the particularities of commercial life, they are based on the logical union of the *totality*. Otherwise, such associations could not be constituted as legal subjects.

This so-called *fiction* is actually a logical determination. The juridical person retreats from its sensual prejudice toward singularity and from its character as a plurality. The juridical person is then constituted as the unity of the legal subject, on the basis of [the idea of] totality. This example, which jurisprudence provides to ethics, is more than an example; it is a paradigm that has no peer in any other form of altruism. Later we will examine this point carefully.

Finally, the law, taking the form of *constitutional law*, brought about, in the concept of the state, the unity of a totality that must serve as the direct paradigm of the ethical personality. We began with the observation that *Plato* presents the human soul for investigation, so to speak, in the soul of the state. For him, the *soul of the state* becomes a new type of world soul. This grand idea has been taken up throughout the ages, and it has yielded new meaning throughout the vicissitudes of world history.

The basic motive of the constant ferment on this question was a paradoxical notion: the human being is not what he believes himself to be when he relies on his sense of self in the realm of sensibility; his individual soul comes to life only in the realm of the state. That is the great paradox, to which one can perhaps apply that sacred verse: "fill your heart with this, as large as it is." One is perhaps permitted to add, "that it grow large."[51] This is the way and the means to enlarge the self and to produce, in it, the concept of the moral human being.

We have already touched on the *antinomy of society and state*. To be sure, we saw that the concept of society brings the original moral force of *societas* to bear on an ahistorical and amoral conception of a state that has ossified in its own laws. Its effect, however, is only to cause movement in a necessary direction. Its effect is never rest and equilibrium. Without presupposing such an *equilibrium*, though it be an ideal, there could be neither an enduring and guaranteed union of human beings, nor even the unity of a human subject. Thus, even though the intense and powerful influence of society is beneficial and indispensable, society must nevertheless transcend itself. It must annul itself and aim for the state, by presupposing the equilibrium that it must presuppose to give meaning to its actions. In logical terms we can express this claim more simply, and perhaps also more precisely, by understanding *society* as *particularity* and the *state* as *totality*. Only then can the state be understood as a *unity*.

Later we will take up the question of the relationship between the concepts of the *people* and the *state*. Here we wish only to note that we mean to derive the unity of the human being not from the serendipitous unity of his people, but from the necessary unity of the state to which a moral human being must belong. From the standpoint of logic, the people derives from the blood of the family; it represents human beings in the naturalness of the sensual realm. State, on the other hand, is a juridical concept, the concept of a juridical person. For the concept of the ethical human being, it is the prime example of the concept of the juridical person. *The primary methodological significance of jurisprudence for ethics lies in the elaboration of law into constitutional law, the law of the state.* In terms of the precision and profundity of its concepts, the significance of jurisprudence brooks no comparison, neither with psychology, nor history, nor sociology, nor even religion.

51. [Cohen plays on—and subverts—Faust's dialogue with Margarete, in which he entreaties her to fill her heart with the fullness of the world. She may call the resulting feeling of bliss whatever she will; it is beyond reason ("name"). Faust concedes that he has no name for this sensation, and in a romantic, antirationalist outburst exclaims: "Call it joy, or your heart, or love, or God! / I have no name for it! / The feeling's all there is: / The name's mere noise and smoke—what does it do / But cloud the heavenly radiance?" (*Faust*, Luke trans., 109, lines 3451–57).]

What, then, is ultimately at stake in ethics as a whole? We may reasonably ignore the solace afforded by hope or by elaborate mythical fantasies. Ethics is not about what one should believe, to be able to hope and desire, or even to fear and despair. No: ethics is concerned only with what I should do so that all my deeds attain the value of a human action. The concept of action consists of unity of action. Unity of action grounds the unity of the human being. *The unity of the human being comes about through unity of action; it consists of unity of action.*

We may regard the unity of the human being as the ultimate goal, as the true object of ethics. In his actions and aspirations, a human being should remain neither conflicted nor confused. He should not, in every given moment, undergo a metamorphosis. In that case, it would not be the human being who is bringing about change in himself, but the things around him, perhaps also the things in him that are changing *him.* Even this description of the matter is imprecise: he does not undergo a metamorphosis, for he is not yet actually present. As long as he is suspended in a plurality consisting of actions impinging on him from without and of reactions proceeding from the plurality within, his self is not yet present. Only unity can provide him with a self and make him into a moral being.

We now know that this unity can be secured for the human being only in a totality, as represented by the state; from the perspective of method, too, the unity of the human being should be grounded in the totality of the state. That was Plato's understanding. The unity of the human being lies not in the singularity and particularity of the sensual world, but rather in an abstract unity, which, though abstract, still generates (*zur Erzeugung bringt*)[52] the purest reality: *in the unity of the totality of the state, in the unity of the ethics of the state.*

Not only power and the capacity for action are ascribed to the state, but also will. The will of the state can be conceived of as a drive only in an inverted metaphor.[53] The purpose here is to construct and compose an ethics as *the ethics of pure will.* We are, of course, acquainted with the concept of "the pure" from the *Logic,* and thus would be permitted to presuppose it in this context. However, we must refrain from applying the concept of "the pure" to the will, for although we have considered the concept of will, we have not yet defined it. *Therefore, the*

52. [*Erzeugen* and *Erzeugung* (meaning generating and generation, respectively) are technical terms in Marburg neo-Kantianism and the key to understanding Cohen's epistemology. Reason "generates" the contents of consciousness.]

53. [Cohen's intent here is obscure.]

introduction will stop here. It will be the task of the exposition itself to develop the concept of the pure will, as the content of ethics.

The only preemptive argument that this introduction could still confront would be the claim that the pure will could not provide an outline for the substantial content of ethics in the same way that the concept of pure cognition provides this for the content of the natural sciences. However, by connecting the pure will to jurisprudence and constitutional law, we preempt skeptical reservations of this kind. Where the task of ethics is under discussion, everything depends on addressing this argument, as a matter of principle.

For nothing will do more severe damage to the task of ethics than the *suspicion* that its content is *subjective*. To be sure, a faint sheen of subjectivity falls upon the foundational distinction between Is and Ought, as we have considered it. Ought, as pure willing, must be able to assert that it has the proven validity of being. Any doubt on this point would be not only to teach false idealism, but would also undermine and defeat idealism itself. The idea is not a fantasy, but rather the fruitful and unfailing guiding concept of world history. The pure will becomes the methodological tool of the content that the idea of ethics — ethical idealism — must make real. *The pure will becomes the will of historical being, of historical reality.* In this historical reality, the concept of the human being will be made manifest by the pure will.

It will be shown that the *distinction between state and humanity* is a distinction in appearance only. In seeking to establish the unity of the human being in the unity of the state, we do not sever the human being from humanity; we only avail ourselves of the right tool for abolishing the distinction between individual human beings and universal humanity. Only when we follow this methodological path will humanity become an ethical idea; otherwise it remains merely a pious belief that, in the best of circumstances, must rely on its opposite, that is, a naturalistic concept. For the teleological principle of the unity of the human race amounts to no more than this.

In the end, however, to ground the idea of humanity in a foundation in this way leads to the same reductionist result as when the state is grounded in the unity of the people. The pure will steers clear of such natural images. It seeks to deploy conceptual constructions in which jurisprudence is able to constitute and to provide the grounding for the unity of the juridical person.

Ethics, as it is now established, rests upon the foundation of logic and extends to the ideal. The fundamental law of truth has coupled ethics to logic. Just as logic is the logic of Idealism, so too is ethics.[1] The method of foundation laying is common to both. All problems must be able to pass muster with this methodology; it alone is the method by which such problems may be treated and resolved.

From the perspective of method, therefore, *Idealism* opposes everything that is called *metaphysics*. This opposition cannot be reconciled. One might think it could be understood by comparing it to marching in parallel—like using different means to serve the same end. This conciliatory view is not valid; it is dangerous. The different means contradict one another, and methods may not do that if they are pursuing the same goal. Metaphysics is a deceptive imitation of Idealism, in that it relates to thought insofar as thought is subsumed under the general concept of *consciousness*. That, however, is also where the distinction lies. Thought dissolves and vanishes into consciousness; it loses its distinctive significance as pure thought, as thought of foundation laying, as thought of Idealism.

First, consciousness encompasses *sensation* just as much as it encompasses thought. For this reason, from Aristotle on, metaphysics has fluctuated in every age—one could perhaps say without exception—between spiritualism and sensualism, extending even to materialism. But consciousness also encompasses the *will*, and the will can no more be conceived of as pure, generating will than thought can be conceived as pure, generating thought. Therefore, drive and desire claim their place alongside the higher faculty of appetite (a name, in the best case, for "the will"). Thus, with regard to ethics too, metaphysics fluctuates between naturalism in its various nuances and the various forms of spiritualism.

However, these forms of spiritualism differ from those employed by theoretical metaphysics. In the latter, rationalism can still retain its position of leadership. The problems of ethics, on the other hand, bring about a change. With the

1. [Implied, but not stated here explicitly, is Cohen's methodological principle that the philosophical discipline of ethics functions as the logic of the humanities. Hence both logic per se and ethics constitute the logic of Idealism as an all-encompassing system.]

problems of ethics, it is characteristic that the difference between the problem and method of ethics and the problem and method of theoretical reason is diminished or even resolved altogether. One overarching concept is given to both: the concept of the *absolute*.

From logic, we know that, in *Plato*, the concept of the absolute arose in close connection with the concept of *hypothesis*. It was an expression of despairing humility from the depth of the human spirit, of reason's ironic sense of itself. Since all being is grounded in a foundation in thought, there arises a profound yearning for a ground that is independent of this foundation: the nonfoundation (ἀνυπόθετον = ἀνυπόθεσις). The preferred way of translating the objective term, which indicates the content, would be to render it by a methodological term (to which the word indicating the content must conform), thus ensuring that the paradoxical nature of the term is unmistakable.[2]

Aristotle built narrower bridges, but only then to eliminate them. The principles,[3] the ancient beginnings, became that which cannot be mediated: the nonmediate (ἄμεσα). Thus, scientific reason was inoculated with the notion that there must be eternal, innate foundations that are firmly established, in and of themselves, and that are rendered subjective, if one concedes that they are innate to the human spirit. In any event, the scientific meaning of *axiom* lent support to this notion of independent foundations that, in themselves, are given and immutable. It seemed then that there was justification for using foundations (ὑποκείμενα) to argue against the grounding of foundations. The grounding of foundations seemed to have only provisional, not eternal, established validity, fixed in itself. And certainly no one wanted to be without the latter. The fact that it was impossible to justify the establishment of a foundation on the basis of *its own* validity was supposed to speak *for* its validity. The aim was to have foundations in hand that could be regarded as more than mere presuppositions.

The aim was foundations, in the identical sense, not just of being and thought, but also of being and consciousness. The aim was to be able to appeal to such foundations of being for all problems of being—for both ethical and theoretical

---

2. ["Nonfoundation" (*Ungrundlegung*) is Cohen's coinage, a negation of *Grundlegung* (meaning foundation or grounding). By "methodological term," in contrast to "objective term," Cohen is referring to the logical operation of laying a foundation, not the foundation that is the result of this logical operation. This is also the distinction between the two Greek terms he cites: the first, *anupotheton* (nonfoundation), is a past participle form indicating the negative result of a negative logical operation *anupothesis* (non-foundation-laying.]

3. [Referring to the Greek *archai* (singular, *arche*), or "first things."]

problems. And these ultimate foundations were never purported to be merely the foundations of consciousness, let alone of thought; they were always purported to be the foundations of being as well. No question of consciousness relates only, or even primarily, to consciousness itself; identity always plays a role. This presupposition was allowed to stand, but not, to be sure, as a methodological presupposition; instead, it was incorporated into being. *Metaphysics* thus encompasses and includes all the problems of reason and grounds them all in the identity of consciousness and being. It is a magnificent domain that metaphysics represents.

However, what was expressed in the grand notion of the absolute was neither solely metaphysics's own biases, as defined by the prevailing principle of identity, nor the problems and methods of metaphysics itself. The actual content of the absolute, the focus of all the problems that dwell in the absolute, is indisputably situated in the concept of *God*.

But what concept—of what God—is it that thus became the Absolute? It is untenable to think that *Anaxagoras*, with his nous, inaugurated the monotheism of metaphysics. After all, if that notion contained a grain of truth, *Socrates* and *Plato* would have caught on. *In this, Plato's report must be authentic, so to speak, and hold for Socrates too.* They would not have been able to disparage *nous* so completely, reducing it to a *deus ex machina*.[4]

However, even *the God of Plato* is caught in the spell of his knowledge of the Ideas. It is very typical, in ancient as well as modern times, to quarrel over the question of whether the idea of the good should be equated with God. If that were true, what would follow from it for God? To be sure, metaphysics would then possess unity with regard to both theoretical and practical reason, for the good is what is also supposed to make being knowable, just as the sun makes it visible.[5] However, it is also the case that the identity of consciousness and being would then be forfeited, for this God, as the idea of the good, would then have been infused with the ambiguous essence of transcendence. With transcendence, however, metaphysics as such, metaphysics based upon the principle of identity, cannot manage all its many paths.

---

4. [Anaxagoras (500–428 BCE), the pre-Socratic philosopher who posited mind (nous) as the cause of the physical world. His thought survives only through fragments and summaries presented by others, among them Plato's "report" on Anaxagoras, delivered by Socrates (Plato, *Phaedo* 97c–d) and characterized here as a deus ex machina.]

5. [Plato, *Republic* 509b.]

Therefore, to the extent that metaphysics is to be directed by the correlate of consciousness, metaphysics must follow paths—with reference to the problem of God—that are far removed from transcendence, and that instead were pre-figured by identity from the very beginning. Transcendence, however, originates not in this term of Plato's, but in the God of the *prophets*. Metaphysics therefore enters into a new kind of dualism, wavering between all the forms of super-natural theology and pantheism.

There is a methodological distinction between idealist ethics and metaphysics; this holds true for idealist logic as well. However, since, in the case of logic, this distinction is conceived of as the difference between what is true and false, idealist ethics can proceed in accordance with the fundamental law of truth only by striving to take possession of those motifs that enjoy sufficient historical re-spect in metaphysics to hold sway over the intellectual interest of the human being. It is not enough just to recognize where the foundation and beginning [in metaphysics] may be fictitious and erroneous and to conclude that the results of this way of thinking must therefore be false. To be sure, ethics has to ground its independence firmly in its method alone—yet without neglecting or ignoring the historical forms and broad range in which moral ideas have presented them-selves with their distinct character. Just as ethics has to attend to such forma-tions in law and state, it must also cultivate sympathy for those moral ideas that have made history in myth and, in particular, in religion. It must not surrender to the form that these questions assume in myth and religion. And yet ethics must give dispassionate attention to those forms in which the cause of morality has expressed its value and importance, accomplishing this outside the realm of ethics, and even in a struggle against ethics.

It is beyond doubt that, among these moral forms of thought, God stands above the rest. Therefore, the fundamental and multifaceted significance of God in the history of ethical problems would give us sufficient cause to consider its value for ethics—even if our methodological considerations and structure had not led us inevitably to the point of contact with the problem of God. Let us reflect, first of all, on the point at which this contact takes place. Let us review the meaning of the question that occupied us throughout the previous chapter,[6] to establish the extent to which the problem of the reality of the ethical has been resolved in the ideal of eternity and in the problem of the actualization of the ideal. At the same time, *let us also examine whether some remainder of that longing for*

6. [The subject of the previous chapter (chapter 8) of *ErW* is "The Ideal."]

reality has been left behind, unresolved. This consideration will lead us to the significance of the idea of God for ethics.

The problem of reality, the chief difficulty of logic, is no less a constant stumbling block for ethics. In our system, this stumbling block is twofold. First of all, we represent the standpoint of Idealism; we take a disinterested view of the power and evidence of naturalism, and no less of the power and evidence of historical empiricism. Yet, on the other hand, we construct the pure will with a view toward law and state; we reject, on principle, any reference to religion. Not only do we find an example of genuine self-consciousness in the juridical person of the state; more than that, by deflecting ethical self-consciousness from natural, personal individuality, we direct it toward the content that is formed and delineated by the state. *Immersing the I in the fullness and the energy of the ethical actions that converge in the unity of the state—this is the directive we give for the cultivation of genuine self-consciousness of ethical personhood.* We avoid the term "community" because it involves too much relativity; the juridical concept of the cooperative is precise and, at the same time, injects a small dose of sociability into the state. Nevertheless, in this approach, it is the formidable power of historical experience toward which moral self-consciousness is oriented.

It is possible that this might give rise to the concern that the pure will, because of this directive, might either be dashed to pieces or not come about altogether. That would call the fundamental concept of purity itself into question. To be sure, one could hold the opinion that this concern is based upon the religious and theological prejudice that the state stands in opposition to the ethical world. However, even apart from this prejudice, the idealist doubt can arise whether ethical purity is possible in the context of the material of the historical state. It could appear that the conditions of positive law and the positive state are incompatible with the conditions of the pure will. Later, we will give this question closer attention: it is a fundamental question of the application of the pure will, and thus of its effectiveness. Here, however, the question prompts us to strike out in another direction.

In spite of our concern, we constructed ethical self-consciousness exclusively with regard to law and the state. Freedom, to the extent that it is the presupposition of this ethical legal subject, was defined in its manifold ramifications.[7] Finally, we raised the question of reality in the context of this problem of pure self-consciousness. Its solution should lie in the direction of the state—it

---

7. [Defined in *ErW*, chapter 6, "Freedom of the Will."]

should. For the question has not been solved—neither in the individual who might carry the living spirit of the state in his heart, nor in the positive concept of the state, let alone in an actual state. *When will that state, the state of the ideal, appear in reality?*

We have availed ourselves of the term "ideal" for this kind of ethical being. And while we forgo the [use of the] term "sensation," we do not therefore doubt that ethical being is being. This is what we call ideal: a being that cannot be delineated as determined by sensation, even if sensation could encompass all the countries of the earth—a being that may not be delimited. It is inimitable to space; does it also resist time?

This is purity's source of reassurance. The will is oriented toward the future. It makes infinity possible. And with infinity comes a warrant and a kind of reality for ethical self-consciousness. *Eternity is mine.* Here we may state the meaning, in principle, of Lessing's saying.[8] Now self-consciousness possesses the reality that is accessible and adequate to it. Could space ever offer a better guarantee and means of securing [reality] than what is here achieved by time—when space would have to take recourse to sensation if it wished to exercise its claim? Eternity is the being of the ideal of ethical self-consciousness, the eternity of ethical humanity.

This is what we were able to produce in the way of reality. *We started from the state but progressed toward humanity.* Later, at the point to which we just referred, we will discuss the notion that state and humanity do not oppose one another in any way: the state finds its completion in a federation of states, just as humanity can be an ethical concept only in a federation of states. *Thus, for us, the problem of eternal peace emerges as the problem of eternal progress in the development of the ethical concept of the state.*[9] Nevertheless, it is possible to object to this version of ethical reality in two ways—on the one hand, that it secures *too much* reality, or, on other hand, *too little.*

8. [The last line of Lessing's 1780 *Die Erziehung des Menschengeschlechts* is, "Is not the whole of eternity mine (Ist nicht die ganze Ewigkeit mein)?" For an English translation, see Gotthold Ephraim Lessing, "The Education of the Human Race," in Gotthold Ephraim Lessing, *Philosophical and Theological Writings*, trans. and ed. by H. B. Nisbet. (Cambridge: Cambridge University Press, 2005), 240.]

9. [Cohen seems to be alluding to a distinction between his own conception of eternal progress toward peace and Kant's vision in "On Eternal Peace" (1795). For an English translation, see Immanuel Kant, *Perpetual Peace and Other Essays on Politics, History, and Morals,* trans. Ted Humphrey (Indianapolis, IN: Hackett, 2007).]

The first kind of objection was already noted. In it, all the weight of ethics seems to be placed on positive law and the positive state in their historical progress. In spite of our explanations of freedom and autonomy, the misgiving could still persist that positivism is being granted too dominant a role here. According to this view, one cannot rely upon law and the state to have the power to produce true ideality—not only as a consequence of its history, but also by the logic of the state. Therefore, eternity, too, has no traction here; it is taken as a figure of speech for the law of inertia. The term "eternity" is taken to be a usurpation, illegitimately transferring its original religious meaning—which, to be sure, is merely mythological—to the temporality of all positive law and all states.

The objection that there is too much reality, then, merges into the other type of objection, according to which there is, in this kind of eternity, too little reality. One can say that it is not worthwhile to dispute, and certainly not to deny *immortality*—but also not to render it ineffective with regard to the principal questions of ethics, just to gain, in exchange, the dream vision of eternal humanity in an eternal state.[10] *What criterion distinguishes this ideal of eternity from the eternal life of immortality?* This criterion is the hypothesis that cannot be sustained in relation to the immortality of the individual soul. Thus, it is still foundation laying on which the highest, ultimate warrant for all ethical being is based. And if one can now also say that all the reality of nature rests upon no firmer ground than foundation laying, then the objection can be raised that in mathematics too the foundation laying is carried out in nature, and that sensation too might also be content if it too were referred to foundation laying. Here, however, it is not merely that there is no mathematics for the grounding of being. Rather —and this is what seems to be the worst of all—law and state take the place of mathematics; the sciences of positive power take the place of the science of pure thought and pure being. Thus, the second kind of objection merges with the first.

If we take up the second objection first, we will be able offer the firmest rebuttal to the first objection, which is serious in every way, serious in what it suspects and what it misunderstands. But we shall do so not to speak in defense of myth and religion, which are intertwined, but to carry out our own methodology. In so doing, we must reflect on the fundamental concept of pure will. For is it really sufficient to achieve purity in its negative sense, to free oneself from false empiricism and conservativism? Does not the positive sense of *purity* lie in applying it

10. ["State" in the sense of a political entity, not a "condition."]

effectively? The logical legitimacy of the pure will for ethics consists only in this —that purity, in this sense, is applied to the subject of the will and of action, the subject that presents itself in history.

Nature and history, then, are indisputably the presuppositions of purity. It is not only the fundamental law of truth that establishes the correlation of the ideal and nature; but it is the very first natural presupposition, from which the method of purity proceeds. The natural will is not the pure will. The natural human being is not the pure human being. The empirical I is not the pure I. But if there were no natural human being with natural will and natural self-consciousness, then the method of purity could not commence; it would have no meaning at all.

If one now sets about to construct an ethics, one cannot be troubled by such reservations. The natural will of natural self-consciousness rages sufficiently clearly in the individual and in history that one need not be concerned about this material foundation. In logic it is no different. When one begins to free one-self from the impertinences of sensation, then one can position pure thought in opposition to sensation. And then, confident that the warrant provided by mathematics suffices, one need not dwell on the question whether the planets whose orbits are described by such pure thought are also actually present. Initially, such a carefree attitude may be innocuous and pose no danger, but in the end, Idealism disrupts such naïveté, and the soundest logic must learn to take responsibility for mathematics and, with it, for physics. How much more urgent must such responsibility for its kind of being weigh in the case of ethics, since not only Idealism is arrayed against it, but also all the powers of theoretical obscurity—and what is still worse, all the powers of the twilight of theory.

Hence, ethics preserves only its own path by taking up the question of Idealism as it is commonly understood—that is, as the Idealism of consciousness, not the Idealism of pure generative thought. In the case of nature, there seems to be little point in calling it into question, or even in leaving it to consciousness, so that nature would stand and fall with the latter. Without consciousness there is no nature. This statement is intelligible only in the more precise form: without pure thought, there is no nature of the natural sciences. However, if one believes one can give an appearance of metaphysical profundity by proposing the thesis "without consciousness, no nature," then one deserves a banal rebuke in the form of the counterthesis "without nature, no consciousness." One should not waste any more words on the matter; tirades on this kind of wisdom belong in popular books on metaphysics. By contrast, in the case of ethics, the question concerning the common type of Idealism assumes an entirely different meaning. It appears to call into question ethics itself.

For is it not the case that ethics is called into question just as much when its end is imminent as when it has no beginning? Such an end would be inevitable if nature—and the natural human being along with it—ceased to be. In fact, there would then no longer be consciousness, and thus no will, no action, no self-consciousness. In such a case is ethics supposed to be content, as perhaps mathematics could be—that it may have had its time and its validity, and thus the meaning of its being? Could ethics be satisfied with validity that is assigned to the past, when eternity, after all, is supposed to form the very being of ethics? If ethics is content with validity of the past, then eternity becomes an illusion and an edifying phrase; the ideal becomes a fiction of being, without reality. This great difficulty lingers over the problem of ethics, from beginning to end. Ethics takes no account of nature and the natural qualities of the human being, because it can achieve purity only by means of abstraction. However, once it has done so, then the question—which extends back to the beginning—transforms its entire structure, as if by a gust of wind, into a chimera.

This is the characteristic fate of ethics: that it must detach itself from nature, and yet seems as if it were chained to it; Prometheus represents its fate. It is all very well for the prophet[11] to say: heaven and earth may pass away, [for] he believes they are firmly grounded in the rock that, to him, God represents. But ethics cannot pass up this question. By engaging it, ethics is not straying into some alien territory; it is a most proper concern of ethics to ensure that nature exists and perdures to secure its own eternity. It must give thorough consideration to the question that ordinary Idealism generally considers: what meaning does this question have for ethics? What would be the consequences for ethics and its fundamental concepts if nature were to possess no reality, or if nature were to pass away? One can see that, from this vantage point, the problem of the eternity of nature assumes an entirely different character. Usually, the eternity of nature is understood in contradistinction to the religious conception of creation; it is, therefore, understood as a position adopted by naturalism. Here, however, this problem serves to extend the question into the infinite past. What was ethics before there was nature?

11. [Cohen is referring not to a prophet, but to Jesus's words in the Sermon on the Mount: "For truly, I say to you, till heaven and earth pass away, not an iota, not a dot, will pass from the law until all is accomplished" (Matt. 5:18).]

However, one might suspect that this turn of phrase is an attempt to anticipate, and thus impede interest in the problem. For now, then, let us leave it aside; let us accept that before there was nature, there was no morality either. However, what about the future? Can nature pass away? Or, since entropy is supposedly imminent, may it be thought of as synonymous with the grand conflagration, the end of the universe? May ethics let this verdict stand, pronounced on all being? Or should it insist on the requirement that nature be infinite, in space and time, because the being of the ideal signifies eternity? If this question must be answered in the affirmative, then there is *a lacuna in the methodology* of fundamental concepts, and it is necessary, methodologically, to fill in this lacuna with a new fundamental concept.

Ethics must admit the concept of God into its theoretical system. But what, in the constitution of ethics, is the methodological character of this concept? Above all, what is called for is a sober logical characterization of the concept of God. This is a necessity if its introduction into the system is not to fall under suspicion as a concession to extraneous interests, but is, instead, to rise above all doubt, as an inherent necessity of ethics.

It is not in dispute that the concept of God has a conspicuous, specific logical character. The logic of pursuing knowledge of nature has no need of it. It was possible to construct our ethics without taking it into consideration at all. Only at the conclusion of our work does the concept turn out to be unsatisfactory. And then it emerges, as was to be expected, that at the start we overlooked the error that, in the end, threatens to thwart our plans; now, a new concept is to be introduced to correct this error after the fact. What, however, was this error that was overlooked at the beginning of ethics?

Strictly speaking, the error was prior to ethics. When the pure will was taken up as a problem, we considered it an acceptable point of departure to assume that human beings, with their will and their actions, were present, so that the purity of their will and of their actions could be taken up as a problem as well. In the end, however, it turned out that for purity the solution must lie in eternity. Thus, the question arose, whether *the natural substratum* that provided the evidence from which we started *corresponds to this eternity*. To decide this question in the affirmative — the question on which ethics depends, to be or not to be — the concept of God suddenly appears. And what is it supposed to achieve?

The concept of God is supposed to secure, for the eternity of the ideal, the eternity of nature analogous to it. Consequently, its significance does not merely lie within ethics but extends back into logic. Yet its significance is not confined to logic alone;

rather, it extends into ethics. This is the great difficulty in attempting a logical characterization of this concept. Indeed, it appears as if this concept, invented to fill a lacuna, must remain suspended between two parts of the system. But then no logical term would probably remain for it, other than the one that *Kant* attempted to use in this context, the "postulate." Yet with this label, the concept took on a task quite different from the one assigned to it here.

However, the situation is not as hopeless as it appears to be. It is not true that we began the construction of our ethics without considering this difficulty; we took substantial precautions against it. *We began with the fundamental law of truth.* It means that a methodological connection must exist between the problems of ethics and of logic. To be sure, at this starting point, the emphasis lay on ethics—that it neither contradict logic nor, in its methodology, assert its independence from it. At first, it was our aim to prevent any harm to ethics, caused by a false independence. Now, however, we can proceed from there in a new direction: that ethics gains the greatest advantage from its connection to logic and from its dependence on it.

Additionally, we can now also shift the emphasis onto logic. Admittedly, logic too must take its point of departure from mathematical natural science, the prototype of pure cognition; but by no means does the latter—or the natural sciences in general—cover the full range of the problems of logic. Rather, logic must extend to the humanities and to their logic: ethics.

If it now turns out that the concept of God makes the necessary connection between eternity and nature, and therefore between ethics and logic, then the methodological character of the concept of God has now proved itself. It has the character of *modality*. It represents an expansion of modality insofar as it no longer merely brings about the necessary combination of concepts in the gradual progress of investigation. More than that, it makes possible the necessary combination of two parts of the philosophical system. This combination of logic and ethics corresponds to the fundamental law of truth. *Thus, in this sense, precisely defined, the concept of God becomes the concept of truth.*

To envision the full value of this concept of truth, one must cross the bridge this concept builds between logic and ethics in both directions. Let us first go backward, from ethics to logic. Is it permissible to do without the existence of nature? Does "dreaming Idealism," as Kant calls it, have any legitimacy or meaning?[12]

---

12. [Kant characterizes as "dreaming Idealism"—and rejects as naïve—a form of idealism that declares the objects of experience to be the things-in-themselves, whereas

Now we can see that it calls into question the content of ethics, the value of the ideal. It could be that at some time there was no world, and it could be that at some time nature will disappear. What purports to be *metaphysics* fantasizes in this manner. Such fantasy is frivolous, for it destroys not only ethics, but the problem of morality altogether. It violates the truth that ensures the connection between both types of cognition. Thought that violates the truth cannot have any legitimacy or meaning. *The truth opens the path that leads from the ideal back to nature.*

However, just as surely, truth also guides nature to the ideal. Logic represents only a portion of the truth. To insist on the idea *"je n'en vois pas la preuve* [I do not see the proof in this]" is to narrow the spiritual horizon. Logic must begin from such a methodological idea and thus from astronomical certainty, but this must not remain the final word. There are questions between heaven and earth. Humanity must not rid itself of these questions; it must not do so, even if it wished and were able to do so. It is contrary to truth to restrict oneself to mathematical natural science. As soon as one touches the territory of biological nature, forces of the problem are awakened, the problem that points away from the earth.

It is an entirely unsustainable restriction to try to base the human being on the biological organism alone—while dismissing the spiritual peculiarity from which the problem of ethics emerges and denying that it is a problem in its own right. Moreover, it is of no use to exacerbate the error, seeking to escape it by reducing the *humanities* themselves to products of natural dynamics. Then, however, there would be no truth any more, for there would no longer be two trajectories in cognition. To this extent, one could concede the consequences of naturalism, but the methodological standpoint remains very dubious.

At the very least, the methodological expediency of such reductionism is very questionable: it is presented as a mechanical monstrosity, not at all as a harmonious uniformity. Try to imagine: law, state, and all morality—in the creations of thought and in historical institutions—are supposed to be nothing other than the result of adapting to natural conditions. A problem of any other kind should not show up in their midst. Breeding and adaptation—there is nothing else, there is no need for anything else.

In the *Logic,* we already considered that the good and proper core of *Darwin-*

Kantian "transcendental, better '*critical*' Idealism" takes the objects of experience only as appearances, which are representations in the mind. See Immanuel Kant, *Prolegomena to Any Future Metaphysics,* ed. Günter Zöller, trans. Peter G. Lucas (Oxford: Oxford University Press, 2004), 99.]

ism lies in is its teleological significance—that is, as the teleology that prepares problems for being treated by means of the causality of mechanics. However, if this preparatory teleology is misunderstood, misinterpreted, and diverted from its proper path, then its effect is worse than the absurd materialistic teleology that it is supposed to replace. The blindness of material causation is then conceived of as seeing; its blindness, however, is supposed to remain unchanged, since the material asserts its place; but, at the same time, material causation is supposed to be seeing, in that it adapts. Adapts to what? It is an error to believe that we have dealt adequately with the concept of *adaptation* by providing it with natural conditions. All that it accomplishes is to provide the correlate to the very concept from which adaptation first proceeds; yet this concept too consists only of a natural condition.

What is omitted from all of this is the concept of fitting itself. Was it not somehow a concept in its own right? Is it supposed to mean, in some way, that adaptation[13] too should not, in itself, represent a goal and end, but rather is just the result of the collision of these two groups of natural conditions? Then adaptation is a very odd term for this collision of elements. In fact, in this line of thinking it is different. The *preservation* of the best, even if it goes by the name of "the fittest," is the motto. That is the goal toward which adaptation strives.

Thus, it is teleology in its good sense that has the guiding function in the notion of end, in the [measure of the] cultural value of the best. And it is a confusion of methodological concepts if adaptation, which is a concept subordinate to the concept of "preservation," is elevated to the superior concept.

With its symbolic terminology, genuine Darwinism seeks to bring together those groups of one problem that belong together to make them accessible to mechanics, or to mechanics as a kind of causality. But it is just a stereotypical [Darwinism] if the value of the method is applied in precisely the wrong way, if the difference between the problems is annulled—if the most diverse problems are all to be treated as one.

According to this view, morality is not supposed to be a problem in its own right, but only a production of nature. If this were correct, what would then be gained? Would it advance, or even bring about, the uniformity of cognition, if

---

13. ["Fitting" is the translation of *Passung*, and "adaptation" is the translation of *Anpassung*. The association in German to which Cohen draws the reader's attention here cannot be preserved in translation. However, the English slogan that serves to sum up Darwinism is "the survival of the fittest."]

the distinction between these problems were annulled in some inadequate way? What is gained methodologically by dropping the distinction between morality and nature, by making morality the progeny of nature? From the start, we have taken into account that any methodology of cognition depends on understanding this distinction. To be sure, if one could say that by depriving ethics of its own specific kind of cognition one would establish the unity of cognition, then our problem of truth would, in fact, be null. But we know full well that this view would be nothing but a medieval error clothed in modern finery.

The honesty of the modern age rests upon a simple insight that cannot be masked: mathematical certainty is one thing and moral certainty another. Therefore, the question of the uniform nature of cognition involves not just the specific character of ethical cognition, but all of logic. For the paradigmatic character of mathematics would also be obscured. And this is the fundamental ill in all the *so-called realism of the natural sciences*—that it is void of the logical guidance of mathematical cognition, that the basic concepts that constitute the conditions of the cognition of nature are not the concepts that provide guidance in these controversies. *The unity of cognition requires the distinction between the pure cognition of nature and pure ethical cognition.* This unity represents the fundamental law of truth.

We had to call to mind once again that it is correct to make a distinction between logic and ethics—that it is equally necessary and beneficial for both of them. *Morality does not emerge by natural coercion or chance.* Nature has other business, with an inherent value of its own. We must readmit this chaste sense of nature to our field of vision to recognize the connection to morality that nature itself reveals. Dreaming Idealism need no longer concern us. Nature will continue to exist. However its forms of movement may change, the preservation of substance for their sake now has the additional significance for us: the nexus of these two [kinds of] *preservation*: of ethical self-preservation along with the conservation of energy. *This truth is what we call "God."*

However the distribution of energy may change, we do not doubt that the eternity of moral progress cannot do without a human race through which moral progress is to be effected. Otherwise, morality would have to cease. But it cannot disappear, for its being, its ideal, has eternity—it is eternity. We do not insist that the human race be of one determinate morphological type. This is neither our concern nor our interest. Our interest aims only at the truth— that is, *toward the unity of the different*. If the entities we think of as human beings possess, first, logic, and second, ethics—not, for instance, only ethics—then adequate provision has been made for the correlation of purity. Then nature, which we require, is present.

From this perspective, we can also understand how, in the age of *Leibniz*, the idea of *a great chain of being* was neither dismissed as mere reverie, nor countenanced as a jest played by understanding. It was thought of, instead, as being in the interest of this, our truth. For *Kant* too, this idea may have emboldened him in his basic intention to bracket the natural human being and the empirical human being in general, to speak of *rational entities*, instead of speaking only and explicitly of the human being. A metaphysician like *Schopenhauer* has only derision and scorn for such profundity in a foundation for an ethics. The issue here is not so much a higher [faculty of] reason as a higher nature—or, more accurately, a greater degree of expansiveness and clarity in the natural concept of an entity to which ethics can have access.

The concept of nature itself, as based upon logic, should not be disturbed. Ethics cannot be firmly established by dislodging, even slightly, its foundation in the logic of nature. We do not know where science, by means of logic, may yet lead us or what contents of nature it will disclose. With regard to nature, truth requires only that the logical foundations of the knowledge of nature remain unchanged, and that nature exist in accordance with these logical foundations. Truth requires this for logic, but not only for the sake of logic. It also requires it for ethics, and primarily for ethics. For logic and nature, if they existed only for themselves, might pass away. But they are connected to ethics. Now the problem of truth appears and becomes fundamental law. This fundamental law is represented by idea of God. *God means that nature will endure just as certainly as morality is eternal.* The ideal itself cannot provide this certainty, just as little as can nature in itself. What is necessary is the methodology by which these concepts, better, these parts of the system, enter into relation to one another. They are, after all, parts of a system.

Nevertheless, one might now think that, although it is necessary to establish this nexus of problems by means of its own concept—and thus the nexus of the ideal and of nature—such a step would still not do justice to the significance of the idea of God. The idea of God—so this argument goes—cannot merely signify a methodological concept, no matter how necessary. To be sure, long ago *Pythagoras* called harmony the law of the cosmos, and Leibniz, too, resolved all opposites in being by means of his idea of preestablished harmony. Here, however, the harmony is purported to relate only to two types of cognition, to two parts of the system, and thus explicitly to the connection between these two problems and their contents. *The concept of God thus seems to be reduced to a methodological concept.*

This critique appears to be more threatening than it is, for one can turn it back on the dogmatic concept of God. All of Scholasticism—in fact, from the Latin Fathers on—endeavors to *interpret the Trinity* in terms of the faculties of the soul. In *Thomas*,[14] the Son of God signifies the intellect and the Holy Spirit signifies the will. Numerous as they are, these interpretations are all just variations on this theme; in *Cusa*, too, the interpretations of the Trinity move in this direction.[15] We can thus see that such a methodological significance attributed to the idea of God was neither unheard of, even in the Middle Ages, nor regarded as a desecration. Furthermore, one should not somehow think that this sober conception is somehow well suited to the medieval obsession with subtlety. For even in *Augustine*,[16] the will stands for love. This continues to be the case in mysticism and in Cusa, with the result that one can see how the most ardent enthusiasm of religious zeal has its source in this seemingly subdued methodology.

According to the critique above, methodology is insufficient for disclosing the ample content residing in the idea of God. However, we should not limit ourselves to the long account of historical examples to counter this objection. The principle of truth itself must refute it.

First, one must always take the negative significance of truth into account. It signifies neither the truth of the cognition of nature nor the truth of moral cognition. *Truth refers only to the agreement of both in the methodology of the foundation.*

The concept of God is beyond any relation to natural laws. Likewise, the concept of God is beyond any relation to self-determination. Nevertheless, the idea of *creation* is in no way exhausted by the laws of nature nor by their unity in the fundamental idea of the conservation of energy. Creation can assume an ethical meaning, if —on the basis of some document that in itself conflicts with [the idea of] self-determination—it is not conceived of as being in opposition to natural law. Creation can assume an ethical meaning, if creation is thus not understood in a theoretical meaning that is not intrinsic to it. If up to this point we have been concerned only with the preservation of nature and, in particular, with the preservation of nature for the sake of carrying out moral life, now we are taking up

14. [Thomas Aquinas (1225–74).]

15. [Nicholas of Cusa (1401–64), a German thinker and cardinal.]

16. [Augustine of Hippo (354–430). Love is the central notion of Augustine's ethics.]

the notion that the existence of nature represents an indispensable presupposition for laying the foundation for ethics.

As a result, however, we have dealt with the false appearance associated with the methodological meaning of God. Now, because of the existence of nature, God has become necessary for ethics. Dreaming metaphysics, which grounds being on consciousness, is thus caught in the act of allowing a gap in the ethical problem. The consciousness in which the being of nature is allegedly rooted must not be self-consciousness understood in its psychological universality. Rather, only ethical self-consciousness has the capacity, admittedly not to guarantee, but to demand unconditionally that nature be thus rooted.

In all of these relations, God proves his worth in nature for morality. The idea of *a great chain of being* too, which we referred to above, confines itself to nature; it extends the limits of nature but does not seek to cross them. In this context, we also have the interest of natural science in mind, how it was animated by the discovery of microorganisms. At that time the conflict did not yet exist—that nowadays is assumed—between *development* and absolute ethics. On the contrary, development was regarded not merely as a vehicle, but rather as a proof that morality is provided for in the arrangement of nature. For this reason, the principle of development assumed such far-reaching significance—such fundamental significance—throughout *Leibniz's* thought. In that context, the notion of the future assumes great power. *Le présent est gros de l'avenir.*[17]

In fact, moral reflection cannot avoid the concern that nature may not follow the path that the eternity of moral progress has set for it. And the question may not be turned on its head, in keeping with the spirit of the times: whether such purported progress is nothing more than the result of ceaseless natural development and of the magnificent material and historical development that accompanies it. Rather, from the perspective of the eternity of moral progress, from the perspective of the idea of moral being, the uneasy concern may arise whether nature, both living and inert, will continue to do its work through developments that are required as negative conditions for the idea of eternity.

What would have happened if humans had come to a standstill at the stage of the anthropoid ape? Is it mere chance that human beings arose, thinking about

---

17. [Leibniz wrote: "The present state of a simple substance is the natural result of its precedent state, so much so that the present is pregnant with the future" (Gotthold Wilhelm Leibniz, *Monadology and Other Philosophical Essays*, trans. Paul Schrecker and Anne Martin Schrecker (Indianapolis, IN: Bobbs-Merrill, 1965), 152.]

truth? Chance? Or is it due solely to a surplus of material from the development of the brain? To be sure, just as it was improper to conceive of creation itself as the creation of natural laws or of their material, one should also not somehow misconstrue development in and of itself as the development of morality. That would contradict the concept of morality, and, as a consequence, the problem of truth could not even arise. Rather, in the fact of this natural development, moral concern sees its demand confirmed; when nature provides for morality, truth asserts its power. The concept of *providence* is confirmed in its universal significance for the harmony of both worlds. Now, however, it is clear that the weight of the idea of God lies within the scope of the problem of morality.

Moral concern also extends to the epochs of history. What would have become of humanity if it had remained, as a whole, in the age of *savagery*? The question applies just as seriously to the residue of savagery represented by subsequent civilized ages. What about the unconditioned demand of the moral ideal in relation to the ages of civilization? Is *pessimism* correct when it claims that suffering is simply an attribute of existence? That existence is, in fact, a form of guilt; death is the penalty, for how could it be otherwise? This is how *Schopenhauer* expresses his piety. Thus, wisdom's final word,[18] as is well known, is the renunciation of life. It is truly distressing that the froth of such misguided and disconsolate brooding can claim an entire generation, spiritually and ethically; distressing that no one notices the theoretical emptiness in these fantasies, the stagnation of all intellectual interests and of all scientific methodology; and distressing above all that the moral spirit does not rise up in protest, so that, as if by a flash of lightning sent forth from the ancient right of eudaimonism, the desolate steppe of such speculation be exposed in its glare.

The idea of God is opposed to all pessimism and all quietism. It is not left to the perverse notion of chance what shall become of the human race, of the spiritual and moral culture of humanity. However, it also need not be left to the laws of nature, for they are not the only laws that account for being. Being is not only the being of thought, but also the being of willing. And this willing is pure willing, the willing of morality. Thus, for being there is a twofold correlation, correla-

---

18. [An ironic allusion to Goethe's *Faust*, part 2, act 5: "Das ist der Weisheit letzter Schluss: / Nur der verdient sich Freiheit wie das Leben, / Der täglich sie erobern muss! (This is wisdom's final word: / only he is worthy of freedom and of life itself / who daily these has conquered)" (Johann Wolfgang von Goethe, *Goethe's sämmtliche Werke* [Stuttgart, Germany: Cotta, 1840], 12:289–90).]

tion to thought and correlation to willing. Their unity is truth—is God. *Thus, the eternity of the ideal is now secured by God's providence in nature and for morality.*

Just as the conception of nature, as governed by laws, offers no guarantee of reality corresponding to moral progress, this insight also dispenses with the ancient Epicurean prejudice, that has again become fashionable in our age, confused as it is and incited by extremes: the prejudice that the progress of the natural sciences, by itself, has brought about ethical progress. This view does not have its roots in religious unbelief, but rather goes back to *Buckle*,[19] who, a half-century ago, became the spokesperson for this new kind of rationalism. Buckle taught that, in principle, there is no theoretical progress in morality—that there can be theoretical progress only in the sciences. He thus denied not so much religion as ethics.

That is the serious danger that lurks in this quite fashionable, seemingly crystal-clear form of enlightenment—that while believing that it is destroying religion, it also endangers ethics and all of philosophy. Of course, we are not unaware that this intention is also in play, since this shallow and narrow idea would never have occurred to such minds if they had had any understanding of or reverence for philosophy. If nature alone cannot guarantee the ideal, then, by the same token, neither can natural science alone—even though the ideal itself could not have been established without the foundation of the knowledge of nature. A god alone could not have accomplished this. However, the God that is truth, that signifies the harmony of natural and ethical knowledge—the God of truth—can guarantee the ideal. Otherwise, no form of knowledge could do so.

It can thus be understood that God has, at all times, been thought of as the original ethical power, as the power and force of morality. To be sure, there is a troubling ambiguity in these terms. A force is a force of nature, and a power is a power of history. Both are medial concepts; they operate in a positive, as well as a negative direction. Both of these directions, each type being one-sided, have been removed from the concept of God. If, for the sake of the optimism of ethical Idealism we place our confidence in the idea of God, then the problem of *theodicy* is solved. The concept of God itself then contains, in itself, theodicy. All the defects and ills present in nature become part of the economy of the divine plan of truth. Yet evil too, which we must recognize in human action—or,

---

19. [Henry Thomas Buckle (1821–62), an English historian who developed his theory of the development of civilization in his unfinished *History of Civilization in England* (London: Parker, Son, and Bourn, 1857–61).]

rather, which the one who acts must himself recognize in his action—can only be such an expression of ethical self-judgment. It may not extend beyond the heart of one's own conscience. However, in the judgment that ethical thought, with ever greater precision, has to exercise on history, on its events, its heroes, and its martyrs, evil should never be the only decisive principle. However corrupt and obscure the ways of the *law* and the governments of states may be, our confidence in eternal progress and in the success of the good must never waver on that account.

This is the practical meaning of the idea of God, perhaps better captured by the expression *the victory of the good* than "the power of the good." The power of the good could also be misunderstood as the power of evil. Manichaeism is, in principle, inimical to morality. The *messianic God* arose in explicit opposition to the double God of *Zoroastrianism*.[20] There is no evil. It is nothing but a concept derived from the concept of freedom. A power of evil exists only in myth.[21] A theology and metaphysics of a diabolical divine power represent a continuation of the dominion of myth. By contrast, the victory of the good cannot simultaneously be conceived as the victory of the evil; here, the contradiction is obvious.

The victory of the good means the securing of the good in the face of all doubts, misgivings, and experiences related to the natural and historical imperfections of human existence. Nevertheless, the ideal of self-perfection persists. Moreover, from the perspective of nature, this ideal cannot be denied the *perfectibility of development*. Truth demands it, and therefore God guarantees it. Self-perfection always remains the pure, independent presupposition. Just as nature is unable, in its development, to bring about such self-perfection, neither is God. Rather, God presupposes it. But the guarantee that *self-perfection* can and must become reality on earth, reality in law and in the state—this guarantee lies in the idea of God.

20. [Cohen adheres to the view (restated in *RR*, 47) that the radical monotheism evident in Deutero-Isaiah reflects the encounter of the Judean exiles with Persian dualism (see Isa. 45:5–7). This view was contested by Cohen's contemporary Bernhard Duhm (1847–1928) in his widely read 1892 commentary on Isaiah (*Das Buch Jesaia*, 3rd ed. [Göttingen, Germany: Vandenhoeck und Ruprecht, 1924], 314).]

21. [Gershom Scholem (1897–1982) cites this passage in *Ethics of Pure Will* as an epitome of the rationalist rejection of the existence of evil, which is affirmed, however, in kabbalistic thought. Scholem writes, "mysticism represents, to a certain extent, a revival of mythical lore" (*Major Trends in Jewish Mysticism* [New York: Schocken, 1946], 34), thus affirming what Cohen rejects. Our thanks to George Kohler for this reference to Scholem.]

It is said by all human beings everywhere, each in his own language. Should we fault our language if we call God an "idea," and in fact the *focus of all ideas, the idea of truth?*

In ethics, there is nothing other than concepts and laws—just as, for that matter, there is nothing in logic either, except for concepts and laws. Is the human being anything more than a concept, a concept of ethical self-consciousness? The character of a human being as a person refers only to this concept. Metabolism cannot give him character; he becomes a person only in conformity with the conceptual paradigm of the juridical person. How, then, could we still find fault in *not describing God as person?*

A person is what God becomes in myth. And religion remains under the spell of myth insofar as it applies the concept of "person" to the essence of God. Then the boundary between myth and poetry becomes porous. For this reason, in the history of religions it is a profound moment when a religion takes ever greater umbrage at *anthropomorphism,* a common occurrence in the history of religions. For this reason, the *theory of attributes* in Arabic-Islamic and Arabic-Jewish dogmatics and philosophy of religion represents a very interesting chapter in the history of religious enlightenment. In this context, *Maimonides* emerges as the teacher and leader of rationalism.[22] *Cusa* relies on him for the notion of *docta ignorantia* [learned ignorance]—for the restriction of knowledge of God to those attributes that concern only man, that is, that concern morality. However, the attributes of morality do not require hypostatization in a person. The person is defined by living. And *Maimonides dared to detach the concept of living from the concept of God.* Thus, the Middle Ages, in true religiosity, long ago pursued this fundamental notion that God is an idea.

The proposition *"God is spirit"* has ethical value only in that it prepares the way for the notion that *"God is idea."* Person, life, and spirit are attributes that are rooted in myth and that are of no use for ethics. Even if we leave aside the theological meaning of the concept of spirit, the concept itself is ambiguous for the

22. [Maimonides denies that "essential attributes" can be predicated of God because any addition, even a nonmaterial attribute, would compromise the concept of God's oneness and uniqueness. Only the so-called attributes of action are admissible, describing the way God acts in the world. In Cohen's reading of God's ways in Exod. 33:13—"God is compassionate and gracious, slow to anger and abounding in kindness and faithfulness"—they define God solely as a moral being (see *RR*, 79–81). For Maimonides, God's ways are identical to the attributes of action (see Moses Maimonides, *Guide of the Perplexed*, trans. Shlomo Pines [Chicago: University of Chicago Press, 1963], part 1, chapter 54, 124–25).]

reason that it intermingles nature and ethics. Any attribute is harmful, unless its function is strictly limited to expressing the harmonious connection of logic and ethics, unless it serves as a sign that God must be the God of truth.

One should only not think that what is at stake in this protective measure [against a personal conception of God] is merely a question of theory and ethical methodology. As is always the case with genuine methodology, it is of direct practical value. *The person of God sets up a false relationship with the human person.* God has the task of securing the ideal, but if it is God not as the idea of truth, but as person, *then the fundamental concept of self-determination and self-perfection is cast into doubt.* In my ethical labor and the discrete steps through which I strive to accomplish it, I must remain completely independent of and unconcerned with the question of success. Only with respect to the eternity that is mine may it interest me whether nature can do justice to my ideal being.

God, as the idea of truth, relieves me of such skepticism. He does not abandon my moral knowledge. Not my knowledge; but it is not my moral labor that is in play here. It is not "sicklied o'er" with such skepticism. This is how it is with the truth. However, if God is thought of as a person, then *two different concepts of person* will face one another here; the result will be disorder and ambiguity in the basic condition that, without a doubt, self-perfection represents.

However, there is another disadvantage linked to the [concept of] person that is no less important: that by this term, religion and its texts are, at the very least, granted priority and predominance over ethics. That step revives the very suspicion that the idea of truth is supposed to eliminate—the suspicion that what is under discussion is just a dull theory, which will never stand on secure ground. This is the way to navigate the fundamental mood and mode of thinking of the modern age, by leveling the difference between these two types of knowledge, by reducing them to the distinction between *knowledge and faith.* One can then indulge in a specious feeling of triumph—a feeling as if in all of these questions we were dealing not with knowledge, but with faith.

Yet if matters were simply to stop there, with converting religion's knowledge into faith, it might make good sense insofar as it would mean that the internalization of ethical notions would be proclaimed in external religious form. But religion is not in the habit of observing this boundary; rather, it forces ethics too into the realm of faith. This, however, marks the beginning of the harm that is inflicted on spiritual culture when, innocently enough, the concept of faith is given precedence. Ethics is then not supposed to be able to include knowledge;

it is not supposed to be a necessary part of the system of philosophy. This is the great ambiguity that inheres in the word "faith."

In this context, we endow the concept of God with new methodological value, as the idea of truth. God is now a fundamental concept of ethics. Moreover, one no longer need take umbrage at the appearance that the concept of God is a mere appendix to ethics. The sequence of the principles truly does not matter. However, one can also see that at the inception [of ethics] the concept of God was already there, in waiting: in the problem of the pure will and in the fundamental law of truth. Only when the fundamental concepts are complete is the concept of God fully formulated. For it is important for its significance that a fully elaborated ethics is the presupposition of the concept of God. The concept of God is thus connected to the methodology of ethics in its entirety, down to the last detail.

God is idea, that is, God is the full, pure, most profound problem of knowledge, of ethical cognition. The intellect, however, has no interest other than knowledge; likewise, thought has no other problem. There is no substitute, by any name, that may take the place of thought and cognition. *Therefore, God is not permitted to become a content of faith, if such faith will then be distinct from knowledge.* Neither caution nor any critique of knowledge should allow us to be deluded about the serious danger conjured up by this distinction.

However, religion is not the only impediment to the integration of the concept of God into ethics. At the very beginning of philosophy itself such an impediment emerged, and it has held its own: in *pantheism*. To be sure, pantheism emerged not as an antithesis to theism, but as its forerunner among the *Eleatics*.[23] And the weight of the idea [of pantheism] was tilted in the direction of universal Idealism. The All is being. Thinking is being. Thus, there is unity and identity between thinking and the All. Likewise, unity is conceived as God; thus, God is the All.

At a later point, however, the concept of the will takes its place alongside the concept of thought. Therefore, the concept of spirit or God can no longer be characterized only by means of reason and thought; the Logos must also include the will, as the divine force. Thus, in pantheism, universal Idealism undergoes refinement, becoming absolute *voluntarism*. The will is not set in relation

23. [A pre-Socratic school of philosophy in the fifth century BCE, it takes its name from the town of Elea, where its most prominent thinkers, Parmenides and Zeno, taught.]

to thought and certainly not subordinated to it; instead, the will, as the most universal force of being, becomes the motive of pantheism. The will is supposed to lend expression to the question that is recognized as the most profound question: whence [came] all being? The will is the universal source. But if one admits not wanting to press on to ask, "*where* does the will come *from*," the question must still be asked, because it is a concept, "*where* is the will going?" But this question is not asked. The will is conceived of not as the specific force of morality, but as the father of all—as absolute being, which contains, in itself, both its goal and its origin.

The Idealist form of pantheism seems to be superior to the dogmatism of *metaphysics*. For this reason, one might think that it is more idealistic than pure ethics, in that, keeping with the model of the *Deus humanatus*[24] of Christianity, it equates God and the human being. First, in this way the spiritualization of the human being appears to be more precise, since it appears to be more universal than is the case when it comes about through the ethicization of self-consciousness. Then, however, the idea of God is not merely secured with respect to method; it is objectified in the human spirit, by the highest form of being. It is difficult enough just to describe all the magic that pantheism has deployed through the ages to ensnare the spirit and heart of humanity.

It is not just that the heart grows haughty when it can feel its unity with all of nature. It appears that ethical feelings issue from nature that could not be elicited from other sources. Love of nature generates love for creatures; thus, the unity of the All proves to be a motivation for sympathy and benevolence. But what inspiration the spirit now derives from this notion! For this reason it has become one of the guiding notions of culture. Could there really be a God, without doubt, who merely pushes in from without?[25] If God is not distinct from the All, then I myself, being included in the All, am included in God. There can be no form of thought in which the value of the human being is elevated higher than it is by means of this share he possesses in divinity.

One often hears the question, what could any ethics want to teach and accomplish that is superior to the immortalization of the human being—his redemption from the dust of the earth, from the emptiness and transitoriness of

24. [*Deus humanatus* (meaning God made human) is a medieval Scholastic designation for Christ.]

25. [The phrase in German ("Was wär' ein Gott, der nur von außen stieße"), sympathetic to pantheism, is from Johann Wolfgang von Goethe, "Proömion" to "Gott und Welt" (*Goethe's sämmtliche Werke*, 2:285).]

his egoistic natural condition? Ethics, taken in this profound way, is characterized most powerfully, clearly, and incisively by the divinity of the human being. It is not beneath those who take this position to appeal to religion, even though doing so will awaken mistrust concerning the clarity and unequivocalness of the idea. In any event, this mistrust is encouraged by another factor: that even religion, making surreptitious use of skepticism, was always in an alliance with pantheism. Yet all these admonitions, abundant throughout the whole history of religion, philosophy, and general literature, have been useless in confronting the charm of the idea that has teased humankind: that one is part of the divinity. It can be demonstrated that, for the philosophers of Romanticism, pantheism was the tool they used to attempt to weaken and idealize the psychological dominion wielded over them by the dogma of the Trinity.

But has ethics gained in the process? Only in this sense may we pose the question whether the idea of God has gained in the process. In the philosophy of identity, the question of God is understood as the question of being and thought. What the philosophy of identity accomplished for the latter question—how it grounded the question and resolved it—it thus accomplished for the question of God. *Schelling*, therefore, shows consistency in his personal development when he acknowledges in myth the full truth of his doctrine of God and divine revelation. In Hegel, too, God is generated and made manifest in dialectical movement.

Now we have already seen that Hegel recognizes that the substance of morality lies in the state. To be sure, he distinguishes the *concept* of the state from the *individual* state. But [for Hegel] it is still the reality of the state on which the substance of morality must rely, and this reality does not signify the eternity of realization. One can see here, in the consistency of such idolatry of the state, the ambiguity [that is] inherent in pantheism and that, because of it, is invincible. And in *Schelling* the problem of freedom is connected with the problem of the origin of evil.[26] This is the difficult point at which *Weisse* too succumbed to the danger of the age, disfiguring and derailing both his *Essence of Christianity* and his *Aesthetics*—because of the power of the evil and the ugly.[27]

26. [Schelling develops the problem of freedom in connection with the origin of evil in his 1809 *Über das Wesen der menschlichen Freiheit*. For an English translation, see Friedrich Wilhelm Joseph von Schelling, *Philosophical Inquiries into the Nature of Human Freedom*, trans. James Gutmann (Chicago: Open Court, 2003).]

27. [Christian Hermann Weisse (1801–66), a professor of philosophy at the University of Leipzig. The two works alluded to here are his *System der Ästhetik als Wissenschaft von der Idee der Schönheit* (Leipzig, Germany: C. H. F. Hartmann, 1830) and, probably, *Philosophische*

In pursuing such an ambiguous direction, *Spinoza* has become the leader of the modern age. All the problems of religion as well as of philosophy seem to arrive at a unified solution. Body and soul, matter and spirit—they are subjected to one term, *modus*. And if the greatest questions of being can be solved all at once, then it is no wonder that the more specialized questions of ethics are dispensed with as well. Spinoza extended *the Stoic concept of affect* to its logical conclusion, so that the ancient Socratic theme of virtue as knowledge became an empty paradox. *The idea of the good* had to consent either to be submerged into an affect, or to vanish, as a subject of thought.

Now, to be sure, we must not underestimate the enduring contributions of Spinoza's divine naturalism to religious enlightenment, and thus to general intellectual culture. However, we also must not overestimate them; in particular, we must overlook neither the deficiencies in this kind of naturalism nor the potential harm to ethics that lurks in it. It is quite instructive that Spinoza gave his teaching this precise name,[28] thus giving expression to the goal of his thought as a whole. At the same time, however, his choice of title suggests that there remained in him a trace of doubt regarding whether his metaphysics is, in truth, what it actually seeks to be. He wants to describe human actions as if they were lines, surfaces, and bodies.[29] *For him, the ethics of emotions becomes a mathematics of emotions.* Is it supposed never to have occurred to him that while, in mathematics, matters always proceed in an orderly fashion, in human actions and emotions this is hardly the case? Are all the errors of human thought and aberrations of human emotions nonetheless supposed to redound to the glory of God? One can now understand that Spinoza, this rigid formalist of identity, also took no offense at the formula that *right equals might.*

With this, we have arrived at the point where it becomes clear that the program of pantheism poses a threat not only to Enlightenment in general, but, with regard to praxis, to pure morality as well. In this context, we can ignore the general title that Spinoza uses for God. His fundamental error is to posit an undifferentiated unity of thought and being. *Identity is correct for logic, but it is a snare for ethics.* It is incorrect, and it is ruinous, to say that *"voluntas et intellectus unum et idem sunt."*[30] It is incorrect—not because psychology does not confirm it,

---

Dogmatik oder Philosophie des Christenthums (Leipzig, Germany: Hirzel, 1860). Weisse did not write a book titled "Essence of Christianity."]

28. [That is, he named his magnum opus *The Ethics.*]

29. [See selection 1, n.13.]

30. ["Will and intellect are one and the same thing" (Spinoza, *Complete Works*, trans.

but because it contradicts the possibility of ethics. If it were true, then the theory of the will would in fact be identical to mathematics and logic; then there would be no ethics. The power that emotion, in itself and of its own accord, is capable of acquiring cannot justify ethics.

Pantheism poses a profound danger to pure ethics, to the radicalism of its principles and its predispositions. If ethics is at risk of being dissolved into mathematics and logic, it is not a source of concern for mathematics; nor is it a source of concern for logic. Even religion and theology have resigned themselves to registering no objection to these human truths. It is only ethics that suffers harm. It would forfeit its ability to deal with and solve the mysteries of existence. It would relinquish its specific character and its independence to *metaphysics*, which then goes by the alluring name of pantheism.

Thus, on the one hand, ethics has been naturalized and materialized, while on the other hand, by this very term,[31] it has been deified. It is quite understandable that pantheism satisfied those trends in ethics that had always operated within the limits of religious questions, no matter how vigorously they may have resisted religious solutions. However, religious freethinkers are less inclined to follow those tendencies in ethics that regard ethics as being vitally connected with *natural law*; but these tendencies operate with clarity and vigor in the territory between natural law and natural teleology. *In this connection, Leibniz and his era, in their robust and creative conception of ethics, are superior to any Spinozism.*

On the other hand, pantheism has animated and nourished the aesthetic spirit. Insofar as the German Enlightenment is aesthetic in nature, it is understandable that it would evince sympathy for Spinoza. Just as *Plotinus* located the source of the beautiful in God, likewise our great poets, in the vigor of their youth, at the start of their development, were filled with enthusiasm for Spinoza.[32] After all, in their art they sought the purity and quintessence of all spiritual being and striving. They yearned for unity; in their opinion, difference was a hindrance to their aesthetic power. This unity is the All of being; it is God. This unity, carried

---

Samuel Shirley, ed. Michael L. Morgan [Indianapolis, IN: Hackett, 2002], *Ethics*, Book II, Prop. 49, 273).]

31. [That is, by the very meaning of the term "pantheism," which equates the "All" (*pan*) with God (*theos*).]

32. [Cohen's "our great poets" include Goethe as well as the Romantic poet Novalis (1772–1801), who called Spinoza the "God-intoxicated man" (*Schriften: Die Werke Friedrich von Hardenbergs: das philosophische Werk II*, 3rd ed. (Stuttgart, Germany: Kohlhammer, 1983), 3:651.]

out with all their materials and all their means, must be the goal and content of all artistic creation. Thus, pantheism also became the watchword for *Schelling's* aesthetic philosophy of identity. However, the aesthetic significance of pantheism posed another danger for ethics. It is thus also *a sign that the concept of God belongs to ethics*—not to logic and general metaphysics.

We have already alluded to the way in which the English, and later *Herbart*, attempted to found ethics upon aesthetics. We are concerned now not with the question of being—whether it can be resolved, from this point of view, for ethical being. We are now interested only in the question whether pantheism, which makes morality into a variation on the beautiful, really supports morality as much as it animates aesthetic genius. As this occurs, love for nature is supposed to be stimulated and kindled. And this love need not be thought of only as an aesthetic delight; it can develop into a joyful benevolence toward animals and human beings. God has mercy upon all his creatures. Even the psalmist takes part in this kind of pantheism.

It should not be disputed that aesthetic pantheism has exercised a beneficent influence on contemplative moral philosophy. However, ethics must not be content with contemplation. It must gather the courage for the deed; it may not shrink from any step that might disturb its contemplative tranquility. The peace that the panegyrists of pantheism portray as so blissful—such peace is deceptive. The human being has to seek his peace not in unity with the All, but only in that limited portion of nature and history allotted to him. Nevertheless, he is not limited to this portion of nature; there is an All in which he can and should seek his home. That All is the being of eternity, the morality of the ideal. It is an All in itself; it must not be confused with the All of nature or taken to be identical with it. There is a unity, however, for these two kinds of All. Pantheism does not possess this higher unity; pantheism precludes it.

The idea of God is this specific kind of unity: it consists of the independent task of uniting nature and morality, of uniting them in the way required and permitted by the fundamental law of truth. It is unity in the ancient, classical Platonic sense of unification (ἕνωσις) [*henosis*], in which the concepts to be united endure in their difference; unification is limited to harmonization. Identity, by contrast, has no particular content of its own apart from the logical judgment and the law to which the judgment corresponds. *Identity expresses an abstract relation, but not a logical action by which this relation is brought about.*

When *Spinoza* says that extension and thought are two of the infinite attributes of substance, each of which, by itself, expresses substance in an adequate manner, then, as a result, the divine substance is made identical to each of these attributes. Substance has no content other than that of constituting a substratum for the attributes, which alone exhaust the content of substance. The significance of identity in that case is that, by means of one of the infinite attributes of substance, it defines substance as a general fiction, a fiction that can be realized by any attribute, each one just as well as the other. Identity thus proves to be just as much a restriction as an expansion of substance. Substance, as we know from logic, is always just the foundation and presupposition of relation. Pantheism collects relations into attributes and, from their correlation, produces identity. That is the judgment: God is nothing other than nature, and also nothing other than morality.

If, on the other hand, the idea of God signifies the unity of nature and morality, then this unity must not be confused with identity, as would be the case in pantheism. Rather, the idea of God signifies, for nature and morality, unity as unification, as the harmonization of nature and morality. No discrepancy is permitted to remain between morality and nature; likewise, no discrepancy between the demand and its possibility of fulfillment, if the latter depends on the former. This *harmonizing unity* is its own content; a content that no identity can possess. It is the content of the idea of God.

What advantage, then, does one believe can actually be derived from pantheism for solving the problems of nature and morality? It should be clear by now that it is neither methodologically nor practically beneficial to level the distinction between nature and morality. Therefore, the advantage that is so universally assumed can only refer to *transcendence*. As soon as a particular, specific content is ascribed to the idea of God, general opinion holds that this specific content can only be represented in the form of a person. But a person—so goes this opinion—must be an individual nature; and this individual nature will irretrievably meld with supernaturalism, against which the only defense is to identify God with all of nature. Now, at least, it appears that anthropomorphism and supernaturalism have been fully overcome. Because pantheism has thus emancipated religion from myth, it is now viewed as a kind of critical philosophy. However, this general opinion does not pay sufficient attention to the stance that pantheism adopts toward the problems of philosophy. Pantheism is naturalism; it assimilates morality into its nature.

We, on the other hand, conceive of the *transcendence of God* to lie in the significance of its independent content. Its independent content constitutes the significance of God's transcendence. It does not have some kind of existence outside of nature—just as an idea, in general, cannot be connected to the concept of existence. An idea can be placed in relation to the concept of existence, but sensation must then be allowed to speak and assert its claim. In cases where, because of the kind of problem, sensation has no place, then existence must be barred. To be outside of nature or to be outside of morality—the significance is the same. The content of the idea of God requires them both.

Nature consists of the sum of its laws. These, in turn, have their foundation in logic. God, however, is not in the game. Morality consists of the sum of its ethical concepts; their foundations, their grounding goes back ultimately to logical methodology. There, too, God is not in the game. In relation to both types of knowledge, then, God constitutes an instance of *transcendence*. As soon as transcendence is canceled out by some sort of immanence, then the two parts —nature and morality—suffer harm to their specific character. The advantage of immanence is an illusion. Transcendence represents a danger only from the vantage point of myth. On the contrary, transcendence is necessary and beneficial insofar as it establishes the specific character of an idea.

Transcendence, then, also offers the protection against the myth of person: the myth of person, in modern thought, leads ineluctably into the metaphysics of pantheism. Then, however, a vicious circle is unavoidable: if a person,[33] then as the All; but if as the All, then the original mythological predisposition has been abandoned—but also the more mature ethical predisposition. This has been, in fact, the actual course of the history of the idea of God: interest in myth was suppressed as soon as prophetic monotheism recognized the essence of God in morality alone. But with this, transcendence arrived on the scene. Transcendence thus conflicts inherently with interest in the person.

The difficulties of theological metaphysics too are exacerbated by the [concept of] person. Transcendence, on the other hand, dispenses with them. The person cannot bear the complications that are linked to the relation to the All: the possibilities of action in the world, and reaction, remain equally unsolvable, whether one assumes identity or difference between God and the world. A second person, Logos for instance, can offer a sort of remedy; but then the door is again thrown open for myth to enter. Transcendence denies all these mysteries the right to enter the house of reason. In so doing, it guarantees genuine immanence for the idea, the immanence of the harmonization of nature and morality.

33. [That is, if God is conceived of as a person, as in Christian Trinitarian doctrine.]

The transcendence of God thus acquires methodological significance. God may be identified neither with nature, nor with morality. God is a principle that is not contained in nature in itself. Just as in the individual case of an action of my own I am not permitted to inquire about its outcome, so too I could imagine that I must be indifferent toward the success of the ideal of eternity. Assuming that there were only ethics (and not also natural science and logic at the same time), and assuming that I could then still construct a methodological, pure ethics, I would not in fact have the right to pose this kind of final question to the ideal—leaving aside altogether the issue of whether this question could, in that case, arise at all. Then, in fact, for ethics, the problem of God would be absent.

The problem of God arises only from the internal methodological connection of ethics with logic. On account of this connection, ethics cannot start making itself into the supreme guide without the fundamental law of truth that establishes this connection. This law is, so to speak, the highest principle of all ethical cognition. With this, however, we anticipate the logical consequence that must be drawn when the fundamental concepts of ethics are completed. If this final question cannot arrive at a satisfactory answer, then ethics itself would collapse, for it is based on logic, and the fundamental law of truth wields such methodological power over ethics. For what would be the methodological value of such a system of concepts if there were no guarantee that they could be applied? It is not that such doubts about their application would never surface; on the contrary, they would haunt every step that ethical progress takes. Suspicion would constantly interfere, casting doubt on whether such momentum of the pure will could ever become reality.

The idea of God brings about the inner methodological congruence between our morality and our nature. Both are ours—both of them creations and productions of our [logical] foundations. And thus the harmony too is ours, the harmony that maintains the difference between nature and morality, but also shields this difference from two erroneous interpretations. One is the view that nature and morality are far removed from one another, two different worlds that have no interest, problem, or methodology in common. The other is the view that presents this difference as a contradiction, as if there were and there will remain an irreconcilable conflict and contradiction between morality and nature, between nature and morality.

No, between nature and morality there is only difference. This difference, however, demands harmony of nature and morality and finds it in the idea of God. Now God, to be sure, is transcendent, above nature and above morality.

However, here transcendence signifies nothing other than this: that now, because of this transcendence, nature is not transcendent in relation to morality, nor is morality transcendent in relation to nature. This is what we gain from the transcendence of God—that the transcendence between nature and morality is eliminated, that morality is permitted to look back at nature, and that it does not do so in vain. What we also gain is that nature is not left desolate, abandoned by morality, and that I do not have to take refuge in aesthetics (let alone in all manner of psychological feelings) to produce a connection between nature and morality. The idea of God establishes this connection. This connection, this unity rests on these two parts of the system of philosophy; unity, as distinct from identity.

II | Lectures and Essays

Prefatory Note to Selections 3, 4, 5, and 6

The essays in this part of the book help make sense of how Cohen related his philosophical project and ethics of autonomy to his Jewish allegiances. In particular, the essays help assess how Cohen built his own canon, fusing philosophical and religious sources and adjudicating among their contributions. Cohen's mature ethics required the establishment of a series of relationships to the greatest thinkers in the Western philosophical canon—not just Plato and Kant, but also Jewish predecessors such as Benedict Spinoza and Moses Mendelssohn.

Perhaps the most accessible presentation of the philosophical universe that Cohen curated for himself is selection 3, originally delivered in October 1916 at a meeting of the Soziologische Gesellschaft (Sociological Society) in Vienna. Cohen repeated it in January 1918, in what would be his last appearance, in a monthly lecture series at Berlin's Lehranstalt für die Wissenschaft des Judentums (Institute for the Academic Study of Judaism), a Jewish institute where Cohen taught after retiring from his philosophy chair. Cohen argued that Plato and the prophets offer indispensable aid to one another and to anyone who hopes to reclaim Western traditions for the modern age of reason and freedom. Plato was the first rationalist, and Cohen's affection for his thought stretched back in his career even further than his labors to reclaim Kantian thought. Not only did Plato invent an idealism that sought the foundations of our knowledge of appearances, but he also placed the idea of the good "beyond being," anticipating the Kantian idea of God that functions as a transcendent guarantee of the realization of ethical action. Meanwhile, the Jewish prophets founded social religion, calling on God as the source of communal ethics and on monotheism as succor for remediable suffering, rather than (as in Greek ethics) treating evil as a tragic necessity and heroism as the archetype of goodness. In combination, Plato and the prophets were forerunners who, once their works were fused together, produced the modern ethics that Cohen defended.

Selection 4 turns to a daring account of how Kant, whose comments on Judaism were dark and stereotypical, in fact was the premier thinker for transmitting its legacy to the modern world. Once one drops Kant's own opinions about Judaism, indebted in part to the mistaken conceptions of Mendelssohn and Spinoza, it turned out that Judaism was best interpreted as a forerunner of modern rationalism. Indeed, as Cohen insisted, earlier Jewish thinkers—especially Moses Maimonides—had contended that God's revelation was not some self-authorizing source, let alone a self-sufficient one. Nor were God's laws binding in virtue merely of the fact that He gave them. Admittedly, Judaism, for all its biblical and later appeals to reason, conferred importance on divine command. But Kant and Judaism converged more than they differed, calling on ethics to counteract egoism and rejecting any anthropomorphic understanding of God to approach him rationalistically. Finally, Kant and Judaism coincided when it comes to the destiny of ethics: what Kant defended as cosmopolitan peace in history is not radically distinct from Jewish messianism.

Cohen delivered the lecture reproduced as selection 5 at the Fifth World Congress for Free Christianity and Religious Progress, held in Berlin, in 1910 —later in the same year that he lectured on Kant and Judaism. His progressive Christian audience affected how Cohen's framed his message, and he daringly singled out Judaism and made it superior as a grounding for a universalistic ethics and politics, once Christian misunderstandings were cleared away. Among other things, Judaism refused to juxtapose and segregate faith and knowledge, which Christianity (especially Protestantism) erroneously did; and even if Judaism was excessively authoritarian in its origins, a kind of personal equivalent of premodern theocracy, it was anything but legalism for its own sake. It called for its own brand of rationalism, and its Sabbath—a theme to which Cohen returned again and again throughout his career—stood for the promise of progress in human affairs.

If that progress continued, it would bring about a kingdom in which human beings increasingly understood themselves and treated one another as self-legislating ends, not means to ends. Autonomy was the heart of both Kantian ethics and Cohen's neo-Kantian rendition of them. "Autonomy and Freedom" (1900), selection 6, was written for a memorial book in honor of David Kaufmann, a rabbi in Budapest and, like Cohen, a former student at the Jewish Theological Seminar in Breslau. Yet in this selection Cohen is at pains to distinguish the notion of freedom in Judaism and Christianity from Kantian autonomy, as a miniature version of the distinction he had long maintained between religion and ethics. Just as in a combative review essay the year before of his onetime mentor Moritz Lazarus's attempt to outline an "ethics of Judaism," Cohen insists that there can be no such thing, except insofar as it anticipates the universal ethics of autonomy. While freedom certainly finds a place in religion, for Cohen, Judaism is based on God's legislation rather than the autonomous self-legislation on which ethics depends.

SOURCES

Selection 3: "Das soziale Ideal bei Platon und den Propheten," in *Der Jude: Eine Monatsschrift* 7, nos. 10–11 (October–November, 1923): 618–36, reprinted in *JS* 1:306–30 and *Werke* 17:300–335

Selection 4: "Innere Beziehungen der Kantischen Philosophie zum Judentum," in *Achtundzwanzigster Bericht der Lehranstalt für die Wissenschaft des Judentums in Berlin* (Berlin: Meyer und Müller, 1910), 39–61, reprinted in JS 1:284–305 and *Werke* 15:311–45

Selection 5: "Die Bedeutung des Judentums für den religiösen Fortschritt," in C. W. Wendte, ed., *5. Weltkongress für Freies Christentum und Religiösen Fortschritt am 10. August 1910* (Berlin: Protestantischer Schriftenvertrieb, 1911), 385–400, reprinted in *JS* 1:18–35 and *Werke* 15:431–54. The English translation by Cohen's student Henry Slonimsky (1884–1970) from *Werke* 15:455–66 is presented here with minor emendations.

Selection 6: "Autonomie und Freiheit," in Marcus Brann and Ferdinand Rosenthal, eds., *Gedenkbuch zur Erinnerung an David Kaufmann* (Breslau, Germany: Schles[ische] Verlags-Anstalt v. S. Schottlaender, 1900), 675–82, reprinted in *JS* 3:36–42

The Social Ideal in Plato and the Prophets (1916)

Plato and the prophets are the two most important sources of modern culture as a whole. But like all sources of culture, they too contain foreign borrowings. These borrowings, however, are brought under control and absorbed by the singular originality of these two sources. Both may be considered peerless examples of historical originality.

Two elements are joined together as the basic conditions of the social ideal: *scientific-systematic pursuit of knowledge* and *morality* in the stable form of religion. Plato is and remains the symbol of the former condition, the prophets the symbol of the latter. Scientific knowledge extends beyond the problem of nature and enters into the domain of morality. Thus, as early as in Plato religious elements intermingle with scientific knowledge. And the prophets too, when they reflect upon the essence of morality, cannot help but look about at the human world around them. Thus, they cannot completely renounce the human pursuit of knowledge, although they limit its purview to the world of the human being. Whereas Plato draws ethics into the domain of the pursuit of knowledge, the field of scientific-systematic knowledge remains alien to the prophets. The only part of nature of interest to them is the nature of *the human being*.

In this outline, these two conditions of social life stand in stark opposition, without any interaction, almost without any connection. This outline is, however, a mere abstraction; historical reality fills this abstraction with the vitality of opposites; their interpenetration produces variety in civilization.[1] When these fundamental historical elements intermingle, the opposites are inevitably both refined and diminished, and the specific character of these oppositions becomes unstable and less distinct. It is therefore appropriate to investigate these two fundamental elements in their particularity.

We can see that the focus of Plato's spirit is the problem of scientific cognition. He was not the first Greek to grasp this problem; nor was he the first to

---

1. [The German word "*Kultur*" has a broader semantic range than the English "culture," encompassing both "culture" and "civilization." In this paragraph, "*soziale Kultur*" is translated simply as "social life."]

have connected the problem of scientific knowledge with that of ethics. In connecting the two lines of thinking, he continues in the footsteps of Pythagoras—but only in connecting and not in uniting them. With respect to knowledge, he is indebted chiefly to Parmenides and Democritus, and in ethics to Socrates. However, although Pythagoras is his predecessor in connecting these two lines of thinking, Plato's originality is not thereby diminished. One could perhaps say that just as, in general, the Greeks learned their mathematics and astronomy from the Orient and were still the first to forge and shape their acquired knowledge into science, Plato's relationship to his predecessors is similar: for him, their philosophy as a whole is like an aggregation of insights. He, however, is the first to shape the insights into cognition.[2] This double meaning contains a fundamental question: what is ἐπιστήμη [episteme]?[3] The question signifies: what is the relationship between science and cognition?

In seeking to define this relationship, Plato becomes the author of the theory of Ideas. For the Idea proceeds as a natural outgrowth just as much from the source of the ethical as from that of science. However, the presentiment and outline of the Idea are elaborated into concepts only in the context of the problem of science. With presentiment and intuition, Plato stands on the original soil of Pythagoreanism, which he cultivates with the conceptual tools of the Eleatics and of Socrates. For Plato, however, the connection between such intuited presentiment and the task of the concept becomes a problem in its own right. For Plato, the mind may not have two separate sources: the idea should be just as much a pursuit of the concept as it is an intuited presentiment. Intuition is thus inescapably detached from the realm of presentiment and drawn over to the side of the concept.

The Idea is therefore not merely the concept of Socrates, much less that of Democritus; rather, the concept itself becomes a question mark, a problem unto itself. Presentiment and intuition remain mystical in character: what is their origin and what is their foundation? Similarly, the concept is also mysterious: whence does it derive its authority? On what foundational truth is it based? This is Plato's question, and by this question, from which emerges the creation of the Idea, he overcomes all previous historical naïveté, from Pythagoras to Socrates.

2. ["Cognition" here refers to the process of pursuing coherent knowledge.]

3. [Elsewhere Cohen states explicitly that he understands "episteme" to mean both knowledge and science (Wissenschaft). To be sure, the question here ("What is episteme?") does not occur in this form in Plato, but a similar form is found in his Parmenides (134a) and Theaetetus (for example, 146c, 147b, and 187a–b). See Werke 6:300n2.]

All of them know not what they do. All of them are the authors of magnificent, eternal creations of the spirit. However, they are all comparable to Daedalus[4] or to a maker of graven images. These conceptual images, too, can neither see nor hear;[5] they lack even the living breath that distinguishes them from mere artifice.

Only the Idea gives the concept the vital generative basis that legitimates its existence and its activity. The concept should then no longer be a mystery: what was an image of God has now become, as it were, an image of the human being, a product of, and testimony to, the intellect. Of all the formulations that Plato uses to attempt to describe his Idea at its peak intellectual level, there are therefore two concepts in particular through which he defines the Idea most profoundly and most clearly: first, through his play on words regarding the concept as Logos, which, in the "*giving of Logos (logon didonai)*," takes on the meaning of a rendering of account. Thus, the concept becomes its own bookkeeper and accountant. Plato would not have chosen this figure of speech if he had not focused his attention strictly on the domain of science.

And thus the other attempt at defining the Idea was added, which concerns the systematic method employed in all scientific research, particularly in mathematics. There, the path for a rendering of account is clearly laid out; Plato himself paved the way for it and illuminated it. It is the laying of a foundation, *hypothesis*, that turns the process of the intellect into the process of science. Even if the hypothesis belongs to the obscure domains of intuition and presentiment, such suspicions and uncertainty do not lead science astray. Science proceeds step by step from its clearly laid foundation and produces its deductions. The rendering of account and hypothesis complement one another: the rendering of account is based on hypothesis, and the hypothesis is aimed at the rendering of account.

With the Idea, then, naïveté of thought ceased, even in its production of concepts: the concept, and with it, thinking about oneself, achieved clarity, through science and its foundational method. The idea grew out of the double meaning of ἐπιστήμη [*episteme*], and, by virtue of this connection to science, the idea became the root of knowledge. What is the essence of the idea? This question allows for a precise answer: an Idea is the concept of scientific cognition, of cognition that is

---

4. [Daedalus is the legendary artist of ancient Greece, whose superhuman abilities as a craftsman enabled him to fashion wings for himself and his son, Icarus.]

5. [An allusion to Ps. 115, which mocks idols for their lifelessness.]

connected to and bonded with science, such that cognition originates in science, and science, in turn, organizes its material as cognition.

Idealism, accordingly, is the idealism of science. Without continuous integration with science, there is no knowledge, no Idea, no idealism. An idealism of intuition and vision is, in its most charitable interpretation, one-sided Platonism. Platonism, however, is the epitome of uniformity, and such one-sidedness conflicts with the unity of its system.

The historical eternity of Platonism rests on its uniformity. With its historical eternity, Platonism also unites science and ethics, ethics and science. The Idea, having originated as mathematical idea, reaches maturity in the Idea of the *good*. In the face of such expansion, all skepticism is struck dumb. To be sure, the good is not being; but it certainly must not, on that account, be denied the validity of an idea: for it is thus, in this way, "beyond being."[6]

Transcendence did not originate in God, but rather in the good, as the Idea of the good. The Idea of the good may be beyond being, but it is by no means beyond knowledge. Despite all the differences that are due to the fact that the question leads beyond the native territory of science, knowledge must still be made into a problem, into a desideratum, for morality. Likewise, morality must be made subject to and must be subsumed under the authority of knowledge.

It is here that the danger of dualism for Platonism sets in, for any idealism of ethics. The Idea is not limited to mathematics and to nature; ethical idealism too is attached to mathematical idealism. The ethical too is simply subjected to the norm of the Idea. Intuition and vision are therefore thrust aside and overcome, even where appearance would yield to them. The norm of knowledge retains fully its exclusive sovereignty. All concerns and requirements of human civilization, without exception, must submit to its guidance. And whatever the principle of knowledge requires must be applied to the problem of morality and executed to the fullest, in all its consequences.

However, since, in the case of ethics, there is a methodological difference, inasmuch as ethics lacks a systematic scientific foundation, it is thus inevitable that the principle of knowledge, when applied, will stray into excesses and errors. On account of these methodological deficiencies, from which Idealism, in the realm of ethics, cannot escape, it is fairly understandable that the other source—that of *religion*—has become and continues to be a productive source for the sphere of morality.

6. [Plato, *Republic* 509b.]

For social consciousness, the pure source of religion lies in *prophetism*. However, let us first give our attention to its limitations. The prophet knows nothing of science. Even in Babylonia, he was not enticed by its charms; how much less would he have lifted the veil of science on his own in Palestine. The starry hosts interest him only for the sake of the God who called them forth by number and name.[7] Thus, for the prophet, nature is present only as God's creation. Even the actual meaning of the first word of Genesis, "in the beginning,"[8] is uncertain, and this is typical. The question what it was from which God created heaven and earth is, for these minds, remote. There is hardly even a chaos; how much less would they have imagined primal elements. From the very start, their poetic view of nature directs our gaze to the universe that confronts us in finished forms, in water and light, in plants and animals. This consciousness of nature has no interest in investigating nature, and certainly not in the question of whether sense perception provides a true image of the reality of nature, to say nothing of conducting an inquiry into the tools of consciousness itself: what thought means, in comparison to sensation, and all the problems of this kind that arise with the awareness of the distinction and the relation between subject and object. All these problems issue from the interest in reality as a truth. For the prophets, by contrast, all reality has its truth only outside of itself: in God, who brought it into existence, but who can also transform it, such that truth does not inhere at all in nature itself. That is the limitation of prophetic thought. It knows of no science, and therefore, in this context, the problem of how to acquire knowledge cannot arise.

Yet the prophets do speak of *knowing* their God, and the word seems an appropriate choice: for this God is beyond sense perception and stands in stark contrast to the realm of sensibility. If, however, we maintain the methodological connection between the process of knowing and science—which, in Greece, was a historical connection—then the expression "knowledge of God" can have only a metaphorical meaning.

It is then understandable that in the spirit of the Hebrew language to come "to know" is identical to "to love."[9] To be sure, love is supposed to express an

7. [Evoking Isa. 40:26.]

8. [In the Hebrew original, this phrase is just one word. On creation, see also *RR*, 59–70, especially 64–65.]

9. [Cohen is referring to the root ידע (meaning to know through intimate connection), as opposed to words from the root נכר (for example, הכיר, meaning to know through distinction or discernment).]

intimacy of comprehension, as a process that approximates union. But it would forever remain a mystery how such an identity of knowledge and love is achieved —how, more generally, it was possible that the notion of love be directed toward an unapproachable God—if the solution to the mystery were not the notion that knowledge was supposed to be surpassed. It was inevitable that God be set up in opposition to all sense perception, both concrete and figurative. Accordingly, knowledge must be positioned in contrast to perception. But to shed any connection between knowledge and natural science, knowledge is transformed into love, which has nothing in common with science.

But how then is it possible to give a positive justification for the prophetic concept of love, of both love for God and divine love? All the dangers of religion issue from this point, likewise all its good and its harmful connections to mysticism. Religion itself is, to be sure, not void of any connection to science, but it wants to be extricated from this connection. Hence love comes into conflict with knowledge. Is it then impossible that religion avoid such a connection to mysticism?

The prophets became the *founders of social religion* and thus of social consciousness in general by severing the love of God from mysticism, and, without making use of guidance from science, seeking to pave the way for knowledge within love. How was this possible? In fact, with God [alone], it would not have been possible. However, the prophets did not stop with God alone but placed him in connection, in relation, in correlation to the human being. In this way it was possible for the problem of love to arise: not originally with God, but in relation to the human being. They wanted to know the human being, not on the basis of scientific knowledge of the human being. Indeed, even Plato failed to achieve the latter. He had to resort to Idea. The prophets resorted to their God.

To be sure, it would be inconceivable that the prophets—and only the prophets among the seers of all nations—would have developed the notion of the unique God without any stimulus from speculation. Yet what is characteristic of the prophets is that in their speculation on God as the unique being, they made do without the support of science: it is precisely this that shifts the emphasis from metaphysics of any kind to the exclusive problem of ethics. The latter, however, is concerned not so much with questions about God as with human questions. And thus it came about, from the first, that the God that originated in Babylonia as the creator of heaven and earth was transformed into the God of the human being, into the creator of humankind.

However, when God was summoned by the prophets, as it were, before a human tribunal, then, for the prophets, their preferred paradigm of a human being was not the son of the gods, or a demigod, or a hero; rather, it was the human being in his weakness. This weakness was above all moral weakness; thus, human sin became the first archetype of the human being.[10] However, just as, for them, philosophy was alien to ethics, so too was tragedy. Thus, they did not stop, neither at guilt nor at punishment as the two sides of fate that form the poetic basis of human existence. Rather, they stripped this two-sided countenance of guilt and punishment of its honored position; they understood *suffering* not as human fate, but as one stage in the development of the concept [of the human being].[11] Thus, by eliminating the fundamental concept of [Greek] tragedy, the primal mythical notion of the envy of the gods is eradicated. God is the one, not the good. If suffering also comes from him, then this is not evil; rather, it takes its place in the development of the good, for which the good God takes responsibility.

The separation of suffering, as punishment for guilt, from guilt itself is one of the most profound consequences of monotheism, laying the foundation, at the deepest level, for the problem of the social. For suffering represents the gravest challenge to God's goodness. But if suffering is thought of principally in connection with death, then myth retains its hegemony. Death is an image of fate, to which even the gods are subject and that, for the human being, extends only to death. There is no role for human morality; confronted by fate, it can persevere only in mysticism. If ethical activity is to be aroused to counter suffering, one's view must be diverted from the common [human] fate of sickness and death. It was necessary that misery be disclosed no longer in the biological, but in the sociological, domain. Thus, the poor man became the symbol of the human being.

The entire development of prophecy can be traced by means of this guiding principle. God is not the father of the heroes, and the heroes are not called beloved of God. Instead, God "loves the stranger."[12] In polytheism, the foreigner —unless he becomes a "guest-friend"[13]—is the opposite of the ideal man, who

10. [The elevation of sin as "archetype" is unusual in Cohen. See *Werke*, 17:308n1. It is an innovation in Cohen's late thought, in which the individual, in becoming conscious of their sin, becomes a new human being, and, in atoning for sin, becomes free. See the discussion of Ezekiel in *RR*, 190–93.]

11. [On suffering, see *RR*, 225–27.]

12. [Deut. 10:18.]

13. [The German *Gastfreund* is a translation of the Greek ξένος (*xenos*), a stranger who is a guest or is otherwise accorded hospitality, as opposed to a friend from one's own people.]

is never other than a member of one's own people. The foreigner is a barbarian. However, if one's own God loves the barbarian, declares the hostile people to be his own, like Israel, his special possession, the horizon of the human being expands and brightens. Messianism demands and accelerates this development, which will lead to cosmopolitanism. In what follows, however, we will follow another chain of development, one that leads to socialism. Just as God, along with the stranger, also loves the orphan and the widow, they are the ones who, with the stranger, bear the burden of social oppression, from which God's righteousness shall free them.

But no matter how much the prophets carry on, invoking justice and righteousness and proclaiming their God to be the God of righteousness, for them this kind of abstraction, a type of knowledge, is not enough. They appeal to the human heart, in their view the unique treasure-house of the human spirit. They draw forth compassion (*Mitleid*) as the form of consciousness that corresponds to suffering (*Leiden*). In the Hebrew language, compassion[14] is a wholly native term, deriving from the word for womb (*rechem*). With the feeling of compassion God is merciful to the poor; with this feeling a human being should discover the poor as human beings.

Compassion is therefore not a passion, not a psychological affect common to both human beings and beasts, but rather a spiritual factor; one might say: a surrogate of the spirit. In it, the full force of a worldview struggles toward consciousness. One would have to despair of God's righteousness, of his goodness and providence, if such compassion were not a force of human consciousness able to defeat anything produced by the so-called spirit in the form of skepticism. Of human suffering, poverty alone is my concern. It is the primary shackle of his existence. Perhaps he could vanquish even death itself, if only poverty did not remain the trademark of the human world. Moreover, it is the most fateful deception to claim that poverty could be the response to human guilt. Through this error, one will not arrive at the truth about God, nor at the truth about the human being, nor even at the first discovery of the human being. Only compassion discovers the human being in one's fellow human being. In compassion, the suffering of another becomes one's own suffering, and the other thus becomes one's fellow human being.[15]

14. [The Hebrew word *rachamim* (רחמים) means compassion or mercy. Cohen elaborates on this point in RR, 150.]

15. [Through compassion, the "human being" (*Mensch*) becomes one's fellow human

It is significant that Plato never specifically refers to an Idea of the human being. And it is equally significant that Philo, the Jew, does bring about this advance in the doctrine of ideas. For him, [the idea of] the human being requires its own specific epistemological validity, just as do mathematical ideas of nature. For him, even the Idea of the good does not suffice. And although Plato himself postulates God as the good one, this notion remains narrow and undeveloped, as long as the human being does not attain his own share of goodness. It was the prophets who discovered this intrinsic worth of the human being. And it is their social conscience to which we owe this discovery. *They equate the poor with the pious.*[16] This identification is the decisive climax in the development of messianism. And the messiah himself consequently becomes the standard-bearer of poverty. He takes all the guilt of humanity upon himself, because he takes all human suffering upon himself. Devoid of the allure of the hero's power and the gods' beauty, he rides his donkey through the world as the symbol of human suffering.[17] He spurns any share in the world's aesthetic allures, but only displays human suffering through his social suffering.

Thus, that Faustian poetical work in the Bible, the book of Job, enters into the orbit of messianism. After the prophets have made it clear to human beings that they neither sin nor suffer on account of their ancestors, they pose the question: from where, then, does the evil in human beings arise? In place of this metaphysical question, they should learn to ask: from where does human suffering arise? That is: what is the meaning of poverty? They should recognize this meaning in the negative as: not guilt.[18] Therefore, the positive insight arose that the poor human being should of course be recognized as the good human being. No concept of God, nor of the human being, nor of any worldly experience should confuse this insight. God is the God of righteousness; he will surely help the poor. He is the God of world history, and he will compensate humanity for whatever suffering the individual had to endure. He is the God of goodness;

---

being (*Mitmensch*). In English, a compact translation that conveys the lexical connection of these two key terms is impossible. See *RR*, chapter 8, "The Discovery of Man as Fellowman."]

16. [See *RR*, 284.]

17. ["Rejoice greatly, Fair Zion; / Raise a shout, Fair Jerusalem! / Lo, your king is coming to you. / He is victorious, triumphant, / Yet humble, riding on an ass, / On a donkey foaled by a she-ass" (Zech. 9:9).]

18. [On innocent suffering, see *RR*, 134–38 and 142.]

thus, he can inflict the suffering of poverty on a human being only out of the light of goodness. And knowledge of the goodness of God brings me to the insight that the poor human being is a pious, God-fearing human being, the beloved of God. This knowledge, to be sure, does not derive from science; it is therefore not an Idea of the good, but neither is it the abstract concept of good, that could also be applied to material objects. Rather, this kind of knowledge of the good is concrete and personal, in the human being. And only in the human being is love for God kindled.

To be sure, we now come to recognize the limitation in this concept of the love of God, both for God and for the human being. Compassion for suffering brought about the discovery of this notion [of love for God]. We understand, as a consequence, why this inadequate form of knowledge was unable to get rid of the metaphysics of death. Human beings always find it more pleasurable to swoon in pious dreams than do good actions.[19] And thus we can also understand that good actions, guided by the magic wand of this religious insight, produced the best that could be achieved by restraining and subduing humanity's demonic nature. At the same time, however, it has become clear to us that compassion alone cannot be the sole motivation of social action, but that the wellsprings of science must finally be dug and pressed into use, if there is to be certainty and steady development in ethical problems. Thus, we must return our attention from the prophets to Plato.

Plato's advantage lies in the principle of knowledge. All Orphic theology[20] will remain untenable if it is unable to master the doctrine of ideas. For human beings, compassion cannot serve as a substitute for knowledge. Without philosophy, suffering will not cease among human beings. Thus, knowledge is the pillar of the social world. Even suffering itself cannot be fathomed without

19. [The wording alludes to Nathan's admonition to his daughter Recha in act 1, scene 2, of *Nathan the Wise*: "But see how far / It's easier to swoon in pious dreams / Than do good actions? see how sluggish men / Are fond of dreaming piously, because— / Although at times of their intent not quite aware—they'd shun the need of doing good?" (Gotthold Ephraim Lessing, *Nathan the Wise*, trans. Bayard Quincy Morgan, 13th printing (New York: Continuum, 1989), 14).]

20. [The existence and nature of Orphic religion, attested to in Greek texts of the sixth and fifth centuries BCE and in archeological finds, was the subject of renewed scholarly discussion in the early twentieth century, spurred by the work of the classicist Jane Harrison (1850–1928) on Greek religion and by Albrecht Dieterich, *Nekyia*, 2nd ed. (Leipzig, Germany: Teubner, 1913). Orphic texts deal mainly with theogony and cosmogony.]

knowledge, to say nothing of the eradication of suffering and redemption from it. The prophetic insight is merely a presentiment, a vision. It is surely no coincidence that the Hebrew word for the prophetic vision has the same meaning as the original root of the [Greek] "idea."[21] However, the deficiency in prophecy is just this: a vision cannot become a foundation. And this shortcoming persists in religion: it does not, as a matter of principle, submit itself to scientific methodology. To be sure, it recognizes the human spirit as the "holy spirit" implanted by God but refrains from equating science with divine knowledge of the ethical. Unless it acknowledges, without reservation, the scientific, philosophical knowledge of the ethical, there will be no potential for truth in the domain of religion as a whole. Here is Plato, the divine Plato who, for all time, will exhort us to preserve truth. He will remain the guardian of scientific knowledge as the sole infallible sanctuary of truth.

However, from the perspective of the brighter side of Platonism, we can also recognize its shadows. The well-known saying, that human suffering will not cease until "the kings philosophize and the philosophers become kings,"[22] exposes the shadow. We take no offense at kings but construe them simply as the ones who govern: but should difference among human beings be as stark as the division between the ruler and the ruled? Should not all human beings one day gain a share in ruling, so that all will be just as much rulers as ruled? Is it possible that Plato would fail to draw this conclusion, which the principle of knowledge must demand for all men, insofar as they have reason?

And if the simply inconceivable were nevertheless the case, one could explain this anomaly only by supposing that the principle of knowledge were at fault for its own limitation, as if it would be crippled if it were required to be applied to all human beings. For do not all human beings possess spirit and reason?

Here one can see the shortcoming in the principles of spirit and of reason, as principles of knowing, which is linked with science. One might, as a consequence, want to take refuge in the fragile principle of compassion. Expressed in scientific terms, here one can see the ambiguity in Plato's concept of reason, insofar as it is ethical reason, identified with and based on scientific reason. But since not all human beings are thought to be capable of science—why not?—

21. [The Hebrew חזון (chazon, meaning vision) is from the root חזה (meaning to see and referring to prophets or seers). Similarly, the Greek idea derives from a root meaning to see.]

22. [A loose quotation of the passage in Plato's Republic 473c–d, where Socrates opines on the advantage of philosopher-kings.]

they are likewise not all capable of philosophy.[23] And since all ethics is based on philosophical knowledge, they cannot all, in practice, acquire the capacity for ethics. For this reason, they must be ruled by the rulers, the philosophers. This conclusion is identical to the principle of the doctrine of Ideas, at least insofar as Plato himself was able to bring the Idea of the good into harmony with the general doctrine of Ideas. But all the advantages of theoretical culture can offer no consolation for the harm that has befallen the world as a result of the overextension of this guiding methodological principle. To this very day, skepticism regarding the social ideal is nourished by the prejudice that human beings are simply not all capable of science and therefore also not all capable of knowledge of the ethical by means of scientific method. Thus, it is clear that, for Plato, the Idea of the human being did not work; for without the fundamental principle of the homogeneity of reason across all human minds, there can be no unitary concept of the human being, and similarly, without this unitary concept, no faith in the realization of ethics in humankind will arise. And yet, without this conclusion, that is, the knowledge of the unity of humankind, what is all scientific idealism? Without the knowledge of the unity of all classes in every body politic, of the unity of all human beings, in that all are called to the good and therefore capable of the good—what is the meaning of idealism altogether, without the Idea of the Good in each and every human spirit?

Here, despite its one-sidedness and despite its lack of scientific grounding, the practical advantage of prophecy is still apparent. It cannot abide any such restriction or selectivity among human beings. Even the *king*, should he someday be desired, is bound by the simple commandment that he himself shall copy out the book of the divine teaching.[24] This act of copying, in his own hand, is the general commandment by which he is placed on the same level as every member of the people. With regard to God and the human being, there can be no distinction between ruler and ruled, nor between philosophers and nonphilosophers. Moses says, "would that all God's people were prophets."[25] A distinction is made here only because of the circumstances, but not with regard to the quality of the mind among human beings. Jeremiah likewise stipulates that, in the future, no

23. [In the *Republic* (474b–c) Plato writes, "to them by their very nature belong the study of philosophy and political leadership, while it befits the other sort to let philosophy alone and to follow their leader" (*The Collected Dialogues of Plato, Including the Letters*, ed. Edith Hamilton and Huntington Cairns [New York: Pantheon Books, 1961], 713).]
24. [Deut. 17:18.]
25. [Num. 11:29.]

one shall teach the other, for all of them, from the greatest to the least of them, will know God.[26] The fullness of ethical knowledge is promised to all humanity: fullness, because it arises from the principle of God, which, to be sure, is not—which most definitely is not—the principle of scientific knowledge. This principle of God is the unitary double principle of God and man.

However, we can discern the reason for the shortcoming in Plato's idealism not only in his principle of the Idea: here too his philosophical theory is linked to science and experience. Karl Friedrich Hermann already recognized the historical foundations underlying Plato's ideal state.[27] As a true idealist, Plato was, in all his speculation, bound up with his interest in nature and experience. In the entire domain of natural science, he was faithful to his role model, Pythagoras. And thus as an ethicist, too, he was equipped with the extensive and detailed knowledge of the politician. Moreover, in his travels through Egypt and southern Italy he not only learned mathematics; but, in Sicily, on the threshold of adulthood, he still harbored youthful dreams of bettering the world according to ideal models, which were by no means merely intuited visions. Rather, as a learned and experienced man of the world, he designed them on the basis of political realities.

The context of historical experience allows us to understand the literary fact that Plato discussed the social ideal not only as an element in the development of individual dialogues—as he did with all other philosophical problems—but that he devoted almost entire dialogues exclusively to it. It is his main subject in the *Republic*. Then the *Laws* offers a new account, and finally the latter are followed by the *Critias*, which is not simply a supplement but a successor, transforming the ethics of the state into a utopia. And in all this, we have not yet mentioned the *Gorgias* and the *Statesman*. It is the instability in the foundation of his political theory that helps account for this restlessness and the changes in its presentation. While his attempts to accommodate political realities gave rise to ever-new discrepancies, his own emendations drove him ever deeper into the materialization of his ideal foundations, until they ended in utopia.

Plato's aristocratic origins should not somehow be adduced as an explanation, since they did not prevent him from lodging a protest against the naval politics of his great-uncle Pericles, in remarks worthy of being recorded for eternity.[28]

26. [Jer. 31:33.]

27. [Karl Friedrich Hermann (1804–55), a German classicist, was the author of, inter alia, *Geschichte und System der Platonischen Philosophie* (reprint, New York: Arno Press, 1976).]

28. [Plato, *Gorgias* 515c–17c.]

On the other hand, the narrowness of the Greek point of view more generally accounted for an enduring bias. Jakob Burckhardt has now drawn our attention to the polis as the foundation of the Greek political system.[29] It constitutes the fundamental element of the particularism of its [the system's] tribes and its cities. However, the polis absorbs the individual no less than does the state. The people, now called the mass, is robbed of individuality. True individualization is replaced by a specious form, a partition into three classes: the guardians, the auxiliaries, and the tradesmen.

The issue of the hereditary nature of these castes is of less importance than the classification of human beings in the state generally into assigned professions, interaction among which would benefit the life of the state but is stifled by these fixed assignments.[30] However, being bound to a specific class is not the ultimate cause of evil. The latter lies in the facts that the class of the guardians is also that of the warriors, and that the warrior class constitutes the true foundation of the state as a whole.[31]

At this point we encounter the gulf that separates this social ideal from that of the prophets. According to Isaiah's distinctive saying, the nations should learn war no more. Moreover, linguistically, "learn" means habituation.[32] War should no longer be given a place among human mores. The suggestion that the warrior class could be the ideal and therefore permanent bedrock and wellspring of political existence for the future without end—such an idea is inconceivable and alien to prophetic thought.

29. [Jakob Burckhardt (1818–97), a Swiss historian, known especially for his history of Renaissance culture in Italy. Cohen is referring to Burckhardt's *Griechische Kulturgeschichte* (Berlin: Spemann, 1898–1902), selections from which have been translated under the title *The Greeks and Greek Civilization* (trans. Sheila Stern, ed. Oswyn Murray [New York: St. Martin's, 1998]). On the polis, see ibid., 37–62. For example, Burckhardt writes: "The polis was the definitive Greek form of the state; it was a small independent state controlling a certain area of land in which scarcely another fortified position and certainly no secondary independent citizenship were tolerated. This state was never thought of as having come into being gradually, but always suddenly, as the result of a momentary and deliberate decision. The Greek imagination was full of such instantaneous foundings of cities, and as from the beginning nothing happened of itself, the whole life of the *polis* was governed by necessity" (ibid., 43).]

30. [Plato, *Republic* 415a–c.]

31. [Ibid., 373d.]

32. [Isa. 2:4: ולא ילמדו עוד מלחמה. The root *l-m-d* (למד) means to become accustomed or familiar.]

Let us recall that, for Plato, knowledge is the root of everything human. Accordingly, the foundation of the warrior class must be complemented by the class of philosophers.[33] If it is already an evil beyond remedy that science and knowledge are handed over to a single specific class—the philosophers—and are not bestowed upon all men, then it is worse still that the class of philosophers is recruited from the warrior class and is united with the latter under the name of watchmen and guardians. This combination is the natural consequence of the division of the people into rulers and the ruled. These are the basic classes. Both the separation and the combination of the rulers into the warrior class and the philosopher class result from this division. Sovereignty within the state is the duty of these two classes alone. To unify them is necessary intellectually, but to separate them is a methodological contradiction. For the Idea requires only the class of those who possess knowledge [the philosophers]. The warrior class hails not from the territory of the Idea but from political reality, which still holds Plato's ideal vision captive.

However, if we now must ask why Plato was spellbound regarding this particular aspect of empirical political reality, while his idealism otherwise so often soars above the limitations of experience, we must see the solution to this puzzle in the absence of a unitary concept, of the idea of man. Just as the notion of the unity of humankind is completely absent from Plato's thought, so too is the notion of a human political community, based on the [concept of] the autonomous individual. For Plato, the concept of the human being does not represent the problem of a unity. The human being is "a toy for God, and truly this is best for him" (*Laws* 803c). This artificial toy stands in starkest contrast to the task [of the human being] and to the hypothesis of the human being within the problem of human culture.

And because the human being is not an idea, not an intellectual unity, he also has no need, in empirical reality, of being produced and protected by means of unity and uniformity. He can thus be segregated and divided into professions. Moreover, it does not contradict this concept of the human being if knowledge is actually assigned only to *one* class. It is likewise no contradiction that the duty of knowledge is also delegated ultimately to the warriors' domain. For the latter, along with the philosophers, share responsibility for the affairs of sovereignty and the administration of the state.

33. [On the notion that guardians also have need of philosophy, see Plato, *Republic* 375e–76c.]

One might still ask what the ultimate reason is for this division of the guardians and watchmen into the knowledgeable[34] and the warriors, and why sovereignty in the state is not placed exclusively in the hands of the philosophers. One could easily imagine a special class for the warriors that would be necessary only for the purposes of national defense—for Plato's vision never reaches beyond the borders of his ideal state, which is in fact merely a parochial state, established and determined by its 4,500 landholders;[35] in Plato the long view, toward humankind, is utterly lacking. Meanwhile, his idealism suffers from even more obvious lacunae and defects. The warriors are organized into a permanent class not merely for the purpose of national defense, for they are also deployed to counter disobedience among the third class within their own state.

Thus, not only is the essence of the warrior class exposed; more significantly, the veil is lifted from the essence of the third class. The character of the third class does not consist of the fact that it is given over to the lowliest occupations of acquisition and trade and thus always exposed to the risks of property ownership, while the upper classes participate in communism; it is not enough that this deepest wound of social existence remains an open wound in the social life of the third class: it also serves as the precondition for the enduring, structural disobedience of the third class toward the laws of the state. Therefore, the rulers must be warriors, who keep the third class in check and mete out punishment to it.

There is a further conspicuous contrast to prophecy: that the sovereignty of the prosperous over the poor is also the sovereignty of the nobler over the baser desires. Plato not only says, and correctly, that the acquisition of goods constitutes a general ethical danger; he also establishes a third class for this profession, isolates it, and identifies in it psychological characteristics based on the manner in which it is constituted.

We thus arrive at a crucial methodological foundation point in Plato's doctrine of the state. It is, in a word, his doctrine of the soul. It is a basic feature of his ethical thought, which we are now better able to understand: the human soul— as much as he defends its immortality—can be recognized not so much in the

34. [Cohen speaks here of "*die Wissenden*" (meaning those who know or the knowing ones). In the context of Plato's vision of the ideal state in the *Republic*, Cohen is referring to the philosophers who are drawn from the warrior class and highlighting their qualification for that class: the pursuit and possession of knowledge.]

35. [Plato assumes, taking "a convenient number," that the ideal state would be somewhat larger, consisting of 5,040 landholders (*geomori*) (*Laws* 737e).]

individual as in the state. The state has no individuality either; its individuality is objectivized only in the three classes. Then, on the model of the specious individuality of the state, he constructs the concept of the human soul, for which, to be sure, he postulates an idea and therefore unity as well, but it is still the analogy of the three classes that is reflected in the three specific characteristics of the soul. This holds, even if Plato's expression "the parts of the soul"[36] is not to be taken literally but simply signifies the soul's specific characteristics.

It is logic that, in a fortuitous intellectual discovery, is making sport here. Perhaps Plato would not have arrived at the discovery of the third mode of the soul had the third class not guided him to it. It does not detract from this claim if the tripartite division of the soul had not happened to correspond exactly to the division [of society] into three classes. Psychology had, after all, already provided for the third class: the acquisition of goods corresponds to the appetitive soul.[37] However, the bifurcation of the ruling class into warriors and knowledgeable ones created a new problem. Knowledge had been provided for ever since Anaxagoras. It was not even necessary any longer that reason be the divine universal reason; rather, its trademark was needed for the class of the knowledgeable, for the ideal human type. Now, however, reason also has, in the warrior class, a practical psychological domain. The latter must be distinguished from general reason just as it must be united with it; both of these follow the model of the warriors and the knowledgeable men, under the unity of the watchmen.

Thus, the archetype of the will came into the world. However, it bears its birthmark in its very name. Plato knows of the will (der Willen) only in willing (die Wollung): the Greek term that represents the will is the word for passion, translated incorrectly. However, there is no better translation than "affect" for this word, which Plato draws from his own language, to use for his new concept. In Homer the word still means "wrath," and it is also connected linguistically to the fire and smoke soul, a primitive form of the soul. Still, affect was henceforth differentiated from both desire and the faculty of thought. Neither the pale cast of thought[38] nor unbridled drive is its essence: the warrior class of the state soul has now given birth to a new basic power of the soul. Mere wild impulse and desire

36. [As Hartwig Wiedebach points out in his annotation on this passage in the critical edition of Cohen's works (Werke 17:323n1), the formulation "parts of the soul" does not occur in Plato, but the discussion of the aspects of the soul in the Republic, book 4, is suggestive (see 436a–b, 439b, and 441e).]

37. [See Plato, Republic 580e.]

38. [The phrase is from Hamlet. See selection 1, note 17.]

and passion no longer rule over man; still less do they constitute his soul. Rather, a mediating power of consciousness has come to light; this power is not simply medial[39] in the sense that it lacks the inherent powers of the other modes of the soul, but it mediates between them. Desire is not extinguished, but it can now be tamed. Moreover, reason is no longer reserved only for knowledge; it is now harnessed together with the steed of spiritedness, and in this pair of horses the soul, through its own preexistence, can espy the eternal Ideas.[40] This new power of the soul unites its two predecessors. And indeed, Plato's ethics demands such a unity of the soul.

The pure ethics of Plato, based on the Idea of the good, demands unconditionally this unity of the human soul. It is otherwise, however, with his applied moral philosophy, with his doctrine of the state, and through the state he aims to render the soul of the microcosm more accessible to knowledge than it is through the human organism. Subsequently, however, Plato's thought is vexed anew by the contradiction that both the warriors and the knowledgeable men serve as the basic elements of the state, and thus of the soul. Thus, the dualism between knowing reason and the practical will comes into clear view. We can thus also understand the fact that the will was discovered only as affect and that, moreover, the unity was not yet achieved that must exist between reason and will. Finally, then, we can also understand why limits were set for reason itself, and that affect was not yet contained within the infinite boundaries of the will. The will, still conceived of only as affect, also imposed restraints on reason and narrowed the horizon of idealism.

The concept of the human being was derived from the concept of the state, and specifically, from the concept of the empirical Greek states. The perspective of the idealist operates within the limits set by reality, the present, and at most the past as well. But is the image of time satisfied by past and present? Is it just some trifling matter if the future is missing?

Once again, a tremendous disparity is exposed here, when we turn to the prophets' consciousness of time. Like Plato, they are hardly unworldly—yet their foreign policy alone is enough to set them apart from the politics of Plato, to whom only Greece is really present, and who, in Sicily, wants to establish his

---

39. [Cohen is using "medial" in a—somewhat obscure—metaphorical sense, as a term from Greek grammar that denotes the middle voice between active and passive.]

40. [Plato, *Phaedrus* 245c–47e.]

ideal state exclusively on Greek models. Likewise, in all his political writings he designs his ideal state on these models alone. The prophets, on the other hand, are also practical politicians, active among their own people. But their state is not the polis, in which every Greek's civic spirit champions its particular character; rather, even the tribe extends beyond the polis, and the twin states of Judah and Israel extend beyond the state itself. And now the prophets come along and design an entirely different image of the ideal state; they crush the state of tribes and establish the ideal image of a state of many peoples, a state of human beings. The present is not adequate for this image, and it cannot be drawn from any past. An entirely new conception of time pervades their consciousness: the infinity of time originates in the future, but in Plato, the infinity of time is not even present, being inert to the continued development of humankind. His view extends beyond Greece only on a spatial level. "But the earth has many and wondrous regions, and, as I have been told by a certain person, it is neither in shape nor in size such as is believed by those who have spoken of the earth" (*Phaedo* 108c). But he has no inkling whatsoever that times might someday be better.

For the prophets, by contrast, the earth and the universe are centered almost entirely on time. For them, space stands for the opposition of two concepts: Jerusalem and the whole earth. They reconcile this antinomy by appealing to the "new heaven" and the "new earth"[41] that will come into being "at the end of days."[42] It is this "end," the infinity of time, that they use to overcome the oppositions in spaces, in the geographical diffusion of humanity.

Therefore, the prophets' [concept of] being knows no stasis; rather, everything is in the process of development, transformation, eternal regeneration. Thus, no power of reality can influence them; even the state, their own state, cannot exercise influence over them. It must be destroyed, and only "the remnant of Israel"[43] shall remain, so that, from it, all peoples may be revived. The transformation extends even to language, which God will one day transmute into "a pure language"[44] for all peoples. Thus, neither nature nor the human world has an absolute permanence; rather, the meaning of divine creation is eternal re-creation.

41. [Isa. 66:20–22.]

42. [A common phrase introducing an eschatological vision. See, for example, Isa. 2:2, Jer. 23:20, and Ezek. 38:16.]

43. [שארית ישראל. See, for example, Isa. 46:3.]

44. [שפה ברורה (Zeph. 3:9).]

Burckhardt reproached Plato for "the stagnation of Greek culture."[45] However, we can see that abstaining from the future results in stasis in *all* culture and history. Plato's greatest failing was not that he did not "evince any grasp of the future or influence it in the slightest,"[46] but rather that he had no concept of the historical future and therefore no concept of historical development at all. Even his utopia in Atlantis lacks this long view. For this reason, preparation for war continues to be an obligation, even in a utopia.

The entire question of education rests upon the principle of development. In a practical sense, the doctrine of ideas does indeed aspire to be a system of education. And yet in this system, which is supposed to bring about a "conversion (περιαγωγή)"[47] of the soul, from reality to the kingdom of ideas, pedagogy in this ideal form still assumes the continued, perpetual existence of the warrior class. War, therefore, is integral to the ideal paradigm of humanity.

Contrast this view with that of the prophets! Not only do they preach the end of war, they even attribute peace to their God as his highest attribute. God is the creator of peace, just as he is the creator of light and of humankind. The priestly blessing culminates in the establishment of peace.[48] The Hebrew word for "peace" is derived from a root meaning "perfection."[49] It is, so to speak, an expression of the ideal.

The predominance asserted by the warrior class helps explain all the weaknesses and shortcomings, the lacunae and contradictions in Plato's doctrine of the state. As we have seen, property ownership is abolished, but only for the upper classes. The philosophers become the rulers, but the priesthood remains, and with it the institution of sacrifice remains unchallenged. By contrast, in the prophets' zeal against the sacrificial cult, they assail the priesthood as well. And although only the Levites are left without immovable property,[50] in no way are they alone assigned a share in intellectual life. Likewise, the contradictions in

45. [Burckhardt, *Griechische Kulturgeschichte*, 1:287 (this is not included in the abridged English version, *The Greeks and Greek Civilization*).]

46. [Ibid.]

47. [Plato, *Republic* 518d–e.]

48. [Num. 6:24–26, especially 26: "The Lord lift up his countenance upon you and grant you peace!"]

49. [Cohen is referring to the root שלם (*sh-l-m*, meaning completion or perfection). The form *shalom* (peace) is actually a verbal noun, indicating an ongoing process rather than a static condition.]

50. [Num. 20–24.]

the institutions of marriage and of the family may ultimately be accounted for by the fact that the warrior class constitutes an essential basis of the state. The rearing of children in common involves having wives in common.[51] Nevertheless, adultery persists, and not only is free love prohibited, but love in general, as the principle of marriage, is not recognized. In its place, a system of state assignments for the purpose of suitable procreation is established as state law.[52]

The militaristic principle governs the political system of education, as well as the legal process; ultimately, it is the legislation governing slavery that is especially offensive. It is in itself noteworthy that it is not asked where the slaves come from at the time of the founding of the state, let alone whether they may continue in that status in perpetuity. But the brutality with which they are punished is intolerable: for example, they receive an additional measure of corporal punishment for every berry that they have plucked while gathering grapes from another's domain. This sophistication in corporal punishment is almost more appalling than the brutality that pervades the laws on slavery as a whole.

The prophetic-Mosaic law on slavery, by contrast, conforms completely to its fundamental principle of the human being. The infamous "eye for an eye" is the most senseless and unproductive example in all of intellectual history.[53] The aphorism should rather be: a tooth for a tooth. For if a master only knocked out the tooth of his slave, he had to let him go free. And there is no ransom among Israel for the manslaughter of a slave.[54] Likewise, a runaway slave was not to be delivered up to his master.[55] Here too the notion of the uniformity of the human

51. [Plato, *Republic* 457d. Family life in the ideal state is to be arranged so that "these women shall all be common to all these men, and that none shall cohabit with any privately, and that the children shall be common, and that no parent shall know its own offspring nor any child its parent" (Plato, *The Collected Dialogues of Plato, Including the Letters,* ed. Edith Hamilton and Huntington Cairns [New York: Pantheon Books, 1961], 696).]

52. [On Plato's state-sponsored program of eugenics involving arranged marriages and the supervision of procreation, see *Republic* 458c–61e.]

53. [Cohen is referring to the so-called *lex talionis* in Exod. 21:24, which, in traditional Jewish interpretation, is construed not as prescribing corporal punishment, but as restricting its extreme forms and substituting monetary restitution, calibrated to the severity of the injury. See the commentary on Exod. 21:23–25 in the *Jewish Study Bible*, ed. Adele Berlin and Marc Zvi Brettler, 2nd ed. (Oxford: Oxford University Press, 2014), 146.]

54. [The general principle that a monetary fine, or ransom, may not be substituted for the death penalty for murder is set forth in Num. 35:31. On the case of the manslaughter of a slave, see Exod. 21:20.]

55. [Deut. 23:16.]

being is at work, conveyed through the concept of the stranger. Plato, on the other hand, remains on Greek soil, holding fast to his distinction between Hellenes and barbarians. The difference between Platonism and prophetism can be stated more precisely in sociological terms in the difference between the *ger*[56] and the barbarian. The Hellene is autochthonous. The Torah demands unity for the native-born and the foreigner.[57] This is the ethical regulation that, admittedly, requires modifications in law and in the state. However, the norm is consummated in messianism. When Meyer[58] seeks to demonstrate that the prophecies of the Egyptians served as the model for the prophets, he overlooks a difference: the prophets predict that the destruction of their own state will be followed by a glorious future. Only then, when ethics achieves unconditional dominion over their own state and their own people, will exclusion from humanity such as is represented by the barbarians be abolished. Only through messianic humanity will God become the father—and no longer only the creator—of humankind; only then will human beings, as children of God, become brothers.

The image of a unified humanity fully inhabiting the future involves yet another significant difference. In the prophets' picture of the moral life, there are only dim shadows and faint echoes of the myth of the *afterlife*; in Plato's moral worldview, however, the myth of the afterlife is its true horizon. In the prophets, the afterlife recedes in the face of the "day to come." Isaiah says of the afterlife, "No eye has seen it, except for you, God, alone."[59] All their concern, intellectual and ethical, is directed toward the "day to come" in the human world. For them, the kingdom of God is bound up with this world; no matter how often it is renewed, it continues to be inhabited by the same human species. Only development and only the future define and secure the existence of human beings.

Plato, on the other hand, sets limits to his idealism in this context as well, by accommodating the reformist endeavors of contemporaneous Orphic theology. Indeed, his ethical rigor proves itself in the fact that he does not depict the afterlife as some kind of paradise, nor as the isle of the blessed; rather, he describes Tartarus as the place of retribution, which also extends into rebirth, when human beings carry the consequences of their punishment with them as they return to the world.

56. [Hebrew for "foreigner." See RR, 125–28.]
57. [Num. 15:16.]
58. [Eduard Meyer (1855–1930), an ancient historian and Egyptologist.]
59. [Isa. 64:3. See also RR, 313.]

In this context it is also characteristic of Plato that punishment is the fundamental problem in his practical doctrine of immortality. These recurring descriptions represent the most important criticisms of his treatment of myths,
and on all sides his account of the doctrine of ideas must tolerate being blended
with myth. And it is obvious that when he makes use of myth his sense of
humor really takes wing. In this he is not unlike Dante: in spite of his patriotism
and medieval piety, Dante would not have been able to describe the punish-
ments in hell and purgatory so mercilessly, had his pen not been guided by a
sense of world-historical humor.[60] Similarly, all the paintings of the Last Judgment would not have been possible without such a sense of humor. Plato too
is an intellectual who, without conscious decision, is mocking the magical and
dogmatic chains of religious fantasy. But even if one acknowledges this, the fact
remains that these warrior myths find their place in Hades, thus confirming his
basic principle of the warrior. The question does not stop at the afterlife of existence, which, although only an offshoot, is nevertheless a likeness of the good.
For the good, it would be necessary that there be a future. For the wicked and
their punishment, however, it is necessary to imagine and accept the afterlife.
Without penalty, without pain and agony in the underworld, it is not possible,
according to the *Gorgias* (525), to be freed from injustice.[61] And although it is
primarily warriors and princes who are presented as examples of the most bale-
ful evildoers, the original notion of war still makes its effect felt in the necessity
of punishment.

In the prophets, conversely, retribution becomes forgiveness. The true task
and vocation of their God is to temper justice with mercy, to grant reconciliation and redemption to the evildoer. According to the text of the Hebrew, he
bears sins, takes them upon himself;[62] it is as if, as the creator of humankind, he
should hold himself accountable for the frailties of human nature. This notion
has direct sociological import, not only for the administration of justice and for
reform of the penal system, but also for our knowledge of the deeper roots of
immorality. If Tartarus and punishment are removed as conditions for rebirth
and resurrection, then the most formidable impediment to the social idealism
of the future of humanity is removed as well.

In retrospect, we find that narrow intellectualism had a crippling effect on

60. [On humor, see *RR*, 297–98.]
61. [See Plato, Gorgias 524b–25d.]
62. [Exod. 34:7. See also *RR*, 222.]

the notion of totality. Philosophy is said to be impossible for the masses. By this principle, Platonic light becomes Aristotelian shadow, and idealism is transformed into empirical realism. The prophets are not philosophers. For them it is enough that human beings know God, and through God, know the human being. The prophets are confident that all human beings are capable of such knowledge of God, and they would despair of God if their confidence were to waver. This is the strength of their idealism, if we may draw on common usage to give a name to their optimism. To be sure, their knowledge of God is limited to their ethical teaching, and since their ethical teaching is not based on the idea of scientific knowledge, one may not, if using terminology with precision, call it ethics.

In its most general outlines, world history is the history of the struggle and interplay between these two fundamental spiritual forces. Social progress must set itself the goal of establishing "general schools" and "unified schools"[63] even if such progress begins with economic reform. In our day, it is essential to achieve the dual understanding that pessimism about the so-called masses' incapacity for science and academic study is the basic evil that stifles all true progress and renders it illusory. The entire people a kingdom of priests—this basic prophetic principle must become the rallying cry of the new world.[64]

Equally, however, one must reject the prejudice that religion alone can establish and ground true ethics. Plato is wrong only in denying the masses the capacity for philosophy; but he is correct when he says that, without philosophical ethics, he can envision no peace on earth. It should be a uniform demand in social science that, for the sake of the schools and the state, academic instruction

63. [Cohen was an advocate of universal compulsory state education, in which the established religious denominations would have no role—a position apparently influenced by the disadvantages to Jewish pupils in the prevailing denominational organization of public education in Germany (ErW, 515–17). He supported the educational reforms proposed by liberal parties at the beginning of the twentieth century. The "general school" (allgemeine Schule) was a proposal for having common, ecumenical elementary schools open to pupils of all economic classes. The "unified school" (Einheitsschule) was a proposal by the reformist pedagogue Johannes Tews to integrate elementary and secondary education and thus likewise counteract the segregation of pupils by class. See Tews's Die deutsche Einheitsschule. Freie Bahn jedem Tüchtigen (Leipzig, Germany: J. Klinkhardt, 1916). On these proposals and their political context, see Marjorie Lamberti, The Politics of Education: Teachers and School Reform in Weimar Germany (New York: Berghahn, 2002), 16–17.]

64. ["But you shall be to Me a kingdom of priests and a holy nation" (Exod. 19:6).]

be made available to the entire people. The objective, but no less the pedagogical basis of all higher academic education, was, is, and will be philosophy, which alone, by combining logic and ethics, can lay the ground for idealism. Thus, the prophets and Plato remain the spiritual leaders of humankind, and only when joined together do they bring the goal of the social ideal within our grasp.

4 | Internal Connections of Kantian Philosophy to Judaism (1910)

The internal connections of Kantian philosophy to Judaism involve the objective relationship that can be identified and documented between the ethics of Kant's system and the fundamental concepts of Judaism, even if this correspondence was neither intentional nor conscious on the part of Kant himself. What concerns us here is an internal logical connection of fundamental ideas, not a question of historical influence. To be sure, to consider how Kant's thinking reflects the Old Testament would be a very interesting question in itself. But that task properly belongs to the field of intellectual history; for the objective philosophical appraisal of his ethics, it could serve only as an ancillary topic, not as a source.

Intellectual history differs, as history, from both the history of philosophy and the history of the sciences in that it accords significance to all content, from any participant in the broad realm of the spirit, and certainly from any creative figure. The history of particular scholarly disciplines, by contrast, has to consider only scholarly production as such. Thus, *Newton's* work on the book of Revelation can hardly be classified as New Testament scholarship, for Newton was no authority on the subject.[1] Similarly, Kant was no expert on the Jewish religion and the scholarly study of Judaism. He does, admittedly, have some familiarity with the Old Testament, in *Luther's* translation, but otherwise he knows nothing of Judaism besides what he learned, partly from Spinoza's *Tractatus Theologico-Politicus* and partly from Mendelssohn's *Jerusalem*. And his judgment, based as it is on these sources, is instructive, but not as the judgment of an expert.

As for Spinoza, first of all, in his biblical criticism he was guided by his fundamental political idea of making *philosophy* independent from the state. For him, however, religion was only philosophy; and philosophy was just religion. He therefore saw in the theocracy of the Jewish state the root of all evil, which consists of the dependence of religion and philosophy on the state, and which

---

1. [Isaac Newton (1642–1727) wrote a work titled *Observations upon the Prophecies of Daniel and the Apocalypse of John* (London: Darby, 1733). "Apocalypse of John" is an alternative title for the New Testament book of Revelation.]

he wanted to abolish completely. Thus, he developed the theory that the Jewish religion was intended merely to establish a people and a state.

Mendelssohn, by contrast, advocated the view that Judaism, in its theological content, was nothing other than "natural religion." This sounded very nice; and this judgment seemed to flow simply from the rationalism of the eighteenth century. The extent to which this view was accurate, especially with regard to Judaism's system of beliefs, could have been understood only by those Jews who were familiar with the philosophical interpretation of their religion. In general, one could consider Mendelssohn's account to be a historical idealization, akin to the many other such attempts in [eighteenth-century] rationalism. It was for this reason that Kant politely expressed his astonishment, when he wrote to Mendelssohn, "You have known how to reconcile your religion with such a degree of freedom of conscience as one would not have imagined it to be capable of, and as no other religion can boast of."[2] This latter clause indicates bitingly enough the skepticism with which Kant actually regarded Mendelssohn's construction.

In light of his own plans for public advocacy, however, Kant himself was hardly a disinterested party on this issue. He wanted to convert the Prussian Church, and with it the censorship authorities, to his philosophy of religion. For this purpose, Spinoza's characterization of Judaism suited him better, in order that he might contrast it to his idealization of Christianity. In his own remarks, therefore, he never gives any indication that Mendelssohn's account persuaded him; rather, in this case, he uncharacteristically followed Spinoza, whom he otherwise found unappealing, summing up his own opinion with the monstrous proposition that Judaism is "actually no religion at all"; since: "[The] Jewish faith was, in its original form, a collection of mere statutory laws upon which was established a political organization."[3] Here then, at the same time, "statutory laws" become intertwined with the concept of a political constitution.

Now in general, it might be no disadvantage at all for a religion to serve as the foundation of a political constitution. However, in this Jewish religion that has been dissolved into a state church, what becomes of the prophets? After all, it is the prophets who, with their political religion, shake up this state and, in so

2. *Briefe*, Ausgabe der Akademie, 1: 325. [The translation of Kant's letter is drawn from Alexander Altmann, *Moses Mendelssohn: A Biographical Study* (London: Routledge and Kegan Paul, 1973), 517.]

3. Immanuel Kant, *Religion within the Limits of Reason Alone*[, trans. and ed. Theodore M. Greene and Hoyt H. Hudson (Chicago: Open Court Publishing, 1934), 116].

doing, reestablish their religion as a new religion. Kant, however, in his under-standing of Judaism, knows nothing of the prophets; for him, the prophets are merely "priests and diviners," who could foretell the downfall of the state easily enough, since they, as priests, brought it about.[4] He therefore saw in Judaism, likewise from this political perspective, nothing but "statutory laws," which, to him, represented the absolute antithesis of purely moral precepts.

It was not only Spinoza and the apostle Paul who led him to this mistaken view; the *second* part of Mendelssohn's thesis supported him in this stance. Mendelssohn maintained that the *ritual laws* constitute the special obligation of the Jews, while, according to Judaism, blessedness and moral equality for all other human beings depend solely on adherence to ethical precepts. To support this notion, Mendelssohn appealed—without thinking of Paul, whose criticism really should have made him more cautious—to the principle that the Torah is "the heritage of the community of Jacob,"[5] as if this Torah were not also, and in fact preeminently, ethical teaching, which Paul subsumes under the "curse of the law."[6]

One can thus discern that Kant's peculiar judgments have a literary and historical connection not only to Spinoza, as Julius Guttmann has pointed out,[7] but no less to Mendelssohn's erroneous philosophy of religion. This theme and the impression that it made on Kant have had their aftereffects everywhere in Kant. To be sure, the thought also occurs to him that religious dogmas are just as statutorily encumbering as external observances, and in his *Religion within the Limits of Reason Alone*, he interprets the purpose of Mendelssohn's *Jerusalem*: "he means to say: first rid your own religion of Judaism."[8] However, Kant regards

4. ["Priests and diviners" seems to be a paraphrase, not a direct quotation from a section of *The Conflict of the Faculties*, which continues: "It was all very well for the Jewish prophets to prophesy that sooner or later not simply decadence but complete dissolution awaited their state, for they themselves were the authors of this fate. As national leaders they had loaded their constitution with so much ecclesiastical freight, and civil freight tied to it, that their state became utterly unfit to subsist of itself" (Immanuel Kant, *The Conflict of the Faculties*, trans. Mary J. Gregor [New York: Abaris Books, 1979], 143).]

5. [Deut. 33:4.]

6. [Gal. 3:13.]

7. Julius Guttmann, "Kant und das Judentum," *Schriften der Gesellschaft zur Förderung der Wissenschaft des Judentums* (Leipzig[, Germany]: Gustav Fock, 1908), 50.

8. ["First wholly remove Judaism itself out of your *religion* (it can always remain, as an antiquity, in the historical account of the faith); we can then take your proposal under advisement" (Kant, *Religion within the Limits of Reason Alone*, 154n).]

Christian doctrine only as the "ordinary conception of Christianity," with which he contrasts his own. But if it should now turn out that his understanding of religion is, in fact, in agreement with the one that can be more properly constructed from Judaism, then one could say, conversely: first rid your own religion of Christianity.

Let us, however, set aside the historical question of Kant's personal opinion and turn our attention to his purpose, which was not biblical scholarship, but philosophy.

One might have thought that the inner connections [between Kant and Judaism] could refer only to *ethics*, since Judaism has, after all, no science and thus cannot of course have logic, like the logic of a philosophical system. However, very early on, Judaism strove to establish a *philosophical justification* for itself. After all, this is the path by which the idea of the Logos entered the world. And because —ever since Saadia[9] in the tenth century, and probably even earlier—thinkers attempted to provide an ethical foundation for Judaism, they were unavoidably driven to provide this ethics with a type of *logical substructure* as well. In this, significantly, an inner correspondence is already unmistakable.

The most fundamental and most radical indication of Kant's character is to be found in a statement in the *Critique of Pure Reason*. Even today, there is controversy over the scope of this motto. But with regard to its immediate meaning there can be no controversy. Its significance is this: that all knowledge must be grounded in fundamental principles, which are to be regarded as fundamental truths. Its significance thus distinguishes the concept of *reason*, and of *pure* reason in particular, from sense perception and experience, insofar as the latter consists of the assemblage of perceptions. If one accepts perceptions as the ultimate ground of knowledge, one has forfeited an objective foundation, such as mathematics possesses in its axioms. At the same time one also loses the unassailable criterion for everything that knowledge wants to be and is permitted to be. Then the doors are flung open to unimpeded fanaticism, superstition, and literalism. The believer in miracles, like the spiritualist, will appeal to the authority of sense experience; the literalist will appeal to the authority of the sensuous fact of the written word. If, by contrast, reason is called upon to critique, then even the holy book must be called to account before it; and our pious philosophers of religion have, in fact, done nothing less.

Maimonides was by no means the first to adopt Aristotle's rational principle

---

9. [Saadia ben Joseph Al-Fayyumi (882–942), also called Saadia Gaon.]

as his guiding standard and to recognize and grant validity to the first principles of reason (מושכלות ראשונות) [*muskalot rishonot*]; rather, this formulation can already be found in clear and definitive form in Saadia.[10] Despite Aristotle's dualism—or indeed precisely because of it—he was better understood by the Middle Ages than was Kant by his immediate posterity. To be sure, the leading figures in all fields of Kant's *own* time understood him clearly, but he was not able to persuade the Romantic movement that was then about to burst forth, because, owing to its obscurantism, it had to evade him. By contrast, Aristotle, as is typical for him, simultaneously embraced the most abstract rational principle and, at the same time, sense experience as the foundations of knowledge. This dualism was well suited to our forebears [the medieval Jewish philosophers], but not on account of its theoretical ambiguity, for they always place the center of gravity solely in reason. What was important to them was not at all the contrast between rational principles and sense experience, but rather the *distinction between reason and revelation.*

The distinction between reason and revelation, however, should in no way be taken to indicate an opposition between two sources of religion that leads inexorably to a twofold consequence: first, the separation of morality from revelation and, second, the dissolution of revelation into ritual legislation, even if it still includes some form of political legal code. Such an arrangement would not do justice to the respect that revelation commands in religious consciousness. It would not even do justice to the respect in which the ritual laws are held, since these laws are construed not to be opposed to ethical teaching, but to serve as its vehicle. On this point, contemporary Paulinism, as it has in the past, takes a subjective stance, and is therefore unfair, however correct, in other respects, its judgment concerning the value of all particular forms of worship may be in principle.

In ancient Judaism, the distinction between moral and ritual law is conceived of, more or less, as *the distinction between pure and applied moral doctrine.* Revelation must therefore consist of both forms of doctrine, as well as that of moral reason, *although the latter remains, in principle, autonomous.* And Saadia expresses the lofty idea: if one were to say that ethical teaching is contained only in the Torah, but

10. [Saadia Gaon,] *Emunot we-Deot* [*oder Glaubenslehre und Philosophie*, ed. David Slutzki, trans. Yehudah Ibn Tibon] (Leipzig[, Germany: C. W. Vollrath], 1864), 7. For an English translation, see Saadia Gaon, *The Book of Beliefs and Opinions*, trans. Samuel Rosenblatt (New Haven, CT: Yale University Press, 1948.]

not in reason, "then any possibility of discussion with such a person comes to an end."[11] Such is the uncompromising commitment to reason in its authority over the Torah.

A similar statement is found in Bahya ibn Pakuda's book *The Duties of the Heart*[12] (eleventh century), which came to be perhaps the most popular philosophical book in all of world literature: "the evil inclination seduces a person by encouraging the skeptical belief that it is enough to concern oneself strictly with revelation, and that the cultivation of reason is unnecessary."[13] To Bahya, being on guard against such insinuation of the "evil spirit" is part of introspection (חשבון הנפש) [*ḥeshbon hanefesh*].

Thus, reason, as the inexhaustible and indispensable source of morality, is acknowledged as the inviolable foundation of religion. This stance even comes close to acknowledging the sovereignty of reason, although, to be sure, the sovereignty of revelation must also remain intact and not be explicitly reduced somehow to a secondary position.

Ultimately, however, the *sovereignty of reason* always depends on its *relation to the senses*. And at this point, a correspondence arises between the philosophy of Judaism and Kant that is all the more surprising, because Judaism deviates from Aristotle here on a fundamental point.

It is particularly characteristic of Kant's ethics that it rejects eudaimonism in

11. [Although the idea certainly resembles Saadia's position, the particular passage could not be located.]

12. [Bahya ben Joseph ibn Pakuda lived in Muslim Spain in the eleventh century. His main work, *The Duties of the Heart*, was written in Arabic around 1080 and translated into Hebrew by Judah ibn Tibbon in 1161. For an English translation, see *The Book of Direction to the Duties of the Heart*, trans. Menaham Mansoor (Portland, OR: Littman Library of Jewish Civilization, 2004).]

13. ואל תשיאך הגאוה שתחשוב שהכרתך לא הוסיפה על מה שהיתה עליו מנעוריך . . . כי זה מפתוי היצר
לך שירשל אותך מעיין ומחקור על אמתת העניינים וידמה בעיניך שאתה חכם גמור . . . והכסיל מתעלם מכל זה.
"Do not allow yourself to be misled into thinking your present knowledge has added nothing to the knowledge you acquired in your youth, for it is one of the methods of seduction used by the evil inclination that it weakens your resolve to ponder and inquire into the truth of things, so that you seem in your own eyes to be a complete wise man; however, only a fool closes himself off to all this (and wanders in the darkness)." Bahya 8:3, Stern edition [*Bachjae Filii Josephi Librum de Officiis Cordium*, ed. Solomon G. Stern, trans. Em. Baumgarten into German (Vienna: A. Schmid, 1869)], 389f.; cf. Introduction, 12 and 1:3, 37ff. [Cohen's version in the text is a paraphrase, not identical to the translation he presents in this footnote.]

all its forms. Kant argues, therefore, that all eudaimonistic moral systems are antagonistic to ethics.[14] *Happiness*, no matter what its nuanced form, cannot be the goal of pure will. There is certainly an inherent harmony in the fact that, from Saadia to Maimonides and beyond, along the entire arc of Jewish philosophy, happiness is repudiated.

Such opposition to the pleasure principle is, first of all, a manifestation of the independence and systematic capacity of the Jewish spirit, but then also an indication of the consistency of the biblical frame of mind that is manifest here and that is more than merely interesting. For it is always the Bible by which all these thinkers test the validity of their opinions. With regard to reason, too, they appeal to the Torah itself, which repeatedly establishes knowledge as the foundation of the heart and of the will. "You shall know and make it fast in your heart" (וידעת היום והשבת אל לבבך, Deuteronomy 4:39). Thus, they also elevate systematic knowledge to a requirement, deriving it from the spirit of the Torah. Mathematics and astronomy have, in reason, a common foundation with ethics. But on the issue of eudaimonism the biblical sources are more abundant. And the fundamental principle of faith itself speaks better than proof texts: the *unity of God* has as its consequences the *"unity of the heart"* (יחוד הלב) and the "unity of action" (יחוד המעשה).[15]

Probably in no other language is there a term for *conscience* more profound than *unity of the heart*. Unity of the heart corresponds to the unity of God. The unity of the human being corresponds to the unity of God. This clearest and most profound leitmotif, drawn from the verse of the Psalms,[16] is also expressed prominently in *prayer*, endowing prayer with a harmonic quality, and it inspires the spirit of atonement during the Days of Awe. Love and reverence for God are made possible by the unity of the heart. "Make our hearts unified, to love and to revere your name" (יחד לבבנו לאהבה וליראה את שמך).[17] If Bahya's *Duties of the Heart* had discovered no other concept aside from that expressed in *the unity of the heart*, in the *unity of action*, and in the *unity of worship* (יחוד העבודה), that alone would

14. *Kritik der praktischen Vernunft.* (S.W. [that is, Immanuel Kant, *Kant's gesammelte Schriften*, ed. Königlich Preussische Akademie der Wissenschaften (Berlin: G. Riemer, 1900–)], 5:21–22). [For an English translation, see Immanuel Kant, *Critique of Practical Reason*, trans. Mary Gregor (Cambridge: Cambridge University Press, 2015), 19–20.]

15. Bahya, chapter 5.

16. Psalm 86:11: "Unify my heart, to revere Your Name."

17. [From the daily morning liturgy. See *The Daily Prayer Book: Ha-Siddur Ha-Shalem*, ed. Philip Birnbaum (New York: Hebrew Publishing Co., 1949), 16.]

account for its very substantial value; the fact that Jewish *learning* revered this book as a treasury of devotion throughout the centuries is quite a remarkable indication of its power and clarity, its inwardness and sincerity.

Pleasure and happiness are confronted by reason, the reason of the will, which wards off disunion and establishes the unity of the will. For Kant, to be sure, this unity, insofar as it relates to the soul and mind, would always have remained suspect, as a psychological disposition. Kant seeks, through *objective conceptual principles*, to establish the *moral will*. Because he rejects happiness as the motive of the will, he introduces a concept, derived by means of logic, as the ground of the determination of the will. This principle of the will is *universal law*. Morality should be conceived of as a *law* that is binding *on* every person and *with regard to* every person, without exception. This law should, to be sure, be based on the self-legislation (autonomy) of reason; however, reason can have no connection to the will other than its imposition, on the will, of universal law. It is not permitted for us to be "volunteers of morality."[18] It is as if Kant learned this expression from a Jewish philosopher and in the Talmud itself. "Greater is he who acts under commandment than he [who acts] without commandment" (גדול מצווה ועושה ממי שאינו מצווה ועושה).[19]

To be sure, there is a difference that must not be overlooked. For Kant, it is ultimately reason itself that must always generate the universal law anew, whereas in Judaism, the unique God would become a useless machine if the moral law did not always retain its eternal origin in God himself. It is argued that there can be no contradiction between God and moral reason. The moral law must and can be the law of God, without ceasing, on that account, to be the law of reason.

God and his law define and establish what is opposite to egoism, to selfishness, and in general to the sphere of the individual. The significance of the law as defining this opposition is in turn common to both Judaism and to Kant. In the

---

18. *Kant's gesammelte Schriften*[, ed. Königlich Preussische Akademie der Wissenschaften (Berlin: G. Riemer, 1900–], 5:87. [The reference is to Kant, *Critique of Practical Reason*, 68: "It is very beautiful to do good to human beings from love for them and from sympathetic benevolence, or to be just from love of order, but this is not yet the genuine moral maxim of our conduct, the maxim befitting our position among rational beings as *human beings*, when we presume with proud conceit, like volunteers, not to trouble ourselves about the thought of duty and, independent of command, to want to do of our pleasure what we think we need no command to do." Cohen discusses this passage in *Kants Begründung der Ethik*, *Werke*, 2:332–33.]

19. *Babylonian Talmud*, Kiddushin 31a.

end, the concept of *universal* law gives methodological expression to the age-old idea of the equality of all human beings before God. The same fundamental concept also constitutes the root of the fundamental commandment of the love of neighbor. Perhaps the correct translation of this commandment is: "Love him, *he is like you*" (ואהבת לו כמוך).[20] And how stirring is the ancient verse: "this is the book of the history of man" (זה ספר תולדות אדם).[21] It is human history that is written with the law of human equality and of love of neighbor: this law is prescribed for all history, or inscribed as its epilogue.

Despite the deep correspondence between Kant's philosophy and Judaism with regard to *autonomy*, we nevertheless were compelled to recognize a distinction in the concept of the law, of law that is both self-given and must also be self-generating. This distinction, however, leads us in turn to a new harmony. *God is and remains the author and the guarantor of the moral law.* But for Kant has God, as such, somehow disappeared? Is Kant somehow saying what the faithful poet says in his outpouring of enthusiasm for the fundamental idea of freedom: "When we God receive into our will, He descendeth from his lordly throne"?[22] This is by no means the case. God is for Kant "the sovereign in the kingdom of morals."[23] And the self-legislation of human reason has neither the intent nor the authority to depose this sovereign. For Kant, there is no kingdom of morals without God's sovereignty. Which function, however, now falls to God in the administration of morality?

It is well known that this question touches upon one of the very weakest points in Kant. It is here that Fichte breached the critical system; at this point,

20. [Lev. 19:34.]

21. [Gen. 5:1. The allusion is to a midrashic source in *Sifra*, Kedoshim 12, interpreted in more explicit depth in RR 119. It concerns a dispute between Akiba and ben Azai on the question of which is the greatest principle in the Torah—the commandment of love of neighbor (Akiba) or the principle of equality (ben Azai)—that makes a universal commandment possible. "Evidently," Cohen writes, "Ben Azai is right" (ibid.).]

22. [Quoted from Friedrich Schiller (1759–1805), "The Ideal and Life," trans. Paul Carus, *Monist* 21, no. 2 (April 1911): 281.]

23. [This exact phrase seems to be found not in Kant but in Cohen's *Kants Begründung der Ethik*: "We are indeed lawgiving members of a kingdom of morals possible through freedom and represented to us by practical reason for our respect, but we are at the same time subjects in it, not its sovereign, and to fail to recognize our inferior position as creatures and to deny from self-conceit the authority of the holy law is already to defect from it in spirit, even though the letter of the law is fulfilled" (*Werke*, 2:270). This is an apparent reference to a related statement in Kant (*Critique of Practical Reason*, 68).]

he felt confident that he could prevail against the very system from which he had drawn his greatest strength. Here, however, we can disregard the fact that Kant, contradicting himself, makes God once again into the "dispenser of happiness," to reconcile the incongruities of existence in the afterlife. This argument is a medieval phrase, not Kant's own. He was able to extirpate it, however, only in principle, not from his own personal thinking. In this, Kant remained beholden to his generation.

By contrast, what is characteristic of Kant's theology is that it is *impersonal* in the usual sense; it is *genuinely spiritual, elevating God to an idea. Nothing less than this is the deepest basis of the Jewish idea of God.*

This thesis is very difficult to formulate as a compelling, persuasive argument, for the reason that it concerns the most profound and the truest claims about God, the most truthful object in the pursuit of knowledge of God. Some would rather resign themselves to materialism regarding God, which, to be sure, merely sets the stage for the final victory of atheism. By contrast, every stage in our intellectual history likewise teaches what is demanded by the concept of the unity of God: that *monotheism can only be monotheism of the idea.*

The struggle against the *anthropomorphisms* contained in the Bible ushers in the campaign that our commentators and philosophers wage against the corporeal, sensual, and mythological conception of God. Even for Maimonides it is not at all a novelty. It is just expressed with such pithy audacity that he even calls into question whether *life* can be attributed to God. Scripture does not set "life" in a *status constructus* in relation to God.[24] Even Saadia had objected to life.[25] The being of God is by principle distinct from all other forms of existence, and thus also from life.

24. [Cohen uses the Latin term for the Hebrew construct state (the equivalent of a genitive construction, in which the first noun in a phrase such as "the life of God" is in the "construct state"). Maimonides cites this Hebrew usage when asserting the absolute unity of God: "I mean to say that there is no eternal thing other than He. For this reason it is said, *by the Lord the living,* and not, *by the life of the Lord"*—that is, using the construct state (*Guide of the Perplexed,* trans. Shlomo Pines [Chicago: University of Chicago Press, 1963], part 1, chapter 68, 163).]

25. [Cohen's language here is elliptic: Saadia objected to *the attribution of life* to God.] ואלו היינו באים לספר עליו בלשון האמתי היינו חייבים לעזוב ולהניח שומע ורואה רחום חפץ עד אשר לא יעלה לנו כי אם הישות בלבד. Saadia, *Emunot,* 59, see also 58, 44. ["Were we, in our effort to give an account of God, to make use only of expressions that are literally true, it would be necessary for us to desist from speaking of Him as one that hears and sees and pities and wills to the point where there would be nothing left for us to affirm except the fact of His existence" (Saadia, *The Book of Beliefs and Opinions,* 118).]

The *doctrine of attributes*, the doctrine of *predicates of God*, presents very important and instructive evidence for this fundamental tendency in Jewish thought. We find uniform direction all down the line. In this, *Maimonides* has become the "guide of the perplexed," even for those who do not recognize that they are perplexed. *Nicholas of Cusa* never tired of citing Maimonides in this connection, and Maimonides was also Leibniz's primary influence on this matter. Thus, *Spinoza* was able to borrow, from as early a source as *Saadia*, the fundamental idea on which he bases his definition of substance. And yet what a deep ethical distinction sets Spinoza apart: here, *only moral attributes* may be predicated of God; accordingly, only such attributes as bear upon *human actions*, for which God and God alone, no man or God-man, should be the archetype for human beings.

God's essence is morality and only morality. Morality is the nature of God. There is no other nature of God. *Nature* is God's *creation*. God is not nature. *His essence constitutes not contradiction, but difference in relation to nature, and nature stands beneath good and evil. The uniqueness of God signifies this difference between God and nature.*

In Kant the intimate affinity between religious thought and Judaism appears above all in his treatment of the *Trinity*, a discussion of which, for political reasons, he must include in his monograph on religion, but of which he accepts only the Son of God, equating the latter with *the idea of humanity*.[26] The *Scholastics* had already reinterpreted the *Trinity* from the moral and psychological perspective, evidence of the urge for freedom in medieval reason. Romanticism, on the other hand, used the dogma of *God's becoming human* to lay the foundation for their *pantheism*. *God is human, since God is nature in general.* Here, the dogma [of the incarnation] becomes the central theme of their entire metaphysics and is in no way used solely for ethics. In the process, however, ethics is destroyed; it is absorbed in the general, natural process of becoming and in the movement of the concept, which, in this case, amount to the same thing.

This is the hidden poison that the educated, cultured public unconsciously imbibes, because it does not know how to examine the fundamental methodological defects that undergird pantheism. God is not human and is not nature. *Creation itself has meaning only for ethics*; it must not, however, be in conflict with *mathematics*. Even God's omnipotence is circumscribed by mathematical and logical reason. This too was a fundamental idea for our forebears, and it also

26. [Kant's "monograph on religion" refers to his *Religion within the Limits*. Kant interprets Christ as the "personified idea of the good principle" and "ideal," or the "archetype of humanity" (ibid., 54–55).]

governed their doctrine of *miracles*. Pantheism, by contrast, reduces nature and morality to a single standard. It therefore leaves theoretical reason in the twilight of symbolism and deprives ethical reason of its distinctive quality and autonomy. The pantheist cannot concede that there might be something that "sets him apart from all other beings we know." In this way, *Goethe*, in this poem[27] liberated himself from that bewitching ambiguity.

It is nothing less than astonishing that an even more intimate affinity between Kant and Judaism comes to light here. In his system, Kant *differentiates ethics from logic*. Both fall within the province of reason, but he distinguishes *practical*, ethical reason from *theoretical* reason. The maturity and originality that set Maimonides apart from his predecessors is nowhere more apparent than in this point. According to Maimonides, ethics belongs to the "first principles of reason"; however, "exact demonstration" (מופת מוחלט) distinguishes it from logical and mathematical principles.[28]

In both spheres our great Moses displays radiant clarity: in the logical and scientific sphere as well as in the ethical sphere. In its principles, morality is not equivalent or equal to science and logic. There is a methodological distinction between ethics and mathematics. Such truthfulness constitutes the first principle of ethics. However, ethics and mathematics still have reason in common: Maimonides associates "service of the heart" (עבודת הלב) with the principles of reason, among which he draws the distinction indicated above.[29]

The *God* of Judaism is the transcendent God. Pantheism faults the God of

27. [The quote is from the poem "Das Göttliche (The divine)" by Johann Wolfgang von Goethe (1749–1832): "Edel sei der Mensch, hilfreich und gut; / denn das allein unterscheidet ihn / von allen Wesen, die wir kennen! (Let man be noble, helpful and good; for that alone sets him apart from all other beings we know!)" ("Das Göttliche," in Johann Wolfgang von Goethe, *Goethe's sämmtliche Werke* [Stuttgart, Germany: Cotta, 1840], 2:67–69).]

28. [In *Guide of the Perplexed* (part 1, chapter 31, 65–67), Maimonides distinguishes between the certainty of mathematics and logic, which is confirmed by exact demonstration, and metaphysics, which is not and is therefore open to difference of opinion. This chapter is probably Cohen's source for his thesis that Maimonides separated ethics from logic.]

29. Maimonides writes: שישים האדם מחשבתו בשם לבדו אחר שהגיע אל ידיעתו. וזאת היא העבודה המיוחדת במשיגי האמתות וכל אשר יוסיפו לחשוב בו ולעמוד אצלו תוסיף עבודתם. (Let us now return to the subject of this chapter, which is to confirm men in the intention to set their thought to work on God alone after they have achieved knowledge of Him, as we have explained. This is the worship peculiar to those who have apprehended the true realities; the more they think of Him and of being with Him, the more their worship increases) (*Guide of the Perplexed*, part 3, chapter 51, 620).

Judaism for its transcendence. The better God would be one that lives in my heart—as if he did not live in my heart already, in the purity of my heart, precisely because he lives enthroned far above all my powers.[30] God's transcendence, above the senses, is the true precondition of ethical efficaciousness, that is, *to serve as the foundation for the moral relationships of humankind and of world history.* Where God and the human being or God and nature are equated with one another, *mysticism* inescapably steps in, making morality transcend the senses and making the transcendent sensible. It leads morality into fanatical confusion and casts a dark pall of superstition over the natural senses of the human world.

Immortality, therefore, is connected with the idea of God; the two of them constitute the limiting problem of the sensible world.

It is well known that Kant excluded both immortality and the idea of God from the sphere of knowledge proper, while nevertheless retaining them as ideas of moral knowledge. Judaism breathes confidence in immortality in all its descriptions of the dignity of man, of the value of human life. "I know that my redeemer liveth!"[31] This hope is alive in Jewish scriptures long before *Job;* it is therefore not dependent on the strict sense of the verse in Job. And as for Kant, so too for the Jew immortality is necessary primarily for ethical recompense.

However, what comes naturally to the philosopher who has come of age in the Enlightenment of the eighteenth century is a mark of honor for the medieval Jewish philosophy of religion and for the rabbinic literature with which it is linked. A subtle and restrained sense of discretion prevails in the Jewish psyche on all of these questions of the afterlife. The eternal torments of hell do not haunt the Jewish psyche; repentance always redeems the sinner. Likewise, reward is described only spiritually; the border of mysticism is only lightly grazed.

For the psychology of the Jewish spirit and disposition it is very significant that we do not take our feelings about *death* lightly, neither in our concern for life, yearning and longing for our kin, nor in our sorrow over their loss.

It is both moving and uplifting when as devout a poet as *Judah Halevi* (eleventh to twelfth century),[32] the author of the *Kuzari,* now somewhat better known, expresses this view: what more could one desire from immortality and resurrection that is not already promised and guaranteed by the psalmist: "the nearness

30. [Cohen is alluding to *Faust:* "And though a god lives in my heart, / Though all my powers waken at his word, / Though he can move my every inmost part— / Yet nothing in the outer world is stirred" (*Faust,* Luke trans., 48, lines 1566–69).]

31. [Job 19:25.]

32. [Judah Halevi (ca. 1075–1141).]

of God is my good" (קרבת אלהים לי טוב, Ps. 73:28).[33] Thus, even in the Beyond, God is not beyond the Jew; *the good One is his good.* No other good interests him, even in the afterlife; and the terrors of hell wield no power over his devout imagination. Immortality is and remains what it should be for someone with sound moral common sense, a discrete act of moral hope.

The third of the ideas proposed by Kant is *freedom.*[34] Freedom, as *autonomy* (of which we have already spoken), is the foundation of his ethics. The problem of freedom dominates the entire Middle Ages, and consequently our philosophy of religion as well. Very noteworthy analogies can be found even in purely theoretical discussion. However, if we confine ourselves just to general issues, we observe, first, that it is characteristic that Hasdai Crescas (fourteenth century), who denies freedom and to whom Spinoza refers explicitly, nevertheless retains freedom *as the positive condition of morality.*[35] For him, as for Spinoza, the "*Love of God*" is human freedom. "Choose life."[36] This sentence from Deuteronomy is for him the commandment of freedom.[37] One should not be disturbed by this apparent contradiction, for God is the lawgiver of morality; he is the one who commands us to choose. To choose the good is the moral power and freedom of the human being.

It is significant that no reference is made to any passage where the sinner is defined by his having chosen evil. To be sure, one cannot deny the negative meaning of freedom, the freedom to choose evil. However, the negative meaning recedes, yielding to the positive meaning of freedom, as if only the latter were important. Indeed, freedom signifies, at bottom, nothing other than the *purity of the soul.* And here, again, the analogy with Kant is unmistakable.

Kant's philosophy of religion suffers from a prejudice that seems to militate against the view that he assumed that the human being is pure. After all,

33. *Kuzari* bk. 1, sect. 113 [The English translation is from Judah ha-Levi, *The Kuzari: An Argument for the Faith of Israel*, trans. Hartwig Hirschfeld (New York: Schocken, 1964), 78.]

34. [Cohen is referring to Kant's three "postulates of pure practical reason": the existence of God, the immortality of the soul, and freedom of the will. See Kant, *Critique of Practical Reason*, 97–114.]

35. [Hasdai Crescas (c. 1340–1410 or 1411), author of the 1410 *Or Adonai* (Light of the Lord), an anti-Aristotelian and anti-Maimonidean work. Spinoza cites Crescas in epistle 12, the so-called "Letter on the Infinite" (*Complete Works*, trans. Samuel Shirley, ed. Michael L. Morgan [Indianapolis, IN: Hackett, 2002], 791).]

36. [Deut. 30:19.]

37. See especially [*Or Adonai*] II: 6, 1, also my article "Autonomie und Freiheit," in *Gedenkbuch zur Erinnerung an David Kaufmann*, 678 [selection 6 in this volume].

although he did not embrace the notion of redemption through Christ unqualifiedly, nor without reinterpretation, he nevertheless retained its dogmatic basis in the idea of *radical evil*. A truer understanding of that chapter, on the other hand, places Kant's view and his intention in an entirely different light: he understands radical evil as the propensity of human nature toward the inversion of moral motivations.[38]

[According to this view,] neither freedom, nor the striving for and ascent to pure morality, nor faith in the will's purity is the motive force of the human being and his actions, but selfishness, the drive for power, for gratification, and for pleasure, even if such pleasure consisted only of the dissimulated ascetic pleasure one might derive from compassion and self-denial. Human beings thus philosophize as sophists that never die out. Radical evil in the human being consists of his unwillingness to believe in the good as the sufficient motive of his will, as the most powerful motive of his will.

In our day, does not all the literature and art in which the world delights—painfully delights—offer convincing evidence of this poisonous outlook? And yet it originates only in a human aberration; in no way does it represent the heart of our essence and will. Therefore, Kant himself says that his doctrine belongs not to "moral dogmatics" but rather to "moral ascetics."[39] Thus, it is proposed not as some kind of fundamental doctrine of the ethical character of the human being, but rather with an eye toward healing his "waywardness." And indeed, we are in need of the preacher in the wilderness[40] who would inveigh unflinchingly against the literary and artistic condition of our time, unperturbed by the reaction of the present age, which has much to learn before it can pass judgment. We are in need of the teacher of the ideal, who can make it clear to this entire cultural world that it should not be surprised at the violation of the idea of *humanity* in our times, if it celebrates the idols that are themselves preachers calling out in this battle.

And above all one must not be surprised if the hatred on the part of the misanthropes and self-idolizers strikes at the Jews in particular: at us Jews who have never acknowledged *original sin*; but who, in our daily morning prayers, thank God for the purity of the soul. "My God, the soul which thou hast placed within

---

38. *Religion innerhalb der Grenzen der bloßen Vernunft*, 124; cf. [Cohen's] *Kants Begründung der Ethik*, 2nd ed. [(Berlin: Bruno Cassirer, 1910)], 338 ff.

39. *Religion innerhalb der Grenzen*, 145.

40. [Isa. 40:3. See also Matt. 3:1–3.]

me is pure."[41] Purity is the most fundamental term for the religious expression of freedom. Purity of the soul is what makes the human being the image of God. The human being is not holy. For us, to predicate holiness of a human being is regarded as blasphemy. The human being is, however, pure; his soul is pure. In its purity it possesses the truest mark of immortality, yet also the paradigm of its freedom.

In Kant, freedom also merges into another concept, through which alone the theoretical question is properly resolved: it passes over into the concept of the *"end-in-itself"* and of the *"telos"*[42] that the human being represents. Is pantheism able, even in its more rational form, to say more than what is contained in this idea: that the human being is the purpose of the world? The human being, as the bearer of morality, gives nature its meaning and inherent unity.

The powers of nature, even in the profound regularity of their mathematical laws, satisfy our intellect only when the human being does not remain their instrument and their plaything. *Morality must be the ultimate object of the world.* That is: the human being is the purpose of the world. Saadia expresses this notion with complete clarity.[43] Maimonides thus substitutes self-perfection [השתלמות] for happiness.[44] Self-perfection is the principle of man. A more profound meaning is not to be found even in the concept of the end-in-itself.

For the practical significance that is inherent in the end-in-itself—that *every* human being represents this end-in-itself, that therefore no human being may be used "simply as a means" but "always at the same time as an end"[45]—this

41. [From the daily morning liturgy. See *The Daily Prayer Book: Ha-Siddur Ha-Shalem*, ed. Philip Birnbaum (New York: Hebrew Publishing Co., 1949), 16.]

42. [Immanuel Kant,] *Grundlegung zur Metaphysik der Sitten*[, in Immanuel Kant, *Kant's gesammelte Schriften*, ed. Königlich Preussische Akademie der Wissenschaften (Berlin: G. Riemer, 1900–)], 4:271.

43. [Saadia Gaon,] *Emunot we Deot* (Leipzig[, Germany: C. W. Vollrath], 1864, 161 [*sic*; the correct page number is 91]. [For an English translation, see Saadia, *The Book of Beliefs and Opinions*), 180–81.]

44. [Maimonides], *Guide of the Perplexed*, part 3, chapter 53, 630–32. See [Hermann Cohen,] "Charakteristik," 59f. [Cohen is referring to the essay he wrote originally for a volume honoring the seven hundredth anniversary of Maimonides's death. It was reprinted in *JS* 221–89 and *Werke* 15:161–269. For an English translation, see Cohen's *The Ethics of Maimonides*, trans. Almut Sh. Bruckstein (Madison: University of Wisconsin Press, 2003).]

45. [From one of Kant's classical formulations of the categorical imperative. See Immanuel Kant, *Groundwork of the Metaphysic of Morals*, trans. Herbert James Paton, (New York: Harper and Row, 1964), 96.]

most profound and crystal-clear significance of the *categorical imperative* could well be said to course through the very veins of the Jew. As everyone knows, the most cursory knowledge of Judaism suffices to indict it as the ancient source of a fanatic advocacy for freedom and equality.

In truth, the prophets would not have been the architects of genuine *political morality* if they had not been aggressive teachers of the idea of the human being as an end-in-itself, prepared to suffer for this idea. The *social legislation* of the Pentateuch is their achievement, the greatest creation of *social and ethical idealism*, and it did not remain merely a utopia. The *Sabbath* has conquered the world: it is the symbol of the idea that the human being, even as a laborer, should remain an end-in-himself; that his purpose is not merely to be a cog in the machine of civilization, if this culture does not benefit him in the same measure and to the same extent as it does every other human creature. One cannot say that the symbol of the Sabbath, with its motto, "so that your servant and your maidservant may rest, as you yourself do" (Deuteronomy 5:14), is any less clear than a philosophical concept. It was certainly no less effective. Moreover, the word used here for *equality* is the same word as for the *love of one's neighbor.*[46]

Judaism's social idealism is connected to its messianism. Here it is obvious that Judaism and Kant are of one mind. Kant wrote his *Treatise on Perpetual Peace.* A *"cosmopolitan"* disposition was the fundamental idea not only of his ethics but also of his view of history. He could not have conceived of a *concept of history* if he had not assumed an aim of history. He calls this *aim of history* perpetual peace. Even *wars* must bring about this peace. The great commanders, who then had to lead our war of liberation against the Corsican titan, did not, for this reason, waver in their love for Kant.[47] Only if one makes a virtue out of necessity itself can one evade the simple consistency of the moral law, denounce those who profess it, and fail to recognize its blessing for every people and every state, no less than for all humanity, for which it is also indispensable.

It was the *prophets* who conceived of this kind of confidence in *world peace* as the purpose and meaning of world history, and by this idea they proved themselves to be the *true teachers of love of one's neighbor.* For war is the Satan of world history.

46. [Cohen is referring to the word כָּמוֹךָ (*kamokha*), which can mean either "like you" or "as yourself." The famous commandment in Leviticus 19:18 can therefore be understood, with equal philological justification, to mean either "love your fellow as yourself" or "love your fellow, who is like you." Cohen's preferred reading is the latter.]

47. [Cohen is referring to the war of liberation against Napoleon, 1813–15.]

To think, as did the ancient Greeks, that war is the father of all,[48] or to think that the true meaning of the life of nations and human destiny plays out in war—this mocks the idea of God as the father of all human beings and contradicts the concept of the human being as an end-in-himself and as telos. Whoever believes in perpetual peace believes in the *messiah*, not in the messiah who purportedly came, but rather in the one who ought to come, and who will come.

The messiah is the "servant of the Eternal" עבד יהוה (Isaiah 42:1, *et passim*). The messiah is the most vivid witness for the God of the prophets, for the God of Israel. He has made clear that the purpose of the human being is the peace of humanity. "Peace," the prophets proclaim; they call their God the "creator of peace."[49]

I did not intend my task here to lead to an inquiry in intellectual history. Intellectual history all too easily runs the risk of assuming that the matter itself, the ideas, are already known and then merely illuminating the reflection of these ideas in the minds of particular individuals. However, I cannot refrain from briefly pointing out—although it may sound like parochial boastfulness—that it is easy to understand that, at the time, some of the best minds among the Jews were immediately drawn to Kant. And although Kant exposed himself to severe criticism on this delicate matter, he still seems to have felt quite at ease with his Jewish students.

His letters to *Marcus Herz*[50] evince a cheerful amiability, such that he could have written to no one else. This Berlin doctor, to whom he also turned for private consultation, was well-versed in general and natural sciences; his lectures on experimental physics were published, and he even had the energy and leisure to compose a treatise in philosophy.

Salomon Maimon's[51] profound and perspicacious works, based on a deep knowledge of mathematics, are the best known. *Fichte*, who was a good judge of

48. [The aphorism is from one of the fragments of Heraclitus. See Hermann Diels, *Die Fragmente der Vorsokratiker*, 4th ed., vol. 1 (Berlin: Weidmannsche Buchhandlung, 1922), 88, fragment 53.]

49. [Isa. 45:7.]

50. [After four years at Kant's University of Königsberg, in 1770 Herz (1747–1803) moved to Berlin, where he joined the circle around Moses Mendelssohn.]

51. [Maimon (1753–1800) was an itinerant scholar. In a letter to Marcus Herz on May 26, 1789, Kant wrote that Maimon was without peer in the depth of his understanding of Kant's philosophy (cited in David Baumgardt, "The Ethics of Salomon Maimon," *Journal of the History of Philosophy* 1, no. 2 [December 1963]: 199).]

philosophical talent, recognized it clearly in Maimon. Research in this domain will have to take on an entirely different character from that which dominates the market today before Maimon's merits, which run somewhat deeper, will gain recognition.

From the very start, the achievement of the honorable *Lazarus Bendavid*[52] was crystal clear. He also philosophized on the basis of mathematical and scientific studies and insights. His lectures extended to all domains of Kantian philosophy, even to aesthetics. It need hardly be mentioned that these men did not resign from Jewish scholarship. Maimon composed a commentary, in Hebrew, on Maimonides's *Moreh*, and Lazarus Bendavid wrote for Zunz's *Zeitschrift*, on the Jewish calendar and also on the messiah.[53]

The philosophizing Jew feels as if at home on the soil of Kant; for in this system, based on the logic of science, ethics has *primacy*. Now ethics is also the vital principle of Judaism. The religion of Judaism aspires to be ethical teaching and it is ethical teaching. To love God is to seek knowledge of God. And to seek knowledge of God is to seek knowledge of the moral telos of humankind.

There is, therefore, an internal correspondence between Kant's systematic structures and the fundamental direction of Judaism set by the prophets. Judaism has always rejuvenated itself by drawing from its prophetic sources. Moreover, its philosophy of religion would suffer from an inner conflict with rabbinic ritualism, which its philosophy of religion does retain, if its prophetic essence did not everywhere struggle to assert itself, and if it were not able to secure its spiritual predominance and prerogative.

There lies the distinction between philosophy of religion and history of religion: the former is able to construct the essence of a religion by means of a conceptual idealization of its fundamental ideas, whereas the history of religion brings the verdict down on its own head by claiming to offer an account of the essence of religion. It is neither the historian's task nor does he have the authority to define the essence. Of course, for the historian there can phenomena he

52. [Lazarus (Eleazar) Bendavid (1762–1832) was an important interpreter of Kant and, in the latter part of his life, an advocate for the reform of Judaism in the post-Mendelssohnian age.]

53. [Starting in 1823, Leopold Zunz (1794–1886), founder of the Wissenschaft des Judentums, edited the *Zeitschrift für die Wissenschaft des Judentums*. Bendavid's article on belief in the messiah appeared in the first volume ("Über den Glauben der Juden an einen künftigen Messias," vol. 1, no. 2 (1822): 197–230). For a biography of Zunz, see Ismar Schorsch, *Leopold Zunz: Creativity in Adversity* (Philadelphia: University of Pennsylvania Press, 2016).]

considers secondary; but actually, for his research there are no phenomena that are inessential. Only philosophy of religion can assume responsibility for distinguishing, in a religion, what is of the essence and what is not.

Moreover, historical developments are confirming the idealization produced by philosophy of religion, in an increasingly clear and distinct way. We now recognize, in the most general sense, the value of Judaism—*its value for the further development of Protestantism*—in its *prophetism*, and thus in its *ethical teaching*, in its *universalism*, in its *humanism*. And for our frame of mind, all of its ritualism is a part of historical development, serving as protection and self-defense; it belongs to the imponderables of religious piety, upon which all poetry rests along with all of the power of human history. We differentiate ritual clearly and vigorously, even if still timidly, from the eternal essence of our religion itself. The contrary position seems to us today to be a partisan evasion and a slogan representing some facile impersonal judgment.

Our just claim and our cultural strength rest on the truth of our ethical ideas. In light of the nexus and harmony that connect our ethical ideas with the paradigmatic ethics of the new era that began with the French Revolution, we may derive consolation and hope for both.[54] The mystics, the obscurantists who pass off the semblance of poetry as philosophy, will gradually be banished, along with the misguided minds of this unfortunate, confused age. The classical spirit will reawaken in philosophy and art. Out of that spirit, and with that spirit, a new orientation in politics will clear a secure path ahead. It is inevitable that this new political orientation will sense that it is related to the ethical purity of prophetic monotheism and that it will learn to acknowledge and honor Judaism as its most natural ally.

Only let us not lose our inherited, our *messianic optimism*. The evil spirits that stir up pessimism for sport will vanish, and ethical well-being, human clarity and sincerity—and thus the creative cultural power of our eternally youthful religion—will surely come to be universally known and acknowledged, as surely as *progress toward the good* is and remains the aim of world history.

In this closing thought from the *philosophy of history*, Kant and Judaism again converge, in agreement: the philosophy that is true by virtue of its method, and the religion that is true by virtue of its God.

---

54. [That is, for both the ethical ideas of Judaism and the paradigmatic ethics of the new age.]

5 | The Significance of Judaism for the Progress of Religion (1910)

The World Congress for Religious Progress[1] has for its mainspring the important fundamental thought that religious progress can in no way be confined to any single religion but must devote itself to the furtherance of religion in general.

This fundamental idea immediately involves a tactical postulate, namely, the demand of a mental readiness for sympathy with foreign religions.

Beginning with this second demand, we may say that without sympathy, without the silent understanding that is in all mature religions, genuine humanity, which is identical with genuine divinity, is continually struggling for expression, [and] it is impossible to comprehend and pass judgment upon any positive religion. With respect to the work of art that we term religion, idealization is as necessarily as elsewhere the primary condition for each of its adherents, but no less so for one passing judgment from without.

Without idealization even the historical ascertainment of facts would be impossible, at least insofar as such an attempt aimed at presenting one collective spiritual view of its matter. To be sure, the countercondition of an exact study of the available sources should never be lost from sight. For without this latter it would not be possible for the process of idealization itself to come into operation: a mere subjective phantom would ensue, distorting our view of general culture.

Genuine idealization represents in each religion the sum of the general religious progress in it. But wherein [and] by means of what criterion is this progress in religion to be discerned and determined? Obviously our means of ascertaining such progress must be an element that all higher religions (*Kulturreligionen*) have in common. Now it would perhaps be natural to suppose that this common element was monotheism. But this concept is avowedly so complicated that it can hardly be made to serve as an unequivocal criterion.

If we merely regard the simple literal meaning of the term progress (*Fortschritt*), we are referred to a goal. Now does this goal lie within the domain of religious

---

1. [Cohen has abridged the full name of the congress, which was the World Congress for Free Christianity and Religious Progress.]

progress, or does it lie beyond it, and thus beyond all religion whatsoever? This is the great difficulty involved in the question of a criterion for religious progress.

It would perhaps be possible, for the sake of preventing purely philosophical differences to come up for discussion on this occasion, to avoid putting this question in its whole severity, that is, with respect to the relation of religion to philosophical ethics. It may perhaps suffice merely to point to the relation already existing between religion and morality to attain to a certain degree of clarity with regard to the nature of religious progress. Religion and morality are not regarded as identical. Morality may then consequently be designated as the goal toward which religion is advancing; and the various degrees of such progress will constitute the criterion of this progress.

Unquestionably, all monotheistic religions, insofar as they have undergone development, have had a part in this moral progress. It is my task to bring the proof of this in the case of Judaism. My thesis as such is bound to encounter many prejudices, many difficulties. But I shall rely on your general religious sympathy and leave them all unconsidered. I am likewise not afraid of being charged with overcoloring my subject, for I am addressing a congress that recognizes in idealization the only means of comprehending and interpreting any religion.

I must, however, at the outset draw attention to a particular circumstance. General Christian culture knows Judaism through the Old Testament. To be able, however, to appreciate the religious progress to which Judaism may justly lay claim involves a knowledge of the postbiblical period, of its literature and of its actual religious usage, as well as a knowledge of living Judaism in its religious present. For with all its development and differentiation, with all its struggles from within and influences from without, Judaism has preserved itself as a living historical unity.

In spite of all ill will, it has always been conceded, whether willingly or unwillingly, that Judaism has maintained in its believers the capacity for culture; and that consequently spiritual and moral forces must lie at its base. But the significance and the value of this insight, with which modern humanity arrays itself, becomes confused and unreliable as soon as this capacity for moral culture (*kulturelle Sittlichkeit*) is not discerned and acknowledged to be inherent in the religion itself.

It is therefore of importance at the very outset to grasp Jewish monotheism in its peculiarity. God's oneness is here meant to signify absolute uniqueness. And this denotes absolute difference from all manner of Being, not merely from all material Being, but likewise and no less from all other mental and spiritual

Being. Only through this means is the unique Being of the one God capable of being raised to genuine spirituality. This may perhaps appear as one-sided from the point of view of universal culture. But this one-sidedness appertains to the very essence of the Jewish conception of God. And since God partakes of Being that is different from all other manner of Being, he represents the most real and genuine Being, in comparison with which all other Being as that of nature and of the world of man is mere semblance and shadow, at any rate until creation and the image of God undertake to transfigure and confirm it.

There is thus contained in the absolute spirituality of Jewish monotheism a general element of culture tending and leading toward moral idealism. All the powers of nature and all the forces of culture lose their puissance in the face of the idea of this single and spiritual God. And all mundane existence becomes incommensurate with this spiritual God. There thus arises of necessity the conclusion that the significance of this single God can in no way consist of a relation to nature, involving thereby a basis of comparison between the two, nor likewise in a relation to nature in man. And there thus ensues the further positive inference that the significance of this spiritual God can lie only in that spiritual force, which, in contradistinction to all nature, constitutes the concept of morality and the problem of the moral world.

Here the objection may arise that if God is to mean merely the law and the prototype of morality, then religion will thereby be straightaway reduced to morality, whereas it should be understood that the two are not one and the same thing. But what can religion presume to vouchsafe over and above morality? It would not only be curtailing the right of morality but also obscuring the light of religion to regard God as having any significance beyond and above the domain of morality. In the nature of God Judaism regards only that part as religion that this nature contributes to morality. His essence consists of his attributes. And the so-called thirteen attributes have reference solely and purely to the love and the righteousness of God, in which he serves as emblem and pattern for human morality. All mysticism with regard to his other qualities is warded off because of the dangers it is fraught with for the fundamental idea of oneness and uniqueness.

The enthusiasm of Jewish religiosity is founded on the consciousness of the decisive importance of this fundamental idea. And this consciousness, in all the varying stages and grades of human insight, is alive in every Jew, as in truth it constituted at all times the center of gravity of the Jewish consciousness. One needs but to have experienced and have witnessed the fervor with which the Jew prays his "Hear O Israel" at the conclusion of his Day of Atonement, or the fervor of these words as he breathes out his soul, to feel the truth of this.[2] It is the same excess of enthusiasm that finds such wonderful expression in the words of the Psalmist. "Whom have I in heaven but thee? And there is none upon earth that I desire beside thee. But it is good for me to draw near unto God" (Ps. 73:25 and 28). Those who would confound the peculiar quality of this Jewish enthusiasm with the mysticism of pantheism, or with the love of Christ, misapprehend its character. For in both of the latter man partakes of the very quality of God, whereas the uniqueness of the Jewish God wards off all comparison with heaven and earth, all connection with man.

Pantheism has not been exclusively a detriment to religion. And far be it from us to deny that the love of Christ, as of the ideal of mankind, has had its manifold share in the progress of religion. But the dangers that pantheism bears in its train for the moral potency of the idea of God are too well known to be overlooked; no less, however, likewise those with which Christianity itself has at various times been threatened through an exaggerated and one-sided love of Christ.

The unique God of Judaism preserves his spirituality in his incomparability with everything of heaven and earth that may likewise be contained in man. Therefore all manner of intercession, which a superior human being might undertake as between God and man, is altogether incompatible with his essence. This leads us to a second factor in the religious progress of Judaism.

The aim of religion as such is atonement.[3] To be sure, atonement with God is for the moral conception of religion only a means; the latter must in reality consist of the atonement of man with himself. But religion would neutralize its own virtue if it were ever to surrender the atonement with God as the indispensable means for this latter end.

It is well known that ancient biblical Judaism still had the institution of sacrifice, to be sure only that of animal sacrifice. The zeal of the prophets against it lends color to the historical surmise that perhaps even without the destruction

2. [The "Hear O Israel," (Deut. 6:4) the opening verse of the Shema prayer, is said at the conclusion of the Ne'ilah service at the conclusion of the Day of Atonement and, according to tradition, is also spoken before the moment of death.]

3. There is some difficulty in translating the German *Versöhnung* in this connection. We have decided to render it throughout with atonement rather than with reconciliation, for although now generally used in the sense of expiation, it had originally the quite literal meaning of *at-one-ment*, [which] is thus much more expressive. The Translator [Henry Slonimsky].

of the Temple the internal development of Judaism would have led to the abolition of sacrifice. Rabbi Yohanan ben Zakkai, as is well known, implored Vespasian not for the preservation of the Temple but for permission to erect a seat of learning in Jamnia. And among all the holy days of postbiblical Judaism, there is none so instructive and so full of significance for the principle of its internal religious development as the Day of Atonement, which came to be and has ever continued [to be] the distinctive mark and the sign of life of modern Judaism.

On this one day many Jews of the present day endeavor to manifest and maintain their connection with their religion. The chief feature of the services is a confession of sins, which, in Oriental fashion, are presented in rigorous and exact enumeration; but ritual commands are not even so much as mentioned. It is solely and exclusively moral transgressions that in solemn array are brought home in an overwhelming appeal to the soul.

There is no need of any divine intervention, trespassing in any way on the nature of God, to bring about the Jews' peace of soul by means of a peace with God. No priest, in the function of a vicar of God, and no God-man is permitted to say on such occasion: I am the way to God.[4] Without anyone to intercede, the soul fights its own battle, and in private penitence, in prayer, and in the resolve to moral action it attains its salvation.

Theoretical morality itself makes a great gain through the means of this independent, eminently human work of salvation, directed as it is toward the God of morality, namely, through the concept of innocent sin (shegagah). This Socratic insight is the crowning triumph of Jewish salvation. Frailty is in the very nature of all human action, frailty and imperfect knowledge; a doing as without consciousness. This insight finds expression in the words proclaimed as the very motto of the Day of Atonement: "And all the congregation of the children of Israel shall be forgiven, and the stranger that sojourneth among them; for the whole people shall have the benefit of shegagah" (Numbers 15:26).[5] Will there be anyone ready to doubt that the purified Jewish consciousness will likewise instinctively have extended this atonement to those nations in the midst of which the Jew now dwells, just as the Talmud had already done to the heathen stranger?

4. [An allusion to the words of Jesus according to John 14:6: "I am the way, and the truth, and the life; no one comes to the Father but by me."]

5. [Spoken at the beginning of the Kol Nidre service on the eve of the Day of Atonement. The Jewish Publication Society translation reads: "The whole Israelite community and the stranger residing among them shall be forgiven, for it happened to the entire people through error" (with shegagah translated as "error").]

Atonement is in his eyes something emanating from the one and only God, who is the "Lord of the whole earth," the father of all mankind; for whom alone it is fitting to say, "I forgive."[6]

Among the various prejudices that make a just appreciation of Judaism impossible, the false translation of Torah with law (*Gesetz*) instead of with doctrine (*Lehre*) is foremost. In the Pentateuch the love of God is by no means the only commandment. This love can at all events manifest itself in the fulfillment of the law. But it is the knowledge of God that is in no less a degree required. "And thou shalt learn it this day, and fasten it in thy heart."[7] The love of God is the love of morality. For God cannot be loved with the love we bear to a human being. Spiritual life consists singly and exclusively of the cultivation of morality. But morality presupposes knowledge (*Erkenntnis*), even if such knowledge is not amplified into a science of morality. And thus the Torah must likewise be the doctrine, the knowledge of morality.

Among all the symptoms afforded by Jewish history, perhaps the most remarkable is the fact that in the Jewish people, even in the days of greatest affliction and persecution, the distinction between poor and rich was never tantamount to a distinction between ignorance on the one hand and education, let alone scholarship on the other.

If it is true that a real proletariat never existed in Israel, the ultimate reason for this lay in the fact that its religion (*Torah*) was never merely law, but always a living body of doctrine. The poor who were compelled to engage in fatiguing labor were not thereby excluded from the scholar's life. Every hour of leisure and particularly the hours of the night were devoted to the study of the Talmud. This fact, little as it is known, and still less appreciated in its great cultural and historical significance for the comprehension of the riddle of the preservation of Judaism, also constitutes one of the most important factors in general religious progress.

For this reason the Reformation, and just as little, in view of our previous remarks, the concept of justification by faith, important as these two factors in their historical influence have been and are for the deepest progress of culture, can in no way be said to constitute an advance in matters of principle over Judaism. Not merely the knowledge of the Bible alone, but likewise the study of the so-called oral doctrine, of the Talmud and of its continuations, constituted the spiritual life content of rich and poor alike.

6. [See Num. 14:19–20. This is also spoken at the beginning of the Kol Nidre service.]
7. Deuteronomy 4:39.

The Talmudic precept that the study of the teaching outweighs all commandments has been included in our very prayers.[8] And thus it was impossible for ignorance ever to be suffered within the nation.

This is likewise the reason why, after the old priestly order had disappeared, it was impossible for a new clerical body to arise having a monopoly of learning. And for the same reason it was impossible for the thought ever to arise, particularly with any semblance of religious sanction, that religion contained as its most precious treasure truths that it was forbidden to endeavor to know, and that were to be taken only as matters of faith. This obnoxious distinction between faith and knowledge has no place in the Jewish consciousness. Faith (the word is built from a root denoting firmness, durability)[9] was always conceived of in consonance with knowledge, nay, more, this consonance is ordained and required. The nature of God is the sole exception to the claims of positive knowledge. But God's Being is a matter of fervent belief, because of clear knowledge, that is, of the knowledge of morality.

This mode of interpreting and of realizing the concept of doctrine has verified and substantiated the longing of Moses: "Ye shall be unto me a kingdom of priests and a holy nation" (Exod. 19:6). But it was not merely the suppression of every form of clergy that was achieved thereby; no, this fundamental thought extended its influence through the whole of the social fabric of this religious community and thus had an immediate and living influence on morality.

Among the Ten Commandments only that relating to the Sabbath underwent any considerable change in the repetition of the Decalogue. In Exodus, creation is the reason assigned for the institution of the Sabbath, which obtained therewith most assuredly no mere apparently religious motivation; for the Sabbath appears thereby in the light of the final goal of the whole of creation. In spite of this, the Deuteronomic version drops this reason altogether, and in its place the great sentence makes its appearance: "That thy manservant and thy maidservant may rest as well as thou; therefore the Lord thy God commanded thee to keep the Sabbath day" (Deuteronomy 5:14–15).[10] If the Jewish religion had no other merits at all, the ordainment of the Sabbath alone, its institution, and its preservation

8. [The morning prayers include a passage drawn from the *Babylonian Talmud*, Tractate Shabbat 127a, that lists a number of ethical commandments and closes with the statement, "the learning of Torah is equal to them all (ותלמוד תורה כנגד כולם)."]

9. [אמונה (*emunah*) derives from the root אמן (a-m-n), meaning firm.]

10. [By contrast, in the version of the Ten Commandments in Exod. 20:11, the observance of the sabbath is justified as an imitation of God: "For in six days the Lord made

would entitle it to the claim of being a pioneer in matters of religious progress. For although the economic conditions of the present day impede and render well-nigh impossible the keeping holy of the Sabbath for almost the whole of the Jewish nation, it is nevertheless still held on high as the social symbol of Judaism. For although this religious institution is perhaps the only one that, invented and introduced by one religion, has succeeded in capturing the whole civilized world, Jews can with the best of will not overlook the fact that the Christian churches, in accordance with their dogmatic basis, have changed this Jewish Sabbath into the Sunday, on which, in express distinction to the biblical motivation in both its forms, it is the resurrection of Christ that is celebrated. Here there is a conflict for the whole of the nation's economic and cultural life that remains to be adjusted at the hands of general religious progress.

If then on the one hand the Sabbath is the very symbol of genuine religious progress in general, which can alone clearly and fundamentally manifest itself in the alleviation and final settlement of social antagonisms, insofar as they endanger the unity of culture, then on the other [hand] this social Sabbath, which in the past endowed the Jew of the medieval ghetto with the comfort and the consciousness of being a civilized being (*Kulturmensch*), has enabled the Jew himself, now and always, to fulfill the primal elements of his religion. For only by virtue of the fact that this day in each week was reserved and consecrated not merely to rest from workday labor, and not merely for so-called religious services, but also and quite as much to the study of the body of doctrine, only by virtue of this was it possible for the whole spiritual fabric of Judaism ever to have been preserved alive. For this reason ignorant superstition was never wholly able to supersede the great religious insight that on the Sabbath there was to be no occupation other than study. And the religious services themselves were not confined to prayer alone; learned discourses were likewise introduced for purposes of edification, in order that the less learned might likewise find some spiritual nutriment. Without teaching, no edification and no devotion: this is the fundamental thought of Jewish religious services, as well as of the whole of Jewish religious life.

It is of course a one-sidedness in the Jewish religion to attempt to dominate the whole of man's life. This propensity is an inward continuation of the old theocracy, which belongs in part to the legendary age; and we must not endeavor

---

heaven and earth and sea, and all that is in them, and He rested on the Seventh day. Therefore the Lord blessed the sabbath day and hallowed it."]

to ameliorate the fact that herein are contained the dark sides of a rigid and indiscreet Jewish ritualism. On the other hand it must be acknowledged that this domination aimed at the thorough permeation of life, so that, just as there existed no difference between priest and Israelite, so also it was intended for the whole of man's life and conduced to do away with all distinction between the sacred and the secular: "Be all thy deeds for the sake of God."[11]

Thus, the conception of religion was to be freed from the idea that represents it as serving only the interests of a world beyond and not primarily and above all things those of the world we live in. Not that the thought of the world beyond was in any way to be curtailed; on the contrary, the concept of the resurrection was soon after the Persian period allowed to assume a place within the Jew's religious consciousness. Nevertheless the whole of Jewish literature shows the marked tendency to fix the center of gravity of religion not in the thought of a world beyond but rather to fasten and establish it in the actual life of man on earth.

In this respect too, ancient Judaism felt itself in antagonism to its heathen surroundings. The polytheistic religions have their center of gravity in the belief in a world beyond, a belief originally derived from their ancestral cults, from which the concept of immortality took its rise. And Christianity likewise, no matter how much it endowed its concept of eternal life with deep meaning, was nonetheless forced to maintain as the foundation of its religion the notions of a world beyond and of a new birth, because it was only thereby that salvation could be achieved and therewith the Christian concept of God realized. For this reason Christian morality is compelled to direct itself to this as its final goal; and [it] attains thereby in point of general culture the great advantage of being removed from the affairs of this world in sublime piety and in world disdain. To be sure, this withdrawal from the world is fraught with very grave ambiguities. Thus, the Middle Ages appear under the dominion of two powers. And only in the most recent days has the attempt been made to revive the historical spirit of the Reformation by adopting the watchword of "practical Christianity."[12]

Even apart from the contents of the social laws and thoughts, with which this new view of Christianity returns to the social legislation of the Pentateuch,

11. [*Mishnah Aboth* ("Be all thy deeds for the sake of God (וכל מעשיך יהיו לשם שמים)," "Sayings of the Fathers"), 2:12.]

12. [Known in the English-speaking world as the Life and Work Movement, "practical Christianity (*Die Bewegung für praktisches Christentum*)" was an effort to advance collaboration among the Christian churches on social and political issues.]

the new watchword itself is deeply and originally Jewish: the penetration of the whole of man's life with the thoughts, the demands, and the emotions of religion. And as a matter of fact, it has been expressly acknowledged on the part of leaders of this social movement of practical Christianity that a return must be made to the social legislation of the Pentateuch.

And it was the return to life of this political conviction, and the historical insight that this had it in its power to awaken, that was not least among the causes leading to a thorough revision of the whole of the customary historical judgment concerning the nature of the prophets, as this indeed has turned out to be the signal service rendered by modern biblical criticism, in other words by Protestant academic theology. In the general consciousness of educated humanity the old Israelite prophets are no longer mere soothsayers, in which case they would have been no more than merely a kind of priests, whereas as a matter of fact they engaged themselves, with all the passion the religious heart of man is capable of, in the bitterest opposition no less to these than to the kings and the nobility; they are in truth the pioneers of a new religion because of a new morality. But this new morality and consequently this new religion is dominated by the idea of the Sabbath. On the Sabbath the toiler is to be relieved from his labor; this is Jeremiah's view of the Sabbath (17:21 f.). And Isaiah has the words, "He that keepeth the Sabbath from profaning it, and keepeth his hand from doing any evil" (56:2), thus comprehending in his sense of social morality the sum of all evil in the profanation of the Sabbath. And thus the Sabbath will ever remain a symbol of the whole of genuine religious life, as of a life that is permeated with the most genuine thoughts of religion, and that by virtue of this interpenetration becomes consecrated to the moral life.

There still remains to be mentioned a particular advantage accruing from the law concerning the Sabbath. Social interest, in this case as everywhere else, has a direct and immediate political influence. Thus, the institution of the Sabbath helped first of all to abolish slavery in principle, and other laws were later enacted to complete the task. But apart from the ancient system of slavery, it is the vital principle of political freedom in general that this institution of the Sabbath secures and establishes, and converts into the very anchoring ground of the whole of religious thought. The words, "Ye are the children of the Lord your God" (Deuteronomy 14:1) attain the validity of a serious truth only in the light of those other words, "Thou shalt choose life" (Deuteronomy 30:19). Only through the means of the demand of freedom of choice, which tradition has based on this verse, is the real consummation of the religious concept of man effected.

On the other hand this religious concept of freedom must not be confounded with the corresponding ethical concept.[13] The religious significance of freedom is determined by the somewhat naïve claims and considerations resulting from the two-sided relation between God and man. It is intended that man should on no account be regarded as simply an animal, or as a natural creature in general, but rather as a creation of God, as a child of God. Therein consists his likeness to God. And consequently he can likewise not be said to be the tool of an evil instinct, just as little as God himself is an evil demon, from whom evil could emanate.

The freedom with which Judaism endows man consequently means purity of heart. This constitutes the contradiction, the denial of original sin. It is therefore instructive to see that the Psalmist conceives of a pure heart as the creation of God and that it is this for which he supplicates. "Create in me a pure heart, O God; and renew a steadfast spirit within me" (Ps. 51:10). The receipt of a pure heart at birth is not to be the subject of our longing, but its creation is the work, is the task of one's whole life. This is likewise the ultimate meaning of ethical freedom: that it be not originally present as fact, as datum, but that it always be conceived as task and always remain so.

If freedom is thus equivalent to purity, it will be impossible to regard the latter as an innate possession or as a gift of God; on the contrary it will constitute the ideal of man. Purity with man signifies the same as holiness with God. But this purity is precept and pattern for the struggle of life, which must be carried on under the guidance of a rational, a moral will, namely, the will of freedom.

This is the freedom of the children of God that Judaism teaches, whereas the freedom mentioned in the Epistle to the Romans (8:21), and which Luther has translated in this sense,[14] has in reality reference to the world beyond and signifies participation in the godhead, in the glory (δόξα) of God. In the first case it is human life that is presented to choice. Therefore: "Thou shalt choose life" (see supra). And this sense of freedom with respect to life has conferred on the religious consciousness of Judaism on the one hand its imperturbable optimism, and on the other its unflinching capacity for martyrdom, which in an endless variety of form constitutes as a whole its historical existence, or at the very least accompanies it.

---

13. [On this line of thinking, see selection 6.]

14. The English version has *liberty* [("because the creation itself will be set free from its bondage to decay and obtain the glorious liberty of the children of God"). The Luther Bible has "die herrliche Freiheit" (meaning the glorious freedom)].

But above all, this freedom has been instrumental in inculcating in the Jew a sense of his personal responsibility for his actions. And this personal conscientiousness is and continues to be the center of gravity of all religious sentiment. Sins are confessed openly before the whole congregation. This was ordained by the Talmud, and therewith the confessional was ever after an impossibility. And only through such means is the distinction between congregation and church to be kept alive. The freedom of the Jewish consciousness knows no other form of community (*Gemeinschaft*) than that of the congregation (*Gemeinde*), the rabbis of which are only teachers and judges and by no means ministrants of a church acting as indirect representatives of God.

The fundamental concept of doctrine has likewise here superseded the character and role of a law for the constitution of the community. For as everybody has to participate in the doctrine, so also will the doctrine endow the man with adequate strength to attend independently to his freedom and his purity. As for general human frailties, the Day of Atonement will lend him the requisite aid. And thus, in this new transformation of the path, the old motto still retains its virtue: "Ye shall be pure before the Lord" (Leviticus 16:30).

There is thus a natural connecting link between freedom in its moral significance and in its social and political purpose. But this connection between the two received later on a still deeper foundation by means of the very highest consummation to which the Jewish concept of God ever attained. I refer to the idea of the messiah.

As in the case of all ideas of all kinds, the occasion for the rise of the messianic idea is to be sought in the particular circumstances of the historical development of the time. But it is the manner of employing historical factors that determines the genuine originality of a historical idea. The prophets would most probably not have conceived of the messianic idea if their attention had not been directed to it, so to speak, by the political history of their people. But is there record of any other nations whose political decline led to the hope of the restoration of their might in some distant future? And it was not after the fall of their state that the prophets proclaimed its future reestablishment; but long before its fall they predicted it as a demand of divine justice. Thus, the political element is merely the occasion that wakened the otherwise altogether independent thought into life.

Furthermore—and herein lies the real significance of the matter—the prophets regarded the restoration to life of their own state as by no means the exclusive or even the chief burden of their proclamations; on the contrary, the restoration likewise of those states and nations that had even fought against their own people was included among their promises. In the face of every past, they conceive of and invent the concept of a future. This concept, as an historical-time concept, is the real meaning of their messianic thought, and the real discovery achieved by it.

It is true that here again it is an empirical concept that is the occasion and the material starting point of their thought. In Israel the kings were anointed. And David was the glorious king who had not only founded the kingdom but who was also the real inaugurator of the Temple, and who, to crown all, had in his Psalms bequeathed it an imposing body of prayer. Just as that distant future naturally centered on the fancy of the restoration of their own people, the decline and fall of which their religious sense of justice had demanded, so also does their hope for the future find concrete embodiment in the ideal shape of this royal figure. And thus the messiah becomes a scion of the house of David; he becomes the anointed, as it were, a king. But soon the view changes. The anointed does not merely remain a king; he becomes the symbolic figure of human suffering, from whom alone genuine hope can issue and who alone can bear within himself the genuine warranty for the restoration and regeneration of the human race.

It is only now that the complete, the enormous content of the messianic idea comes into full play. It is not their own people that is in question here. "It is too light a thing that thou shouldst be my servant to raise up the tribes of Jacob, and to restore the preserved of Israel: I will also give thee for a light to the nations, that thou mayest be my salvation unto the end of the earth" (Isaiah 49:6). Thus does Deutero-Isaiah, in spite of all the depth of his patriotic sorrow, characterize his universal task; and the same universal spirit pervades throughout the prophetic conception of the messiah long before the exile. He is to them the symbol of the peace of mankind, in which all men will have assembled into one flock to do adoration to the one and only God, and as indispensable proof thereof to cultivate morality upon earth, in sign of which, and as primary fulfillment, to abolish warfare from the face of the earth, and to develop in concord and in righteousness the life of the future man.

It was in this connection that the concept of mankind that is humanity was born; in no other connection could it have arisen with historical significance. Of a truth, if the Jewish religion had brought forth nothing else save this one messianic idea of the prophets, it would thereby alone have proved itself the deepest fountain and wellspring of culture for moral mankind. But the prophets would never have been able to conceive of and invent this idea of a single humanity, united "at the latter days,"[15] if their one and only God had not served them in the light of a creative and guiding thought, if the concept of the only God had not made a united humanity its necessary corollary. And thus is the messiah absolutely and irrefragably the innermost attribute of God.

It is difficult at such a point to distinguish between religious progress and the general progress of human culture. For it is nothing less than the concept of universal history [*Weltgeschichte*] that constitutes the content of the messianic idea. Nevertheless we propose to confine ourselves to a brief discussion of the religious progress involved here.

The chief difficulty for the concept of religion lies in its complication with *myth*. Now every linkage of a religion to a person exposes it to the danger embodied in myth.[16] For the final meaning of myth is the personification of the impersonal. Here is manifested the value of the distinction that Judaism everywhere attempted to draw between itself and myth; for it refuses absolutely to expect from a person the highest deed that can ever be hoped for from God, namely, the union of his children in concord and faithfulness. The temptation toward such a personification lay near enough at hand; the longing for a scion from the house of David dominated for a very long time their patriotic sentiment [of the Jews]. But the logic of the fundamental idea of their religion obtained the upper hand in the end, and thus they eliminated the figure of King David, and in his stead they raised upon the throne "the servant of Yahweh,"[17] who, through the mediation of Israel, of "the remnant of Israel," can signify nothing else but the people of the future, the humanity of the future. And whereas the messiah was originally meant to designate a dynastic personage, the internal development of this thought brought it to pass that at this highest stage of monotheism, the cult of persons, hero cult in general, not to mention the cult of a divine person, was entirely suppressed.

The whole of civilized humanity has come now to believe in this significance of the messianic idea, although it has not yet acknowledged this, its highest thought, to be the messianic thought. It remains for it to elevate itself to this insight. The ethical humanity of future history—this alone is "the anointed of the Lord," this alone is the messiah. We must therefore not hesitate in giving

15. [Isa. 2].

16. [Cohen is returning to a frequent theme in his thought: any personification of God leads to myth.]

17. [See "Servant Songs" in Isa. 40–55.]

expression to the fact that, if we are to accept this genuine prophetic meaning of messiah, the translation embodied in the name of Christ is no longer tenable. For it was not to save individual man from sin that the messiah was conceived; this individual religious aim was not included within the original intention of the messianic thought. Man's salvation, according to the teaching of the prophets, must, with the support of religion, be achieved by man himself. But the salvation of the world, the purification and elevation of the human race from its historical sins, the peace of mankind in the fear of God, in faithfulness and in righteousness—this is a task for which the human resources of the individual must ever remain inadequate.

Now this task signifies nothing less than the ultimate problem of the reality of morality: that it remain no mere fond thought but attain and maintain the currency and the validity of a truth. Ethical morality unites at this point with religion, for in the end morality itself cannot but proclaim the idea of God: not for the personal salvation of the moral individual, *but as the pledge and warrant for the future realization of morality upon Earth.*[18]

This and nothing else is the plain meaning of the messianic idea of the prophets, and therefore it can be said to embody the final perfection of the idea of the one God. "Can morality become a reality on earth?" is the great question that morality must ask. And the prophets answered this question affirmatively with their idea of the messiah. This messianic idea has been accepted by civilized humanity. But it must likewise be accepted by philosophical ethics. And therewith the prophet's concept of God will have found a place in the body of doctrine formulated by philosophical ethics. For this concept constitutes the pledge for the assurance of historical reality that is made by the messianic idea. And the question as to reality is one that philosophical ethics cannot presume to neglect.

These considerations have led us somewhat beyond the limits of our subject. But from the very beginning we have had to take general progress into consideration, and we may now say that herein is manifested the greatest triumph of religion, in that it is seen to coincide with the consciousness of culture and with philosophical ethics. As regarding the internal religious progress within Judaism itself, we may in conclusion draw attention to one more circumstance: through the agency of the messianic thought an emotion was ennobled that elsewhere in

18. [See selection 2, page 83: "*God means that nature will endure just as certainly as morality is eternal.*"]

antiquity signified only an idle striving. The messianic idea, however, deepened the roots of hope and broadened its bed. Hope has come to be the historical confidence, yes the absolute moral confidence; for he who cannot believe in this future is in truth lost to all idealism. It is known to what an extent the Jewish religion has had need of the anchor of hope, and how much even at the present day it has need of this emotion; it will therefore not permit itself to be deprived of its honor. Under all manner of persecution and oppression, from without and (what is more rarely thought of) internally within the soul, the Jew maintains his religiosity by force of the messianic emotion of hope. His messianic hope is his comfort and his assurance. And as for sufferings, terrible as they are and not merely for him who undergoes them, they have never yet been able to bring about the fall either of an individual or of a nation, if only the requisite spiritual and moral forces are present to resist the influence of suffering.

In the history of nations it is likewise by no means the summit of outward power that saves them from ruin. For this reason the path of suffering that the Jews have had to traverse in the course of the world's history is a sign and symptom of religious progress, because it is proof of a religious power capable of withstanding all persecutions and all unscrupulous enticements. The hope and the confidence on the one hand, and on the other the strength to bear and to suffer, are at once traces and forces of religious progress, seeds of development, inherent within religion for the whole of historical life.

I must not be afraid of touching upon one point more. It is well known how often in the present day the question has been put within the educated and the learned Protestant world: "are we still Christians?"[19] The discussion that has arisen on this point leaves no doubt as to the fact that it is not the concept of God that is controverted here, but the person of Christ. On the other hand, hazy, indistinct, and confused tendencies in politics and likewise in the sciences and humanities are making themselves felt, all directed toward undermining the concept of God. Now psychology can certainly be treated without the need of soul. But surely religion will be impossible if the concept of God is to be excluded. Thus, the thought of God is at the forefront of debate in general culture. And within Protestantism it is really not this question that is meant when dissatisfaction is expressed with the difficulties that are always involved even in an idealized conception of the person of Christ.

19. [This is the title of the first chapter of the last book written by David Friedrich Strauss (1808–74), *Der alte und der neue Glaube* (Bonn, Germany: E. Strauss, 1873).]

In the face of all this, Judaism—harassed, insulted, calumniated, and politically cheated, as unfortunately is the case not merely with Russia, daring all the dangers, the injuries, the allurements on the part of the state—still stands upright as a rock of religious progress. Within its community it is impossible for the question to arise: "are we still Jews?" The saying of the Talmud still retains living currency: "He who utters 'Hear O Israel' is a Jew."[20] We modern Jews cherish our Judaism only as the faith in the one God, and we acknowledge only those duties that stand in a necessary connection with this fundamental faith. The warranty offered by such religious faithfulness in times in which the faith in God is exposed to such serious attacks, and in which, within the religion that in point of culture stands highest, dogmatic difficulties are beginning to envelop the basis of the belief in God—this, I say, should be taken into consideration as a deep and significant problem.

It is neither my task nor my purpose to assume the role of a prophet and to map out the probable course of historical development. Nevertheless the nature of my theme compels me to draw your attention briefly to that element of religious progress that is contained for religion in the concentration of modern Judaism upon the prophets' idea of God. Only through interest in, and understanding of, this concentration can the genuinely scientific, the genuinely historical, insight in the points involved be disclosed. Just as little as Christ is the prophetic messiah, just so little can the God who is bound up with Christ be said to be identical with the one God of the prophets. To comprehend fully the old and still living religion, the mind must free itself from what later times have added. The fundamental thought of the old religion is not sequence but the future—in their own language, "the latter days." We must unlearn and relearn; we must begin anew.

And what science demands is doubly called for by the needs of the age. Faith must be regained in the moral renascence, in the moral future of mankind. This faith must be regained in antagonism to the selfishness of the nations and to the materialism of the classes. The genuine living God, whom the prophets of Israel made to be God of Israel and to be God of mankind, breathes only in social morality and in cosmopolitan humanity.

20. [This particular saying is apparently not to be found in the Talmud.]

The difference between the concepts of autonomy and freedom enables us to determine the difference between ethics and religion. Not between morality and religion, for religion is also morality, and only as morality is it religion. Ethics, however, is the philosophical discipline of morality, and religion is not a philosophical discipline.

This is the reason why autonomy cannot be part of religion. For autonomy is the fundamental proposition of ethics as a philosophical discipline, just as axioms are the fundamental propositions of mathematics. It was Kant who coined the concept of autonomy as a fundamental proposition, using a term that, since the Renaissance, had referred to rational independence, and more narrowly to political sovereignty. Kant gave it the precise meaning of a fundamental proposition. The possibility of ethics as a philosophical discipline depends on the possibility of this fundamental proposition.

Long before, however, Plato anticipated this thought when he established the *idea of the good*, despite his pronounced tendency to distinguish between its value and that of other ideas. In spite of this distinction, the general value of the idea of the good must be maintained. Since the significance of the idea of the good lies in its being the foundation (*Grundlegung*) (ὑπόθεσις—*hypothesis*) of ethics, ethics thus rests on an idea, as required by the system and method of the doctrine of ideas. That is, ethics rests on a foundation or a fundamental proposition. Just as, for Kant, it was autonomy, for Plato it is the good that serves as the fundamental proposition of ethics as a philosophical discipline.

The two founders of ethics therefore agree in their assertion of the value of this fundamental proposition. But the concepts to which they attach this valuation are as different as one may expect, considering the millennia that separate them. Hence, from the very start to the present day, the symptomatic debate has existed on the relation of the idea of the good to God. Alas, one cannot say "to the idea of God," and one would not want to say "to Zeus or Apollo." It is the methodological function of the idea of the good that gives the idea its particular determinacy, its function as the foundation of the philosophical discipline of the good, of ethics as a philosophical discipline.

Kant's disposition of the system of critiques[1] makes it transparent that autonomy has the function of a fundamental proposition. To be sure, Kant considered *freedom* and autonomy to be interchangeable concepts. Freedom, however, as a historical concept, is the origin of autonomy. It was necessary that freedom first be salvaged in the concept of autonomy. It was the fundamental concept of medieval ethics and remained so in modern times. Ancient philosophy did not place freedom at the center of the problems of ethics. In pre-Platonic Socratic thought, freedom merely expresses the demand that ethics is a philosophical discipline, that virtue is knowledge. No one, therefore, can be voluntarily bad.

It is only in the Christian world that freedom advances to become the shibboleth of morality. This occurs when it encounters the conflict between religion and morality and its resolution. It is characteristic that not even Plotinus argues in favor of freedom as energetically as does Origen. Thus it remained throughout the Middle Ages. The arguments pro and contra on freedom remained a contested subject in the quarrel between religion and philosophy. Freedom is both the expression and the measure of the share that religion seeks to seize and retain in philosophy. But freedom ought not signify or mean more than this share. It is the share, therefore, not only that religion has in philosophy, but that philosophy has in religion as well. Nothing could be further from the religion of the Middle Ages than to grant morality its own independence. Thus, from the perspective of relations between disciplines, freedom is connected to the merit of the human being, deserving either reward or punishment. This connection is a more urgent and serious concern than the problematic connection with divine omniscience.

More recently, divine omniscience has been superseded by the natural necessity of causality. The conflict between the two fundamental concepts[2] constitutes the ethical theme of the *Critique of Pure Reason*. The antinomy is resolved by rigorously distinguishing between the two concepts as *two kinds of fundamental proposition*: causality is the fundamental proposition of mathematical natural sciences; freedom is the fundamental proposition of ethics. However, the *Critique of Pure Reason* only prepared the ground for this distinction. It is the *Critique*

---

1. [A reference to Kant's three major critical works, *The Critique of Pure Reason* (1781; 2nd ed. 1787), *The Critique of Practical Reason* (1788), and *The Critique of Judgment* (1790).]

2. [That is, the conflict between freedom and necessity. This was the subject of Cohen's published doctoral dissertation, *Philosophorum de antinomia necessitatis et contingentiae doctrinae* (The doctrines of the philosophers on the antinomy of necessity and contingency), (Halle, Germany: Ploetz, 1865; reprinted in *Werke* 12:1–90.]

of Practical Reason that was decisive, developing freedom into autonomy and thus distinguishing between autonomy and freedom. Freedom expresses the connection between morality and religion. In autonomy the problems are sundered from one another. Ethics becomes a philosophical discipline.

Just as for religion in general, for the Jewish religion too autonomy is a foreign concept, methodologically incompatible with it. God must be regarded as the author and source of revealed morality. Either morality would be diminished in value, if it were merely a human invention; or God would be diminished in his supreme value, his only value, if he had any function other than the revelation of morality. But just as the problem of freedom was not exhausted within ethics when autonomy took its place as a fundamental proposition, freedom also affords religion a wide and long playing field for its labor on behalf of morality. To seek a historical understanding of Judaism from the perspective of autonomy would result in a misrepresentation, for Judaism would cease to be a religion of God.[3] The principle of freedom is the most natural and fertile perspective if we want to understand Judaism's moral history and wish to develop its moral force in the future.[4]

Freedom is the freedom of the *will*. Freedom is thus a twofold problem. For what is the will? In ancient philosophy the will too is only a latent potentiality. For its power is associated with knowledge. Thus, the will raises the problem of *the relationship between knowledge and drive or desire*. For medieval philosophy, the profound conflict over the identity of *voluntas* and *intellectus* is thus not just a question of psychology, but rather one of dogmatics and ethics. It is a misunderstanding of Spinoza and an injustice if one judges him on the weakness of his phrasing, which connects him to the Middle Ages, while he managed to blind himself to this weakness as he waged his battle against theology. His strength rests in the claim that the knowledge of the good is an affect. In affect, the best part of the will is preserved. The possibility of freedom rests henceforth on the power of affect.

Here we recognize that Spinoza, more than quotations can support, has a deep and intimate connection with the religion and philosophy of Judaism and is in harmony with its moral spirit. Freedom is commanded in the Pentateuch

3. [This is a barb aimed at Moritz Lazarus. On Cohen's blistering review of Lazarus, reprinted in JS 3:1–35, see selection 8, 212–13.]

4. [The following paragraph makes it clear that this comment is directed against Spinoza's interpretation of Judaism, according to which Judaism is a religion of unfreedom.]

itself; this would amount to a contradiction, if religion mistook freedom for autonomy. "You ought to choose life."[5] Freedom of choice refers to the will, to the heart, to the soul, to the spirit. All of these terms, even knowledge, signify the will. The old saying is more than symbolic wordplay: freedom was engraved upon the tables of the law.[6] It was engraved not only on the tablets, but also in flesh and heart. However evil the urges of youth may be, "the soul which thou hast placed within me is pure."[7] This is what Spinoza prayed every morning. Purity of the soul: *that* is freedom of will. "The soul is the good inclination." Thus, the soul turns into will, and purity into freedom of will.

It is instructive that Crescas—whom Joël[8] identified beyond any doubt as the closest forerunner of Spinoza (Spinoza read his "*Or Adonai*" before reading any other Scholastic author, and when he read it he still lived, heart and soul, in the "light of the eternal," the *species aeterni*[9])—argues against the Scholastic notion of the freedom of the will. At the same time, he teaches a sharply defined interpretation of the freedom of choice in the Jewish religion: "the true worship of love" (העבודה האמיתית והאהבה). He limits the freedom of knowledge, but the power of love, the power of worship, is without limit. For Maimonides too, the duty of self-perfection approaches the edge of the divine.

The meaning of freedom in the Jewish religion is revealed in the character of Jewish worship, in the manner in which God is worshipped in Jewish religious practice. The veneration of God does not consist of dogmatic contemplation of the divine being, the knowledge of which is supposed to serve as a substitute for mystery and yet still as its representation as well. The magnificent meaning of Jewish transcendence and its orientation toward the world of human beings is this: that our worship of God has almost nothing in common with the knowledge of his absolute being and his substantial nature. The duty and freedom

5. [A paraphrase of Deut. 30:19.]

6. [Cohen is alluding to *Mishnah Aboth* 6:2: "It says, 'And the tablets were the work of God, and the writing was the writing of God, graven upon the tablets' (Exod. 32:16). Read not *haruth* [graven] but *heruth* [freedom]. For there is no free man but one who occupies himself with the study of the Torah."]

7. [From the daily morning liturgy. See *The Daily Prayer Book: Ha-Siddur Ha-Shalem*, ed. Philip Birnbaum (New York: Hebrew Publishing Co., 1949), 16.]

8. [Manuel Joël (1826–1890), a professor at the Jewish Theological Seminary in Breslau and the author of *Spinoza's theologisch-politischer Traktat auf seine Quellen geprüft* (Breslau, Germany: H. Skutsch, 1870).]

9. [An allusion to what, according to Spinoza, is the goal of human life: to live "*sub specie aeternitatis* (under the aspect of eternity)."]

of the worship of God is entirely limited to the will. In this limitation worship carries out its perfection and its freedom. For the will is not just a drive. Affect bears within itself just as much of the intellect as it needs for the will. The transcendent God, sought by the loving will, does not therefore contain the human being within himself. But he does contain the *relationship* with the human being. Transcendence precludes the immanence of the human being and God, yet it includes the immanence of the relationship of God and human being. The love for God is therefore the love for the father of humanity. It is thus love of humanity as such. And thus the love for God becomes the freedom of the moral will.

What is the actual difficulty in the problem of freedom? Why does it seem to be a catchword of pious hypocrisy, while the statistician,[10] who seems to refute it, actually affirms it by preparing the ground for its production? Long ago Ezekiel was compelled to fend off the proverb of the sour grapes by invoking the *individual* both as sinner and as free being.[11] The Ate[12] of guilt chains the generations together, and social circumstances[13] yield their effects, with the causality of natural law. Does it not seem like a residue of theological metaphysics if one nonetheless argues for the freedom of the individual?

Within ethics, freedom obtains only in the realm of autonomy. In religion, however, God may command freedom only for the sake of summoning it to life and truth. In the realm of autonomy, freedom is not a marionette that constantly pulls itself up by its own strings, without realizing that it is actually being manipulated from the outside.

Under the fundamental law of autonomy, freedom is an idea, not a sensory reality. Idea does not mean that it is a figment of the imagination, a pious notion. Idea means that it is a task and always a task. Once equipped with this insight by the philosophical discipline of ethics, we can also recognize the religious value

10. [The word *Moralstatistik* (meaning moral statistics) frequently appears in Cohen's polemics against the reduction of ethics to the empirical social sciences.]

11. [The proverb "parents eat sour grapes and their children's teeth are set on edge" (Ezek. 18:2) is rejected by Ezekiel (and Jeremiah) in favor of a doctrine of individual responsibility. Cohen's use of the verse here is one of the earliest occurrences of this trope in his writings. It appears as the pivotal systematic point in his posthumous work (see *RR*, chapter 11, "Atonement").]

12. [Greek ἀτή or Θεά Ἀτη, a Greek goddess responsible for random acts of destruction and human ruination.]

13. [The reference is to milieu theory, which explains the prevalence of crime among the poor as resulting from the circumstances of poverty rather than from an intrinsic moral failing.]

of freedom not in the simple possession of freedom, which would be worthless even if it were a hereditary possession; but in the *duty* of freedom. We therefore also recognize its religious value in the faculty of freedom within the human being driven by instinct. Freedom is the freedom of the will. But the will is not inclination, which can also be evil. It is the good inclination that is equivalent to the soul. The freedom of the will means the uplift of the will, the uplift in which the will becomes will toward the ideals that are the content of the love of God.

Freedom does not paint the entire individual as free. Rather, it *idealizes* the human being, drawing on the moments of elevation, on the lines that guide him toward the divine path. Freedom does not consist of any particular sensory moment of his empirical existence. Its reality is not ideal as commonly understood; it is idealization. The ideal human being, projected by freedom, is the idealized human being, a human being that idealizes himself. Such self-idealization is accomplished by freedom.

The fruit of this idealization is not only the individual. It goes further by transcending individuals, just as before it transcended the actions and feelings of particular individuals. It breaks through such limitations. It permeates human beings and peoples and remakes them as a new unity, an enlarged self, a moral *community*. Community too, which is the actual content of the moral law, is the creation of freedom. To the immoral spirit that wants to believe that individuals and peoples live by the law of the jungle, community too appears to be a chimera. Humanity is the freedom of human beings. Without the freedom of all human beings, no individual human can be free. The most succinct and most original product of the Jewish spirit is probably the *idea of messiah*. The belief in the idealization of humanity: that is the most certain attestation of the power of freedom in Judaism.

For the moral community, as for the needs of the religious individual, the idealizing meaning of freedom comes to the fore in the most important forms of the Jewish liturgy. God is not venerated in the mystery of the eucharist and the last supper. Such mysteries are neither the apex nor the principal and prevalent content of the liturgy. These are kinds of knowledge that seek to elevate both lay people and priests beyond ordinary human measure. There is one day, called "the Day of Judgment,"[14] whose distinctive ritual seems to include what every prayer throughout the year is meant to accomplish for the reconciliation of the

14. ["Yom Ha-Din" in Hebrew; one of the names for Rosh Hashanah, the Jewish new year.]

human being with God. The only aspect of the divine being revealed on that day is this: his judgment on human beings. Therefore, the *precondition of atonement is freedom*. We are but dust and ashes, but "You made us little less than divine."[15] What we lack is not autonomy. For not even in ethics does autonomy mean that a God is not needed. Neither does the law of nature render the power or the matter of nature unnecessary; nor are human beings created by the moral law. Hence, freedom cannot do without the idea of God. Autonomy demands only that we need to discover ethics on our own. Just as we need to construct ethics as a philosophical discipline from fundamental principles we think up ourselves, we ought likewise to strive to generate the moral law in every moment of our existence and in every approach to an action. This "ought" is the autonomy of the law. That, and insofar as, we are also able; that is, insofar as we succeed in the idealization of our moral self and of the human community—this is the meaning of freedom.

The liturgy of atonement rests on this right of freedom. Sacrifice is merely a faint national memory. We sacrifice to no God. And no God sacrifices himself for us. Hence no priest can produce a mystical representation of a divine sacrifice. The essence of God is of interest to Jewish liturgy only to the extent that freedom can use it for the idealization of the human being: "Before God you ought to be pure."[16] Purity before God: this is the freedom of the human being.

15. [A paraphrase of Ps. 8:5.]
16. [Lev. 16:30.]

III | Coda

When Cohen died in 1918, his followers soon began to dispute how to interpret his philosophical legacy. Ernst Cassirer, his internationally most famous disciple, spoke at his funeral, in remarks published later that year alongside a famous letter from the front by Franz Rosenzweig, one of Cohen's younger associates. Cassirer, a former student of Cohen's at Marburg, resigned his professorship at the University of Hamburg when the Nazis came to power in 1933 and fled Germany, arriving eventually in the United States, where he died in 1945. In his graveside speech, translated below as selection 7, Cassirer presented Cohen's trajectory as continuous and smooth, and his combination of Judaism and neo-Kantianism as one that allowed for personal equanimity and grace.

Very different was the interpretation of Rosenzweig, who published his major work on Jewish thought, *The Star of Redemption*, in 1924 and who died tragically young of amyotrophic lateral sclerosis. Selection 8 is Rosenzweig's elegant, lengthy, and passionate appreciation of Cohen, whom he had known in Berlin after the latter retired there, as it appeared as the introduction to the compilation of Cohen's Jewish writings over the decades. In his text, Rosenzweig forged an enduring and potent reinterpretation of the self-undoing of Cohen's philosophy—one that has controlled most subsequent readings of Cohen, to the point of consigning the philosopher's intended contribution, as he had formulated it in his own words, to relative neglect. Brilliant in its own right, even if its argument is open to question, Rosenzweig's essay supplies a dramatic overview of Cohen's entire life as a Jewish thinker. And it also offers a precious sense of how the cultural and philosophical past of German Jewry could look to one of its most talented members after World War I.

Pivotal in Rosenzweig's interpretation of Cohen's trajectory was the notion of correlation, which Cohen had introduced in his logic and which figured throughout his later philosophy, not only in his final book (on which Rosenzweig dwelled in his introduction). What was at stake in the concept, Rosenzweig suggested, was Cohen's slow approach to the ineffable individuality characteristic of later existentialist thought, making the concept something of a Trojan horse that Cohen welcomed into his neo-Kantian system but that portended its overthrow.

In selection 9, Alexander Altmann rebuts Rosenzweig's argument in a classic essay in its own right that has never before been translated into English. Altmann (1906–87) was born in the Austro-Hungarian Empire but moved to England in 1938, where he lived for twenty years before he settled in the United States and began teaching at Brandeis University. A prolific scholar, Altmann is remembered for his authoritative biography of Moses Mendelssohn. In the essay translated here, Altmann perceptively argues that Cohen developed the concept of correlation on rigorously neo-Kantian terms. In this way, both selections 8 and 9 are crucial aids not only in interpreting Cohen's posthumous *Religion of Reason out of the Sources of Judaism* but also in making sense of the shape of his entire career.

SOURCES

Selection 7: Ernst Cassirer, "Hermann Cohen: Worte gesprochen an seinem Grabe am 7. April 1918," *Neue jüdische Monatshefte*, May 10, 1918, 347–52

Selection 8: Franz Rosenzweig, "Einleitung," in Hermann Cohen, *Jüdische Schriften*, ed. Bruno Strauss (Berlin: C. A. Schwetschke und Sohn, 1924), 1:xiii–lxiv. Reprinted as "Einleitung in die Akademieausgabe der jüdischen Schriften Hermann Cohens," in *Zweistromland: Kleinere Schriften zu Glauben und Denken*, in *Franz Rosenzweig Gesammelte Schriften: Der Mensch und Sein Werk*, ed. Reinhold Mayer and Annemarie C. Mayer (Dordrecht, the Netherlands: Martinus Nijhoff, 1984), 3:177–223

Selection 9: Alexander Altmann, "Hermann Cohens Begriff der Korrelation," in *In Zwei Welten: Siegfried Moses zum fünfundsiebzigsten Geburtstag*, ed. Hans Tramer (Tel Aviv: Bitaon Ltd., 1962), 377–99

7 | Ernst Cassirer: Remarks at Hermann Cohen's Grave, April 7, 1918

At the present moment I cannot presume to speak of Hermann Cohen's contributions, as thinker and scholar, to philosophy and to the world of academic research. That judgment will be the task of history, and the more widely known, the more deeply understood Cohen's works come to be over time, the more certain and unambiguous will be history's judgment on his life's work as a whole. At the present moment, I can only speak of Cohen from a more limited and modest perspective, from the perspective of his student and friend. At this very moment, when we are losing him forever, what comes to my mind are the days when he first approached me as a teacher, more than twenty years ago. I permit myself to open with these personal reminiscences, for they are also typical, and of general value for understanding his character. I first became acquainted with Cohen and his philosophy through his books on Kant. Thus, it was not an easy or smooth path that led me to him, for these books were regarded then, and, in some quarters, are still regarded today as the most difficult books in philosophical literature. Then, as a neophyte in philosophy, I entirely lacked the preparation or training in method necessary for understanding these books. To a great extent I lacked essential historical and systematic background knowledge as well. Hence, I was unable to gain ready access to the difficult conceptual apparatus of his works. Only gradually could I comprehend and appreciate the system as a whole. But what I grasped from the start was the image of the great personality that shone forth from these books. That was the motive for my firm resolution not to rest until I had fully mastered them and penetrated their depth. I was not yet able to follow the substance of Cohen's ideas in all their profundity, but the character of the thinker was clear to me from the start. His unconditional striving for the truth, his audacity and the unique character of his conception of things, his courage to pursue ideas to their ultimate systematic conclusions: this is what led me back to these works over and over again. This is what accounted for their irresistible and enduring claim on my attention. All of this was confirmed for me and yet, at the same time, it all appeared in a new and more brilliant light when, two years later, I stood in the presence of Hermann Cohen himself. To be sure, at that first moment of our acquaintance I found neither the confidence nor the right words to approach him in a more personal manner. Standing face to face with the man who meant so much to me, my timidity and reserve nearly prevented me from talking about myself and about my personal relationship to his philosophy. He was the man in whom I had, for so long, seen the very embodiment of the subject of philosophy and its objectivity. However, it took him little time to discern and understand my state of mind, without uttering so much as a word. I will never forget how he then responded to me with incomparable warmth and with all the exuberant vitality of his nature, how he conquered every last trace of my bashfulness, and how he neither rested nor relented until I had completely yielded and bared my soul. The flood of affection that emanated from him overcame all barriers of convention; he swept aside all external obstacles; he overcame all distance and differences between the young disciple and his elder, the master and the pupil—until eventually the relationship between the teacher and the student evolved into the deepest and most intimate friendship. That friendship endured for more than twenty years, and in all these years it never faltered. It was never darkened by even the most fleeting shadow.

Only in the course of our friendship was Hermann Cohen's true character revealed to me: its mystery lay in the incomparable unity of his will and intellect, of the human and the intellectual aspect of his being. In him both were forged together and inseparable. His thought was borne and animated by his strong power of will, which endured unbroken even into old age. His temperament and his personal love were present even in remarks on purely theoretical matters. It often seemed that in his philosophical inquiries as in his life he was propelled by an invisible inner force; but this force possessed the clarity and certainty of that *daimonion* that lives in the nature of all truly great personalities. In him a passionate will was at work that, at the same time, constantly strove to understand himself with the greatest possible objective clarity, to render an account of himself, to himself. He understood philosophy as a rendering of an account about oneself, as a λόγον διδόναι[1] in Plato's sense of the phrase. He sought to grasp the ultimate, supreme abstractions of thinking, in order to understand the grounds of the moral and religious motivation of his own being. In this way he combined the zeal and ardor of an ethicist with his drive to attain a supreme level of critical circumspection. However, as a logician and a dialectician, he never spoke of

1. [λόγον διδόναι (*lógon didónai*) is Plato's term for "giving a rational account," meaning to explain a thing through its causes and to place it within a system.]

theory as if it were severed from life. Just as his philosophy grew out of life itself, his philosophy also intervened in life, directly and repeatedly. The fundamental law of truth determined his conception of ethics and prevailed in its construction: idealism of the concept became, for him, idealism of the deed. Whatever his ideas could achieve was directed beyond the orbit of ideas alone and sought confirmation by being applied to the great ethical problems, the problems of nation and society. There was no line of separation between "theory" and "praxis," for here theory itself strove not merely to describe or represent, but to form and reform reality.

Only from the perspective of this central point can one grasp the deep inner connection between Cohen's religious and philosophical development, between his concept of God and his concept of truth. For me, this connection was never clearer, never more alive than when I first read the beginning of his last, great work of philosophy of religion, just a few weeks ago. Now of course Cohen will not see the finished work in print. He gave the book the title *The Religion of Reason out of the Sources of Judaism*.[2] Goethe once said that when belief in one God appears in history, it always elevates the spirit, because it directs the attention of the human being to the unity of his own being. Cohen understood the concept of monotheism in the same way. For him, the idea of God was the means of developing and perfecting the pure concept of the human being, the idea of the ethical personality. In this context Cohen cites a passage from the book of Exodus. Probably no one else has interpreted this passage with such profundity and feeling. When Moses stands before God at the burning bush and asks which name of God he should give the people when they ask for the name of the God who sent him, God answers him with the words: "I will be who I am. Tell them, 'I am' sent me to you."[3] Here the "I" has reached the ultimate and highest level of abstraction, in a concept of person that is utterly removed from the realm of

---

2. [As Steven S. Schwarzschild has explained, *The Religion of Reason out of the Sources of Judaism* "was the title when the book was first published, while in all later editions, though unfortunately not in all references to it, this fundamental mistake was rectified" ("The Title of Hermann Cohen's *Religion of Reason out of the Sources of Judaism* (1986)," in Steven S. Schwarzschild, *The Tragedy of Optimism: Writings on Hermann Cohen*, ed. George Y. Kohler [Albany: SUNY Press, 2018], 141). The correct title is *Religion of Reason out of the Sources of Judaism*, without the definite article, for Cohen wished to avoid the implication that Judaism was the only possible religion of reason. However, Rosenzweig (selection 8), consistently refers to the book by the incorrect title, as did Altmann as well (selection 9).]

3. [Exod. 3:14.]

things. The pure spiritual principle of personality has overcome sense perception or image. The root of the true power of monotheism and its world-historical mission lies in this ultimate abstraction of the "I." Polytheism deifies nature in the abundance of its many individual forms; pantheism expresses the unity of the world in terms of the unity of God. But only monotheism penetrates to the core of the "I," to the principle and foundation of human self-consciousness, and discovers there the meaning and content of the divine. When the prophets discover a new concept of God and a new concept of the world, a new heaven and a new earth, it is because a new concept of humanity was revealed to them, new in its meaning for the individual and for society, for ethics and for religion.

From here the path leads us directly to what Cohen called his fundamental conviction in the realm of systematic philosophy. In the *Critique of Judgment*, in the "Analytics of the Sublime," Kant once said that in the Old Testament there is no passage more sublime than the prohibition against the worship of images, than the command: Thou shalt make no image, neither of anything in the heaven above nor on the earth beneath, nor under the earth.[4] He felt the sublimity of these words completely—for his philosophy too rests on a foundation that is imageless and entirely separate from sense perception. It is based on what is produced in pure thought, on what can be grasped only in thinking and in the inner autonomy of the will: on that which he calls the noumenon of freedom. This fundamental idea permeates all the components of the critical system. And moreover, this is the point at which Cohen launches his endeavor to understand Kant's thought. The saying "determine yourself from within yourself,"[5] which Schiller considered perhaps the greatest and most profound utterance ever spoken by a human being, became Cohen's key to Kantian philosophy as well. He understood it as the great doctrine of the autonomy of the spirit: of the logical, ethical, and aesthetic spontaneity of consciousness. He had thus embarked upon a path on which he sought to go beyond Kant in his own systematic works, in the *Logic of Pure Cognition*, in the *Ethics of the Pure Will*, and in the *Aesthetics of Pure Feeling*. Employing a method that was to be pure[6] and comprehensive, he

4. [Exod. 20:4. See Immanuel Kant, *Critique of Judgement*, trans. J. H. Bernhard, 2nd ed. (London: Macmillan and Co., 1931), 143 (B124).]

5. [Friedrich Schiller, "Kallias or Concerning Beauty: Letters to Gottfried Körner," in *Classic and Romantic German Aesthetics*, ed. J. M. Bernstein (Cambridge: Cambridge University Press, 2003), 153.]

6. [In Cohen's terminology, "pure" indicated a method of deriving knowledge solely from consciousness. It thus expresses the Marburg neo-Kantian idea that all knowledge

sought to carry out the implications of giving priority to activity over passivity, to the autonomous spirit over the sensual thing. Invoking the "given" was to be stopped; the grounding [of knowledge] in things was to be eliminated and replaced by a pure grounding of thought, of will, of the artistic and religious consciousness. Thus, Cohen's logic became a logic of origin. Metaphysical and religious thought invents the concept of creation, to refer all physical and natural being to an ultimate [and] primal spiritual ground. The philosophy of critical idealism thus establishes the concept and the postulate of the "origin" to anchor firmly all that we call existence, to fix unsteady Appearance firmly in everlasting Thought.[7]

This was the basic conviction that animated Cohen as a thinker. It also made him the great teacher that he was. For a great teacher can only be one who proceeds from autonomy of action and influences the autonomous action of another. Cohen had neither ambition nor any idiosyncratic urge to be an "original" at any cost. In the preface to *Kants Begründung der Ethik*[8] he argued in sharp and pithy language against being a philosopher detached from the great and constant history of philosophy as a whole, against philosophizing on one's own. And what freshness and vitality he was able to lend these historical connections. He took a kind of modest pride in considering himself to be a link in the great chain of philosophical idealism: in that golden chain that leads from Plato, by way of Descartes and Leibniz, to Kant. On the strength of this systematic connection the entire historical past became, to him, the immediate present. He never merely narrated the history of philosophy. He never rendered an account of it as if it belonged to an irrelevant past. On the contrary: he stood in the current of thought, examining and weighing, evaluating and taking his own positions. One could often disagree with his judgment, or even with his understanding and interpretation of the sources. However, there was one constant: in his presence

---

is "given" in consciousness; there is no Kantian "thing-in-itself" that is assumed as "given" and yet beyond the scope of reason.]

7. [Cassirer is invoking a well-known verse from the "Prologue in Heaven" in Goethe's *Faust*, Part One, in which God charges the angels with rendering the realm of appearances permanent and enduring: "Und was in schwankender Erscheinung schwebt, / Befestiget mit dauernden Gedanken! (And fix unsteady Appearance / firmly in everlasting Thought!)" (Johann Wolfgang von Goethe, *Goethe's sämmtliche* Werke [Stuttgart, Germany: Cotta, 1840, 11:17].

8. [Hermann Cohen, *Kants Begründung der Ethik*, 2nd ed. (Berlin: Bruno Cassirer, 1910), reprinted in *Werke* 2.]

one always gained insight into the enduring, grand motives that dominate the history of philosophy and constantly give it new strength. One could feel that Cohen did not just teach the history of philosophy; he was a part of this history himself. He represented its essence; he was its concrete, living embodiment. What he offered as a teacher were not bare dates and facts, to say nothing of mere general topics and terms—we believed we could sense the breath of the spirit itself out of which the great systems emerged and grew.

And yet even this effect of his seemed abstract when compared to another, that emanated from Hermann Cohen the human being. It revealed not only the most profound, but also the most tender, intimate, and kind aspect of his being. Whoever did not experience this side of him did not know him. His spirit was always directed toward the universal and the most universal of all,[9] yet he could also focus his warmth and sympathy on the most personal and individual detail. Only those knew him knew how this austere and unyielding thinker could become all compassion, patience, and kindness when concerning himself with individual human affairs. When he was defending his own position on an issue, he possessed unshakable faith, robust obstinacy, and grand self-confidence. And yet with what childlike modesty, with what touching reserve, with what gratitude he himself would accept even the slightest human gesture of concern. His thinking strove for the greatest heights. It touched upon the most remote problems still within the scope of human comprehension. But he was one of those rare human beings who also possessed love of and devotion to detail. His entire being was always ready to do battle, and as fate would have it, he had to do battle against narrow-mindedness and limits on intellectual freedom. And yet what an abundant need and capacity for love, what patience and indulgence for human frailty this man possessed alongside his passion for battle. Only when one combines these seeming contradictions, which in truth are contradictions only in the abstract, and not human contradictions, can one gain a clear picture of the personality of Hermann Cohen. The fact that this union of supreme objective and supreme personal qualities should now be dissolved is what stirs us so deeply at this hour of parting. We know that his work will remain what it is. Indeed, the further we probe into his work, the deeper it will draw us in to its riches. But our mourning for him, for the man himself, whom we loved for every individual utterance, can never and will never die out. Thus, as we face the body of the deceased, feelings unite and intermingle that, as in those words of

9. [That is, to the idea of God.]

Goethe's, are elicited both by the death of a youth and of an elderly man. This elderly man, now at peace, lies before us complete and finished, a splendid exemplar of humanity. Yet in spite of it all, we are seized and overcome by an unending longing for him. For in spite of his seventy years we still knew him as if he were a youth, and we loved him as a youth. What we cannot grasp and what we cannot yet understand is the fact that we can no longer touch his kind, fatherly hand, nor see the smile on his face, nor see that face suddenly light up with joy, nor hear the sonorous warmth of his voice.

And still we must not allow the pain of his loss to overwhelm us, for even our pain is just a shell that we must shed to arrive at a true, spiritual perception of his essence. The highest personal qualities and values, like the highest objective ones, are inextinguishable and indestructible. In the case of Hermann Cohen, that which truly moved us and affected us cannot perish. What Hermann Cohen has left to us, his pupils, is no mere aggregate of individual philosophical teachings or truths, no matter how significant. He himself never construed the effect of his work in this way. Indeed, he recently articulated this view by dedicating his book on "the concept of religion"[10] to "the Marburg school," for he regarded this school as an association for scholarly work and research that derived its coherence not from shared results, but from a common idealist[11] orientation in research and inquiry. Many of us may, while sharing in this particular orientation, arrive at results completely different from those of Cohen himself. But the bond that unites us with him will not, on those grounds, be diminished. In all the restlessness of seeking and in the joy of discovery, his image will be present before us; when we encounter doubts or inner difficulties, we will think we can hear him cheering us on, encouraging us. For his gift to us was the best that a teacher of philosophy can give to a student. He bequeathed to us no teachings or dogmas. Instead, he showed us by his example how a great man, working from the center of his being, could discover for himself—and open the way for others to discover—a new form of being and deeper, richer content in life.

10. [Cassirer is referring to Cohen's programmatic monograph *Der Begriff der Religion im System der Philosophie* (Giessen, Germany: Töpelmann, 1915).]

11. [The word in German is *ideel*, referring to German Idealism as a philosophical approach.]

8

Franz Rosenzweig: Introduction to the
Jewish Writings of Hermann Cohen (1924)

The Academy for the Academic Study of Judaism[1] has given a great gift to
German Jewry, to Jews throughout the world, and to many others of goodwill.
The gift—these three volumes—encompasses everything Hermann Cohen
ever wrote for publication dealing explicitly with Jewish questions and Jewish
topics. It does not include everything he ever said on the topic of Judaism, for
there is much more and much of consequence scattered throughout his other
works, some of it occasional in nature and some of it contained in more extensive discussions. Nor do these three volumes include letters, conversations,
and lectures—to the extent they are known—and what they could contribute
to the topic. Nor, of course, do they include the most important of all, his great
posthumous work, *The Religion of Reason out of the Sources of Judaism.*[2] The task of
this introduction arises from these three omissions. First, it is to depict the uni-

---

1. [Rosenzweig prefaces the notes to his introduction with the following comment:
"Aside from the present introduction, two essays by me have been published on Cohen: in
the [*Neue*] *Jüdische Monatshefte*, nos. 15–16 (1917–18): 376–378: 'Der Dozent: Eine persönliche
Erinnerung [The teacher: A personal reminiscence]' . . . and in *Jüdische Rundschau*, Hanuk-
kah issue 1921, 'Hermann Cohens Nachlaßwerk: Ein Brief' ["Hermann Cohen's posthumous book: A letter]." The Academy for the Academic Study of Judaism (Die Akademie
für die Wissenschaft des Judentums) acknowledged here was proposed by Rosenzweig in
an open letter to Cohen and then established by Cohen in 1918 for the primary purpose of
research. It was distinct from the Lehranstalt für die Wissenschaft des Judentums—the
Institute for the Academic Study of Judaism established in Berlin in 1872, originally called
the Hochschule für die Wissenschaft des Judentums, which, although founded primarily
as a research center, soon evolved into a seminary for aspiring rabbis and teachers. Permission to use the name *Hochschule*, which implies university-level status, was withdrawn
during the antisemitic agitation of the 1880s, restored during the Weimar period, and
revoked again by the Nazi regime, which forced the closure of the institution in 1942. For
Rosenzweig's open letter, "Zeit ist's," see Franz Rosenzweig, *Kleinere Schriften*, ed. Edith
Rosenzweig-Scheinmann (Berlin: Schocken, 1937), 56–78. For an English translation, see
"It Is Time: Concerning Jewish Education," in Franz Rosenzweig, *On Jewish Learning*, ed.
Nahum Norbert Glatzer (Madison: University of Wisconsin Press, 2002), 27–54. Rosen-
zweig gives his own account of his open letter in this selection.]
    2. [See selection 7n2.]

verse of Cohen's oeuvre, of which these Jewish writings are only a part. Second, the introduction must hazard an attempt, as best as it can, to render visible the figure of the personal demiurge behind this literary universe. For his life may come to be recognized as a life that, in its fateful progress, will seem more Jewish, and Jewish in a still deeper sense, than all its individual intellectual articulations. Finally, although this introduction can and may serve, in a broader sense, as an introduction to the reading of that classic posthumous work, it should not preempt but only anticipate the day when, on every bookshelf where these three volumes of *parerga* and *paralipomena* have found a place, Cohen's magnum opus will be found next to them. In accomplishing all this, and although it accomplishes all this, the introduction also seeks to help the reader tackle the double and seemingly contradictory difficulty in Cohen's style of thinking and writing: that the difficult appears more difficult and the simple appears simpler than it is. Surfaces obscure depths; depths lurk beneath the surfaces. They are joined in the unity of the man himself.

The German university, as it existed until the end of the war,[3] owed its significance to a unique combination of national and world-historical developments. As a thoroughly modern phenomenon, its significance is unparalleled in the other countries of our cultural sphere. The university in Berlin,[4] founded in 1811, gave institutional expression to this new type for the first time since the University of Jena put it on display for all to see during the last decade of the old century: it blossomed in splendor, but would soon wither and wilt. Perhaps Göttingen can be regarded as a precursor of this type into midcentury, and Halle for somewhat longer. However, at the beginning of the new century, the new spirit, the spirit of Jena, spread as its faculty dispersed, initially among the universities of the south, both to new institutions and to those experiencing a renaissance. Starting with the founding of the university in Berlin and into the two subsequent decades, the spirit of Jena extended to all German universities, lending enduring form to their intellectual physiognomy.

What, however, was the novelty that made the German professor of the nineteenth century distinct from both his predecessors in the eighteenth century and his counterparts beyond the German cultural sphere, distinct both in his

---

3. [World War I.]

4. [The university was established in 1810 (though Rosenzweig writes 1811) by Wilhelm von Humboldt (1767–1835) and was named Humboldt-Universität in 1949 after him and his brother, Alexander (1769–1859).]

own sense of himself and in the eyes of his fellow citizens? That is, how did he become the appointed[5] guardian, responsible for the soul of the nation, a sort of "philosopher-king" as in Plato's *Republic*? He was the teacher of the youth, who were preparing for careers and a livelihood, and who also liked to live it up when they could—after all, these are the sober quotidian facts of the academic profession, as they have been and remain, here and everywhere. How did the German professor come to have such a celebrated self-image? And how did it come about, just because the nation celebrated its professors with such respect, that his self-image took on the power to shape reality in turn? Around the year 1900 the status of the professor was still so specifically German that a German professor touring America felt compelled to explain to people that they should regard him not as a schoolmaster for nineteen-year-old boys, but as, well, in a word, a German professor.

The answer to this question was anticipated in the decisive position occupied by Jena in the historical process just described. In Jena of that decade, a unique convergence took place: a great moment in the history of thought that, by its nature, is always world-historical, and a great moment in the history of language that, by its nature, is always national-historical, like two clock bells in harmony, striking at the same hour. Plato was compelled to banish the great art of his nation from his perfect state; medieval thought, and even Renaissance thought, had to play itself out in the heavens of a lingua franca far above the living vernacular languages below. Even during the period just before the great moment in Jena, it was still possible that a Kant could write his aesthetics without knowing anything of importance about Goethe, and it was possible that Goethe could take his first tepid notice of the *Critique of [Pure] Reason*, published about a decade earlier, only after setting out for Italy. Only then could the world-historical miracle occur, initially in the encounter between Goethe and Schiller, and then in the profession of loyalty that Fichte and Schelling rendered to Goethe, accompanied by Schlegel's fanfare, and followed finally by Hegel who, in his profession of loyalty to the two great poets in turn, here as always had the last word: universal philosophy celebrated its reconciliation with national culture, while the language of the poets embodied the ideas of the thinkers. Thus came into being what is called "German Idealism," Germany's legal title to intellectual dominance, which it did in fact hold for the duration of the nineteenth century. Kant could not have wielded such power, nor Goethe before his encounter with

5. [University professors were paid by the government.]

Schiller, even if each of them, Kant and Goethe, taken in isolation, makes a more powerful impression on the mind than any of the later figures. It was only when the two streams issuing from these two men converged that the world power of the German spirit was established.

This convergence occurred in a university, not at a court. Weimar was once again no longer a "court." And not in a city; Jena was then less of a city than it is today. Rather, it occurred in a university. It was the first time since the age of Parisian High Scholasticism that creative philosophy found its place at a university. Even Kant did not believe that he should teach the best of his knowledge to his young students. Instead of teaching his own philosophy, he taught the very philosophy that he himself had overcome. Now, for a while, the professor of philosophy and the philosopher could be one and the same person—Schopenhauer's famous diatribe shows just how short a while it was.[6] It was out of the question, especially in philosophy, that this phenomenon could be widespread or long lasting. Yet it did serve to ennoble the profession as an entire class; it accomplished this in the way that a class ennobles itself, by increasing the demands that it makes of itself as well as the demands made of it by others. True, the German professor of the nineteenth century did not want to be a philosopher, yet he wanted to treat his subject philosophically, with the profound seriousness of philosophy. He too believed that his right to be a teacher was now predicated on his status as a scholar and thinker. Thus, men such as Ranke, Savigny, Grimm, and Helmholtz[7] assumed that empirical inquiry of the kind they conducted was itself philosophy. The profession as a whole and every member of it felt, on a small scale, what every one of those great thinkers felt on a large scale at the beginning of the century. One can hardly put it any other way; they felt they were intermediaries between the world spirit and their own nation, called to the task of interpreting for the latter the ways of the former, and of conveying the messages of the world spirit to their own nation.

6. [Rosenzweig is referring to Arthur Schopenhauer's, 1851 essay *Über die Universitäts-Philosophie* (On university philosophy), which is included in *Schopenhauer: Parerga and Paralipomena: Short Philosophical Essays*, ed. and trans. Sabine Roehr and Christopher Janaway (Cambridge: Cambridge University Press, 2016), 125–76.]

7. [Leopold von Ranke, a historian (1795–1886); Friedrich Karl von Savigny (1779–1861), a legal scholar and cofounder of the "historical school" of jurisprudence; Jacob Grimm (1785–1863), a linguist who, with his brother Wilhelm (1786–1859), compiled collections of folktales and music; Hermann von Helmholtz (1821–94), a polymath who made contributions especially to the fields of physiology and philosophy.]

This is the profession Hermann Cohen entered when, as the thirty-one-year-old son of the cantor and teacher of the Jewish community of the small city of Coswig in Anhalt, he completed his second dissertation in the winter semester of 1873.[8] He thus earned the right, as *Privatdozent*, to lecture in philosophy at Marburg. His earlier attempts to advance to *Privatdozent* in Berlin had failed, but honorably enough, on account of the bold originality of his first major work. On the basis of that same book, however, he was accepted in Marburg with unusual enthusiasm. After only half a year, the faculty nominated him alone for a chair (*Ordinarius*); three years later the position was his. What was it that affected Cohen's scholarly contemporaries so deeply that Friedrich Albert Lange,[9] after reading Cohen's first book, wrote to him: "You send us all back to the beginning!"? What was it that gave the young scholar such a proud launching into his academic career that even in his old age he would remember it as a "model in the history of academic appointments [*Habilitationen*]"?

The great systems had collapsed. But the empirical sciences were now set free, and, like all of culture at the time, were still trailing the strands of the unraveled twine that had once bound them all together. In part, philosophy withdrew to explore its own history, thus contenting itself with being one discipline among others. In part, where philosophy still presumed to have a task of its own, it sounded the call "Back to Kant!,"[10] but it understood this call only as a summons to critical deliberation, a call to clear away the systematic debris left scattered about by the post-Kantians. Philosophy was so ill equipped to deal with this situation that Schopenhauer, the latecomer to the post-Kantian movement, was

8. [The German academic career includes, after a candidate receives a doctorate degree, the writing of a second dissertation (called a *Habilitationsschrift*), on the strength of which the candidate may be granted permission to lecture (*venia legendi*) as a *Privatdozent* (that is, an unsalaried lecturer). The next stage would be appointment as an *Ordinarius* (that is, an "ordinary" professor).]

9. [Friedrich Albert Lange (1828–75), a philosopher and social reformer, was instrumental in bringing Cohen to Marburg and played a role in the beginning of the Marburg school. He wrote the classic *Geschichte des Materialismus und Kritik seiner Bedeutung in der Gegenwart* (Iserlohn, Germany: Baedecker, 1866), which went through no less than ten posthumous editions that, from sixth edition on, included Cohen's "Einleitung mit kritischem Nachtrag" (introduction and critical supplement). See n46.

10. [Nearly every chapter in the 1865 *Kant und die Epigonen* (Kant and the epigones) (reprint, Berlin: Reuther und Reichard, 1912), by Otto Liebmann (1840–1912), concludes with the refrain, "We must therefore return to Kant (Also muss auf Kant zurückgegangen werden)."]

able to celebrate his own triumph. Then Cohen's book appears, *Kant's Theory of Experience*,[11] apparently attempting to use philosophy to reassemble the disparate forces of the intellectual life of the university, all the while preserving contemporary trends in academic philosophy: the restoration of Kant and the study of the history of philosophy. Cohen opened a path forward, for himself and his contemporaries, by means of two discoveries: the first was his demonstration, bold and yet justified by the sources, that Plato's theory of ideas was itself critical idealism and that critical idealism was thus as old as philosophy itself. This discovery then developed in a natural way, leading Cohen to unfurl a presentation of the entire history of philosophy from this point forward. The other discovery was systematic, accomplished by means of an impressive deployment of Kantian philology: Cohen argued that the essence of Kant's critical method was not its "power to crush," but its "power to lay foundations."[12] In this view, Kant's only purpose in cautioning against exceeding the limits of experience was to bind philosophy all the more tightly to experience. Experience, meanwhile, was equated with science, a claim adequately supported by numerous passages in Kant himself. But as Cohen pursued his discovery further, experience came to encompass the whole range of human culture. It is clear that Cohen satisfied the demands of the times mentioned above. As a historian of philosophy and a Kantian he was the equal of any member of the academic guild; however, in the way that he was both of these and was thus in tune with the times, there was something more that propelled him—and his time—still further. Certainly, he was a historian of philosophy, but the history of philosophy of his design, despite his insistence that the philological "must always be squared away,"[13] was something fundamentally different from the history of philosophy to which his contemporaries aspired: to them, the history of philosophy consisted of a series of meticulous monographs on individual thinkers or, going a step further, on a succession of individual questions. Cohen's goal, however, was a history of philosophy that was no more and no less than a history of human reason as a unity,

11. [*Kants Theorie der Erfahrung* (Berlin: Dümmler, 1871).]

12. [The original is: "nicht ihre 'Zermalmungs'-, sondern ihre 'Grundlegungskräfte.'" Rosenzweig is echoing Moses Mendelssohn's epithet "der alles zermalmende Kant (the all-crushing Kant)" in his 1785 preface to *Morgenstunden oder Vorlesungen über das Daseyn Gottes*, in Moses Mendelssohn, *Gesammelte Schriften, Jubiläumsausgabe* 3.2, ed. Leo Strauss (*Schriften zur Philosophie und Ästhetik*) (Stuttgart-Bad Canstatt, Germany: Fromann, 1974), 3.]

13. See Robert Arnold Fritzsche, *Hermann Cohen aus persönlicher Erinnerung* (Berlin: Bruno Cassirer, 1920), 10.

and thus nothing other than what, according to Hegel, is the core of a system. Of course, Cohen was a Kantian. And although his Kantianism was consistent in its emphasis on the cautiousness of the critical approach—a cautiousness that Cohen too never abandoned—it was not at all an act of bittersweet resignation over his inability to ascend to the level of a system, as if a system were a fruit hanging high on a tall tree, out of reach. Cohen placed Kantianism on a trajectory to become a system, a system of culture, like the system that Hegel had finally just established. Cohen accomplished this by elaborating the positive element in Kant's concept of experience and then filling out the concept of experience thus defined with the world-historical experience of human culture.

He was thus the only member of his guild in those years to follow a path to a system. He did so both as a conscious opponent and as an unconscious successor to the great thinkers who, by combining Kant's thought and Goethe's life, created the cultural power of German Idealism at the beginning of the century, drawing especially on Hegel, who reverberates in Cohen's ideas again and again. The unconscious element gave him the strength to achieve this great task, yet his conscious rejection of German Idealism was justified. Hence it is not only that he never lost sight of the Kantian restraints that he, as well as his era, took as a point of departure; the goal of his thinking lay beyond the boundaries of the century that those thinkers had established, farther beyond than he could have known. Here, we are approaching the focal point of this discussion. Where did this man's thinking extend beyond his conscious and unconscious connections with the past, becoming creative in the highest sense of the word?

The titles of the three parts of Cohen's system have one term in common, seemingly clear, yet actually very difficult: "pure." When Cohen uses the word its meaning differs entirely from its meaning in Kant. Whereas for Kant pure reason is reason detached from experience, which therefore can be "critiqued," for Cohen pure cognition is cognition as it relates to experience. Cognition contains everything required, without remainder, for its own operation, in a structure regulated by laws. Or: whereas Kant's pure practical reason, detached from all internal and external conditions, sets forth the law of ethical action, Cohen's pure will is the ethical will, both the real will and the will that realizes, which is animated and sustained by all the ethical powers of the soul, by passion, and by "affect." Here, therefore, "pure" still means "pure of" something, but not, as in Kant, "pure" of all else. Here "pure" means "pure" only in the sense that it is pure of anything that would disrupt its properly regulated operation, which is the very purpose of purity. "Pure," in the Kantian sense, would be chemically pure alcohol, while "pure" in Cohen's sense would be pure wine, where purity consists of the properly regulated mixture of its ingredients.

This turn to the positive and concrete in the concept of purity is evident in the inscriptions over the portals to the edifice of Cohen's system; it then influences the architecture of the whole. Because of the systematic tendency of his thought, Cohen does not tire of hanging up the threads that bind together the three parts of the system, thus ensuring the mutual relationships among them. More than that, Cohen draws up plans for a cupola that will arc over the three parts of the system that were predefined for anyone succeeding Kant. The cupola was to be a psychology of cultural consciousness. As the fourth part of the system, it would encompass the whole. Moreover, it would overcome any unreality still adhering to the individual disciplines in spite of their connection to culture, just because and to the extent that they are still only individual disciplines, whereas the human being who lives in a culture is a unitary human being. Cohen's Hegelianism was unconscious and thus was really ingenious, unlike all the feeble attempts at a renewal of Hegelianism that had appeared in the preceding decades. This neo-Kantian's Hegelianism would have led, by means of such a psychology of the objective spirit, to a grand summation of the achievements of the nineteenth century, just as a grand summary of its preconditions was provided by Hegel at the beginning of the century. It would have, that is, if Cohen had ever written such a cupola. But he never did. It was replaced by another book instead. To be sure, the author was not conscious of this substitution, for he would speak of the book on psychology even in the final days of his life.[14] The book that replaced it, when viewed in the context of Cohen's life and destiny as a whole, would have ruptured the architectonic of Cohen's system were it not for some special contrivances that held it in check. It is a book that will live on, even when Cohen's system too will one day have gone the way of all systems: *The Religion of Reason out of the Sources of Judaism.*

As great as Cohen's philosophical oeuvre was—and in those years academic philosophy produced nothing that bears even a remote comparison—he was himself even greater than the sum of his works. His work gave form to the spirit of the century, the century of German Idealism, but was not consumed by it. Even if his oeuvre, like the crown of a tree, cast its shadow only over the space of a century, its roots extended deep into the ages. Seeking happiness in culture and in the this-worldly sphere—what the historian of contemporary Germany

14. As reported by Leo Rosenzweig.

called "the great idea of immanence"[15]—was the very fabric of this century. Although Cohen drank deeply from its spirit, he was never intoxicated by it. One could easily be tempted to ascribe this to what I have called the Kantian restraints that he never abandoned. But there were plenty of Kantians: why is it that their protests against the "great idea of immanence" never sound as if they actually come "from over there," from an actual, and therefore unmistakable "Over There"? This is the sound of Cohen's voice when, confronting all the magic of pantheism—no matter how spiritualized it may be—he asserts that there is one unique God, the origin of nature and of reason, beyond comparison to any creature. Cohen's voice also asserts, against all claims of culture, the inalienable right of the soul. Both of these ideas were given systematic form in Cohen's late works; they are the golden keys that alone grant access to the vaults of treasure that lie concealed beneath the rationalistic concepts of truth and of humankind visible on the surface. He was always in possession of these keys, even if at times they were misplaced. Whoever saw and heard him had to notice the depth behind his words. Cohen surrendered the keys to the world at large only in his old age, actually only after his death. His rationalism had no need to shun irrationalism, for reason itself was for him a miracle; his ethical system had no need to recognize individualism, for the humanity in which he believed grew in the soil of his soul.

It was, however, a long journey that led to this moment of self-discovery and self-revelation. And it was both, and yet more the latter than the former. It was a journey of completion and a journey of return and homecoming. The Talmud says of the penitent or the one who returns home—in Hebrew one word covers both—that he occupies a place in heaven that not even the completely righteous can attain.[16] At a banquet held in his honor during the remarkable journey to Russia that Cohen undertook just shy of his seventy-second birthday, a speaker called him a *"Ba'al Teshuvoh,"*[17] referring to Cohen's renewed attention

---

15. [The scholar of contemporary German history was Heinrich von Treitschke (1834–96), whose reputation was based on his five-volume *Deutsche Geschichte im neunzehnten Jahrhundert* (German history in the nineteenth century), (Leipzig, Germany: Hirzel, 1879–94). Rosenzweig attributes "the great idea of immanence" to Treitschke not only here, but also in his *Hegel und der Staat* (Hegel and the state) (Munich: Oldenbourg, 1920), 2:203. However, Rosenzweig gives no source, and the phrase does not appear in Treitschke's magnum opus. For these details we are indebted to Frederick Beiser.]

16. [*Babylonian Talmud*, Berachot 34b.]

17. [The Hebrew term (literally, one who returns) refers to one who returns to an

to his coreligionists. Cohen, with his fine ear for tone and subtlety, interjected loudly: "I have been a *Ba'al Teshuvoh* for the last thirty-four years!"[18] Thus, he dated the beginning of his "homecoming" to the moment when—in 1880—he wrote his "Confession on the Jewish Question,"[19] his intervention in the controversy of the day. By opening two fronts, against Treitschke[20] in one direction and Graetz[21] and Lazarus[22] in the other, he must have infuriated his own party more than his antisemitic opponent. He was aware, however, that at that moment in 1880 he had embarked on the very path that he was now still traveling. He saw the path as a unity. Thus, we too may treat it as such.

Hermann Cohen's youth overlapped with the most intellectually dynamic years of the emancipation of German Jewry. They began with the Berlin *Kulturverein* and Zunz's program for the academic study of Judaism (*Wissenschaft des Judentums*)[23] and extended from Hirsch's *Nineteen Letters*,[24] Geiger's early works, and Riesser's appearance on the scene to the systematic philosophies of religion offered by Steinheim, Samuel Hirsch, and Formstecher[25] and the

---

engaged Jewish life, incorporating the term *teshuvah* and thus connoting both "return" and "repentance."]

18. According to an oral account from Boris Pines.

19. JS 2:73–94 ["Ein Bekenntnis in der Judenfrage (A confession on the Jewish question)." In his introduction to Cohen's *Jewish Writings*, Rosenzweig noted in the margin the volume and page number of every text of Cohen's to which he was referring, weaving them into his biographical essay. These references are retained here in the form of footnotes. The title of each text has been added, in German and English.].

20. [Treitschke's 1879 "Unsere Aussichten (Our prospects)" unleashed the Berlin antisemitism controversy to which Cohen's "Confession" was a response.]

21. [Heinrich Graetz (1817–91), a historian and the author of the monumental eleven-volume *Geschichte der Juden* (History of the Jews) (Leipzig, Germany: Oskar Leiner, 1853–76).]

22. [Moritz Lazarus (1824–1903), a philosopher and psychologist.]

23. [*Kulturverein* is shorthand for the *Verein für Cultur und Wissenschaft der Juden* (the Society for the Culture and Critical Study of the Jews), founded in Berlin in 1919 by Leopold Zunz (1794–1886) and others. Zunz's "program" refers to his visionary 1818 essay, "Etwas über die rabbinische Literatur (On rabbinic literature)," which set forth in stunning breadth the outline of Jewish studies for generations to follow.]

24. [Samson Raphael Hirsch (1808–88), *Neunzehn Briefe über Judenthum* (Nineteen letters on Judaism) ed. Ben Usiel (Altona, Germany: Hammerich, 1836). Ben Usiel is Hirsch's pseudonym.]

25. [Abraham Geiger (1810–74), a leading thinker in the nascent Reform movement in Judaism; Gabriel Riesser (1806–63), a lawyer and judge who was active in the campaign for the emancipation of the Jews; Salomon Ludwig Steinheim (1789–1866), author of *Die*

rabbinical synods of the 1840s and 1850s. By around 1860 the movement had run its course. German Jewry, having achieved political emancipation, sank into a sated somnolence. In a physical sense, it was awakened by the new wave of antisemitism at the end of the 1870s. Intellectually, however, it would be awakened only by the Zionist movement of our own day. At the Breslau rabbinical seminary[26] Cohen would count among his teachers many of the leading minds of that lively period. He had attended secondary school (*Gymnasium*) until his sixteenth birthday and also acquired the fundamentals of a Talmudic education, including the philosophical works of Maimonides and Bahya. In the essay[27] that Cohen composed for the celebration of the fiftieth anniversary of the founding of the seminary he crafted a beautiful memorial to his teachers. In the famous controversy between the revered director of the seminary, Zacharias Frankel, and Samson Raphael Hirsch, Cohen intervened with a letter[28] in

---

Offenbarung nach dem Lehrbegriffe der Synagoge (Revelation according to the doctrine of the synagogue), (Frankfurt am Main: Siegmund Schmerber, 1835); Samuel Hirsch (1815–89), a rabbi, leader of the Reform movement in Germany and the United States, and author of the *Die Religionsphilosophie der Juden* (The philosophy of religion of the Jews) (Leipzig, Germany: Heinrich Hunger, 1842); Salomon Formstecher (1808–89), a rabbi, philosopher active in the Reform movement, and author of *Die Religion des Geistes—Wissenschaftliche Darstellung des Judentums nach seinem Charakter, Entwicklungsgang und Berufe in der Menschheit* [The religion of spirit: A scientific description of Judaism according to its character, development and vocation in humanity] (Frankfurt am Mein: J. C. Hermann, 1841).]

26. [The *Jüdisch-theologisches Seminar* (Jewish Theological Seminary) was founded in 1854 by Zacharias Frankel and led by him until his death in 1875.]

27. JS 2:418 ["Gruß der Pietät an das Breslauer Seminar (A pious salute to the Breslau seminary)].

28. Hirsch's interesting response can be found in the section "Letters to the Editor" of Hirsch's *Jeshurun* 5621 (1861), vol. 7, no. 5, p. 297f. [In *Jeshurun* the letter appears under the heading "Briefkasten der Redaktion (Editor's mailbox)"] The beginning is reproduced here:

To Mr. H. C. in B. The opinions expressed in your letter do such honor both to you and to your revered teacher that I do not hesitate to respond publicly.

It would indeed be terrible, if attacks such as those directed at the scholarly principles of your teacher in our last and in the present issue did not distress his students and friends. I have utmost respect for your sense of duty, that you felt compelled to testify, for my benefit, that your revered teacher lives in the traditional orthodox fashion, "stands in synagogue with the *talit* [prayer shawl] over his head, sings *zemiroth* [Sabbath songs] with you on Friday evenings, and even during a *shi'ur* [lesson] will, on occasion, fervently remark: here a *yerei shamayim* [a God-fearing man] has to be *mahmir* [stricter]!

which he sought to convince Hirsch of Frankel's piety. Hirsch then quoted and commented on a sentence from Cohen's letter in his own journal; thus, Cohen appeared in print for the first time, even if with no mention of his name. Cohen's encounter with Graetz, to which he alludes in the jubilee essay mentioned above, was not as naïve. Instead it was rather characteristic in its maturity.[29] The great historian, seeking to place figures of Jewish history in their respective eras, had presented a historically balanced characterization of David Kimchi[30] to his students. In so doing he had insulted this particular student, who had just arrived from his father's tutelage and whose traditional Jewish sensibilities were ahistorical, transcending history. Such a one does not go back to the past, but gathers the past into the present, so that "Rashi," "Rabe," "Rashbam," [and] "Ramban" are not Shlomo Yitzhaki, Abraham ibn Ezra, etc., who lived in this or that particular place and at this or that particular time. They are the illustrious company gathered on the page of the Pentateuch I have open before me for the purpose of explaining the page to me as a present-day reader. The young neophyte gave expression to his feeling of insult, asking with feigned uncertainty: "Herr Professor, are you referring perhaps to the world-renowned Radak?"[31]

This was the Cohen, half still a child, who had arrived at the seminary. Seven years later, his patron Steinthal[32] introduced the young doctor to the great Zunz with the following words: "Dr. Cohen, a former theologian, now a philosopher." Whereupon the acerbic elderly man immediately replied, "a former theologian

---

    I consider myself obligated, just as I acknowledged those attacks publicly, likewise to acknowledge publicly that your letter with contents as described above has reached me.

    However, you do not comprehend that this is not at all the matter under discussion. . . .

29. JS 2:420; JS 2: 453.

30. [David Kimḥi (ca. 1160–ca. 1235), a Provençale grammarian and exegete whose biblical commentaries are part of the traditional Jewish curriculum.]

31. According to an oral communication from Dr. Bruno Strauss. [Strauss (1889–1969) grew up in Marburg, where his father, Abraham, was a friend of Hermann Cohen's and a teacher at the Jewish school. After Cohen's death, Bruno Strauss edited *Religion of Reason out of the Sources of Judaism* for publication.]

32. [Heymann Steinthal (1823–99)—a professor in Berlin who, with his brother-in-law Moritz Lazarus, edited the *Zeitschrift für Sprachwissenschaft und Völkerpsychologie* (Journal for linguistics and ethnopsychology)—took an early interest in Cohen. Cohen published several articles in the *Zeitschrift*.]

is always a philosopher!"[33] Cohen himself would one day provide a living example of the reversal of this statement. Today there are numerous examples, but at the time Zunz's statement was correct. At the time Cohen really did feel as if he had escaped the life of a man of the cloth. What connected him with Judaism were the feelings of piety for a certain "ineffable kind of elevated mood"[34] that, even against our better knowledge, "inheres in the things among which we are raised" and the strong feelings of sentimentality that Cohen, self-critical as always, kept in check. Even Cohen, however, seems to have been overwhelmed by these moods while once in his parents' house on the holidays. (As his father grew older, Cohen took his place as cantor during the morning and the afternoon service on the "Long Day."[35]) But these were only moods. Even on such holidays, "through which the role models of our youth assume saintly status," he attributed these moods, almost anxiously, to the feeling of being in the circle of one's family. He once protested to an older married couple with whom he was friendly that at the Passover seder he felt nothing more than "the feelings of a son tenderly loved by his aging parents, nearing the age of thirty, sitting at their brightly lit table while holding his father's hand and, trembling with joy, shifts his gaze from his father to his mother and from his mother back to his father." It was made easier for him, he continued, because his father, "without any evidence of genuine Jewish sentiment," "would fly through the first part of the Haggadah in about twenty minutes." To judge the monstrous extent of the alienation evident in these words one must be familiar with the sequence of emotions, of laughter and tears, that fills the first part of the Haggadah. Cohen's soul thus still seemed to walk familiar paths, at times quite timid and shy or at times turning defiantly to say "e pur si muove."[36] But in spirit Cohen had left home and burned his bridges behind him.

33. As related by Cohen himself. I once asked Cohen about Zunz, for, although I am filled with inherited respect for him, I harbor my own doubts about the greatness—in the full sense of the term—of this man and scholar. He then gave a lengthy description of Zunz, consisting of pure antitheses—antitheses in value judgments!—of which I can remember only the last: "He could have been a great historian and yet was only a collector."

34. These words, and those immediately following, are taken from an as-yet-unpublished letter to Mr. and Mrs. Louis Lewandowski (Cohen's late parents-in-law) around Pesach 1872.

35. [The "Long Day" (*der lange Tag*) was, among German Jews, the common expression for Yom Kippur, the Day of Atonement, "long" because of its regimen of prayer and fasting beginning at sundown on the eve of Yom Kippur and continuing through sundown of the next day.]

36. In this paradoxical usage in a letter to Cohen's young friend, Hermann Lewandow-

Except for one. It is very telling which bridge it was. There is one component of Judaism that developed, remarkably, in two parallel tracks: First it manifested itself as a traditional Jewish idea, developing new forms of expression under the bright sky of the nineteenth century and within the sphere of German Judaism. But it also manifested itself outside of Judaism, through offshoots that emerged both from within Judaism and, like the first track, from within Judaism's German branch: this second track was socialism, and it developed into a deed of world-historical significance. More precisely, it was Cohen's messianic socialism, as an aggregate of the commandment to love one's neighbor and the demand for justice, the same socialism that Abraham Geiger and S. R. Hirsch, both at the same time, rediscovered as the legacy of Judaism, the same socialism that was at work as a latent motive in Lasalle and in Marx as well, but only to the extent that Marx was blessed with the gift of inconsistency. The two earliest essays in the present collection, the anonymous essay on Heine[37] of 1866 and the 1869 lecture on the Sabbath[38] are guided by Cohen's messianic socialism. He identified himself as a democrat and socialist to the end of this life. During the war of the 1870s[39] he was cosmopolitan and reserved, in contrast to Berthold Auerbach, but in agreement with Johann Jacoby,[40] both of whom were in the audience at Cohen's lecture on the Sabbath. He made his peace with Bismarck, but only conditionally: on the condition of securing democracy and socialism.

The essay on Heine frames the problem of Heine at the high level where it always belonged, while the lecture on the Sabbath frames its question in an unmethodical way. They both allow the deeply personal and humane roots of Cohen's socialism to shine through, and they both obscure these roots almost as much as they reveal them. This was and remained typical of Cohen as an author: in stating his thoughts he set them at a certain remove from the matrix of feeling where they arose. Was this due to his self-critical bashfulness about his

---

sky. [The words (meaning "and still, it moves")] were purportedly uttered by an obstinate Galileo Galilei (1564–1642), after he was forced to renounce his hypothesis that the earth revolved around the sun.]

37. JS 2:2–44 ["Heine und das Judentum (Heine and Judaism)"].

38. JS 2:45–59 ["Der Sabbat in seiner kulturgeschichtlichen Bedeutung (The Sabbath in its significance for the history of culture)].

39. According to letters to the Lewandowskis [sic].

40. [Berthold Auerbach (1812–82), a politically active German-Jewish writer; Johann Jacoby (1805–77), a doctor who was active in the causes of Jewish emancipation and liberal democracy.]

own "sentimentality"?[41] Was it his concern for the clarity of his own philosophical style? Whatever it was, fortunately he did not succeed in detaching thought from feeling. Yet he succeeded often enough that someone who did not know him personally might confuse the Cohen of the printed word with someone who speaks in abstract terms for lack of anything concrete to say. But to return to the socialism of his twenties: when Cohen was already seventy years old, he was visited in Berlin by a man who was also getting on in years, a well-known philanthropist. As a young doctor of philosophy Cohen had, for a time, served as the man's private tutor. In the course of their conversation the visitor told Cohen that he owed whatever he had become in life to an utterance of Cohen's. He was certain Cohen himself would have forgotten it. They had been strolling through the Tiergarten,[42] where Cohen occasionally conducted his lessons, when a vagrant approached, begging. "And you gave him a coin. I then asked: 'Doctor, why did you give that fellow anything at all? He'll just waste it on drink.' And you said: 'Silly boy, don't you ever like a little treat?!' Those words have remained with me for my entire life."[43] — This was Cohen's socialism.

To be sure, his socialism was lacking something quite essential before it could be called messianic socialism in the true sense, and in the sense in which Cohen, the mature Cohen, intended it. Both the essay and the lecture steer clear of God. The Heine essay takes a history-of-ideas approach, presenting Spinoza's pantheism as the mature fruit of an older Jewish monotheism; one may note that, at the time, Cohen, who would later be an ardent foe of any pantheism, still professed pantheism of a kind, even though he occasionally stresses that he is unwilling to commit to a position. It was not the pantheism of Spinoza, but a pantheism of mind, like that to which Heine subscribed, along with the entire Hegelian century. Against that backdrop the older monotheism was forced to recede to the childhood of world history. In the lecture on the Sabbath it is unsettling how Cohen adopts the impartiality of a history-of-religions approach, moving from Saturn to "Jehovah"—what angry words he later used, admittedly much later, when he lashed out at the misuse by biblical scholars of the appellation "Yahweh" to refer to the God of the Prophets and the Psalms![44] While invoking Saturn and Jehovah, the Sabbath lecture makes it abundantly clear that the speaker believes

41. In a letter to Hermann Lewandowsky.
42. [A park in the center of Berlin.]
43. Cohen's own account.
44. JS 1:206 [in the essay on "Gesinnung (Conscience)"].

no more in the one than in the other. He appears to be certain of his argument, as only a "former theologian" could be. As his studies of Kant progressed—after finishing the book on *Kant's Theory of Experience,* he moved on to *Kant's Grounding of Ethics*—he made a discovery about which he was himself astonished, reporting to the intimate friend of his youth:[45] he would "take along" the Kantian God, a position that, at the time, was generally held to be a mere concession in Kant's ethical system. Even more than that: he was now persuaded that any attempt at ethics would be vacuous and wanting in principle if carried out without such a God. In his next letter he had to protest that what he meant was not just "any edifying God" and that it had nothing whatsoever to do with common sentimentalism. On the contrary, he reports that, because of the so-called Rosh Hashanah mood—it was just the high holidays and he was at home in Coswig—it was impossible to work on these questions. To draw these exceedingly subtle distinctions and make them clear, one must be cool tempered and focused.

That was a year before Marburg. The importance of the event should be neither overestimated nor underestimated, and in the life of a philosopher it was certainly an event. Cohen's own timidly qualified report, which we already heard, protects us from the first of these two dangers—from overestimating the event's importance. However, our present day is much more susceptible to the danger of underestimating such experiences in the realm of thinking. On account of faith, feeling, and relationships, people act as if human thought is located on the moon and is not just as much a part of the human being as anything else. A healthy human being requires both: faith and thought. Where faith believes it can stake its claim without compelling thought to take cognizance of it, in the long term either faith will be paralyzed or thinking will atrophy. For the sake of the wholeness of the human being, therefore, faith and thinking may not be strangers to one another. Which of the two takes the first step may vary in individual situations; but a first step has to be taken. And here that is precisely what had occurred.

When he came to Marburg, he had that conversation with Friedrich Albert Lange, who had recruited him to come. He later described the conversation himself.[46] Lange asked, "On Christianity do our views differ?" Cohen replied, "No,

45. In letters to Hermann Lewandowsky around Rosh Hashanah 1872. [Published in Hermann Cohen, *Briefe,* ed. Bruno Strauss and Bertha Badt-Strauss (Berlin: Schocken, 1939), 42.]

46. In his "Einleitung mit kritischem Nachtrag [introduction with critical supplement]" to Lange's *Geschichte des Materialismus* [(history of materialism), 9th ed.] (Leipzig[, Germany:

for what you call Christianity, I call Prophetic Judaism." The author of *The Labor Question*[47] understood how the comment was meant; he was able to show Cohen the passages in the Prophets that he had underlined in his Bible. Cohen himself finished the story: thus, it was ethical socialism that united us in one fell swoop, overcoming religious barriers.

For the next seven years he was able to live and teach, firm in his belief in this accord. These were the years when Falk[48] was minister, but it was not only Falk who made it possible for Cohen to ascend to the rank of professor. The prevailing mood in educated Protestant circles in those years was favorable to Jews. Cohen himself, who owed his admission to the [German] nation to the liberal movement of his century, was a testimony to the amalgamation of the national and liberal will. And the Jews entered this newly accessible national community with open hearts. It was only during his Marburg years that Cohen too found his inner connection to the new empire [*Reich*]. During this period of civic peace, it was possible for his Judaism to retreat into the shadows, to be taken for granted and cultivated with pious loyalty. There was no need for Cohen to profess it in public. In a letter written sometime after his lecture on the Sabbath he expressed his intention to speak of these things "more often and more publicly," but during the ensuing decade he does not appear to have acted on this declaration of intent.

Judaism, however, must be professed, and when its children believe they are allowed to shirk this duty, what occurs is what the Talmud once said in response to the question whether salvation will occur at a predetermined time or only when Israel "repents":[49] The Holy One, Blessed be He, will set a harsh king over them and then they will repent.[50] Toward the end of the 1870s the new wave of antisemitism began, and in 1880 Cohen published the essay from which he later

---

Friedrich Brandstetter], 1914), 104. See also *JS* 2:197 [in the essay "Der Jude in der christlichen Kultur (The Jew in Christian culture)"].

47. [Friedrich Albert Lange, *Die Arbeiterfrage in ihrer Bedeutung für Gegenwart und Zukunft* (The labor question in its present and future significance) (reprint, Hildesheim, Germany: Olms, 1979).]

48. [Adalbert Falk (1827–1900). As *Kultusminister* (minister of education and culture) from 1872 to 1879, during Bismarck's *Kulturkampf* against the Vatican, Falk was responsible for the May Laws limiting the authority of the Catholic Church.]

49. [Cohen uses the German verb *umkehren* to indicate that he has the Hebrew *teshuvah* in mind. See note 17.]

50. [*Babylonian Talmud*, Tractate Sanhedrin 97b.]

dated the beginning of his own "return." It opens with the words: "so once again it has come to this: we must confess our faith and loyalty."[51]

The essay is a strange confession—and it is one of Cohen's most brilliant writings. It appeared with the same publisher that had, up to that point, published his philosophical books and is addressed equally to Christians and Jews. The voice of a philosopher at a Prussian university speaks through this essay. Moreover, because his essay on Heine was anonymous and because the lecture on the Sabbath was not yet in print, Cohen's "Confession on the Jewish Question" was the first occasion on which Cohen presented himself as a Jew to the wider public. What was the call to which he was responding? By then the antisemitic movement had been active for about two years. As long it was Stöcker's business, the liberal educated classes could believe that they did not need to take heed.[52] That changed when Treitschke intervened, the great national liberal historian and popular author: the movement now shed any restraining sense of shame, in Mommsen's pithy phrase.[53] Cohen had responded to Treitschke's first article, which appeared in the November issue of the *Prussian Yearbooks*, the journal that Treitschke himself edited. Cohen's response, in the middle of December, intended as an open letter to Treitschke, trembles with suppressed indignation, not just on the part of the Jew in Cohen, but also of the liberal German. But he also seeks understanding and, consistent with his whole position, expects to find it, for in the positive and the negative he is confident, as we are about to see, that he and his adversary are in broad agreement. Accordingly, Treitschke's reply was courteous but hardly touched upon the substance of Cohen's letter and pointed instead to the future discussion of the topic in the *Yearbooks*. And most importantly, he simply passed over Cohen's request that his letter be included in Treitschke's journal without a word. Cohen was enraged but responded on the very same day, subduing his anger, writing once again a lengthy letter that explained his first letter once again and closing with a forceful repetition of his request that his first letter be published in Treitschke's journal. It took Treitschke six weeks to decline this request. In place of a response Cohen found, in the January issue of the journal, what he must have taken as a malicious quotation from his last letter: "a Jewish colleague at a small university, however, a well-meaning man,

51. ["Ein Bekenntnis in der Judenfrage" (Confession on the Jewish question," JS 2:73.]
52. [Adolf Stöcker (1835–1909), a politically active Protestant theologian and Berlin preacher, was notorious for inciting antisemitism among the low and middle classes.]
53. [Theodor Mommsen (1817–1903) coined this phrase in his response to "Unsere Aussichten (Our prospects)," by Treitschke.]

has expressed to me his hope that the pejorative term Jew will cease entirely to be used and that, in the future, one will speak only of Israelites." Since his adversary denied him the platform Cohen had sought, he set about to publish his two letters[54] as a separate booklet, for it was precisely Treitschke's second essay, and the way he was quoted in it, that finally motivated Cohen to state explicitly what he actually considered pivotal in the discussion. For in the new article Treitschke had shifted the question from the domain of the politics of race, to which he had limited himself up to that point, to the domain of religion—animated perhaps by some allusive passages in Cohen's letters? Treitschke characterized Judaism as the national religion of an alien ethnicity (*Stamm*) that therefore has nothing to contribute to the German Christian on his path to a new "purer form of Christianity." The manner in which Cohen, in this booklet, mounts his defense allows us to see how much his thinking had matured since the pronouncements we just considered above.

Cohen probes the question at the deepest level, without a trace of petty denominational polemics or apologetics. He ferrets out the ultimate secrets of his opponent's stance, secrets that have apparently only now become clear to him, and produces a fittingly deep response. To be sure, the response neither satisfies his own side in the controversy, the side he sought to "defend," nor does it silence his opponent, who wanted only to tiptoe over these depths. That he was able to speak at all and to speak in this way was due to a decisive event in his development as a thinker: two ideas, that of the spirituality of God and that of the messianic promise, have coalesced: "the two grow out of one another." For Cohen the character of "Israelite monotheism" now emerges from these two ideas and the nexus they form. This is the monotheism he can profess. This confession of faith grants him the security he needs to accommodate his opponent to the extent that he does in his letters and that he reiterates, sometimes word for word, in his booklet. However, what is new, and what Cohen only touched upon in the letters, is the theological and world-historical context of the problem that he now elaborates. From the perspective of cultural history the significance of Christianity consists of this: by providing a dogmatic cloak for the humanization of God it humanized religion for humanity and thus laid the foundation of the modern "idea of moral autonomy" as it took shape especially in the German

54. The two letters to Treitschke, the drafts, and Treitschke's responses are in the possession of Mrs. Cohen [Frau Geheimrat (Privy Councilor) Cohen]. [Martha Cohen's personal papers were lost when she was deported to Theresienstadt in 1942.]

Reformation and in the philosophy of Kant. At the hand of Hegel and his school, this nexus of ideas, world historical in its significance, becomes the common property of German culture and thus influences Cohen. Seen in this context, all modern Jews, and German Jews in particular, are Protestants. However, to the extent that a kernel of the ancient God of the prophets must always resist being rendered human—"To whom, then, can you liken Me? To whom can I be compared?"[55]—to the same extent, "all Christians" are also "Israelites."

Thus, the common religious life that Treitschke demands for the sake of national unity is already present. Cohen adds—in a thoroughgoing polemic against Lazarus—that such a demand is both possible and necessary. The common religious life can then grow steadily in mutual give-and-take. As in the letter he wrote for the *Yearbooks*, he addresses his fellow Jews, reminding the Orthodox of the very fact of this unity and reminding liberal Jews of the fact that this unity must be religious in nature. He abandons Graetz, the target of Treitschke's attack, as he had already done in the letters. He has nothing in common with Jewish nationalism. And as for Treitschke, although Cohen had initially seemed to be seeking an understanding with him, even in the booklet, following the example of the letters, in the end he settles his accounts with Treitschke too. For behind Treitschke's demand that Jews become German—a demand that Cohen accepts, emphatically, only in the form of a demand *to be* German—he now discovers the demand that he undergo a political baptism as well. Out of a sense of religious indignation, he rejects this demand, not only as a Jew, but also for the sake of the state, the nation, and even for the sake of Christianity itself.

In all this he had marked out a road from which he never had to deviate. Up to the end of his life he liked to recall the Catholic colleague who, in 1883, sought his advice, asking his thoughts about attending the Luther ceremony at the university.[56] Cohen responded: "If I didn't go, who should then?"[57] However, along some stretches of the road, due to the all too straight consistency of his thinking, he was unable to make it around the curve. In the essay at hand that occurs primarily when he treats the problem of race. He seeks, at a minimum, to bring the problem closer to resolution, along with the central problem of religion. Here too, as in his first letter, he makes a concession to Treitschke the patriot—again differing with Lazarus and departing from then-dominant political theory: he

55. [Isa. 40:25.]
56. [The year was the four hundredth anniversary of Martin Luther's birth.]
57. Cohen's account, as told to my mother in September 1917.

concedes that Treitschke is right to strive for a representation of "the racial type of his people that shows it in its most glorious realization." Cohen asks only for a bit of "patience"—it is not necessary that one day a wiser man appear to decide this case.[58] Neither Cohen's approval, in principle, of mixed marriages [between Christians and Jews] nor his recommendation to shift the Sabbath to Sunday, as the national day of rest, were intended as a forfeiture of religious particularity. He made the latter recommendation in the "Afterword" to his old lecture on the Sabbath, published at long last in the following year.[59] His approval was an implicit consequence of the fundamental principle of the "Confession," but the sort of straightforward consequence that is oblivious to the fact that Judaism, as a minority religion, cannot afford to draw all the possible consequences of any particular extreme standpoint—not only Cohen's standpoint, but also any other possible standpoint. Cohen himself later abandoned these two perilous consequences, one of them without a word and the other explicitly.[60] However, these two proposals[61] heightened the risk of misinterpretation to which the essay was already exposed on account of its bold and peculiar discussion of the relationship between Judaism and Christianity. These proposals are also partly responsible for the fact that the essay did not enjoy the success in Jewish circles that it otherwise might have. Without these proposals the main idea could not have been as easily misconstrued. To be sure, Treitschke and his ilk were, in general, quite satisfied, and Treitschke himself, in the February issue of the *Yearbooks*, referred to Cohen's essay as the most profound, warmest, and most thoughtful response. Although it contained many misunderstandings, Treitschke wrote, he was nevertheless in agreement with many of its essential points. He expressed the wish that German Jewry would take to heart these warm and urgent admonitions offered up by a sensible coreligionist. German Jewry itself, however,

58. [Rosenzweig invokes—and negates—the words of the judge in the "parable of the three rings" in act 3, scene 7, of *Nathan the Wise*, intended to defer to the far distant future any judgment about the superiority of one religion over another: "I bid you, in a thousand years, / To stand again before this seat. For then / A wiser man than I will sit as judge / Upon this bench, and speak" (Gotthold Ephraim Lessing, *Nathan the Wise*, trans. Bayard Quincy Morgan, 13th printing (New York: Continuum, 1989), 80).

59. JS 2:66 ["Nachwort (aus dem Jahre 1880) (Epilogue [from the year 1880])].

60. Compare the note on the lecture on the Sabbath (JS 2:469) and especially his posthumously published book. [Rosenzweig is referring to the source notes in JS by the editor, Bruno Strauss, who gives an account of Cohen's change of heart on moving the Sabbath from Saturday to Sunday.]

61. [That is, to condone mixed marriages and to move the Sabbath to Sunday.]

was unanimous, all its factions, in its rejection of an advocate who appeared to be joining their opponent, arguing his cause. In the February following the publication of the "Confession" a hailstorm of letters of denunciation from old friends[62] descended upon the "confessor" who, in Marburg, secluded from the world, had hardly anticipated the effect of his "Confession." The month after the excitement of the correspondence with Treitschke was difficult. Cohen did write one rejoinder to a response published by an old companion from his years in Breslau, Rabbi Moses, who had ended up in the United States.[63] He sought to explain, hoping to win some understanding for his essay, which he conceived of as both a "polemic and a bid for peace,"[64] all the while holding fast to his position.

Like the letter on the essay on the Sabbath mentioned above, this "Defense" would lead one to expect that Cohen would repeat the core idea of the "Confession" in a multitude of other forms. However, if one scans the list of his *Jewish Writings*[65] after these publications starting in 1880–81, there is nothing until 1888: the expert testimony he submitted in Marburg on the Talmud,[66] combining, in an extraordinary way, both his philosophical profundity and his apologetic power. Most of the essays that follow thereafter, from the end of the century on, are occasional writings, first in intervals of several years, and then ever more frequently. However, he wanted to say it "in a multitude of other forms." Hence, we are allowed to search elsewhere as well. The period from 1883 to 1912, the span of a generation, saw the publication of Cohen's own system. It began with his propaedeutic work on infinitesimal calculus.[67] The book was of epochal biographical significance, a fact brought home to Cohen himself by the painful experience of observing the sluggish progress of his oldest student, Stadler.[68]

62. His friendship with Steinthal also broke off over the "Confession."

63. JS 2:95, "Prof. Dr. Hermann Cohen in Marburg und sein Bekenntnis in der Judenfrage. Eine Reminiszenz und Kritik von Rabbiner Adolf Moses, Mobile, Alabama," *Zeitgeist* (Milwaukee, Wisc: 1880). [*Zeitgeist* was a German-language periodical published in Milwaukee. Rabbi Moses's critique appeared in the issue of August 5, 1880, 256–57.]

64. Cohen's phrase, describing his essay, in a letter from January 1880.

65. [Rosenzweig is inviting the reader to scan the chronological list of Cohen's "Jewish Writings" that precedes his introduction in volume one of the three-volume 1924 edition. See JS 1:ix–x.]

66. JS 1:145–74 ["Die Nächstenliebe im Talmud (Love of neighbor in the Talmud)"].

67. [*Das Princip der Infinitesimal-Methode und seine Geschichte. Ein Kapitel zur Grundlegung der Erkenntniskritik* (The principle of the infinitesimal method and its history. a contribution toward the foundation of the critique of cognition) (Berlin: Dümmler, 1883).]

68. [August Stadler (1850–1910), a philosopher and Kant scholar at the Polytechnikum

Cohen's system concluded with the publication of the *Aesthetics*, the significance of which was likewise epochal and, in retrospect, obvious, in that he left the university that very year and relocated to Berlin. And in response to a letter from the Frankfurt Lodge, congratulating him on the completion of *Ethics of Pure Will*, he expresses his sense of good fortune at the opportunity to present his concept of Judaism within a philosophical system before producing works of greater length on this subject. Cohen continues that, in his Jewish thinking, he has relied for guidance not on his instinctual sense of attachment to religion and tribe, but only on philosophical method and historical verification: "My Judaism is situated in the context of my philosophical insights."[69] Thus, we may venture to present the substance of those texts in these three volumes[70] that are drawn from the period of Cohen's mature thought—the period that usually comes to mind when Cohen's name is mentioned—in the context of his system, and especially of the *Ethics*.

The idea of God, which was the source of the penetrating power of the "Confession" of 1880,[71] is located at the epicenter of all these Jewish writings. Where, however, is it located in the system? Not at the epicenter, for the epicenter is occupied by reason, just as in the great idealistic systems of the beginning of the century. Cohen is prevented from identifying God with reason, as these idealists did, by two factors: one is his Kantian sense of truth. For in this regard Kant is still the great teacher of thought and thinking: from Kant, thinking can always learn and learn again that it should not always allow itself to be propelled by its own momentum. It should also honor the realities of truth when they bid it to halt its flight. The second factor is his Jewish knowledge of God, that God cannot be "identified." If, then, God is not the epicenter of the system and cannot be the "foundation," what then is he? Cohen had not simply "taken along" the Kantian God at the age of thirty, without further ado. To his own astonishment, he was

---

in Zurich. The context of Rosenzweig's observation is not clear. For the correspondence between Cohen and Stadler, see *Hermann Cohen: Briefe an August Stadler*, ed. Hartwig Wiedebach (Basel, Switzerland: Schwabe, 2015).]

69. ["Im Zusammenhang meiner wissenschaftlichen Einsichten steht mein Judentum."] This response, dated December 11, 1904, was published along with the letter from the lodge in the "Report of the Great Lodge for Germany U.O.B.B" (*Unabhängiger Orden Bne Briss*) of February 1905, no. 2. [Rosenzweig presents the full text of Cohen's response (not included here) in the notes to his introduction (see JS 1:333).]

70. [Of JS.]

71. ["Ein Bekenntnis in der Judenfrage," JS 2:73–92.]

compelled to recognize the Kantian God as a requirement of any philosophical ethics. Kant "postulated" God for the sake of guaranteeing the harmony of virtue and felicity, which could not be insured in any other way. This was a concession to the sentimental eudaimonism of the time that Cohen certainly could not repeat; it encompassed, at best, only a small part of the meaning of trust in God. Hence, this postulate served only as an ornament in Kant's ethics, and not as a structurally necessary part of the edifice. With Cohen it is otherwise. His idea of God is the keystone, provided by ethics. Without it the entire vault of the system would collapse. What trust in God means, when taken to its final consequences, is actually translated here into the fresco terminology of a philosophical system: God guarantees the realization of ethics, the ethical transformation of nature. Without God, ethics would be just a beautiful thought, a mere utopia. And without God, nature would have reality, yes, but not truth. The "basic law of truth" in this system denotes not the concluding chapter of the *Logic*, but the opening chapter of the *Ethics*![72] The idea of God functions as the "keystone" of the system, in a dual role as guarantor, supporting the forces of cognition seeking truth as well as the forces of the will seeking realization.

Even in the circles of those who believed themselves to be close to Cohen, the idea of God was understood such that God was therefore "just an idea," as if what the prophets and psalmists said to and about their God was only a "poetic expression" of the position adumbrated above. No greater misinterpretation is possible, neither of the thinker nor of his thought. Quite apart from the fact that for Cohen an idea is not "just an idea," God himself is no more a "poetic expression" for the *idea* of God than the fact of mathematical natural science is a poetic expression for the logic of pure cognition. Cohen's philosophy always scrupulously avoids identifying with its objects, although it acknowledges its relation to an object at every stage. The sublation (*Aufhebung*) of an object into its philosophical idea—that interpretation may apply to Hegel, but not to Cohen. The word "idea" indicates what kind of philosophical statements can be made about God; it indicates therefore that one can neither describe, measure, nor comprehend God. For an idea is neither a thing, nor a relation defined by laws, nor a concept. However, one can say what would not exist were it not for God, or put another way, what it is for which God "lays the ground." To give an account of such "ground layings" is, to Cohen, to give an exhaustive account

72. [Rosenzweig is referring to the first chapter of *Ethics of Pure Will*, titled "The Basic Law of Truth" (Das Grundgesetz der Wahrheit).]

of the content of an idea. By giving an account of its content, however, one is not finished with an idea. On the contrary: now begins what Cohen called its inexhaustible fertility.[73] To be sure, philosophy can identify such "fertility" in individual examples, but only as a fact.

For Cohen, "fact" was powerful. Occasionally it could erupt with volcanic force through the veil of his philosophical jargon. One just has to be able to read Cohen as if listening to him. His speech possessed an astonishing musical expressiveness. He once told me the story of a Protestant professor of theology in Berlin who had attempted to persuade him that there is a kind of devotion to God that grows only out of one's relationship to Christ. "What?? I said,—the Eternal is my shepherd; I shall not want!" I can still hear him today, as if he had just spoken, that thundering "What??," the faint emphasis on the "Eternal," and the triumphant "I shall not want!" pronounced as if one word.

What is it that God "guarantees"? The realization of the ideal. The term "ideal" indicates the other, older focal point of his Judaism, from an earlier period of his biography, as we know. The ideal is the goal of historical development, to be realized for the most part in the state. In assigning such a central role to the state on the one hand, and in orienting himself toward social justice and the idea of a league of nations on the other, Cohen is again the successor both of Kant and of Kant's great idealist followers. Cohen would group these notions together under the term humanity; for him the ideal of humanity would be fulfilled when the state was ordered, internally, in accord with social justice and directed, externally, toward the unification of humanity under international law. Humanity can thus be realized only in a state and nowhere else, not, for example, in the organizations of the church, which address humankind without intermediary. Although the state is an individual state, it is in essence a totality, because it addresses the human being as an ethical being. The churches, however, although they are also universal, are only pluralities because they conceive of human beings only in their limited status as members of a religious denomination. Ethical culture reaches its peak in the human being conceived of as a member of humanity and as a member of a state, where both are understood strictly as tasks to be realized in the eternity of ethical progress, and yet are never fully realized.

73. [Rosenzweig may have Cohen's essay on "The Idea of the Messiah" ("Die Messiasidee," JS 1:105–24) in mind, where Cohen proclaims that the universal acknowledgment of the one God would demonstrate the "inexhaustible and indestructible fertility" of the idea of the Messiah (119).]

Humankind owes this zenith of ethical culture and its ultimate foundation to monotheistic religion and prophetic Judaism.

Now here too it is necessary to guard against a misinterpretation, or actually a "hearing impairment," that any brief presentation—including this one—will inevitably bring about. Even Cohen's own presentations, especially when they are short and formulaic, may lead to misinterpretation, as if what is under discussion here were the concept of progress, which the literary youth of our day cannot mention without adding the epithet "dreary." But the issue is not quite that simple. Whoever reads the brilliant chapter on "The Ideal" in *Ethics of Pure Will*[74] will find the most profound response possible to that "dreary" concept of progress in Cohen's exposition of the concept of eternity. And one will then see that, for Cohen, eternity is a very fertile concept, without which human life would be dreary indeed. For Cohen, eternity is not the sum of all time. It was Cohen who, in his *Logic of Pure Cognition*, defined time in such a way that it precludes any such summing up. What constitutes time is the future. Eternity is the most distant future, related to the moment, the distant future "realized" in the "acorn" of the moment. This is not some sort of pedantic accounting of the "progress of civilization."[75] It is, instead, the fervent advance of the will toward realization. For Cohen what is at stake in all these considerations is realization. That is the reason for his struggle against anything that might distract humankind from the will to action, the reason for his struggle against all quietism, even if it appears in the garb of religious hope for immortality. Hence, this is also the reason for his determined appeal to the state as the visible, public site of the testing of morality. In the anthology published on the occasion of the seven-hundredth anniversary of Maimonides's death, Cohen devoted a comprehensive "Characterization" to Maimonides's ethics.[76] He regarded Maimonides as his predecessor, a potential ally in refining the concept of God into an idea and also in distilling from messianic prophesy its exclusively this-worldly, political character, distinguishing it sharply from the hope for immortality. As an ethicist he withholds his loyalty from the prophets, granting them his loyalty only as aestheticist, where the prophetic hope for the future fades into "mythological" images of nature at peace; the ethical struggle must never cease. No, although the present may never measure up, the ideal should not therefore be postponed

74. [Chapter 8.]

75. [Rosenzweig uses the English phrase "progresses [sic] of civilization" in the original.]

76. JS 3:221–89 ["Charakteristik der Ethik Maimunis"].

into the misty future. On the contrary, for that very reason it must be planted in the present. With this kind of ardor in his soul, Cohen witnessed the great Jewish event of the turn of the century, the Dreyfus Affair. In two remarkable essays he instructed his coreligionists to experience the event "as redemption."[77] At the time he was in high spirits, as he always was whenever it was possible to construe events as the birth pangs of the messiah. This was reported by his friend from Giessen, who knew him well in those years and whose book, "Reminiscences of Hermann Cohen," is a pearl among the literature on Cohen.[78] His "messianism" was certainly not an excuse for inactivity, deferring the goal into an infinite future while we settle into a finite life of aimless comfort. He always held out hope for salvation "speedily and in our time." Such hope was the bedrock from which Cohen the logician and ethicist mined his concepts of time and eternity. Elsewhere[79] I have recounted the conversation in which he said he believed that he would yet experience the advent of the messianic unification of religions, thus silencing my own meek doubts.

In chapters 8 and 9 of *Ethics of Pure Will* Cohen integrated messianism and monotheism into his system of philosophy. This did not signify, as one might believe, a concession to religion. It was consistent with the trend toward rendering religion superfluous once and for all, as with the great idealist philosophers of the beginning of the century, only here it was more explicit. We will address this more thoroughly later; here it has to be mentioned only so that it can be understood that from these two vantage points it is possible to survey the entire range of Cohen's Jewish writings during this period. To this extent, toward the beginning of this period nothing had changed. What is significant is the very fact that he now fulfilled, in magnificent form, the promise he had made in the essay "In Defense"[80] of 1881: for the first time in a universal system of philoso-

77. JS 2:346–51 ["Unsere Ehrenpflicht gegen Dreyfus (Our debt of honor to Dreyfus)"; 2:352–59 ["Der geschichtliche Sinn des Abschlusses der Dreyfus-Affäre (The historical meaning of the conclusion of the Dreyfus Affair). Cohen homiletically compares Dreyfus's release with the liberation of the Israelites from Egypt, both being manifestations of redemption (JS 2:346).]

78. The "friend from Giessen" refers to Robert Arnold Fritzsche, author of the small book cited above [n13].

79. In my *Judah Halevi*, 159f. [Rosenzweig is referring to the first edition of his annotated translations of the poetry of Judah Halevi. In the second edition, *Jehuda Halevi: Zweiundneunzig Hymnen und Gedichte*, trans. and ed. Franz Rosenzweig (Berlin: Lambert Schneider, n.d.), the anecdote is related on 239.]

80. "Zur Verteidigung," JS 2:95–100.

phy, the elements of philosophy of religion were oriented on the Jewish concept of religion. This fact made an impression on both friend and foe. Here Judaism was registering a claim, loud and clear, that it had something more to say to the world. Cohen himself was led further, step by step, by the consequences of this fact. The moment when religious community would be supplanted by the philosophical and ethical concept of humanity was still far in the distance. The night was not yet over; indeed, antisemitism in all its forms was the symptom both of the ongoing night of world history and of the continuing necessity of our distinct existence. What was it, then, in his "Confession" that was so confusing, even for those who were close to him and to his views? It was, in addition to his views on the nexus of politics and religion, the appearance that the author of the "Confession," out of a desire for reconciliation, neglected to stress the differences that set Judaism and Christianity apart. The essays of the period we are now considering, however, would give no more support to this criticism. Thus, in the second half of this period, Cohen gradually became the trusty Eckart[81] of German Judaism, making his voice heard both intramurally and in public, in public for purposes of defense, and intramurally to give counsel, to admonish, and to teach. Counsel and admonishment coalesce into a Jewish deed in the founding of the Marburg Home for Students and Apprentices,[82] which he conceived of as a paradigm and in a broad context—as is evident in his "Two Proposals for Securing our Future" of 1907.[83] Counsel and admonishment also coalesce in his work on behalf of the establishment of the Society for the Advancement of the Academic Study of Judaism[84] as well as in his successful advocacy for creating professorships specializing not in Arabic, but in Jewish philosophy of religion.[85] Cohen the teacher is never silent and always offers glimpses into the deeper context of the topic at hand. But in some of the longer essays, above all in the essay

81. ["Trusty Eckart (Der getreue Eckart)" is the title of a ballad by Goethe that is invoked here because the magical figure of Eckart protects a group of children from harm on a nocturnal errand and also from a scolding after their return home.]

82. JS 2:102–7 ["Die Sprüche im Israelitischen Schüler- und Lehrlingsheim zu Marburg a.L. (The inscriptions in the Israelite Home for Students and Apprentices in Marburg an der Lahn)].

83. JS 2:133–41 ["Zwei Vorschläge zur Sicherung unseres Fortbestandes"].

84. [Gesellschaft zur Förderung der Wissenschaft des Judentums.]

85. JS 2:108–25 ["Die Errichtung von Lehrstühlen für Ethik und Religionsphilosophie an den jüdisch-theologischen Lehranstalten (The establishment of professorships for ethics and philosophy of religion at academies for Jewish theology)"].

on "Religion and Ethics" of 1907[86] and as early as 1900 in the particularly beautiful and forward-looking essay on "Love and Justice in the Concepts of God and Man,"[87] his teaching begins to assume the form of the systematic sketch of his philosophy of religion,[88] which then turns out, in content, to be just the execution of the basic plan outlined in the ethics. Cohen once outlined a brief essay on method in self-defense,[89] half serious and half mocking.[90] But the topic of self-defense frequently appears in conjunction with those other elements, admonishment and instruction, as in his powerful reprimand to Noeldeke,[91] lending greater emphasis to the former and greater relevance to the latter, while itself drawing strength from admonishment and depth from instruction.

From a biographical perspective, the particular quality of this period—what it was and what, though latent, yet promised to emerge from it—could be discerned from that magnificent critical discussion in which Cohen, as scholars are wont to do, was anticipating his own path forward as he then envisioned it: that critical discussion is his devastating review of the first volume of Lazarus's *Ethics of Judaism*[92] in the *Monatsschrift für die Geschichte und Wissenschaft des Judentums* in 1899. Cohen is not able to do justice to the merit of Lazarus's book, Lazarus's attempt to feel his way toward what we nowadays understand to be sociology of religion. To Cohen that tendency appears to be nothing more than an effort to court vulgar popularity. However it is noteworthy that, in this essay, he out-

---

86. JS 3:98–168 ["Religion und Sittlichkeit"].

87. JS 3:43–97 ["Liebe und Gerechtigkeit in den Begriffen Gott und Mensch." English translations of this and other essays by Cohen on the love of neighbor are being prepared by Dana Hollander of McMaster University.]

88. [An allusion to Cohen's 1915 BR.]

89. [That is, against antisemitism.]

90. JS 2:360–68 ["Über die literarische Behandlung unserer Gegner (On the literary treatment of our adversaries)"].

91. JS 2:369–77 ["Das Urteil des Herrn Professor Theodor Nöldeke über die Existenzberechtigung des Judentums (Professor Theodor Nöldeke's judgment on the justification for the existence of Judaism)"]. [Nöldeke (1836–1930) was a German Orientalist and an authority on the Koran, comparative Semitic philology, biblical religion, and early Judaism.]

92. [*Moritz Lazarus, Ethik des Judentums*, vols. 1 and 2 (Frankfurt am Main: Kauffmann, 1898 and 1911). For an English translation see Moritz Lazarus, *The Ethics of Judaism*, trans. Henrietta Szold, *The Ethics of Judaism*, (Philadelphia: Jewish Publication Society of America, 1900–1901). For Cohen's critique ("Das Problem der jüdischen Sittenlehre: Eine Kritik von Lazarus' *Ethik des Judentums* (The problem of Jewish ethics: a critique of Lazarus's ethics of Judaism)" see JS 3:1–35.]

lines the program for the future scholar of Jewish philosophy of religion, which had lain fallow for fifty years. To Cohen, it must have seemed that Lazarus had selected his sources randomly, that he had deliberately demoted the status of our medieval Jewish thinkers, and that he had attempted, though without success, to sever the connection [of Judaism] with the philosophical culture of the world. By contrast, Cohen will construct his own work on a "foundation of historical research into the sources, including our dogmatic literature, aware that the sources are universally bound up in a living nexus with systematic philosophy."[93] Just a year later, in his long essay on love and justice,[94] he made his first attempt at carrying out this plan.

His engagement on behalf of Judaism reached its pinnacle, on the intramural front, in his speech at the conference of the Association of German Jews in 1907,[95] and, for an external audience, at the World Congress for Free Christianity and Religious Progress in 1910 in Berlin.[96] Seen in context, however, his engagement in Jewish affairs constituted but a small part of the work of the Marburg professor. Toward the end of this period, in 1911, Cohen himself articulated his position in the memorial volume for Ludwig Philippson:[97] the German Jew has a duty to undertake a division of labor between one's labor on behalf of German culture, free of reservations or extraneous motives, and labor on behalf of the future of his Jewish prophetic religious life. Only such a division of labor "is what grants our minds true unity and, indeed, gives our spirit its natural orientation and focus in life."[98] Cohen lived his life true to these words. They also indicate an unmistakable shift in accent when compared to the connection he presented in his 1904 letter of thanks to the Frankfurt Lodge,[99] not without a certain anxiety in the face of "his own sentimentality." It is a result of the weighty circumstances,

93. [The closing words of Cohen's critique of Lazarus, JS 1: 35.]

94. JS 3:43–97 ["Liebe und Gerechtigkeit in den Begriffen Gott und Mensch (Love and justice in the concepts of God and man)"].

95. JS 1:1–17 ["Religiöse Postulate (Religious postulates)"].

96. JS 1:18–35 [Selection 5. Although Cohen refers to the conference as "Der Weltkongreß für religiösen Fortschritt (The world congress for religious progress)," its full name was "Der Weltkongreß für freies Christentum und religiösen Fortschritt (The world congress for free Christianity and religious progress)."].

97. JS 2:439–45 ["Über die Bedeutung einer philosophischen Jugendschrift Ludwig Philippsons (On the significance of an early philosophical work by Ludwig Philippson)"].

98. [JS 2:444.]

99. JS 1:332–33 ["Antwort auf ein Glückwunschschreiben der Fankfurtloge (Response to a letter of congratulations from the Frankfurt Lodge)"].

however, that this harmony and equilibrium held sway really only in his psyche and that in his external life his "cultural work" dominated by far. Only when engaged in such work, and alongside it, do we have to gather and sustain "time and strength, composure and leisure, interest and passion, love and enthusiasm for working on behalf of our Judaism."[100] Nevertheless it was his lot, in the end, to make that "focal point of his life"[101] the focus of his public life as well and thus to achieve complete equilibrium. For the four decades since the end of his journeyman years,[102] Cohen's life had flowed gently in the same riverbed. At the beginning of his eighth decade, however, it overflowed the riverbanks and, with its accumulated force, dug out a new channel.

In a certain sense, this powerful turn in Cohen's life came about very quietly, inconspicuously, and without drama. For it was occasioned not by what was to emerge as the substance of the approaching, final five years of his life, but by what had occupied his life for the preceding forty years. Perhaps it is always this way: that the greatest things that occur in a human life begin invisible to the eye. To be sure, Cohen found himself in the position of having to defend his Judaism more and more frequently before a new generation of colleagues. In the [university] senate and among the faculty, his Judaism also imposed a harsh isolation on Cohen, assuaged only by Natorp's loyalty,[103] starkly different from his first decades, marked by harmony and a happy social life. To be sure, he no longer gave his lecture course on Schiller. The student body had been infested with antisemitism, and his sense of dignity and pride would not allow him to offer such an intimate confession of loyalty to the German spirit in the presence of those who regarded his Germanness with a mistrust that was beneath him.[104] To be sure, the times had changed so that the professor who made the quiet rural university into an intellectual center of international reputation was never elected its rector. All of these factors probably made it easier for him to be uprooted from the soil of Hesse, to which he had become attached and where,

100. [JS 2:444.]

101. [Ibid.]

102. [*Lehr- und Wanderjahre*—the metaphor alludes to the title of Goethe's late novel, *Wilhelm Meisters Wanderjahre*.]

103. [Paul Natorp (1854–1924), with Cohen the main representative of the Marburg school of neo-Kantianism.]

104. This is the justification he gave me himself. ("Look, I cannot speak about Schiller in the presence of these people, who look at me asking themselves: what does the Jew have to say?!")

after forty years, he felt at home. However, in the end, personal reasons such as these are not what brought about the break. Not the Jew, but the professor, was locked in a struggle with the government and the faculty for the legitimacy of systematic philosophy that he had championed his entire life, a struggle in which the living forces of his time fought on his side, a view that, today, is probably beyond doubt. With honor in defeat, but furious, Cohen left the place that owed its fame to his career.

He went to Berlin. Ever hungry for art, music, and companionship, he had always yearned for the life of the big city. Dear friends beckoned. By virtue of his justified sense of his own importance and of his own ineradicable faith in human beings, he assumed that the university and the Academy[105] would take note of his presence. But what was foremost in his mind was something else, now liberated from any constraints or disguises. Only a short time before he had himself described it as the "focus of his life": he wanted to serve "his Jews." [106] The metropolis, the place where "his Jews" were most endangered, would be his field of activity. His base of operations would be the Institute for the Academic Study of Judaism,[107] of which he had long been a supporter and which was permeated by a spirit of freedom of inquiry. Finally, the Jews of the big city would have a need to hear the voice of the Prussian privy councilor; they would flock to the famous thinker, even if only out of sensationalism or curiosity.

This was what he assumed. He was mistaken. The circle of those touched personally by his activities was very small. He did not conquer the "West." The "West" sought out other altars where worship was less demanding. In general, however, even his listeners in the circles where he was heard were not fully aware of Cohen's towering status. He sensed all of this keenly. In his human relationships he was no Stoic. Nor did he suffer any illusions. He was capable of giving himself over entirely to complaining; his voice then took on something of the whimpering of a child. But then it was magnificent to observe how he could pull himself together after such decrescendos of vitality, often with a single word. What followed was then always a fresh start. He was never exhausted, because he was inexhaustible. When Berlin—soon enough—proved to be a mistake, he occupied himself with another plan: the tour of Russia. Difficulties with his

105. [The Academy for the Academic Study of Judaism.]
106. For this and the following the source is Cohen's own remarks, in conversation with me.
107. [Lehranstalt für die Wissenschaft des Judentums.]

passport forced him to delay several times, but the tour took place in the spring of 1914. The immediate reason was the introduction of a *numerus clausus* limiting the admission of Jews at higher schools to a fixed percentage. To oppose this brutal measure Cohen planned to organize a separate educational system for the Jews of Russia. He believed he would be able to bring about this grand project in self-help by the power of his name and reputation among Russian Jewry in particular. He would not have been the man he was if he had not seen this plan too as part of a larger context. Among his numerous Russian students he had observed how effortlessly these students from Russia could travel the road from Orthodox constraint to nihilistic radicalism. He hoped to alleviate this danger, now obvious for all to see, and thought he could do so if liberal Judaism[108] existed in Russia, as it had for a hundred years in Germany, and if it had the power to attract those who had escaped these old constraints for new, spiritual constraints that would replace them. He wanted to work toward that goal, in conjunction with the immediate plan and through it.

From the outside the tour appeared to be a lecture tour by a scholar. As such it was a triumph. Russians and Jews vied to outdo one another in celebrating the philosopher, who was read more widely in Russia than in his own country. The great centers of Jewish population in the East, especially Vilna and Warsaw, made a deep impression on Cohen in turn, even though he had known and appreciated Eastern European Jews[109] from his childhood on. Two essays bear equal testimony to this: his beautiful essay for Buber's journal *The Jew*[110] and his decided protest against the "Closing of the Border,"[111] advocated even then by German Jews out of a false conception of patriotism. Full of enthusiasm, he would tell the story of a young boy to whom he put a question during his visit to a heder in Vilna, "Now, what will be *b'acharis hayomim*, at the end of days?" The

---

108. Cohen was a liberal Jew—who, if not Cohen! But he deliberately avoided committing to any particular denomination. There exists a letter from him to the Association for Liberal Judaism in Germany (*Die Vereinigung für das liberale Judentum in Deutschland*) in which he declines a request to join. The letter would be worth publishing.

109. [Rosenzweig uses the adjective "*ostjüdisch*," common among German Jews, to refer to Jews from Eastern Europe.]

110. JS 2:162–71. ["Der polnische Jude (The Polish Jew)." The journal *Der Jude* was founded by Martin Buber (1878–1965) and edited by him from 1916 to 1924.]

111. JS 2:378–80. ["Grenzsperre." For an account of this episode, see Hartwig Wiedebach, *The National Element in Hermann Cohen's Philosophy and Religion* (Leiden, the Netherlands: Brill, 2012), 17–19.]

boy answered promptly, "Nu, everyone will be yiden."[112] When Cohen retold this story, he added, "What more can you want?" But the war and then the Bolshevik Revolution swept over all the grand plans of that tour—and we know with what result.

But even in those years, before the war, the great turn in the life of the old man began to bear intellectual fruit, confirming again the truth of the saying of Goethe's, which he coined at the same age: the springtime of the soul. This intellectual fruit recouped all the energy that had dissipated in those unfulfilled plans and gave it some staying power. Indeed, what is collected in these three volumes represents, for the most part, the Berlin years. But these are the foothills and the spurs that surround the mountain peaks, his magnum opus on the philosophy of religion and the study on religion in the system of philosophy.[113] The foothills also often afford the most beautiful views both of the countryside and of this mysterious alpine world. Thus, to understand these shorter writings, we must now turn to the center of this landscape.

The author of *Ethics of Pure Will* believed that, by introducing the idea of God into ethics, he had provided, at the same time, a philosophy of religion. Thus, he did not shrink from the conclusion that religion could have no greater task than to merge, finally, into pure ethics, and that ethics, in its prophetic purity, neither can nor may aspire to any other goal whatsoever. How was it possible that this thinker could fail to perceive the particular form of the deepest forces living within him? Could he really have thought that, in this distant vision of God and the human being of messianic humanity, he had given an exhaustive account of all that can transpire between God and the human being? Did he know nothing of the love of God, nothing of human misery and sin, nothing of all that happens in the world, arising from the mutual relationship between God and the human being and among human beings themselves? Certainly this would contradict what has been revealed to us of his personality thus far. And yet the contradiction is eliminated if one takes a more general view of Cohen's thought, and, in this context, considers the fact highlighted above, that Cohen completed the third part of his system, his *Aesthetics*, just before the onset of the turn in his thinking.

112. ["Nu, alle Menschen werden sein Jüden." By both the syntax and the phonetic transliteration, Rosenzweig is indicating that the young boy responded in Yiddish.]

113. [*Religion of Reason out of the Sources of Judaism* and the 1915 monograph *The Concept of Religion in the System of Philosophy.*]

Though a systematic thinker through and through, Cohen is not at all an architectonic thinker. His system is not some structure in which the architect, once having built it, then conducts a tour for the interested visitor. Rather, his thinking begins by spinning the threads of connection in the system that were initially not visible. Very few presuppositions are taken as given. Actually only two: the two that arise by distinguishing between the task of logic and the task of ethics. The threads of the web are suspended between these two. Moreover, it is apparently not the web itself that is important, but the act of spinning. The points where the web is attached are strong, even rigid. Yet between them everything is slack, as if it were an intellectual experiment: the fundamental presuppositions, those very "points of attachment," are justified retroactively because it is possible to suspend threads of connection between them, drawn from the material of cultural facts. If the experiment is successful, then the experimental apparatus can simply be dismantled; it served only an experimental purpose. If someone was not already familiar with the field of culture from which the material for the particular experiment was drawn, he will hardly come to know it from following the rapid work of this talented researcher. He may not even get a glimpse of it. Here lies the reason for the difficulty of Cohen's major works and the reason, too, why he himself did not believe they were difficult: if the reader knows everything that Cohen knew (and even better, also does not know what Cohen did not know), his books are not difficult. Therefore, Cohen's books were really not difficult for Cohen himself.

Thus, Cohen's thinking is experimental. It never actually proves and rarely produces anything; it just thinks. This fundamental characteristic of his thinking expresses itself in the fact that it *thinks* only when it is—thinking. It regards its own thinking, at most, as a task, never preempting it by anticipating its result. The biographical sequence of his works is actually the sole expression of their architectonic quality. Thus, the contradiction indicated above, between his discussion of religion in the *Ethics* on the one hand and his deeper knowledge of religion on the other, is apparently due to the circumstance that he intended to accommodate these discrepancies in his *Aesthetics*. Cohen the thinker had to write the book first, carrying out his thought experiment, before he could be persuaded that a discrepancy remained even then. For his biography, it is of providential significance that the date on the title page of the third major work of his philosophical system coincides with the year of his move from Marburg to Berlin.

The *Aesthetics* itself—this too is characteristic of the abruptness of his biographical turn—rejects throughout the notion that religion can make any systematic claims of its own; this can be seen both in the details of the structure of the book and in its execution. In the first volume, which deals with first principles, there is a chapter on Dante, the length of which exceeds that of all the other chapters of the book. He is presented as a secular poet, in a very wide-ranging discussion, profound in its insights, and bold in its interpretive turns. Only logic and ethics may serve as the preconditions of "pure feeling." The latter is now defined in rapturous terms both as the real feeling of the self, before which the self of logic and the self of ethics are pale abstractions, and as true love of humankind, the love of the human being as the totality of body and soul, love for "the nature of the human being and for the human being in nature." This is the true locus of the love of the human being, which was rejected, in the *Ethics*, as being "ambiguous." In carrying out this idea, which had led Cohen—in his discussion of lyric poetry—to the discovery of the I and You, he interprets all the great material and spiritual confluences of art history and history of religion as aesthetic humanizations of the religious, so that no one might entertain the notion that this dependent relationship could be reversed. This approach can also yield profound insights, as is demonstrated in the case of Judaism in particular by his sections on the lyrical poetry of the Psalms, on the Sistine Chapel, on Michelangelo's Moses, and on Rembrandt's Jewish models.

But now, after the experiment has been carried out, one can recognize that something still remains, something that could not be accommodated even in the realm of art. There was still buried treasure concealed within Cohen the man that had not yet yielded to the spade of Cohen the systematic philosopher. We learn what kind of treasure this was, free of any trace of positive religion, from that remarkable passage in a letter that Cohen wrote to Stadler after the death of Gottfried Keller and that was published a few years ago:

What is honored in the academic-bourgeois mode of thinking is the thinker within the soul, and, similarly, what is recognized as the most important capacity and the real worth of the wretched human individual is his ability to transport himself intellectually into the eternal realm of culture. However, if one is liberated from this mode of thinking, then what endures as the genuine abiding element, as the value of the human being and as the eternal in the this-worldly, is the ineffable and transitory element in the mood of one's fellow human beings, or, better, in their mentality. . . . Religion is after all the sphere where one adorns the futility of the world with the glory of the eternal. What ethics ever advised that we should not abandon the ruins of obsolete reason to its heterogeneous fate as soon as possible—just to fulfill our duties toward the other scarecrows of the moral law? We are actually just wasting our time if we shed a tear over human weakness![114]

These words, written in 1890, use passionate irony to assert the status of the "individual himself" ("individuum quand même") confronting the bourgeois academic narrow-mindedness of an ethics that is oriented solely toward the eternity of culture and the moral law. Nonetheless, it would take decades of development and require his withdrawal from the "academic bourgeois" milieu of the university before Cohen the thinker found the language for the certainty that Cohen the nonbourgeois man had long been fervently defending. From this letter it seems not a road of twenty-three years, but just a single step to the basic idea of the philosophy of religion that he presented in his lectures at the Berlin Institute in the winter of 1913 to 1914 and published in late 1915 in the journal of the Marburg school, *Philosophische Arbeiten*.

To be sure, at this point certain influences began to shape Cohen, but not until this point, as is evident in the book just mentioned, *The Concept of Religion in the System of Philosophy*: the influence of Protestant theology, of the critique of *Ethics of Pure Will* by Wilhelm Herrmann, Cohen's Marburg colleague and friend, and of Hermann's concept of "the reality of God."[115] Cohen's formulation of his new ideas was apparently also influenced by his need to set himself apart from the mystical subjectivism then taking shape in Natorp's thought. These factors, however, were not decisive. What was decisive was that he had now reached a point in his life when he could and did give voice to the fullness of his heart. That he could do so in this book in particular, while preserving the substance of the system that he had produced through a lifetime of labor and for which he bore responsibility in the eyes of the Marburg school—this was nothing to be taken for granted from a psychological point of view. It was grounded in the latent

114. The letter is included in *Gabe Herrn Rabbiner Dr. Nobel zum 50. Geburtstag dargebracht* [A gift presented to Rabbi Dr. Nobel, on his fiftieth birthday], Frankfurt am Main, 5682 [1921], p. 10, edited by me and dated July 17, 1890. [Rosenzweig's contribution to the volume is "Hermann Cohen: Briefe über Gottfried Keller (Hermann Cohen: Letters on Gottfried Keller)," 9–11.]

115. [For Wilhelm Herrmann, see his 1886 *Der Verkehr des Christen mit Gott* (for an English translation, see *The Communion of the Christian with God* (Philadelphia: Fortress Press, 1971). The experience of "the reality of God" is a central theme in his theology.]

connections of his system to these new, complementary ideas, ideas of which he was only now becoming aware. Of course, he could not proceed without correcting or retracting some of his own ideas. Up until this point, he was able to add the threads of each new part of the system without disturbing the strands of the web that were already in place. Now, however, the new turn meant that Cohen could only insert new threads with one hand if, with the other, he raised a thread here, lowered one there, or sometimes added yet another thread that was entirely new. Not for nothing is the 1915 book dedicated to the Marburg school. It was at once a programmatic text and a rendering of account—the first half of the title, *The Concept of Religion*, representing the former, and the second half, *in the System of Philosophy*, the latter.

The new fundamental concept—new, even if Cohen occasionally reaches for it in his essay on love and justice[116]—is "correlation," the mutual relation between the human being and God. At an earlier stage, consistent with *Ethics of Pure Will*, he had defined the concept of monotheism in contrast to all forms of polytheism. Polytheism was directed toward the gods and the divine, whereas monotheism was directed exclusively toward the human being. Now, however, he offers an explicit correction: monotheism is characterized by its strict orientation toward the correlation between the human being and God. Only what God is for the human being, and what the human being is for God, falls within its field of vision. From this, however, follows the discovery both of a new concept of God and of a new concept of the human being. The human being in the presence of God is no longer the self of ethics, which, in itself, can only be an eternal task. The human being in the presence of God is the actual human being in his suffering and distress, entangled in the sins of his present moment, for whom the solace of eternity offers no comfort. The "individual himself" of that letter[117] is disclosed here by philosophical means, the individual who, in his sin and remorse, is not able to envision the totality of humanity, but who must regard himself as a being as unique as—God. Now, God can no longer be merely the God of *Ethics of Pure Will*, serving the pure will as the guarantor for the

---

116. "Liebe und Gerechtigkeit in den Begriffen Gott und Mensch [Love and justice in the concepts of God and man]," *JS* 3:43–97.

117. [The letter to August Stadler quoted above.]

118. [From the beginning of the Avodah service on the Jewish Day of Atonement (Yom Kippur), that moment in the afternoon liturgy when the drama of the high priest's atonement for the sins of the congregation is reenacted. The text is based on *Mishnah Yoma* 3:8.]

perdurance of humanity. Now, when the unique individual cries in distress, "before You alone have I sinned,"[118] God must give him the only response that can help him, the unique response that only he, the unique one, can give: "I pardon, according to your word."[119]

This twofold discovery also casts new light on the moral life of humankind and its history. Suffering becomes the focus. It was necessary that it be neglected in the *Ethics*, even if it does suffuse reality, the suffering of body and soul, of the individual and of nations. The result is thus the emergence of a new doctrine of the human being, in coordination with ethics to be sure, but also in sharp contrast to it: the doctrine of the human being with God and before God. Only then is the human being a real, present human being who cannot be merged into the humanity of the future and does not desire to be a "scarecrow of the moral law." This is the human being whose love of humankind becomes love of God through his certainty that this God loves the human being in return. In the years when Cohen was discovering correlation, he never tired of polemicizing against Spinoza's famous statement, even though it was not Spinoza who uttered it, but Nicholas of Cusa: "also a more pious man."[120] Now it is the human being thus conceived who occupies the bright center of his [Cohen's] field of vision and no longer the human being of the *Aesthetics*, who once seemed able to do so. Now the human being of the *Aesthetics* is reduced, in all his aesthetic individuality, to a "mere type." The aesthetic love of the human being, when compared to the earnestness of the love of suffering, is exposed as mere play. Now these terms are sharply delineated from the fundamental concepts of aesthetics that had taken possession of them (we have seen why this was so) and must again become fundamental words. When God entered into the realm of art, he always remained but a conduit; the human being was not only the alpha but also the omega of this world; creative movement originated with the human being; and creative movement returned to him, creating him in turn. How different it is in the realm of correlation, where God cannot be God without the human being nor can the human being be a human being without God, and both exist in equal measure

119. [Num. 14:20: "I have pardoned, according to your word," recited at the beginning of the liturgy for the eve of the Day of Atonement.]

120. In the lectures of 1913–14. See note 131. [Rosenzweig is apparently reporting that Cohen, in an aside during one of his lectures, noted that Spinoza was not the first to propose the immanentist idea, "God or nature (*Deus sive natura*)," but that he was preceded by Nicholas of Cusa. Moreover, Cohen, harboring a deep animosity for Spinoza, quipped that Cusa was the more pious of the two.]

in their mutual dependency. Now the historical relationship between religion and art must also emerge as quite different from the grossly narrow version of it claimed in the 1912 book.[121] Now, finally, Cohen acknowledges—no, more than that: he seeks out the primal religious forces in the artistic activity of humankind. This tendency is evident in almost all the examples from art history cited in his 1915 book on religion; it comes into play in "Germanism and Judaism";[122] and it deeply influences two of the most precious gifts in the present collection of writings, the two unpublished manuscripts, one on the lyric form of the Psalms[123] and the other, considerably older, on the style of the prophets.[124] This tendency is also at work in the manuscript of his lecture, also published here for the first time, on the aesthetic value of our religious education.[125] It is evident in Cohen's general remarks, in his numerous examples, and finally in his advocacy for the use of the original language in scripture and in prayer, for which he gives a deeply reasoned argument.

Not that Cohen himself would have allowed this new content to dislodge the supporting pillars of the system. They remained where they had been sunk into the ground. Moreover, the shaft that had already been dug for the fourth pillar of his system, psychology, remained open. Cohen summons all his mental acuity to demonstrate that religion, while it has a particular form, has no independent place within his system. It does not constitute its own systematic component within consciousness, corresponding to cognition in logic, to the will in ethics, or to feeling in aesthetics. Nor may religion presume to encompass these powers of consciousness. That remains, without any change, the task of the unity of cultural consciousness, to be carried out by psychology. And yet although, or rather just because, Cohen maintains this clear and consistent concept of culture and its parts, he manages to prevent this philosophy of religion from becoming a—philosophy of religion, that is, he manages to prevent religion from being assigned its own place among the divisions of culture, like one stone element among others in the tracery of a Gothic window. Or from becoming an argument between religion and culture as a whole, the former alternative being the Scylla, the latter the Charybdis of a century of philosophical labors concerning

121. [*Aesthetics of Pure Feeling*.]
122. ["Deutschtum und Judentum," *JS* 2:237–301 and 2:302–18.]
123. "Die Lyrik der Psalmen [The lyrical style of the Psalms]," *JS* 1:237–61.
124. "Der Stil der Propheten [The style of the prophets]," *JS* 1:262–83.
125. "Über den ästhetischen Wert unserer religiösen Bildung [On the aesthetic value of our religious education]," *JS* 1:211–36.

the concept of religion. It is precisely his refusal to grant religion any independence within his system that gives religion—it cannot be put any other way—its systematic omnipresence, a faithful expression of its full presence in the thinker Cohen himself. This omnipresence is given expression in the pivotal sentence of *The Concept of Religion in the System of Philosophy*: "Therefore the love of God must surpass all cognition . . . it must connect all things and all problems of the world with the concept of God."[126] In this context Cohen gives his bold and yet true interpretation of the commandment in Deuteronomy: "I cannot love God without my entire *heart*, as it lives for my *fellow human beings*, without my entire *soul*, as it is turned, using all the trajectories of the spirit, toward the world around me, without deploying all my *might* for God in his *correlation* to the human being." Thus, one can say: "Nothing remains in the consciousness of the human being if he loves God."

But we must dig even deeper. Cohen's awareness of what he had done extended only this far; yet his deed anticipated the future more than he knew. Now that we have defined his place in the development of nineteenth-century philosophy differently than he defined it himself, we must show how he made a forceful advance beyond the nineteenth century, into the terrain of the philosophical future. His new foundational concept, correlation, secured religion's particular form; Cohen stressed this point himself. Now it is true that the concept of correlation played a methodological role elsewhere in Cohen's system, but nowhere as a foundational concept.[127] The foundational concepts of the system were always concepts of generation and origin. Nature as an object of cognition, humanity as the task of the will, the love of human nature, condensed into a work of art, as a production generated by feeling: Cohen the thinker saw it as his task to generate these three, in their original purity. Nature, humanity, and art are thus shown to be productions generated by reason, where "reason" is taken in that broad and profound sense in which German Idealism used the term. But in this way nature and humanity could be understood only as generated entities, as if in a conceptual *status nascendi* [a state of being born]. They were derived, conceived, explained, and their foundations were laid; however, no consideration was given to the possibility that they existed prior to all derivation, explanation, or founda-

---

126. [BR, 81–82, is the source for this and the following two quotations.]

127. [Rosenzweig anticipates here the counterargument to his interpretation that will be mounted decades later by Alexander Altmann in "Hermann Cohen's Concept of Correlation" (selection 9).]

tion laying, that their facticity was prior to their givenness as object or task. To give consideration to such facticity would have demolished the charmed circle of Idealism, which, even after Hegel, was spellbound, unswerving in its faith in the "great concept of immanence." For Cohen, however, the charmed circle had ruptured, for the simple reason that he believed in God and that his inherited Judaism had become the dominant force in his life—no other philosopher of the modern era shared such a faith and destiny. It is true that he built the idea of God into his ethics, as the idea appears within the horizon of Idealism. But to articulate his faith, he required methodological tools other than those provided by the foundational concepts of Idealism—methodological tools, because it is a philosophical statement that is at stake here. At this point, he discovered correlation. Where two entities are in a mutual relationship, there is no danger that one will contest the reality of the other, as is almost necessarily the case of the relation, in Idealism, between the generating concept and the thing generated. The thing generated would be the sawing off of the very branch that supports it. In its relationship to the other, the one respective entity gains, by philosophical means, the "explanation" that is available only from its respective other. The reciprocity of the relationship protects each side in this relationship against the dissolution of its own being into the "more authentic" being of the other. In this way the facticity of each side of the correlative relationship is secured.

First this operation is carried out for God and the human being. Thus, from the vantage point of God, the "individual *itself*" can be apprehended, and ethics can be renewed in its full scope. Second, however, because the human being is also part of nature, that other correlation is disclosed, the correlation of God and nature, anticipating the concept of creation. It is no coincidence that in his major work of philosophy of religion[128] Cohen liberates the correlation of I and You from the golden fetters of the aesthetics of lyric poetry. Then, taking correlation as the point of departure, Cohen discovers, unconsciously and with prosaic gravity, the foundations of a new logic. Thus, the last great heir of Idealism was the one who breached its boundaries, indeed, the boundaries of all previous philosophy, if one considers that Descartes's *raison* replaced only the God of the Middle Ages, just as the latter had replaced the cosmos of the ancients. In each case one possessed the power to render the other less authentic. This view, ascribing such great significance in the history of philosophy to the emergence of correlation as a foundational concept, is not an overstatement, as is demonstrated by the final

128. [*Religion of Reason out of the Sources of Judaism.*]

step that Cohen takes in his posthumously published book, a step that is almost alarming in its naïve genius. For in the fifth chapter[129] of that book he gives an interpretation of reason, the ultimate ground of all Idealism, and, since Idealism expresses what is the tacit secret of all previous philosophy, the ground of all philosophy: reason is a creation of God. It is created reason.

First of all, he had now given philosophical voice to his faith in all its vitality; but it was not just that: he could give freer expression to his [sense of] destiny, more unrestrained and less formulaic. Certainly it was significant that, when Cohen gave his great rendering of account to the [Marburg] school,[130] it was completely natural that he developed the concept of religion on the basis of Judaism and mentioned Christianity only rarely and mostly only as a foil to Judaism, as if it could not be otherwise. However, that was not necessarily anything new. His *Ethics* had been dismissed by the philosophical professoriate on the ground that it was just a Jewish philosophy of religion. What is new, however, is Cohen's repeated expression of wonder, or actually of solemn amazement, at the miracle of the Jewish people, its career in history, and its possession of revelation. Now, when Cohen speaks of this, there is something in his words of the prostration of the worshipper during the Avodah service on Yom Kippur at those passages that tell of the moment when the divine name, which is otherwise never pronounced, is proclaimed over the people assembled in the Temple. Cohen's lectures during the winter semester of 1913 to 1914, which my ears had the good fortune to hear, were replete with such outbursts.[131] On the Sabbath: "These are all miracles!" Or on the love of one's neighbor: "This is removed from any process of development. Here there is no place for concessions to evolutionary thinking. It cannot be allowed to have developed—this is what the philosophers call 'a priori.'" On the willing acknowledgment of suffering by the pious: "Can we conceive of this? Isaiah responds, 'See, O Israel!'" And again, on the servant of the Lord, in Isaiah:

129. ["The Creation of Man in Reason."]

130. [Referring to the 1915 treatise *The Concept of Religion in the System of Philosophy* (BR), which was dedicated to the Marburg school.]

131. These quotations are from notebooks in which, even then, I sought to preserve —but to preserve word for word—only the most significant moments. It was not possible to keep a real notebook. While trying to take notes, one would have missed the best parts. Sometimes he would conclude an entire train of thought with a hand gesture. It was the real conclusion, more persuasive than all conclusions. I attempted to record my impression of [Cohen as] teacher in the brief essay of 1918, mentioned above [see this selection, note 1].

"how we make bold to grasp such things from a human historical perspective. . . ." On the origin of prophetic thinking: "How? When? We will never want to be able to understand it." And then the powerful lecture on unity, this "most abstract of all," "for the sake of which we let ourselves be slain every day":[132] "as far as I'm concerned, God may be whatever he wants, but he must be one." "On this point we will never be able to reach agreement with the Christians—I have to say it." "Balaam's oracle of a people that dwells apart[133]—the civilized human being cannot grasp this. Nature in its entirety, the model of art, is presented in the second commandment and—locked away." And again: "We have not been forgiven for that up to the present day," and then, after an emotional pause: "It is beyond understanding." Cohen's great lecture on the lyric poetry of the Psalms puts it this way: "Monotheism is a psychological mystery. Whoever does not recognize this does not understand it in its profundity."[134]

Thus, the miracle of his faith, as the legacy of his nation, has now become intermeshed with the miracle of his nation, as the product of his faith. Once, when a Christian friend spoke to him of the nearness to God that he possessed through Christ, Cohen responded: "Christ is to you what to me is my connection with the prophets—and the Pharisees."[135] Mark: he does not appeal to the prophets and the Pharisees, but to his connection to them. And this connection has now become so universal that Cohen, the vanguard of "prophetic Judaism," is able to give his Christian friend a gentle slight by stressing the word "and." Now it has become the general case. In a departure from the monistic tendency of all philosophy before him, the concept of correlation had helped Cohen to discover that little word "and," until then unknown to philosophers: God *and* the human being, the human being *and* God, God *and* nature, nature *and* God. Similarly, now the "and" of connections comes into view within his Judaism, connections in which Cohen himself is situated. The prophets remain, joined now by the Pharisees. The teaching remains, joined now by the law, a step that was anticipated in Cohen's critique of Lazarus[136] but is completed in the eighteenth chapter of Cohen's posthumous work in a series of deliberations that are so fruitful on account of the circumspection that accompanies them at

132. [Ps. 44:23.]

133. [Num. 23:9.]

134. ["Die Lyrik der Psalmen," *JS* 1:237–61 and *Werke* 16:165–98. For the quote, see *JS* 1:239 and *Werke* 16:167.]

135. Cohen's own account.

136. *JS* 3:1–35.

every stage. Among the prophets, Amos, Isaiah, and Michah remain the great promulgators of social ethics and messianic peace among nations. But they are joined now by Jeremiah and Ezekiel, the discoverers of the individual and his soul. Ezekiel, in particular, unfairly eclipsed by Protestant scholarship, is now lovingly embraced in all his seeming contradictions. For although Cohen, like all of us, felt indebted to Protestant scholarship for restoring the image of the prophets, he also protested its narrow-minded bias against the "special character of Old Testament religion"[137] in his essays, for instance, on the "Neighbor" and on "Conscience."[138] Cohen knew himself that he was paying back our debt to Protestant biblical scholarship, to which he renders full homage in his essays on Baudissin and Bertholet.[139] I can still see him, when he had once again convalesced after an illness, lying on the sofa, and saying, in a quite happy mood, "I, Ezekiel number thirty-six"—it was his Hebrew given name—"had to come along to restore the honor of Ezekiel number one!" and then, in Hebrew and half talking to himself, "Cast away from yourselves all your sins ... and get yourselves a new heart and a new spirit,"[140] repeating it over and over, almost inaudibly, "... cast away ... and get yourselves ... get ..."

This too was something that had remained and was simply joined by something new. As his essay for the Kaufmann jubilee volume[141] demonstrates, Cohen never sought to conceal the difficulties posed by the concept of autonomy for religious thought by draping them in some well-chosen passages from the Talmud, a possibility that was always open. Now he has found a simple solution, even if it is all too simple. Moral labor, human self-purification in the presence of God, remains entirely free. Its success is guaranteed only when divine reconciliation, purification, joins in. In Rabbi Akiba's blessing of Israel, God himself serves as the purifying bath for Israel's sins.[142] Cohen arranged his magnum opus so

137. JS 2:404–9 ["Zwei Rektoratsreden an der Berliner Universität (Two rector's addresses at the University of Berlin)"].

138. JS 1:182–95 ["Der Nächste (The neighbor)"] and 1:196–210 ["Gesinnung (Conscience)"].

139. JS 2:404–9 ["Zwei Rektoratsreden an der Berliner Universität"] and JS 2:410–15 ["Die Eigenart der alttestamentlichen Religion (The special character of Old Testament religion)"].

140. [Ezek. 18:31.]

141. JS 3:36–42 ["Autonomie und Freiheit (Autonomy and freedom)," selection 6].

142. [Mishnah Yoma 8:9. Cohen also quotes this passage in the chapter in RR on "The Day of Atonement": "Blessed are ye, O Israel, who purifies you, and before whom do you purify yourselves? It is your Father in Heaven" (RR, 223).]

that it opens with this blessing as its motto. In it Cohen saw not only the conjoining of religion and ethics, which, as correlation would have it, binds God and the human being to one another, but also sets them apart. He also saw in it the shibboleth that distinguishes Judaism from Christianity. In so doing, he also grants recognition, now as in 1880, to the cultural and historical significance of Christian dogma for its discovery of the concept of moral autonomy, and thus for the greatest contribution for which humanity is indebted to philosophical ethics. But the reconciliation of the conflict between religion and ethics is possible only if there is a strict distinction between the role of the human being and the role of God within their reciprocal relationship, as is the case in the pure monotheism of Judaism.

To be sure, in his "Thoughts on Readings for Youth" of 1906,[143] Cohen offered an interesting treatment of the problem posed, for Jews, by the person of Jesus. But, in general, it is only now, from the perspective of religious depth anchored in the concept of correlation, that dialogue with Christianity really bears fruit. Of course Maimonides remains "our great guide," Cohen's epithet for Maimonides in the course he gave on him in 1913–14. Nevertheless, in his 1915 treatise on religion, Cohen tellingly finds it necessary, at an important point, to cite a liturgical poem by Maimonides's great opposite, Judah Halevi.[144] As a boy he had read Maimonides with his father. As a grown man, writing his open letter to Treitschke, he had "felt no calling whatsoever"[145] to interpret Maimonides's philosophy. But now, in his old age, at the Institute in Berlin, he gave courses on Maimonides for several semesters. He had always lived in very direct connection to Maimonides. When, in January 1918, he gave me the first pages of his magnum opus and asked for my first impression, I answered by invoking the verse with which the circle around Virgil welcomed the *Aeneid*, then in progress: "Cedite, gentiles scriptores, cedite, nostri! Nescioquid maius nascitur Maimonide."[146] Cohen then responded, pleased, but also tempering my excess: "Yes, that's what I also thought: Rambam[147] would be satisfied." Now, however, as he conceived of

143. *JS* 2:126–32 ["Gedanken über Jugendlektüre"].

144. [See *BR*, 61-2.]

145. At the beginning of the letter. See this selection, note 54.

146. ["Make way, gentile writers, make way writers of our own! Something is being born greater than Maimonides," a play on Propertius's prediction that the *Aeneid* would surpass the *Iliad*: "Make way, Roman writers, make way ye Greeks / something is being born greater than the *Iliad*" (*Carmina* 2.34.65).]

147. [Maimonides (an acronym formed from his Hebrew name).]

the notion of the correlation of God and the human being, another philosophi-cal figure from the Jewish past would appear before him, the oldest of them all: Philo, not as a guide, but misguided instead. At the crossroads of correlation—this is how his latter-day colleague sees it now—Philo went astray, leading oth-ers down a world-historical detour. He had neither the faith nor the courage to accept the two poles of correlation as mutually dependent, but believed instead that he had to argue for a special mediating force. "If Philo had not conceived of the Logos, no Jew would ever have doubted." In his course in the winter of 1913–14, this is how Cohen spoke of both the demonic and monstrous dimensions that Philo, the first of all Jewish philosophers, had now assumed in his eyes, and the deeply un-Jewish character of Philo's world-historical idea.[148] In this context, through his need to deal with Philo, Cohen arrived at the exegetical discovery to which, in those years, he returned again and again: that the holy spirit of the Old Testament is the human spirit. He even devoted an entire essay to this discovery in the jubilee volume for Guttmann.[149] God places the holy spirit in the human being and will not retract it, not even from a sinner. In the holy spirit correlation is solidified. In correlation, God and the human being converge for the very rea-son that, in essence, they remain separate: the human spirit is the holy spirit, and God—this is Cohen's bold formulation in the 1913–14 lectures—would have no need of spirit, if human beings had no need for their share of it. Correlation thus emerges as an expression of the Jewish feeling that must yearn for the unique-ness of God to overcome the infinite chasm and come directly before the eternal. It thus runs counter to "the entire concern of the scientific world, in its specific and absolute sense, which simply cannot tolerate the difference between God and the human being and thus is fundamentally incapable of understanding

148. One very intimate point deserves mention here. Cohen never forgave Kant his mistaken judgment about Judaism; his [Cohen's] long essay [selection 4] deliberately avoids it. Christian bias, against which he took up arms his entire life—here it struck him in his most vulnerable spot. He wrote a brief essay on the subject, which was intended for publication from his papers, after his death. The matter was very important to him. I hap-pened to join him once as he was reading the essay aloud to Mr. S. Brünn; I still remember the energetic tone in which he read, but no longer the details of the content. I can still hear him saying, "This should be published one day, out of my literary estate!" In September 1917 he told my mother of the essay, of his decision that it be published posthumously, and of his peace of mind, knowing that it lay ready. Unfortunately, the noteworthy document appears to be lost.

149. JS 3:176–96 ["Der heilige Geist (The holy spirit)," 1915, in *Werke* 16:437–64. The jubi-lee volume honored the seventieth birthday of Jacob Guttmann (1845–1919).]

those who confess belief in the uniqueness of God." These words are taken from the essay in that jubilee volume and sum up his settling of accounts with Philo: "The Greek spirit, and it is the model of the philosophical and scientific world-view, seeks an 'in-between,' as they call it, between God and the human being. Philo the Jew, with his Logos, fell victim to this Greek charm."

Cohen felt a deep shudder, even horror, at the Christian anthropomorphosis of God, the very feeling expressed first by the high priest when he tore his garments[150]—and it never left him, in spite of the philosophical idealization of the Christ idea, in spite of the recognition accorded to the Christ idea in cultural history, and in spite of the multifaceted, deep influence of Christian theology that Cohen deliberately wove into his 1915 treatise on religion. If, in his presence, someone defended the idea that a Jew might undergo baptism out of genuine belief in Christian dogma, he could fly into a rage, "*No one* has *ever* believed in it!"[151] That was a paradox of the kind that he loved, yet grounded in a profound seriousness that restored gravity to the much abused word "belief,"[152] gravity that it derives, for us, from the harmony that reigns between faith and thinking spirit and between faith and mute existence. With the same profound seriousness, shortly before his death, Cohen went to the rescue of one of his pupils who had dared cross swords with the foremost champion of the new sociological school of theology. He went into battle with a "great question mark" etched on his shield as a threatening escutcheon. And if he sought to rescue not the pupil himself from the merciless hands of his opponent, then at least the armor that the pupil had borrowed from him.[153] Cohen, noticing an unprotected spot, raised his arm to deliver a powerful thrust: "Gentlemen, what position do you take, in your minds and in your hearts, on the God of the prophets, who created the world to rule over it?"[154] The thrust did not abide by the rules, but it sealed the victory.

150. [Matt. 26:65.]

151. In conversation with me.

152. [The German word *Glauben* encompasses both belief and faith.]

153. JS 2:398–401 ["Der Prophetismus und die Soziologie (Prophecy and sociology)." The "champion" of the sociological school is Ernst Troeltsch (1865–1923). Cohen had deputized his pupil Benzion Kellermann (1869–1923) to respond to Troeltsch's 1916 essay, "Das Ethos der hebräischen Propheten (The ethos of the Hebrew prophets)," which Cohen regarded as an "aberration" (JS 2:401).]

154. JS 2:465 [Cohen's eulogy for Julius Wellhausen, "Julius Wellhausen, Ein Abschieds-gruß ("Julius Wellhausen, a farewell)"].

And alongside Philo, another figure emerges: Spinoza. After the Spinozistic sin of his youth, the anonymous Heine essay of 1867,[155] Cohen seems to have regarded Spinoza as his adversary for the rest of his life. But only now is he able to articulate his deepest motive for this adversarial relationship. For it would be a mistake to attribute it simply to his Kantianism. His Kantianism always contained such an admixture of post-Kantianism Idealism, in the spirit of the nineteenth century, that on that account alone he could have continued along the path of that essay of his youth. That essay, after all, was able to follow a Spinozistic path only because it spiritualized Spinozism, reading in place of the Natura sive Deus of the century of Galileo and Newton, the Deus sive Spiritus[156] of the century of Hegel and Ranke. But in the struggle against any form of pantheism, including a pantheism of the spirit, his Judaism stiffened his resolve, and his Judaism alone had the word now. Here too correlation emerges as the conceptual tool that allows his faith to speak. In the short but rich essay on the holy spirit[157] Cohen now finds the "advantage of Judaism over pantheism in the concept of the individual."[158] God must remain God; the human being must remain a human being. Neither may God dissolve into the human spirit—after all, in keeping with Cohen's powerful utterance in that lecture, which will outlast the century, God would have no need of spirit, if he did not want to give the human being a share of it—nor may the human being dissolve into the being of God, if and because the "nearness" of God is my good, as in that verse from the Psalms that is now so widely quoted.[159] Since his old opposition to Spinoza had now found its mooring in religious consciousness, Cohen turns to a new examination of Spinoza's relationship and attitude toward Jews and Judaism. He was enraged by the uncritical glorification of Spinoza that was then rampant in modern Jewish circles and that had just led to the naming of a B'nai Brith lodge after Spinoza. His lengthy essay of 1915[160] grew out of the seminar at the Institute in which he dealt with the *Theological-Political Treatise*, out of earlier and recent research on Spinoza, as well as out of his own research, illuminating the contemporary po-

---

155. JS 2:1–44 ["Heinrich Heine und das Judentum (Heinrich Heine and Judaism)"].

156. ["Natura sive Deus," "nature or God," is a version of Spinoza's dictum, whereas "Deus sive Spiritus," "God or Spirit," is Rosenzweig's invention.]

157. JS 3:176–96.

158. [JS 3:193.]

159. ["As for me, nearness to God is good" (Psalm 73:28).]

160. JS 3:290–372 ["Spinoza über Staat und Religion, Judentum und Christentum (Spinoza on state and religion, Judaism and Christianity)"].

litical background of the *Treatise*. In the essay, his opposition to Spinoza rises to the level of enmity, which, in oral remarks that do not bear repetition, could rise to the level of hatred.[161] What came out in those temperamental eruptions, beyond the religious opposition just described, was the emotional estrangement between a passionate Ashkenazic Jew, filled with sympathy, the very emotion so reviled by Spinoza, and this late product of Sephardic Jewry scorched by generations of suffering—"He is cold, like a Sephardic Jew," Cohen once said to me. Yet even in his hatred the connection was so direct that it spanned the centuries as if they were mere seconds.

At this juncture too he achieves a connection to an ultimate and most intimate point of faith, that, until then, had eluded him. This development is related to his expanding literary horizon: it now encompasses not only the prophets but the Psalms as well, to which he accords great weight. In the summer of 1914 Cohen gave a magnificent, unadvertised class at the Institute on the Psalms.[162] In his 1915 book on religion he even went so far as to assert that the prophets are actually still ethics; only the Psalms are religion. On the basis of the Psalms he was then able to allow himself access, modest but certain access to the notion of immortality, which he had long dismissed. The *Ethics* had led him to think it necessary to reject the notion of immortality, in favor of messianic progress toward [the realization of] humanity. The *Ethics* even led him to criticize prophetic messianism on the ground that its conception of its goal was too idyllic, whereas its goal was supposed to consist only of laboring continually, for all eternity. Here too the task fell to the *Aesthetics*—the occasion was Goethe's *Elective Affinities*[163]—to fashion this "most sacred crown of the human soul": the eternity of love—this is the meaning of "poetic immortality." In the lectures of 1913–14 Cohen's tone was still harsh, denying the individual's longing for immortality any fulfillment other than fulfillment of this aesthetic kind. In 1915, however, in the monograph on religion, and especially in his essay on the holy spirit, the "distinction between religion and aesthetics" is also reflected in the "distinction between the human soul and human nature." Faith in God is now itself unmediated confidence in deliverance, in the preservation of the human soul by God. The human being comes from God and returns to God. And the question, what

161. In conversation with Martin Buber.

162. Following the announced class on Maimonides. In each session he would read only one psalm, reading and translating himself. For interpretation he relied heavily on Graetz.

163. [The 1809 *Wahlverwandtschaften*, Goethe's last novel.]

then becomes of the spirit of the human being when it is with God, is settled for the human being by the final words of the Psalm, final in every sense: "Every soul praises God" [Ps. 150:6]. It is likewise settled by that "treasure of the soul" unearthed by Psalm 73: "Whom else do I have in heaven? / And having You I want no one on earth; . . . As for me, the nearness to God is good."[164] Now there is no need for any other form of ethical action. Piety is fully satisfied if it can just serve God and delight in being near him. The goal of human existence as consisting in the return to God is so far beyond any mythology of immortality that its earthly, all-too-earthly fantasies collapse of their own accord. In "nearness to God," the yearning for a "reunion" [in the afterlife] must be silenced, because desire "on earth" is silenced. Heavenly fulfillment requires denying the desire that our own miserable, earthly heart pursues by necessity. I recall an occasion seven weeks before his death: the widow of a Christian friend had posed the question to Cohen whether he believed in reunion [in the afterlife]. Her deceased husband had believed it would be so. To my inquiring glance he responded that he had once stood at the deathbed of a man he loved dearly. One last time, the man embraced him with an expression on his face that summed up a life of love but also conveyed a certainty: now we are seeing one another for the last time. There was something indescribable in this story, a story that precluded any further questions: in the earthly "no" that appears to be the whole substance of the story, Cohen's eternal confidence was so clearly audible that the "no" vanished entirely into this "yes."

Then, in the midst of the developments described here, the war broke out, but it did not influence them significantly. Cohen did not live to see the war's end. In the days leading up to it, being the old socialist and democrat that he was, his attitude was cautious and deliberate. However, then the exchange of telegrams between the Emperor and Czar were published and amazed him.[165] Now his own state was justified before the forum of ethics. "Our cause is as pure as the angels," he would tell me again and again, "as pure as the angels!" He delivered his confession of loyalty to the German war effort, once in his lecture on the special character of the German spirit, at the Kant Society in the fall of 1914, and again in his pamphlet on "Germanism and Judaism" in 1915 and 1916.[166] There is

164. [Psalm 73:25 and 28.]

165. [The private telegrams exchanged on the eve of World War I between Emperor Wilhelm II and Czar Nicholas II were published in 1914 and later reprinted as the *Willy-Nicky Correspondence*, ed. Herman Bernstein (New York: Knopf, 1918).]

166. [Rosenzweig is referring to two essays by Cohen that have the same title, "Deutsch-

little mention of the war itself, but it is typical of that genre of the literature of war, authored by professors, like the speech that Dubois-Reymond gave in 1870 and that had once elicited Cohen's derision.[167] For that reason, today, after the bitter end, "Germanism and Judaism" is difficult to read, as it was for the younger generation even at the time. The details of the pamphlet were not planned haphazardly. He did not forget[168] that his *Aesthetics* had closed with an homage to France as the land of social revolution and the land that portrayed labor in painting. But the organization of ideas was intentional and the conclusion was overstated; what was lacking was the living breath of an event legitimated by personal experience. The living breath of personal experience, for example, hovered over Cohen's discussion of this question in his farewell to Wellhausen, obviously imbued with love for his friend, who died shortly before Cohen himself. Only personal experience makes it possible to give an answer to a question that, as a theoretical matter, can be answered only in a way that would be harmfully forceful. He once made a direct approach to the government when the issue at hand was courting American support.[169] It was thought that Cohen should make a journey for propagandistic purposes; all that came of it was his essay for the *New Yorker Staats-Zeitung*.[170] He wanted to instill in the hearts of the Jews of America, and indeed of the whole world, a loyalty toward Germany as toward a second fatherland. After all, Germany was the matrix of the spiritual renewal of Judaism, from Mendelssohn onward. It was military service in the good and plain sense when Cohen, now elderly, but undeterred by the exertion of the journey from Berlin, would lecture in Marburg, as he had done in 1915 and 1916, a guest lecturer in his old professorship. However, the course of the war ultimately weighed on him terribly. The steady increase in antisemitism frightened him, especially as it was taken up by the state itself in the "Jewish census."[171] Cohen,

---

tum und Judentum"—one published in 1915 (*JS* 2:237–301 and *Werke* 16:465–560) and the second, responding to critics, in 1916 (*JS* 2:302–18 and *Werke* 17:109–32.]

167. In the letters to Lewandowsky. See this selection, note 36. [Emil Heinrich du Bois-Reymond (1818–96) was a professor of physiology in Berlin.]

168. He emphasized it in conversation with me, to demonstrate his impartiality.

169. According to a communication from Dr. Bruno Strauss.

170. *JS* 2:229–236. ["'Du sollst nicht einhergehen als ein Verläumder': Ein Appell an die Juden Amerikas ('You shall not go around as a slanderer': An appeal to the Jews of America"), *Werke* 16:299–310. The *New Yorker Staats-Zeitung* is a German-language newspaper that has been published in New York since 1834.]

171. As reported by my mother, Cohen was very annoyed by the timidity of the "councilors" [*Justizräte*] and would have liked to see a more decisive and self-confident protest. [The

after all, like all of German Jewry, had regarded the war against Russia as a war against the czarist abuse of the human rights of the Jews. Yet, to repeat, he did not live to see the end.

It would be a mistake to seek the reason for his attitude toward Zionism in such excesses of German patriotism. To be sure, his first public statement might suggest such a connection: he was one of the signatories of a declaration in a newspaper in early 1914 in which the leading personalities of German Jewry disavowed any common cause with the Zionists.[172] His valiant participation in a milieu far beneath his own resulted in difficulties for him later. It was not until 1916 that he fully developed his own position on Zionism, when he was asked by the anti-Zionist Jewish fraternities to write on the subject for their monthly *Blätter*.[173] Following a rejoinder by the spiritual leader of the new Zionist youth, Martin Buber, which Buber published in his journal *Der Jude*, Cohen responded, again in the *K.C.-Blätter*, whereupon Buber, with yet another rejoinder, closed the conversation. A fruitful encounter might have come of it. At the time, Buber was about to turn away from mysticism, the basis of his fame, and to discover a concept of religion that, by deploying the fundamental word "relation" placed him in proximity to Cohen — to the Cohen of correlation — that was more than a matter of terminology. It was not just that Cohen had developed the concept of nationality in his beautiful chapter on "Loyalty" in the *Ethics* — nationality is not necessarily identical to a political nation: the individual nonetheless owes his loyalty to his nationality, and the state owes him forbearance. It was not just that he had begun to apply this concept of nationality to Judaism. More than that: Cohen had already undergone the development described above, making explicit in his writings what until then could only be read between the lines. As it was, however, neither Cohen nor Buber saw the other as a partner. The younger one was at an advantage in the defense, insofar as he at least expressed himself clearly, while his elder, when on the attack, was often only able to grab hold of

---

"Jewish Census" (*Judenzählung*), a census of Jews serving in the Germany army during World War I, was ordered by the German command in 1916. German Jews, the vast majority of whom supported the war effort and served with pride, regarded the census as an affront to their patriotism.]

172. *JS* 2:477 [The full text of the newspaper declaration is included by Rosenzweig in his notes but is not included here.].

173. [The *K.C.-Blätter*, a monthly journal published by the Kartell-Convent der Verbindungen deutscher Studenten jüdischen Glaubens (Association of fraternities of German students of the Jewish faith). It ran from October 1910 to February 1933.]

the cape his opponent had cast on the ground. In a word, Cohen was only able to see the Zionism that he had once, in a conversation with Ahad Ha'am,[174] easily dismissed. Then, Cohen had invoked the universalism of the prophets, to which Ahad Ha'am responded by citing the verse from Isaiah that specifically addresses proselytes: "These I will bring to my holy mountain. . . ."[175] Whereupon Cohen responded by citing the continuation of the verse, "and make them joyful in my house of prayer"—only in my house of *prayer*. When he encountered a different kind of Zionism, such as in the person of N. A. Nobel,[176] for a long time the only Zionist among the German rabbis, his antipathy was subdued. Cohen sought to place him in a most prominent position, albeit without wanting to acknowledge the seriousness and the chthonic amalgamation of Zionism and Orthodoxy in this Goethe-intoxicated mystic. And in the two essays for Graetz's centennial celebration[177] Cohen still firmly maintains, in principle, his own position in all its purity, even while invoking "our Graetz," as he is now called. The essays represent, in themselves, a magnificent palinode of the cruel attack that Graetz's old pupil, thirty-seven years before, had directed against the Palestinianism of the great national historian. However, even in the debate of 1916, the most serious reason for Cohen's rejection of Zionism never came to light. It comes into view only in a single passage in his magnum opus, where, in passing, he mentions Zionism as an "episode."[178] What he meant by this can be elucidated by something he said to me, reproaching me for my all too tolerant attitude toward Zionism, while I sought to defend it. He interrupted me midsentence, thrusting his enormous head forward, framed by the most delicate curls. Intimidatingly close to my face, he said: "I want to tell you something," and then, toning down his voice to a thundering whisper, "those fellows want to be happy!" The future of Zionism will be decided by the question whether these words speak for it or against it. Cohen would be right if he were arguing against a Zionism that limited its

174. As reported by Cohen himself. [Ahad Ha'am is the *nom de plume* of Asher Ginsberg (1856–1927), a central figure in the *Hibbat Zion* (Love of Zion) movement.]

175. [Isa. 56:7.]

176. [Nehemiah Anton Nobel (1871–1922), a rabbi in Frankfurt from 1910, had studied under Cohen in Marburg and was a major influence on Rosenzweig and his circle. A charismatic speaker, he was also known for lacing his sermons with quotations from Goethe.]

177. ["Zur Jahrhundertfeier unseres Graetz (On the hundredth anniversary of our Graetz)," JS 2:446–53; "Graetzens Philosophie der jüdischen Geschichte (Graetz's philosophy of Jewish history)," JS 3:203–12.]

178. [RR 360.]

methods and goals to the scope of an episode, a Zionism that was unaware that we would never have arrived at the notion of messianism if our national history had been happy—a phrase from an oft-quoted lecture. Not only would Cohen be right: Zionism will, I hope, refute him, proving him right.

Once again, shortly before his death, an opportunity presented itself for him to have an active role in Jewish affairs. This time the impetus came from me. When I addressed my open letter[179] to him, I had no notion how closely the substance of my proposal would align with the "Two Proposals for Securing our Future"[180] that Cohen had circulated in 1907 in the report of the *Großloge für Deutschland*.[181] I had proposed coupling educational reform with subsidies for scholars. Together, these two measures, which would be mutually beneficial, both intellectually and in a practical sense, constituted the essence of my proposal. Cohen was kind enough to take up the idea anew and assume responsibility for it as his own, devoting the last weeks of his life to it. The *Neue jüdische Monatshefte*,[182] in which he had collaborated on almost every issue since its founding, published his call for the establishment of an Academy for the Academic Study of Judaism.[183] Unlike the Society for the Advancement of the Academic Study of Judaism, the task of which was only to publish works of scholarship, the purpose of the academy would be, above all, to establish salaried academic positions. These positions would be held by those people who, at the same time, would meet the needs of large urban congregations for advanced instruction and continuing education, in their role as "senior religion teachers." Thus, among these congregations they would foster a direct interest in jointly supporting the positions at the academy. This final plan of Cohen's too was only half successful. When it was implemented, only the academic aspect received attention; of the integration of the theoretical with the practical component of the plan,[184] so typical of Cohen, nothing was left.

179. [On Rosenzweig's open letter, "It Is Time," see this selection, note 1.]

180. "Zwei Vorschläge zur Sicherung unseres Fortbestandes," JS 2:133–41.

181. [The Großloge für Deutschland U.O.B.B. was the German chapter of B'nai B'rith (Unabhängiger Orden Bne Briss [the Independent Order of B'nai B'rith]), the Jewish fraternal benevolent society.]

182. [Cohen was one of the founders of this magazine (New Jewish monthlies), which was published from 1916–17 to 1919–20.]

183. "Zur Begründung einer Akademie für die Wissenschaft des Judentums [On the establishment of an Academy for the Academic Study of Judaism]", JS 1:210–17.

184. In his personal advocacy, of course, it was appropriate to emphasize now the one, now the other.

Thus, his attempts, in the magnificent final five years of his existence, to conquer life head-on for the sake of an idea all ended in failure. He felt it; it affected him and yet did not defeat him. In those years Lessing's proverb, "Is not the whole of eternity mine?"[185] which his *Ethics* has entered into the family records of humankind, took on an increasingly concrete meaning for him. In his posthumously published book the "sources of Judaism" were allowed only a certain personal and incidental meaning in relation to the "religion of reason." He actually seems to concede this point in his treatment of the general question of the history of religion. The sources of Judaism thus unexpectedly turn into original sources for Cohen, in the systematic sense of "purity." Now, analogously, it is Judaism, his Judaism, that has become the living guarantor of humanity. The lecture on Plato and the Prophets,[186] the transcript of which is being published in this collection, concludes with a passionate shout of joy: "But we—are eternal!"[187] These were the last words he uttered from his lectern in the lecture hall of the Institute.

In the transcript they are lacking. But that too is of their essence. He did not speak them; they welled up and then overcame him. A certain pathos, which was always aphoristic and thus always credible, was one of his forms of expression; the other was his sense of humor, mostly in conversation. His sense of humor always—I have no other word for it—had its eyes on the systematic and was thus present in every utterance, full of meaning and inexhaustible. As dissimilar as both these modes of expression are, they were mutually complementary, elucidating one another. I can hear the burst of laughter, interrupting the shout of eternal joy—it must have been around the same time—when he recalled that not only Dante, no, Plato too, his beloved Plato, apparently took great delight in describing the torments of hell. He then invoked that verse from the Psalms "What is man!" in a tone of deep resignation[188] and immediately after that, still trembling with fright over Plato's and Dante's damnations of hell, let out a serene sigh of relief: "if he isn't a Yid!" This was the personal, humorous side of his eternal pathos.

Of course, all this did not mean that he withdrew into a spiritual ghetto. The rich breadth of his interests was undiminished. At the Institute he also

185. [See selection 2, n8.]

186. ["Das soziale Ideal bei Platon und den Propheten (The social ideal in Plato and the Prophets)," JS 1:306–30 (selection 4).]

187. I was present myself.

188. [The allusion is to Ps. 8:4: "What is man, that you are mindful of him?"]

lectured on the history of Greek philosophy. And when he refuted and reproved Schmoller in the *Monatshefte*[189]—one of the most brilliant works of journalism he produced in his last years—he was speaking equally as a professor emeritus and as a German Jew. When he argued for retaining or reinstating Hebrew in Jewish religious education and liturgy, he sensed a parallel between that struggle and the struggle for Greek in the gymnasium, in which Cohen likewise felt called upon to take a public position in those same years. And above all else: his psychology, the fourth part of his system, was still pending; in his last days he still spoke of it, that he hoped, finally, to write it "this summer."[190] But now that sentence from the year 1912 would become fully true in his life: his spirit had found its natural point of orientation, the center of his life; his mind had found true unity. Multiplicity, manifold trajectories, a delineated periphery—all of this remains in place. In fact, now it all came alive, now that the beating of his heart was audible. To be sure, he achieved this unity of the heart—it was he who defended the metaphysical profundity of this foundational concept of Bahya's work against Bacher's scholarly Arabist objections[191]—he achieved this unity of the heart at a high price: forsaking the world that, for four decades, was his own. He had to bear the full, external consequences of the step he had taken in 1912. In the face of the scant attention paid to him by official Berlin, he would say, mockingly: "But I'll have a beautiful *levayah* (a beautiful funeral)."[192] However, in this too he was mistaken: when he died, Marburg sent his old companion from the capital city of the Marburg school to bid a final farewell, but in Berlin neither the university nor the Academy of Sciences took any notice that the sole philosophical thinker who had salvaged the honor of the German university in the age of Nietzsche was being brought to his final resting place in Weissensee.[193]

189. *JS* 2:381–97. ["Betrachtungen über Schmollers Angriff (Observations on Schmoller's attack)." Gustav von Schmoller (1838–1917), a widely read economist, published several essays that Cohen criticizes as attacks on the status of the Jew in the modern state. See Wiedebach, *The National Element*, 37–38. *Monatshefte* refers to the *Neue jüdische Monatshefte*.]

190. As reported by Leo Rosenzweig.

191. ["Die Einheit des Herzens bei Bachja (Unity of the heart in Bahya)," *JS* 3:213–20. Cohen's debate with Wilhelm Bacher (1850–1913) on the origin and meaning of the concept of "the unity of the heart" in Bahya starts with Bacher's "Zu Bachja ibn Pakudas Herzenspflichten (On Bahya ibn Pakuda's *duties of the heart*)," *Monatsschrift für Geschichte und Wissenschaft des Judentums* 54, no.3 (1910): 348–51.]

192. As reported by Leo Rosenzweig.

193. [The vast Jewish cemetery in Berlin-Weissensee, dedicated in 1880, where Cohen is buried in the *Ehrenreihe* (honor row).]

Of course, representatives of Jewish Berlin were present. And Eastern European Jews, driven to Berlin in great numbers by the war, followed the great son of our people to his grave by the hundreds.

During Cohen's lifetime, the *Monatshefte* published a series of articles, most of them weaker versions of the parallel individual chapters in "The Religion of Reason: Out of the Sources of Judaism,"[194] the book that appeared two years later, published from Cohen's literary estate. In this work, which will still be read when the language in which Cohen wrote it is understood only by scholars, the entire Jewish harvest of this life is preserved. And thus it is, in the end, the harvest of his entire life. Cohen's concerns have been assuaged, the concerns about systematic classification that had determined the structure and content of that major preliminary study of 1915. To be sure, he skirts no difficulties, and the path of the argument is laid out upon a base consisting of the concepts that he had formed in that preliminary study. However, a kind of supreme naïveté holds sway over the entire book, the kind of naïveté that otherwise erupts only in brief moments in Cohen. It is a naïveté of consciousness: it knows that the sources are entrusted to him, both for their protection and for the purpose of slaking the thirst of his own soul, and that, once released through the channels of reason, they will irrigate the entire earth. The homecoming that began in 1880, precisely at the midway point of his life, reached its goal when the second half of his life was completed. The book is both the sign and the fruit of his homecoming, now complete. It is dedicated neither to a philosophical school, nor to anyone whom the author encountered just because of the path his life happened to take. It is dedicated to the memory of the man to whom he was indebted for his connection, in body and soul, to that homeland of blood and spirit that can never be lost. It is dedicated to his father.

194. [See selection 7, n2.]

9

Alexander Altmann: Hermann Cohen's Concept of Correlation (1962)

Franz Rosenzweig has presented an impressive argument[1] that in Hermann Cohen's two late works, his programmatic monograph of 1915[2] and his 1919 book,[3] published posthumously, a "new fundamental concept" makes it appearance. To be sure, this concept played a "methodological role" in Cohen's earlier thinking, but it was not a fundamental concept. We are referring to the concept of "correlation," which secures the peculiar character of religion. Whereas up to that point Cohen had striven to show that religion merges into ethics,[4] now religion shifts, for him, to the center of cultural consciousness. To be sure, the "principle of unified scientific truth," the "methodological matrix" (BR 114), is not undermined by religion. Religion does not possess "independence," but only "particular character." It is only "associated" with the three "trajectories" of cultural consciousness (logic, ethics, and aesthetics); it is placed neither above them nor beneath them as their matrix. However, as Rosenzweig correctly emphasizes, religion thus attains an "omnipresence" unlike what any other philosophy of religion, as one component among others, could ever achieve.

The methodological tool that Cohen uses to work out his new concept of religion is the concept of correlation. There is no doubt that this fundamental concept leads to the discovery of a new concept of God and of the human being and that it gives Cohen the philosophical voice to speak of his deep religiosity and love of Judaism. But does this concept mean more than that? Rosenzweig interprets it as the overcoming of Idealism, as a "forceful advance" beyond the philosophical movements of the nineteenth century and "into the terrain of the philosophical future," that is, toward the path of the "new thinking" that Rosenzweig was following himself. He does not deny that the "supporting pil-

---

1. In his introduction to *JS*, 1:xlv–l [selection 8, pp. 221–26].

2. *BR*.

3. *(Die) Religion der Vernunft aus den Quellen des Judentums* (Leipzig[, Germany: G. Fock], 1919). [By enclosing *"Die"* in parentheses, Altmann indicates he is aware of the error explained in selection 7, n2.]

4. See Hermann Cohen, *Ethik des reinen Willens* (Berlin[: Bruno Cassirer], 1904), cited by the 4th ed. [corresponding to *Werke* 7, abbreviation: *ErW*].

lars" of Cohen's system remain untouched, that the concept of correlation is a "methodological tool," for "it is a philosophical statement that is at stake here." But, juxtaposing this new foundational concept to the foundational concepts of the system, he presents it as something entirely different: "The foundational concepts of the system were always concepts of generation and origin." Nature, humanity, art were "derived, conceived, explained, and their foundations were laid; however, no consideration was given to the possibility that they existed prior to all derivation, explanation, or foundation laying, that their facticity was prior to their givenness as object or task." The concept of correlation, however, as Rosenzweig construes it, is not a generative concept. It does not contest the reality of what it generates, as is "almost necessarily" the case with the concept of generation in Idealism. Where the relationship is one of mutuality, then it is impossible that one side be derived from the other. The "charmed circle" of Idealism is broken. "Facticity" is secured for both sides of the relationship. "Thus, the last great heir of Idealism was the one who breached its boundaries, indeed, the boundaries of all previous philosophy. . . ."

Does this presentation of Cohen do justice to the issue? Does Cohen's concept of correlation really signify a breakthrough that leads beyond Idealism into dialogic thinking, as Rosenzweig and, after him, Samuel Hugo Bergman[5] understood it? Or is Julius Guttmann correct in his judgment that Cohen's new turn to religion does indeed change the content of the idea of God, but not its methodological character?[6] The purpose of this inquiry is to clarify that question.

Let us begin by defining terms. The correlation of God and the human being refers first of all to the mutual connection of the concepts of God and the human being: "Neither of the two can be thought of in isolation. When I think of God, I must also think of the human being at the same time, and I cannot think of the human being without simultaneously thinking of God" (BR 96). "God is conditioned by correlation with the human being. And the human being is

5. See his [Bergman's] essay in the memorial volume, *Between East and West — Essays Dedicated to the Memory of Bela Horowitz*, ed. Alexander Altmann (London[: East and West Library], 1958), 43: "Cohen's path led from the idealistic ego to the correlative I-Thou." See also Bergman's presentation of Hermann Cohen in *Faith and Reason: An Introduction to Modern Jewish Thought*, trans. and ed. Alfred Jospe (Washington, D.C.[: B'nai B'rith Hillel Foundations], 1961), 49.

6. Julius Guttmann, *Philosophie des Judentums* (Munich: Ernst Reinhardt, 1933), 361. [For an English translation, see *Philosophies of Judaism*, trans. David W. Silverman (New York: Holt, Reinhart, and Winston, 1964), 366–67.]

conditioned by correlation with God."[7] "His [the human's] being consists of the concept of God" and "thus God too is conditioned by the human being."[8] Thus, correlation expresses a relationship between the *concepts* of God and the human being. We are dealing with concepts, as Cohen stresses time and again: "They are both total concepts and therefore authentic logical abstractions, the logical value of which cannot be produced by a species of feeling" (BR 96). Correlation "resides in the concept of God"[9] and of the human being.

The term "correlation" is therefore, in principle, a concept of logic. Cohen establishes its logical character beyond all doubt.

How did I arrive at the notion of correlation at all, to which we here ascribe foundational significance and have now tried to prove? Correlation is a basic form of philosophical thought, in our terminology of judgment. Its general name is purpose. Wherever a concept is in formation, there a purpose is established. It is a teleological relation that we set up between God and the human being, just as between God and nature. If we were to ask how we arrived at the correlation between God and the human being, the answer is: that is how judgment proceeds in the determination of purpose, which has its general form altogether in the formation of concepts. Thus, if I seek to form the concept of God, I must establish a teleological relation between God and the human being and thus also derive the concept of the human being from the structure in the content of the concept of God, and the other way around. This is, in general, the elementary significance of purpose for a concept (BR 47).

In Cohen's posthumously published book as well the term correlation retains this general meaning, relating to logic: "our philosophical language calls it correlation, which is the term for all concepts of reciprocal relation" (RV 100 / RR 86).

The "logic" in which Cohen anchors the concept of correlation is not formal logic, but Cohen's own "logic of origin." It overcomes the medieval concept of the absolute and, with it, medieval metaphysics.[10] "Absolute substance is thus not only a presupposition of relation; it is now correlation" (LrE 517). The "methodological core" of logic consists of "the idea of hypothesis" in the sense in which Cohen understands and elaborates this Platonic concept: as "foundation laying,"

7. "Der heilige Geist [The holy spirit]," JS 3:191.
8. BR 136. As early as in his essay "Religion und Sittlichkeit" (1907) Cohen states that the "idea of humanity" constitutes the "correlate of the unity of God" (JS 3:150).
9. JS 3:190.
10. LrE, 516–17.

as the "thinking of the origin."[11] "Thought may have no origin external to itself" (*LrE* 11). "Only thought itself can generate that which has validity as being" (*LrE* 67). The "laying of a foundation is the cast of the anchor" that secures the basis, the ultimate ground of cognition (*LrE* 73). But the concept of generation proves itself only in relation to its object, that is, in correlation. Thus, Cohen remarks in his discussion of the problem of space:

> In the case of space, the correlative value of thought for being is actually given meaningful expression for the first time. . . . The problem of nature requires the correlation of something external to something internal. The concept of pure generation is based on this correlation. Pure cognition contains the relationship to nature as object. In all such postulates . . . space was already *thought as well, simultaneously;*[12] for it gives independent expression to the necessary correlation of the internal and external. (*LrE* 161)

One can see how tightly linked are the concepts of correlation and foundation laying in Cohen's thought.

At the same time, the concept of correlation rules out the concept of immanence. Cohen's treatment of the concept of God in his religious writings is not the first time that he draws a distinction between correlation and immanence. The distinction is already present in his "logic of origin," offering a noteworthy proof of the continuity and coherence of Cohen's thought. It is imprecise to say: permanence is immanent in motion, just as it would be imprecise to say motion is immanent in substance. "Correlation must take the place of immanence; and it must be conceived of not formally, but methodologically. The two concepts in themselves require one another; when they correlate, they bring about cognition" (*LrE* 202).

As we saw, when Cohen linked the religious concept of correlation to his logic, he stressed the connection between concept and purpose. What is the meaning of this connection, and how is it consonant with the concept of correlation? The answer to these questions is provided in the chapter on the "Judgment of the Concept" in the *Logic of Pure Cognition*. "Purpose"—as Socrates first

11. See Walter Kinkel, "Das Urteil des Ursprungs [The judgment of origin]," *Kantstudien* 17, no. 3 (1912): 274–82; Josef Solowiejczyk [Joseph Soloveitchik (1903–93)], "Das reine Denken und die Seinskonstituierung bei Hermann Cohen [Pure thought and the constitution of being in Hermann Cohen]," (PhD diss., University of Berlin, 1932).

12. See the sentence cited above: "When I think of God, I must also think of the human being at the same time . . ."

discovered purpose, through its concept—describes the form of the question through which Cohen defines "concept." Purpose is the eternal question mark of the conscience, including the theoretical conscience. Thus, the entire description of "concept" transpires through "purpose" (*LrE* 304). In a magnificent historical overview, Cohen shows how purpose, for Aristotle, becomes the principle of motion, the prime mover, how this hypostatization leads, in the Middle Ages, to personification; how then Spinoza, with his disdain for the *causa finalis*, "throws out the baby with the bathwater"; and how, finally, Kant, in the *Critique of Practical Reason*, rehabilitates the significance of teleology, at least for ethics (*LrE* 305–8). Cohen, however, both elaborating on Kant's concept of purpose and yet going beyond it, presents the connection between purpose and concept. "The metaphysics of purpose must be resolved into the logic of the concept" (*LrE* 314). "The concept is a question and remains a question, nothing other than a question. The answer too, which it contains, must be a new question, pose a new question" (*LrE* 326). Cohen speaks of a "reciprocal interaction" of question and answer that transpires in the system of the concept (*LrE* 326). Thus, concept, purpose, and correlation are all intrinsically connected. This emerges most clearly in Cohen's distinction between the philosophical and the popular concept of purpose. In popular thinking it is the correlation of means and purpose that dominates. Purpose is the higher concept, to which the means are then connected. By contrast, philosophical thinking requires that they be "terms that are equal in rank." It requires correlation, that is, purpose is not independent, superior to the means, but it is at best a means itself, with which the first means is associated, in correlation. This idea of correlation gives expression to the general character of the concept: it is the "unity of solution and problem" (*LrE* 335–37). This interpretation of "concept" is based upon the logic of origin as generative thought.

Cohen applied this idealistic principle—in Idealism's most profound sense —in all three trajectories of thought, in *Logic of Pure Cognition, Ethics of Pure Will* and *Aesthetics of Pure Feeling*. He adheres to it no less forcefully with regard to religion. In his programmatic monograph of 1915, deviating fundamentally from the position he took in the *Ethics*, he assigns religion a "particular character," but not "independent status." "Religion attaches to these generative trajectories of consciousness, bringing to them the particular character of its special contribution to the cultural consciousness of humankind. It does so inasmuch as cultural consciousness culminates, with regard to all its concepts of the human being and of God, in the correlation of the human being and God" (*BR* 136). For this reason, we cannot ascribe any reality to God (beyond being), since such reality would negate the unity of the systematic concept of God. "For reality presupposes existence, and existence presupposes that phenomenon of consciousness that constitutes sensibility. By contrast, the systematic unity of consciousness is directed . . . solely at the purposeful generative trajectories of the contents of the system." "In this way religion is grafted into the system of philosophy" (BR 136). It is the main goal of the programmatic monograph to secure legitimacy for the specific character of religion "from within the system," that is, to delineate it from the other elements of the system and to demonstrate that the specific character of religion "provides a new kind of completion to the system of philosophy" (BR 14). Cohen's posthumously published book makes no change in this basic position. Likewise, correlation does not upset the idealistic structure. Here too correlation is understood as a basic methodological norm (RV 410), as "our guide" (RV 244 / RR 207); as "the main scaffolding of religious knowledge" (RV 244 / RR 207); as a "fundamental equation" (RV 132 / RR 114), from which certain requirements arise. Correlation thus "requires" that God plants his spirit in the human being (RV 104 / RR 89); thus, correlation "brings it about" that the human being is conceived of as the "fellow human being" (RV 132 / RR 113–4) and "generates" the fellow human being (RV 188 / RR 161).[13]

As Cohen elaborates and draws out the substantive implications of correlation, his idealistic position remains constant. Correlation, as a norm, proves to be extraordinarily fruitful for the interpretation of "Religion of Reason" out of "the sources of Judaism," sources of which he makes loving use. Although it discloses new meaning, this mode of interpretation does not, in principle, go beyond the realm of thought understood as the generation of concepts. Let us follow the stages in this disclosure of meaning, as we encounter them in the programmatic monograph of 1915 and in Cohen's posthumous work.

The concept of correlation of God and the human being, by virtue of its intrinsic meaning, demonstrates that the specific character of religion cannot be reduced to ethics. Ethics is not capable of meeting all the "needs" of this correlation. Instead, religion is entitled to its "own combinations in this correlation" (BR 43–44). These represent new content that justifies incorporating religion into the [philosophical] system (BR 44). Not only with respect to ethics, but also in

13. See RV 193 / RR 165: "For the purpose of establishing the correlation of God and the human being, we have previously established the human being as a rational being and, further, as a fellow human being."

the context of the other elements of the system (logic, aesthetics, and psychology) religion proves to be sui generis and, at the same time, situated in relation to these elements [of the philosophical system].

1. RELIGION AND LOGIC

God means in religion what being means in philosophy (BR 45). In religion the being of God ("I am who I am") is the "unique being." But it does not declare all other being to be mere appearance, or to be naught, or to be identical with itself (BR 21–26). Instead, by virtue of the principle of correlation, all other being can be conceived of as created being. "Although God alone thus represents true being, there must nevertheless inhere in him a connection to the being of nature because of its necessary correlation to the human being. For this reason, with regard to being too, religion will require, in addition to the true being of God, the being of nature as well" (BR 45–46). Drawing directly upon earlier lines of thinking in *Ethics of Pure Will*, Cohen requires the creation of the world and its perdurance for the purpose of ensuring the possibility of the realization of morality. The innovation in the argument in the 1915 book is that they are now required under the perspective of correlation, whereas until then this requirement operated solely under the perspective of the idea of God. "*God means*," Cohen wrote earlier (ErW 450),[14] "*that nature will endure just as certainly as morality is eternal.*" In this new version, nature is not only the field of ethical realization. It is creation. The concept of correlation, which has now been made the basis of all foundation laying, is still oriented toward ethics, but it now opens up ontological perspectives as well. It encompasses the correlation of God and world and thus leads to the notion of creation (BR 47), dealt with at greater length in Cohen's posthumous book. Creation is "the consequence of uniqueness."[15] It signifies "the being of God, which is the being of the originative principle (*Ursprung*)" (RV 75 / RR 65). The being of God is juxtaposed to the becoming of nature as its "foundation" (RV 76 / RR 67). Seen in this ontological perspective—Cohen describes it, in keeping with his method, as "logical"—the concept of correlation appears as an analogue for the logic of origin (*das Denken des Ursprungs*). But Cohen does

14. [See selection 2, page 83: "*God means that nature will endure just as certainly as morality is eternal.*"]

15. RV 76 / RR 67: "Creation is God's primary attribute; it is not only the consequence of the uniqueness of God's being; creation is simply identical with it."

not leave it at that. The specific character of religious thought is expressed in "God's determination of the purpose of the future of existence." It answers the question: "What purpose does God have for the existence of nature? Or, also: what purpose does the existence of nature have for God?" (BR 49). This problem transcends the logic of the concept, pointing in the direction of the idea, to the idea of God as well as the idea of the human being, which are in correlation to one another. The substance of this question, Cohen says, presupposes ethics. Nevertheless, the problem as such belongs in the sphere of religion that here both merges with logic and differentiates itself from it at the same time (BR 49).

In *Religion of Reason*, the analogy of religion to logic is elaborated further in the concept of revelation. The correlation of human being and God provides the ground for both creation and revelation (RV 95 / RR 82). The general meaning of revelation is "that God enters into relation with the human being" (RV 82 / RR 71). This relation, however, is understood not in a metaphysical sense, but in the sense of a foundation laying. "Just as being is the necessary prerequisite for becoming, so too is [the problem of revelation], in an eminent way, the necessary prerequisite for the becoming of the human being. It is only by virtue of revelation that the rational creature, the human being, comes to be. This statement is of the same logical power as the one about the uniqueness of being . . . as the presupposition of becoming" (RV 82-83 / RR 71). This is not a case of "causality," but of its "precondition," which is "contained" in being (that is, as we might say, is posited) (RV 83 / RR 72). "For being has the immanent meaning of revelation as well as of creation. Revelation is the creation of reason" (RV 84 / RR 72). "The uniqueness of God determines his relation to human reason. And human reason, as God 's creation, determines the human being's relation to God as a rational relation and therefore also determines the consummation of this rational relation in revelation, which together with creation establishes the correlation of the human being and God" (RV 95 / RR 82). "Creation and revelation take effect only through reason. Both of these concepts turn out to be expressions of correlation, and therefore both of them are based on the concept of reason. . . ." (RV 103 / RR 88).

Cohen sees correlation, expressed in creation and revelation, as having its "ground" in the concept of unique being as the presupposition of becoming (RV 102 / RR 88). That is, from the perspective of logic, correlation is identical to the logic of origin. Only "with the notion of purpose" is it that "the concept of correlation moves from the realm of theoretical knowledge into the realm of the ethical" (RV 108 / RR 93). Thus, we may distinguish between two concepts of correlation in Cohen: a theoretical concept (which is identical to the logic of origin) and an ethical concept (which involves purpose). In his presentation of the theoretical concept, to which the concepts of creation and revelation belong, Cohen is careful to exclude all metaphysical concepts (such as emanation, or causality as a form of communication). On the other hand, just because of the concept of correlation, he cannot avoid speaking of God and the human being as discrete essences and thus create the appearance that they have become meta-physical absolutes. "The spirit of the human being can . . . not be the spirit of God" (RV 104 / RR 89). "The human being is spirit. And spirit comes from God, 'who placed it,' who planted it in the human being" (RV 105 / RR 90). But in the same breath we hear: "However, God gives his spirit to the human being, as correlation requires" (RV 104 / RR 89); "through knowledge . . . God enters into necessary correlation with the human being" (RV 105 / RR 90). "Correlation is the decisive concept" (RV 104 / RR 89); "spirit becomes . . . the mediating concept, the concept that effects correlation between God and the human being" (RV 103 / RR 88). Thus, it is clear that Cohen has prevented these concepts from becoming metaphysical absolutes.

2. RELIGION AND ETHICS

In ethics correlation means the correlation of God and humanity: "To en-able humanity to act in accord with the eternity of the ideal, ethics requires the idea of God" (BR 60). But the concept of the human being is "hardly defined, in every respect, by ethics" (BR 56). The individual as such cannot be dissolved into the pure idea of the human being as it is represented by the totality of the state and the union of states. In such a totality, the individual still remains an individual. "Ethics itself requires this concept and its generation" (BR 56), that is, it requires religion. However, the "conceptual origin" of religion resides in the individual's consciousness of sin. This is where the "new concept of the human being" comes into effect (BR 58) and, "in accordance with the new concept of the human being," there emerges, in tandem, "a new concept of God" as well. The correlation of God and humanity, which is peculiar to ethics, expands to encompass the correlation of God and the human being. This is the "particular characteristic of religion" (BR 60). The uniqueness of the human being corre-sponds to the uniqueness of God (BR 61). In this "transition to religion" (BR 61), a new concept of God is required for the new concept of the human being as sinful individual (BR 62). "The unique God thus brings about a significance of its uniqueness: it is unique for the human being, insofar as the human being must be conceived of as unique" (BR 61). In other words, the concept of the unique God is a correlational concept that expresses a purpose. It derives its meaning from the question, "What does the unique God accomplish . . . for the unique human being?" (BR 61). The answer is: "the redemption of the individual" (BR 63), not in the sense of a gift of grace or even of mere divine involvement in ethical labor,[16] but in the sense of a "mark" of "success" (BR 63–64) of such labor. God is "conceived of as the goal" toward which the striving of the sinful human being is directed (BR 63). This is the "new meaning of God" that corresponds to the new concept of the sinful individual (BR 64). In this "new correlation" liberation comes about, that is, the redemption of the human being (BR 64). In redemption the concept of God "is completed" as "the God of religion" (BR 64). No further demonstration is needed that here too we are moving within the sphere of pure idealistic thought.[17]

In the rest of the analysis, the meaning of correlation is defined solely as conceptual and idealistic. Correlation "becomes active" in repentance and forgiveness. "The correlation of God and the human being, as it proceeds here, brings about this *logical consistency of concepts*" (BR 65). In analogy to the generation of the concept of God in the *Ethics* (*ErW* 442), it is stated here: "The sinfulness of the individual would be a chimera, if it were not that its goal, forgiveness, shines like a beacon from God" (BR 65). We may formulate it this way, that God guarantees the meaningfulness of repentance: "without forgiveness repentance would have no meaning" (BR 65). Thus, it is clear that correlation turns out to be a function that grants meaning. It encompasses the positing of the God of grace and forgiveness. At the same time, it places a limit on the horizon of the validity of the concepts posited. "Correlation is thus situated in a clear structure: here the human being, the individual in his isolation, and there God in his uniqueness" (BR 66). Correlation establishes the "transcendence" of God in the sense of the human being's capacity to declare his humanity. God is not involved in the ethical labor of the human being. The God of grace and forgiveness "has only this

---

16. See Immanuel Kant, *Die Religion innerhalb der Grenzen der bloßen Vernunft* [Religion within the limits of reason alone], in *Immanuel Kants Werke*, ed. Ernst Cassirer (Berlin[: Bruno Cassirer], 1923), 6:192, 264, 289, 324, and 328.

17. Compare, however, BR 92, where the concept of the individual is derived directly from correlation: "The individual is neither a logical nor an ethical concept in the narrower religious sense; it thus does not belong to a plurality, and also not to the totality. Instead, it arises, originates, in the correlation to God."

significance: to guarantee the goal, the success, the victory of the ethical labor undertaken by the human being himself" (*BR* 66). Cohen deploys the concept of correlation to develop, through it, the "pure monotheism of Judaism," in contrast to Christianity (*BR* 66–68).

Correlation also proves itself as theodicy. The suffering that the human being takes upon himself as punishment "transfigures" both God and the human being. It serves to advance the work of repentance and therefore no longer calls the essence of God or the human being into question (*BR* 69–70). But "how can God assume responsibility for the suffering of the pious?" (*BR* 74). As a "consequence of correlation" the love of God is "inherent" in love between human beings. "The suffering (*Leid*) of the pious must not be a matter of indifference to me. It awakens compassion (*Mitleid*) within me, and compassion is transfigured into love of the human being (*BR* 76). "In this way the concept of the fellow human being (*Mitmensch*) and the love of the fellow human being is based on knowing the poor as the pious." At the same time, the concept of God expands to become the concept of the "loving God." Just as human love is "the religious form of the social relationship between one human being and another," arising out of compassion, "with God too love only becomes active in religion" (*BR* 79). "The religious God can only decree sufferings of love." "Divine love appears only as it is conditioned by human love" (*BR* 80). The meaning of correlation is such that God's love for the human being is "inherent" in human love: God must love "poor human beings, because the human being must love his poor fellow human beings" (*BR* 80). In this "practical faith"—as Kant would call it—one can say nothing more about God than that he should be the motive of ethical and religious action. Again, correlation turns out to be a teleological relationship: human love points toward divine love.

In the *Religion of Reason*, we encounter the same kind of deployment of the concept of correlation. Only the order of topics is different; the direction is the opposite. First Cohen treats of "The Discovery of Man as Fellowman" (chapter 8) and "The Problem of Religious Love" (chapter 9), then "The Individual as the I" (chapter 10), and finally "Atonement" (chapter 11). In a pointed formulation, Cohen writes that the correlation of the human being and God "is in the first place that of the human being, as fellow human being, to God." The "significance" of religion—the "fundamental equation" of which is correlation (*RV* 133 / *RR* 114)—"proves itself" in that, initially, the human being, as fellow human being, "becomes a problem" and is "generated." Only "when the correlation between human being and human being is included" can the correlation of the human being and God "come into effect" (RV 133 / RR 114). Under the symbol of the covenant with Noah, "God places himself into an unceasing, a conceptual correlation with nature and with humankind within nature, with the human being as fellow human being" (RV 135–36 / RR 117). Relationships between one human being and another form the "inner correlation within the correlation of God and the human being" (RV 154 / RR 132). As the concept of the human being grows in the mutual correlation of human beings, "accordingly the content of the correlation of God and man also grows" (RV 155 / RR 133). "The correlation of the human being and God is built only upon" the basis of the social relations between human beings (RV 157 / RR 135). Cohen also uses the inverse formulation: religion, through its particular characteristic, that is, the correlation of the human being and God, generates the fellow human being (RV 188 / RR 161). We encounter this formulation in the chapter on the problem of religious love. Compassion and love transform the next human being (Nebenmensch) into the fellow human being (Mitmensch). That is the work of religion (RV 170 / RR 144). Only now, "after the human being has learned to love the human being as a fellow human being, is his thought turned back to God . . . that God loves the human being, and, indeed, the poor with the same favor as the stranger" (RV 172 / RR 147). "The formulations of correlation may be said to be the expression of this, God's love" (RV 175 / RR 150).

The concept of the individual, which Cohen's programmatic monograph of 1915 identifies with the sinful human being in need of salvation, is conceptualized more precisely in his posthumous work as the "absolute individual" (RV 193 / RR 165).[18] Through correlation the human being is generated, first as a "rational being" and then as a "fellow human being." The peculiarity of religion is shown in "that the correlation of God and the human being takes on the narrower meaning in relation to the human being, as individual and as I" (RV 194 / RR 166). In social morality the I is generated through the Thou (RV 209 / RR 179). Suffering and compassion disclose the Thou in the human being (RV 22 / RR 22). However, the I-Thou relation and the love of God toward the human being, which grows out of the I-Thou relation by means of correlation, does not exhaust the entire depth of correlation. The absolute individual, that is, the "isolated" human being (RV 197 / RR 168) in his guilt and desperation has need of correlation with God (RV 195 / RR 167–68). In this "new sense" of correlation, God has the meaning of the "redeemer from sin" (RV 244 / RR 207). The forgiveness of sin is "the most

18. "Absolute individuality" is mentioned earlier, in BR 92.

important content of the correlation of God and the human being" (RV 251/RR 213). "It is the meaning of God, and as well of the human being, that God has to grant atonement to the human being" (RV 252/RR 214). Hence, by the very meaning of correlation, there can be no mediator between God and the human being. "It is necessary for the notion of the correlation with God . . . that he and only he be the redeemer" (RV 244/RR 207–8). "Correlation is fitted to and concluded between the human being and God, and no other link may be inserted" (RV 236/RR 201). It is thus shown again that correlation generates the *concept* of God, in this case of God as the forgiver of sin. It is the "meaning" of God to grant reconciliation. In this God expresses his "goodness." This "meaning" circumscribes the "essence" of God, insofar as essence is understood in correlation to the human being: "for its essence consists of correlation with the human being," as Cohen interprets the medieval doctrine of "attributes of action." God is "the paradigm for the actions of the human being" (RV 252/RR 215). In chapter 6, "The Attributes of Action," we learn more explicitly how correlation and these attributes are logically connected. The concept of correlation is a "teleological concept." In the question, "what does purpose mean in the case of God? . . . The problem of correlation is implied." The purpose of action in relation to God is now defined so that the attributes of action come to be conceptually determined models for human action (RV 110/RR 94–95).[19]

3. RELIGION AND AESTHETICS

The concept of religion in the system of philosophy has been presented in two realms thus far, both of which operate with the concept of correlation. In relation to the logic of origin, correlation represents both creation and revelation. And in relation to ethics, it means, as we just saw, redemption. In what way can a border be established that separates religion from aesthetics, the third systematic division of (Kantian-) Cohenian philosophy? More precisely, what is the particular characteristic of religion in relation to aesthetic feeling?

The correlation of God and the human being, Cohen says, is not given directly to aesthetic consciousness. For "the sole objects of art" are the human being in

19. See also BR 106: "Only in correlation to the human being is the essence of God definable. Only those attributes may be ascribed to him that ground human morality and advance his emulation of God."

nature and the nature of the human being (BR 85). "Aesthetic objectivity," that is, the world that is generated by the aesthetic consciousness, is exhausted in the human being in nature and the nature of the human being. When God appears as a special object of the plastic and graphic arts, then it is not a case of generation by aesthetic feeling, but of direct religious correlation that is thus indirectly expressed in art. That God may appear as an object of art is "only an illusion" (BR 85–86). Nevertheless, the concept of love always poses the "danger of intermingling" art and religion. The pure feeling of aesthetics should be defined as "love," "out of fidelity to the ancient usage of the word eros" (BR 86). But, as we saw, religious consciousness of correlation is also recognized as love. It is important, then, to determine "the differences between the aesthetic and religious concepts of human love" (BR 86). It then becomes apparent that religious love takes hold of the human being as an individual, is "ignited" by his suffering, and expresses itself as compassion, whereas the aesthetic love of the artist sees in the individual only a type and transforms his suffering aesthetically. Thus, in tragedy, the suffering individual becomes a rising god (BR 88). The familiar distinction between eros and agape coincides in many respects with the distinction made here by Cohen. In aesthetic creativity, feeling possesses "all the force of activity" (BR 88). Feeling is thrown back by the work of art into the self, which in turn arises only in the act of aesthetic creation itself. Feeling in its "generative purity" is the "systematic means" (BR 88). In religion the fellow human being is discovered, is "situated alongside his 'I', and both are then directed toward God, from whom this illumination shown forth" (BR 89).[20] In art the self is constructed by pure feeling; in religion it is constructed by double correlation (the correlation of God and the human being and of human being to human being) (BR 89). Aesthetic love is therefore, in spite of its creative power, still "only fantasy," the "magic of eros" to which only magic itself matters; it is "just abstraction," just "a game of ideas that catch fire in the ardor of the heart"; whereas religious love has an "earnestness" "that, in its sublimity, exceeds even this sublime game" (BR 92).

20. The formulation above means that the fellow human being arises from the correlation of God and the human being. This contrasts with the other formulation, which states that compassion leads to God (see above in this selection, 253) and the passage (BR 98): "Thus, compassion leads, with the human being, to the other pole of correlation, to God." The seeming contradiction can be resolved by noting that the human being is led, by correlation, to the fellow human being, but that the love of one's fellow human being generates the loving God.

Religious feeling is thus recognized as compassion, that is, "as the discovery of the human being in suffering, as the discovery of the individual in the suffering human being, and as the discovery of his correlation with God, who is fitted into place, so to speak, by suffering and compassion" (BR 94). This is the "creative activity" of religious feeling. Schleiermacher's interpretation of religion as surrender to the universe, as "immediate consciousness," and as the "epitome of all higher feelings" is pantheistic (BR 95) and contradicts the meaning of correlation. His definition of religion as "yearning for love" (in his *Speeches*)[21] and (later, in his book on dogmatics) as the "feeling of an absolute dependence," juxtaposed to pantheistic identity, also does not do justice to the significance of religious feeling. "In this term one can just recognize the indeterminacy of this kind of consciousness, that has no objective content other than itself. . . . The whole objective indeterminacy of pantheism manifests itself here, no less than the conceptual barrenness of Romanticism" (BR 95–96). We may say, following Cohen's lead, that Schleiermacher transfers aesthetic feeling to religion. Yet God and the human being, as religion conceives of them, are essences and thus genuine logical abstractions, whose status as contents of consciousness cannot be generated by any kind of feeling (BR 96).

Correlation between the human being and God achieves its "fulfillment," "its vital and true completion," in yearning for God (BR 98), which has found its classic expression in the religious lyric poetry of the Psalms (BR 99–100). This is where the genuine limit is located between religion and aesthetic consciousness. Religious yearning—in Cohen's definition of the concept—is nothing other than the "passion" of compassion for the human being that then rises up to God (BR 98). It "arises not out of the pity of the lover for himself, seeking love in return, but the other way around. Love is the response, so to speak, to the compassion that is awakened by the soul one encounters and that is then reflected radiantly from one's own soul, directed toward God. Without compassion, this radiance toward God does not arise. Yearning for God is, first, the response to compassion; it is testimony to God" (BR 99). We can state that this is not roman-

---

21. Cohen is apparently thinking of the passage: "to perceive the world and to have religion, the human being must first have found humanity, and he will find it only in love and through love. It is for this reason they are so inwardly and inextricably connected: yearning for religion is what helps him to come into possession of religion" ([Friedrich] Schleiermacher, *Über die Religion: Reden an die Gebildeten unter ihren Verächtern* [On religion: Speeches to its cultured despisers], 2nd ed. (Leipzig[, Germany: Felix Meiner], 1911), 57.

tic yearning, which Hegel characterized as mere "exuberance."[22] This yearning is a fulfillment of correlation. "Whereas human love was defined in connection to compassion, love for God, as yearning, as desire of the soul, as a neediness of the individual that can be satisfied only by God, is defined in connection to religion (BR 99). The religion of the prophets is still just the religion of ethics. It is—this is Cohen's paradoxical formulation—not yet actually religion, but only ethics (BR 100). "Only in the Psalms is ethics transformed into religion," "does the human individual reveal itself in his correlation, in his yearning" (BR 100). "Only then does the correlation between God and the human being arise, in which we see the fundamental condition of religion" (BR 100). "Thus, it is yearning that ultimately brings about [the] correlation between God and the human being, and, as a consequence, religion (BR 102). For the God of yearning, as the God of redemption, is the God of the individual (BR 102). Thus, in Cohen, the yearning for redemption, which begins in the soul of the individual "in the distress of his sin" (BR 99), merges with the yearning for God, which erupts in compassion. In this way yearning joins with love and with the awareness of the nearness of God. All these terms—compassion, yearning, love, nearness—serve no purpose other than to indicate the "problem" that religion represents, as a particular characteristic of consciousness (BR 106–7).

In the *Religion of Reason*, the same arguments reappear, in part in modified form. The yearning for God, as expressed in the Psalms, is "the soul's confession of love." "The soul dissolves in this light, in this purity of yearning." "And despite this, the border of the mystical is never touched. Union with God is nowhere desired" (RV 249 / RR 212). The nearness of God remains the highest good for the human being, as the psalmist has said (Psalm 73:28). Such nearness is achieved through desperation (RV 249 / RR 212). To Cohen prayer is the expression for wrestling to achieve nearness to God. "Prayer is longing" (RV 442 / RR 374). The object of the human being's search will always remain a distant vision, as with any yearning. "For God can never become actuality for human love. The quest is an end in itself of the religious soul. Longing signifies and fills the entire inner life of the soul, to the extent that it is focused on correlation with God, for the purpose of engendering religion" (RV 442 / RR 374). The fact that Cohen is not prepared to forfeit the idealistic conceptual framework in favor of a mysticism

---

22. See *Briefe von und an Hegel* [Letters to and from Hegel], ed. Johannes Hoffmeister (Hamburg[, Germany: Meiner], 1952) 1:352ff., cited in Otto Pöggeler, *Hegels Kritik der Romantik* [Hegel's critique of Romanticism] (Bonn: H. Bouvier, 1956), 105.

of feeling is clear from the sentence in which he distinguishes the logical component in religion from the psychological component: "the fundamental form
of religion, the logical expression of which is the correlation of man and God,
is, psychologically, the love for God" (RV 441 / RR 373–4). "The love of God," as
Cohen put it in an earlier passage, "is the love for an ethical ideal." *"How is it
possible to love an idea?"* Cohen asks, and his answer is, "how is it possible to love
anything but an idea? Does one not love, even in the case of sensual love, only
the idealized person, the idea of the person?" "Pure love is directed only toward
archetypes, toward models upon which pure moral action can be established"
(RV 187 / RR 160). "This idealistic [!] meaning is the clear, exact sense of the love
for God" (RV 189 / RR 162).[23]

4. RELIGION AND PSYCHOLOGY

We have seen that the concept of correlation functions on three planes, according to whether its relation to logic, ethics, or aesthetics is under consideration. One could be tempted to characterize it as metalogical, metaethical, and
meta-aesthetical. As a metalogical concept it is merely a concept (creation, revelation); as a metaethical concept it extends to a teleological idea (redemption).
As a meta-aesthetical concept it can be understood through psychology, in compassion and yearning, but it cannot, on that account, be reduced to psychological
phenomena. Cohen makes this issue clear in his discussion of the relationship of
religion to psychology (chapter 5 of the programmatic monograph). Compassion
and yearning are "concepts" that, here, are employed with "systematic intention"
for distinguishing, that is, for rendering a conceptual definition of the individual.
The psychological processes of compassion and yearning are "illuminated" by
these concepts but may not be equated with them (BR 108). Only the "old naïve
view of psychology" can address these concepts as "their sole property." Cohen's
critical psychology, which is now called into action, is not a psychology of the
processes of consciousness. Its task is the problem of the unity of consciousness,
as the unity of cultural consciousness (BR 108–9). Its task is the "ideal unity of
consciousness," in which "all the main trajectories, the highways and byways"
of cultural consciousness are assigned their normative classification.[24] As far as

23. [The exclamation point following "idealistic" is Altmann's editorial flourish.]
24. See BR 134: "However, feeling thus proves to be the wrong term for this correlation,
for it acquires its methodological meaning only as systematic correlation."

religion is concerned, the problem should be formulated along these lines: by what methodological means can the correlation between God and the human being be allowed to take place—correlation being the peculiar characteristic of religion—without diminishing the rights of the three independent divisions of the system (logic, ethics, and aesthetics)? (BR 110). In the present context it cannot be our task to follow, in detail, the treatment of this problem and its solution. This brief account will deal with Cohen's presentation only to the extent that it can further illuminate the methodological meaning of correlation.

Conflict is not permitted between religion and systematic knowledge. The foundations of religion can be "nothing other than the positing of foundations" (BR 111).[25] Revelation, which we saw is given its foundation through correlation, "must therefore regard it as its most ideal interpretation when it is compared and set in analogy to the a priori of cognition and ... is understood as the eternal, as that which is the foundation of all development" (BR 111). In relation to ethics, in which the autonomy of the human being is argued, religion may not signify heteronomy. The God of religion is determined by ethics, in Cohen even more so than in Kant. Correlation, which is the basis of the peculiar character of religion, concerns the personal relationship of the sinful individual to the God of redemption, to God as the "personal surety" for the success of the individual's autonomous ethical task (BR 116–17). "The result, for the human being, of correlation with God consists of the concept of the human being as an individual, as an individual in his most intimate moral life" (BR 118). Cohen again devotes a thorough discussion—not without its share of repetitions—to the difference between religious feeling and aesthetic feeling. The concept of correlation, however, is illuminated in a new way in Cohen's debate with his friend Paul Natorp. Natorp defined religion as "the unmediated life of the soul," as the "original concretion of unmediated lived experience," and in this way sought to prove the "superior power" of religion over all other tasks, strengths, worries, and elevations of the human spirit. "The difference between us," Cohen says, "consists of this: that ... [for me] the correlation of God and the human being is the problem, whereas Natorp ... takes only the interpretation of human consciousness as his point of departure, probes its depths, and in so doing spares no effort to seek support in human consciousness for the supreme autonomy of

25. ["Die Grundlagen der Religion können daher auch nichts anderes sein als Grundlegungen" (BR 111). The "positing of foundations" (Grundlegungen) refers to Cohen's use of the notion of hypothesis as the basis of all knowledge. See, for example, BR 28–31.]

religion" (BR 122). As Cohen emphasizes, correlation requires that religion have a particular character, but not that it be independent. "Correlation . . . places the life of the soul in a balance with the being of God" (BR 122). On the basis of this "rigorous notion," any analogy with "any particular sector of the unity of consciousness is out of the question: with cognition, morality, and to say nothing of art" (BR 122–23).

Cohen defines the "ultimate meaning" of correlation as the separation, and therefore the preservation, of God and the human being (BR 134). In pantheism the human being is consumed by the all of the divinity, and his individuality is annihilated. "Saving individuality, however, is the actual task of religion" (BR 134). Religion is therefore not only the feeling of the infinite, but the feeling of the finite at the same time. "Correlation alone expresses the methodological connection between God and the human being" (BR 134). The unity of consciousness is guaranteed only by means of correlation. "Pantheism has no unity of consciousness" (BR 134). For—we can interpret it thus—the unity of consciousness encompasses a structure of the spheres of culture within itself, whereas pantheism—Cohen is thinking primarily of Spinoza—dissolves this structure into identity (see ErW 464). Spinoza's doctrine of divine substance knows no self-consciousness, to say nothing of cultural consciousness (BR 134). Thus, from the perspective of the unity of consciousness, what religion accomplishes cannot be overestimated. As opposed to logic, ethics, and aesthetics, "which all require that the finite merge into the totality of the infinite," religion secures the human individual in his finitude; "it places the human being on equal rank with God" (BR 135). Religion thus gives "conceptual precision" to what the biblical metaphor says about the human being: created in the image of God (BR 135–36).

Our analysis has shown that Cohen maintains his fundamental idealistic position throughout, and more than that: he applies all his energy to producing a "systematic concept of religion" (BR 137). "True religion," he stresses, is based "upon the truth of systematic philosophy, and, seen subjectively, true religiosity is based, accordingly, on the maturity and clarity of systematic knowledge" (BR 137–38). In his programmatic monograph Cohen concedes—to be sure, it is toward the end—that correlation is not simply a reciprocal relationship. Rather, God is its center of gravity. Being is transferred to this center of gravity. "Serving as this center of gravity, God alone supports being; he alone signifies and guarantees being. Therefore, in relation to nature and the human being, he is the unique one" (BR 137). And yet the transfer of the center of gravity to God does not mean that correlation is shattered. The definition of God as the unique being does not represent an excursion into the realm of metaphysics. Cohen immediately gives an interpretation of himself: "God's uniqueness is placed on a logical foundation only by the systematic concept of the human being" (BR 137). That is, God stands in correlation to the human being, to human cognition, which establishes the foundation of being itself, and for itself. "For all being of cognition, cognition itself establishes the foundation of absoluteness, of transcendence. To be sure, the latter winds its way back into cognition on account of correlation" (BR 137).

Thus, for Cohen the concept of correlation signifies a methodological concept in the precise sense that method possesses in idealistic thinking. Correlation is and remains a concept of origin and of generation and cannot, therefore, be interpreted after the manner of dialogic thinking. God as one pole of correlation is not a personal "Thou" but an idea,[26] however much this concept, methodologically deduced, may tend to assume personal features when it meets its psychological fulfillment in lived experience. Cohen's concept of correlation is also radically different from Paul Tillich's, although and exactly because the concept of correlation is the central methodological concept of theology for Tillich as well.[27] Tillich characterizes correlation as "a mutual dependence of question and answer,"[28] a formulation that, superficially, has a similar ring. However, for him the questions are those of human existence, and the answers are those that are "spoken into" human existence from the sources of revelation.[29] The correlation consists principally in this: that the form of the theological answer depends on the way in which the question is posed from out of the questioner's existential situation. "The human being cannot receive answers to questions he has never posed."[30] But the answer "cannot be derived from the analysis of existence." In this, Tillich is taking sides with Karl Barth, quite apart from all other differences, and against all idealistic interpretation of religion.[31] The contrast with this con-

26. This was recognized clearly, and early on, by Walter Kinkel, in *Hermann Cohen, eine Einführung in sein Werk* [Hermann Cohen, an introduction to his works] (Stuttgart[, Germany: Strecker und Schröder],1924), 224–25.

27. See Paul Tillich, *Systematische Theologie*, 2nd ed. (Stuttgart[, Germany: Evangelisches Verlagswerk], 1956), 1:73.

28. Tillich, 78. See Cohen's definition of concept in general as the "reciprocal interaction" of question and answer, discussed above (see page 246).

29. Tillich, 78.

30. Tillich, 79.

31. See on this point Walter M. Horton, "Tillich's Role in Contemporary Theology," in *Theology of Paul Tillich*, ed. Charles W. Kegley and Robert W. Bretall, the Library of Living

cept of correlation makes the contrast with Cohen's concept of correlation, conceived within the frame of Idealism, especially clear.

The question whether Cohen's argument shatters the frame of what can be generated within Idealism, the question whether it make demands of his method that exceed its capacity, is another matter. Especially Cohen's concept of God as the "unique being"[32] and the concept of the human being as the "absolute individual"[33] have been read as forays into the metaphysical. Yet our analyses have shown that both concepts are developed as genuine concepts of correlation. They are not metaphysical entities, but ideas in the sense of the a priori of Idealism. To be sure, going beyond Kant, Cohen concedes to religion its "own stratum as a category," but he does not concede [its] independence. Thus, he does not breach the "border" of "pure formalism."[34] Religion remains religion of reason. It is constructed, not received. As in Kant and Fichte (in his *Critique of All Revelation*),[35] reason prescribes to religion, a priori, both the content and the scope of its validity. Whatever the increase in content available to lived experience, religion remains within the "charmed circle" of idealistic and critical philosophy.

Theology (New York: MacMillan, 1959) 1:29, and further inquiries into Tillich's concept of correlation in the same volume, 98 *et passim*.

32. See Siegfried [Sinai] Ucko, *Der Gottesbegriff in der Philosophie Hermann Cohens* [The concept of God in the philosophy of Hermann Cohen] (Berlin[: Reuther und Reichard], 1929), 30–49.

33. See Walter Kinkel, 267.

34. Th. Siegfried, in his review of Cohen's *Jüdische Schriften* in the *Theologische Literaturzeitung* (53[, no. 8 (1928)]: 177–79), states that Cohen was "perched at the border," prepared "to forfeit his pure formalism and to concede to religion more than its meaning as a symbolizing function, that is, to concede it its "own stratum as a category." This characterization, however, does not do justice to Cohen's further development as represented in his two late works.

35. [Johann Gottlieb Fichte, *Versuch einer Kritik aller Offenbarung* (Königsberg[, Germany]: Hartungsche Buchhandlung, 1792).]

Suggestions for Further Reading

HERMANN COHEN'S WRITINGS IN ENGLISH

The Ethics of Maimonides. Translated by Almut Sh. Bruckstein. Madison: University of Wisconsin Press, 2003.

"Martin Buber and Hermann Cohen: A Debate on Zionism and Messianism." In *The Jew in the Modern World: A Documentary History,* edited by Paul Mendes-Flohr and Jehuda Reinharz, 571–77. 2nd ed. New York: Oxford University Press, 1995.

"The Polish Jew." Translated by Joachim Neugroschel. In *The Jew: Essays from Martin Buber's Journal "Der Jude" (1916–1928),* edited by Arthur A. Cohen, 52–60. University, AL: University of Alabama Press, 1980.

Reason and Hope: Selections from the Jewish Writings of Hermann Cohen. Translated by Eva Jospe. New York: W. W. Norton, 1971.

Religion of Reason out of the Sources of Judaism. Translated by Simon Kaplan. 2nd ed. with new introductions by Steven S. Schwarzschild and Kenneth Seeskin. Atlanta, GA: Scholars Press, 1995.

Spinoza on State and Religion, Judaism and Christianity. Translated by Robert S. Schine. Jerusalem: Shalem Press, 2014.

"Truth: The Connection between Logic and Ethics." Translated by Steven S. Schwarzschild. *Judaism* 15, no. 4 (1966): 466–73. [An excerpt from chapter 1 of *Ethics of Pure Will.*]

MAJOR SECONDARY LITERATURE IN ENGLISH

Batnitzky, Leora. *Leo Strauss and Emmanuel Levinas: Philosophy and the Politics of Revelation.* Cambridge: Cambridge University Press, 2006.

Batnitzky, Leora, and Shira Billet, eds. "Spinoza, Hermann Cohen and the Legacies of German Idealism." Special issue, *Jewish Studies Quarterly* 25, no. 2 (2018).

Beiser, Frederick C. *The Genesis of Neo-Kantianism.* Oxford: Oxford University Press, 2014.

———. *Hermann Cohen: An Intellectual Biography.* Oxford: Oxford University Press, 2018.

Billet, Shira. "The Philosopher as Witness: Hermann Cohen's Philosophers and the Trials of Wissenschaft des Judentums." PhD diss., Princeton University, 2019.

Bouretz, Pierre. *Witnesses for the Future: Philosophy and Messianism.* Translated by Michael B. Smith. Baltimore, MD: Johns Hopkins University Press, 2010.

Cassirer, Ernst. "Hermann Cohen and the Renewal of Kantian Philosophy." Translated by Lydia Patton. *Angelaki* 10, no. 1 (April 2005): 95–108.

Cohen Skalli, Cedric. "Cohen's Jewish and Imperial Politics during World War I." In *Cohen im Netz,* edited by Hartwig Wiedebach and Heinrich Assel, 173–93. Tübingen, Germany: Mohr-Siebeck, 2021.

Derrida, Jacques. "Interpretations at War: Kant, the Jew, the German." Translated by Moshe Ron. *New Literary History* 22, no. 1 (Winter 1991): 39–95.

Erlewine, Robert. *Monotheism and Tolerance: Recovering a Religion of Reason.* Bloomington: Indiana University Press, 2010.

Fackenheim, Emil. "Hermann Cohen—after Fifty Years." In *Jewish Philosophers and Jewish Philosophy*, edited by Michael L. Morgan. 41–56. Bloomington: Indiana University Press, 1996.

Gibbs, Robert, ed. *Hermann Cohen's Ethics*. Leiden, the Netherlands: Brill, 2006.

Gordon, Peter Eli. *Rosenzweig and Heidegger: Between Judaism and German Philosophy*. Berkeley: University of California Press, 2003.

———. "Science, Finitude, and Infinity: Neo-Kantianism and the Birth of Existentialism." *Jewish Social Studies*, n.s., 6, no. 1 (Fall 1999): 30–53.

Guttmann, Julius. *Philosophies of Judaism: The History of Jewish Philosophy from Biblical Times to Franz Rosenzweig*. Translated by David W. Silverman. New York: Holt, Rinehart, and Winston, 1964.

Köhnke, Klaus Christian. *The Rise of Neo-Kantianism: German Academic Philosophy between Idealism and Positivism*. Translated by R. J. Hollingdale. Cambridge: Cambridge University Press, 1991.

Liebeschütz, Hans. "Hermann Cohen and His Historical Background." *Leo Baeck Institute Year Book* 13 (1968): 3–33.

Munk, Reiner, ed. *Hermann Cohen's Critical Idealism*. Dordrecht, the Netherlands: Springer, 2005.

Myers, David N. "Hermann Cohen and the Quest for Protestant Judaism." *Leo Baeck Institute Year Book* 46 (2001): 195–212.

Nahme, Paul E. *Hermann Cohen and the Crisis of Liberalism. The Enchantment of the Public Sphere.* Bloomington: Indiana University Press, 2019.

Poma, Andrea. *The Critical Philosophy of Hermann Cohen*. Translated by John Denton. Albany: SUNY Press, 1997.

———. "Hermann Cohen: Judaism and Critical Idealism." In *Cambridge Companion to Modern Jewish Philosophy*, edited by Michael L. Morgan and Peter Eli Gordon, 80–101. Cambridge: Cambridge University Press, 2007.

———. *Yearning for Form and Other Essays on Hermann Cohen's Thought*. Dordrecht, the Netherlands: Springer, 2006.

Schwarzschild, Steven S. *The Tragedy of Optimism: Writings on Hermann Cohen*. Edited by George Y. Kohler. Albany: SUNY Press, 2018.

Seeskin, Kenneth. *Autonomy in Jewish Philosophy*. Cambridge: Cambridge University Press, 2001.

Weiss, Daniel H. *Paradox and the Prophets: Hermann Cohen and the Indirect Communication of Religion*. Oxford: Oxford University Press, 2012.

Wiedebach, Hartwig. "Aesthetics in Religion: Remarks on Hermann Cohen's Theory of Jewish Existence." *Journal of Jewish Thought and Philosophy* 11, no. 1 (2002): 63–73.

———. *The National Element in Hermann Cohen's Philosophy and Religion*. Leiden, the Netherlands: Brill, 2012.

Willey, Thomas C. *Back to Kant: The Revival of Kantianism in German Social and Historical Thought, 1860–1914*. Detroit, MI: Wayne State University Press, 1978.

Zank, Michael. *The Idea of Atonement in the Philosophy of Hermann Cohen*. 2nd ed. Providence, RI: Brown Judaic Studies, 2020.

Index

absolute, the: cognition as establishing foundation of, 261; Hegel's ethics in highest form as, 38; practical and theoretical reason as being, 70
absolute ethics vs. concept of development, 85–86
absolute individual, 253, 262
absolute voluntarism, universal Idealism in pantheism as, 91–92
Academy for the Academic Study of Judaism, 184, 215, 238
action(s): compassion as not sufficient for moral, 114; correlation and attributes of, 254; drive to externalize, 50; God as guarantor of realization of ethical, 101, 141–42; God as motive for human ethical and religious, 252; human being defined by pure will and, 41; problem of intellect as sole determinant of, 16–17; and problem of psychology, 60–61; as realm of jurisprudence, 54–55, 61–62; unity of action, 61, 67, 136–37; and the will, 60
actuality vs. reality, 23
adaptation, 81
Adler, Felix, 42n35
aesthetics and aesthetic feeling: eros vs. agape, 255; and pantheism, 96; and psychology, 49; and relationship of art to religion, 48–49, 95, 218–19, 222–23, 254–58; as trajectory of consciousness, xxiv, 242. *See also* art
Aesthetics of Pure Will (Cohen), 206, 218–19, 222, 233
affect, Platonic will as, 121–22
afterlife, 126–27, 139, 142–43, 158
agape vs. eros, and aesthetics, 255
agnosticism, metaphysics of, 19–20

Ahad Ha'am (Asher Ginsberg), 237
All as being of eternity and morality of the ideal vs. All as nature, 96
Altmann, Alexander, on correlation, 242–62; aesthetics and religion, 254–58; compassion as generating love of God, 255–57; as counterargument to Rosenzweig, xx, 176; cultural consciousness, 242, 246–47, 258–59; ethics and religion, 247–48, 250–54; foundational concepts vs. methodologies, 244–45; logic and religion, 248–50; psychology and religion, 258–62; purpose and correlation, 244, 245–46, 249–50; redemption, 251–52, 256–57; religious yearning, 256–57; on Rosenzweig, 242–43
amor intellectualis, 21
Anaxagoras, 71
anthropological and psychological reductionism, 1, 9–26
anthropomorphizing of God, 89, 139–41, 231
antinomy of society and state, 66
antisemitism, xiv–xv, 194, 200–204, 211, 214, 235–36
appearances, Platonic, xiii, 23–24, 101, 181n7
appetite. *See* will
a priori, philosophy of the, 55–56
Aquinas, Thomas, 84
Arabic-Islamic and Arabic Jewish philosophy of religion, 89
Aristotle, 48, 70, 134, 246
art: defined, 49–50; drive to externalize in, 50; and pantheism, 95–96; reason as generator of, 224; religion's relationship to, 48–49, 95, 218–19, 222–23, 254–58;

death of, xix, 240–41; defense of Judaism in later years, 201–4, 214–15; education in Judaism, 194–95; as experimental thinker, 218–19; at Institute for the Academic Study of Judaism in Berlin, 215–20, 229–41; introduction to his life and thought, xi–xxii; on Kant's theory of knowledge, xiv; legacy of, xix, 182–83; letters to Treitschke, 202; loyalty to Germany during WW I, 234–35; and Maimonides, 209–10, 229; at Marburg University, 188, 199–215, 220–21; opposition to Zionism, xi, xv, xviii, 194, 203, 236–38; philosophical development of, xvi, 187–96; politics of, xviii, 128, 197–99, 200; reconciling religion to Kant's philosophy, xi, xiv, 47n38, 195–96, 199–201, 211–12, 215–36; Rosenzweig's personal reflections, 208, 226–27, 228, 229–30, 234, 237, 239; Russian tour and mission, 215–17; as teacher, 181, 211–12. See also *specific works by title*

Cohen, Martha Lewandowski (wife), xx

community, role in moral and religious thought, 63–64, 172

compassion: employed to render conceptual definition of individual, 258; as generating love of God, 255–57; vs. knowledge as pillar of social world, 114–15; prophets' call for seeing the poor as human beings, 112–14

The Concept of Religion in the System of Philosophy (Cohen), xvi, 220–21, 224, 242–44, 246–47, 248–49, 250–53, 254–57, 258–61

concept (per se) as discovered in the concept of the human being, 6–7. See also *specific concepts by name*

"A Confession on the Jewish Question" (Cohen), 193, 200–206, 211

congregation, as distinct from church, 63–64, 161

conscience, ethics of, 17, 136–37, 161, 246

consciousness: art as expression of pure, 49; autonomy as grounded in as opposed to senses, 181; basis in relationship of ethics to intellect, 34; and concept of law, 27; correlation's impact on, 246–47, 258–59; as encompassing will, 69; ethical self-consciousness, 73–74, 85, 89; as foundation of being, 70–71; and identity, 71; Jewish extension of purified consciousness to all nations, 154–55; power (social and political) as drive of, 50; as precursor to nature, 76–77; psychology of cultural consciousness, 191; pure, 49, 154–55; reality and pure self-consciousness, 73–74; reason as generating contents of, 67n53, 180n6; religion's relationship to, 242, 250–52; social, 110–11; trajectories of, xxiv, 242; unity of, 223, 258, 260

constitutional law: Cohen's ethical and parliamentary socialism, xviii; and ethical culture movement, 42; existentialism and loss of Cohen's ethical vision, xx; and ideal of the wise man, 27; and state as moral actor, 30; and state as unity of totality, 65, 66

correlation: as conceptual and idealistic, 251; defined, 244; as generator of God concept, 254; of individual, plurality, and totality, 6–7, 9–16, 62–63; relation to concept and purpose, 244, 245–46, 249–50; Rosenzweig on, 175–76, 221–36. See also Altmann, Alexander

cosmopolitanism, xv, xviii, 112, 146, 197

creation: ethical meaning of, 84–85; mathematics and logical reason as necessary for, 140, 249; nature as God's, 109; as nature vs. ethics, 248

Crescas, Hasdai, 143, 170

critical Idealism. See transcendental Idealism

Critique of Judgment (Kant), 180

Critique of Practical Reason (Kant), xv, 168–69

ethical knowledge, as promised to all humans by idea of God, 117

ethical personhood, path to supported by state, 73

ethical self-consciousness, 73–74, 85, 89

ethical socialism, xi, xviii, 200

ethics: as the absolute, 38, 70; absolute ethics vs. concept of development, 85–86; applying to suffering, 111; and art, 18–19, 257; and autonomy vs. freedom, 102–3, 140–41, 167–73; and concept of the soul, 10–11; of conscience, 17, 136–37, 161, 246; correlation of individual and totality as true task of, 62–63; creation as nature vs. ethics, 248; as doctrine of the human being, 4–5; emotion as incapable of justifying, 94–95; and eternity, 77–78, 83, 84–85; vs. eudaimonism, 13, 135–37, 207; evil and self-judgment, 87–88; focused on plurality over individual, 63, 65; as form of knowledge, 26, 41, 105; and fundamental law of truth, 79, 82, 83, 84, 87, 99; God's relationship to, 72–100, 101, 141–42, 199, 207, 252; Greek, xvii, 57; as hinged on action rather than belief, 67; human being as object of, 3–4, 5, 9, 19, 44, 45, 82–83; idea and thing-in-itself, 24; and Idealism of consciousness, 76; idealist ethics, 72; ideal of the wise man as found in, 14, 27, 29; identity as problem for, 94; and Jewish prophets, xvii–xviii, 101, 148–49; Judaism as ground for universalistic, 102, 150–66; and jurisprudence, 1, 53–55, 59–67; Kantian, xv, xviii, 23, 57, 137–42, 199; and law, 56, 57, 59, 89; logic's relationship to, 1, 2, 10, 20, 26, 33–34, 38, 39, 55, 61, 69, 72, 79, 83, 133, 219; Maimonides on, 141, 209–10; and meaning of creation, 84–85; Mendelssohn on, 132; metaphysics' relationship to, 15, 16, 95; naturalism's methodological danger for, 12–15; natural science's relationship to, xiii, 33–34, 56–

57, 61, 77–78, 87, 115; nature's relationship to, 13, 69–100; pantheism's relationship to, 91–98; as path to the ideal, 209–10; philosophical status of, 3–4, 8–9; Platonic view of, 3, 10, 17, 101, 105, 106, 108, 115–16, 167; politics and the state, 32, 35, 50, 53–68, 73–75, 128, 208–9; as precondition of history, 34; as precondition of sociology, 37; and psychology, 9–26, 43, 45, 62; and purity, 82–83; rational basis for, 4–5, 18–19, 133–34; reality problem for, 73, 74–75; reason vs. God as origin of, 137–42; religion's relationship to, xv–xvi, xviii, 1, 20, 40–53, 62, 72, 87–91, 102, 128–29, 134–35, 137–42, 148–49, 152, 208–9, 229, 247–48, 250–54; secular threat to, 87; and spirit, 34, 89–90; as trajectory of consciousness, xxiv, 242; and unity of cognition, 82. *See also* action(s); individual; Is and Ought; morality; practical reason; totality; will

Ethics of Judaism (Lazarus), 212–13

Ethics of Pure Will (Cohen), xv, xvi, 1–100; completion of, 206; eternity in, 209; idea of God, 69–100; introduction, 3–68; prefatory note, 1–2

Ethics (Spinoza), 14–15

ethnonationalism, xviii

ethnopsychology, 11–12

eudaimonism vs. ethics, 13, 135–37, 207

evil: as derived from concept of freedom, 88, 160; and freedom, 93; God as responsible for good and evil, 111; prophets on source of, 113; radical evil, 144; retribution and forgiveness in afterlife, 127

evolutionary biology, 85–86

evolutionary socialism, xviii

existentialism, xi, xii, xix, xx, 86, 175–76

experience concept, Kant's, 189–90

facts, power of, 31, 50, 59, 208

faith: afterlife, 126–27, 139, 142–43, 158; vs. ethics, 42, 90–91; vs. Idealism, 225; vs.

faith (*continued*)
  knowledge, 2, 41–42, 90–91, 155–56; and
    thought, 199, 231. *See also* religion
Falk, Adalbert, 200
family, not juridical person, 65
fate, 40, 41, 42, 44
federation of states, as leading to humanity,
  74
Fichte, Johann Gottlieb, 13, 22, 23, 58, 138–39,
  147–48, 186
Formstecher, Salomon, 193–94
foundation laying: cognition as foundation
  of absoluteness, 261; concepts vs.
  methodologies, 224, 244–45; generation
  and origin as criteria, 243; God as
  foundation of morality, 47; grounding
  of foundations, using foundations
  to justify, 70; Idea of the Good as
  foundation of ethics, 167; international
  law as foundation for natural law, 58; vs.
  metaphysics of God-human correlation,
  249; religion as foundation for law,
  58; thought and consciousness, 70–71.
  See also logic
Frankel, Zacharias, 194
freedom of the will: as duty, 172; and ethical
  self-consciousness, 73; and ethics,
  159–61; as grounded in obligation,
  xviii; as idealization of human being,
  172; Kantian, xv, 143–45; in religion, 16,
  143–45, 159, 160–61, 169–71; separating
  from autonomy, 102–3, 140–41, 168–69
Fritzsche, Robert Arnold, 210n78
fundamental law of truth: as guide
  for nature to obtain the ideal, 80;
  as harmony of natural and ethical
  knowledge, 87; idea of God as, 83,
  84, 87–88, 89–90, 96, 99–100, 207; in
  methodological connection between
  ethics and logic, 79, 82, 83, 84, 99

Geiger, Abraham, 193, 197
generation and origin: as criteria for

foundational concepts, 243; judgment of
  origin, 55, 244; logic of origin, 181, 246,
  248, 249; relationship to correlation,
  244, 245, 246, 248, 249
German Idealism, 15n14, 190–92, 224
"Germanism and Judaism" (Cohen), 234–35
German-Jewish synthesis, xi, xv
German Jewry: and antisemitism, xiv–xv,
  194, 200–204, 211, 214, 235–36; Cohen's
  career in midst of emancipation, 193–95;
  division of labor between German
  culture and Jewish prophetic religious
  life, 213–14; and Kant, 130, 147–48;
  rejection of Cohen's accommodations
  in "Confession," 204–5
Gierke, Otto von, 64n48
God: anthropomorphizing of, 89, 139–41,
  231; attributes of, 47–48, 89n22, 140, 163;
  as beyond sense perception, 109–10;
  Christian equating of human being and
  (Jesus), 92; compassion as generating
  love of, 255–57; as content of absolute,
  71; in correlation with human being, 221,
  225, 227, 228, 229, 243–44, 249, 251–53,
  254, 259, 260; equality of all humans
  before, 116–17, 138; eternity of the ideal
  as secured by, 78–79, 87; as ethical
  cognition, 91; ethics' relationship to, 72–
  100, 101, 141–42, 199, 207, 252; as father
  of all human beings, 111–12; freedom of
  pure human being before, 173; and the
  Good, 71, 113, 167; as guaranteeing the
  realization of the ideal, 208; holy spirit
  as human spirit, 230; human being as
  defined in relationship to, 47; and idea,
  110, 258; Idealism and knowledge of, 128;
  as idea of truth vs. mythological person,
  79–80, 89–90, 98, 163; immanence of
  relationship to human being, 171; and
  individual, 14, 221, 222, 252; Kantian view
  of, 137–43, 199, 206; logical character
  of concept, 2, 78; love as service to, 48;
  love of God as love of morality, 155; as

methodological concept, 83–85; as moral foundation, xvi, 46–47, 72–73, 82, 86, 111, 152, 156, 252; as motive for human ethical and religious action(s), 101, 141–42, 252; as natural necessity of causality rather than omniscience, 168; nature's relationship to, 84, 85, 87, 98–99, 109, 140, 225, 248–49; opposed to pessimism and quietism, 86; in pantheism, 92, 97; as person, 47–48, 89–90, 98, 140, 163, 221–22; reality of, 220; reason's relationship to, 46–47, 137–42, 226; as redeemer from sin, 253–54; as responsible for good and evil, 111; Spinoza's, 94–95; spirituality of, 202; and suffering, 113–14; transcendence of, xvi, 47, 71, 100, 101, 141–42, 171, 251; truth's relationship to, 179; uniqueness of Being, 151–53, 248, 251, 260–62; unique relationship to human beings, 110–11; unity as revealed by, 47, 97, 136; as unity of will and intellect, 86–87; yearning of human being for, 257. *See also* idea of God

Goethe, Johann Wolfgang von, 140, 179, 182–83, 186–87

Good, Idea of the. *See* Idea of the Good

Graetz, Heinrich, 193, 195, 203

great chain of being, 83, 85

Greek ethics, xvii, 57

Grotius, Hugo, 58

Groundwork of the Metaphysics of Morals (Kant), xv

guilt and the problem of human suffering, 86, 113

Guttmann, Julius, 132, 243

Halevi, Judah, 229

harmonization of nature and morality, 96–97, 98, 99–100, 136–37

harmony and the idea of God, 83–84, 96, 97

Hegel, Georg Wilhelm Friedrich, xiii, 15, 16, 38, 93, 186, 190, 191, 203, 257

Heidegger, Martin, xx

Heine, Heinrich, 197, 232

Herbart, Johann Friedrich, 14, 96

Hermann, Karl Friedrich, 117

hero cult as basis of polis, 27, 34

Herrmann, Wilhelm, 2

Herz, Marcus, 147

Hirsch, Samson Raphael, 193, 194–95, 197

historical materialism, 32

historiography, and antagonism of material power and ideas, 31

history, 26–35; dialectical movement applied to, 38–39; ethics as precondition of, 28, 34; Kant's social idealist aim for, 146; and morality as necessary, 86; of philosophy, 181–82; vs. philosophy of religion, 130–33, 148–49; as presupposition for purity, 76; of religion, 46, 130–33, 148–49, 219; socialist conception of, 32–33; totality and the state, 31; and transformation of actions into passions and feelings, 54

holy spirit as human spirit, 230, 232

Hugo, Gustav von, 58n46

human being: as all equal under God, 116–17, 138; biology in concept of, 9–10, 35–36, 45; as central to morality, 43, 105, 145–46, 170–71; Cohen's doctrine of human being with God and before God, 222; concept (per se) as discovered in, 6–7; in correlation with God, 225, 227, 228, 229, 243–44, 252–53, 254, 259, 260; defined by pure will and actions, 41; development of, 8, 35, 111; as ethical self-consciousness, 89; freedom before God, 173; God as defined in relationship to, 47; God as father of, 111–12; God as person vs. idea in relationship to, 90; immanence of God's relationship to, 171; Judaism's idealization of, 172–73; as knowing subject, 39; logic and ethics together as provision for purity of, 82–83; as mathematical construction, 15; as member of humanity and the state, 208; moral weakness and relationship

human being (continued)
to God, 111; naturalism's loss of concept, 15–16; as object of ethics, 3–5, 9, 19, 44, 45, 82–83; pantheism's error in concept of, 16, 92–93; Plato's lack of an Idea for, 113; Plato's lack of unity perspective on, 119–20; as presupposition covering entire field of inquiry, 59; and psychology, 17, 20–21; as purpose of the world, 145; reason as agent of agreement and reconciliation with God, 46–47; Socrates on concept of, 3–4, 5, 7; and suffering, 111, 252; uniqueness of God's relationship to, 110–11; will of human being vs. will of nature, 19; yearning for God, 257. *See also* plurality; totality; individual

humanity: as central to unity, 180; as ethical idea, 68; future unification of, 126; as generated entity, 224–25; human being as member of, 208; religious failure as moral path of, 53; Son of God as idea of, 140. *See also* culture and civilization; totality

hypothesis, 70, 107, 244

Idea, the: love for idea, and love for God, 258; monotheism of, 139; Platonic, 23, 106, 107–8; as power of nature, 39; vs. representation, 23; and thing-in-itself, 23–25

Ideal, the: All as being of eternity and morality of, 96; development as goal of, 208; ethics as path to, 209–10; fundamental law of truth and, 80; idea of God as guarantor of, 87, 88; individual as, 27–29; as undetermined by sensation, space, and time, 74. *See also* eternity of the Ideal; totality

Idealism, philosophical: Cassirer on Cohen's, 179, 183; Classical Greek, 14; of consciousness vs. pure generative thought, 76; correlation's relationship to, 224–25, 242; dreaming Idealism, 79, 82; vs. faith, 225; German Idealism, 15n14, 190–92, 224; and idea of God as truth, 87–88; integrating religion into Cohen's, 2, 246–47, 251, 257–58, 260, 262; Kant and Christianity, 131; and knowledge of God, 128; logic of as encompassing logic and ethics, 69n1; vs. materialism, xiii, 1, 12–13, 34; vs. metaphysics, 69; pantheism and universal Idealism, 91–92; and pure will of historical being, 68; and religion's role in morality, 108

idealization's value for all religions, 150

ideal of the wise man, ethics as found in, 14, 27, 29

idea of God, 69–100; Cassirer on Cohen's interpretation, 179–80; Cohen's reclamation for modern philosophy, xvi; vs. correlation in God's relationship to nature, 248; in correlation with idea of the human being, 221–22, 249, 261; and eternity of the ideal, 83; ethics value of, xvi, 72–100, 101, 117, 141–42; as fundamental law of truth, 83, 84, 87–90, 96, 99–100, 207; harmony and, 83–84, 96, 97; as Kant's and Jewish interpretation, 139; Maimonides on, 209; and messianic idea, 88, 164; as more than methodology, 84; pantheism as threat to, 16, 153; Platonic, 71; in religious philosophy, 89–90; Rosenzweig on Cohen's, 192, 206–7; as within scope of morality, 86; as truth and pure will, 91; as victory of the good, 2, 88

idea of humanity, Son of God as, 140

Idea of the Good: as foundation of ethics, 167; God's role in, 71, 113, 167; reason as necessary for understanding of, 116; Spinoza on, 94; transcendence as originating in, 108; unity of soul as requirement for, 122; validity of Being as guaranteeing, 24

idea of truth, God as, 79–80, 89–90, 98, 163

identity, philosophy of, 16, 39, 71, 72, 93, 94, 96–97, 260

immanence, 98, 171, 191, 245

immortality, 75, 120–21, 142–43, 158, 209, 233–34

"In Defense" ("Zur Verteidigung") (Cohen), 210–11

individual: absolute, 253, 262; biology as prior to social individual, 35–36; as Christian focus, 14, 27–29, 40; classical Greek philosophy's focus on, 14; Cohen's challenge to academic ethics, 220; compassion in conceptual definition, 258; in concept of the human being, 7, 12, 250; in correlation of human being to God, 221; correlation with plurality and totality, 6–7, 9–16, 62–63; as counterpoint to pantheism, 232; as enduring within plurality, 8; ethics' relationship to, 34n27, 46, 53; and freedom of will, 172; and God, 14, 221, 222, 252; and the ideal, 27–28; lack of recognition by Plato, 121; and mythology's conflict with ethics, 40; psychological perspective, 9–16, 43; redemption as focused on, 259, 260; religion's origin in consciousness of sin, 250–52, 253; representing ethics in, 26–35; in sociological methodology, 37; soul as extension of self, 10; unity of moral, 65

infinitesimal calculus, 205

innate, the, 45, 70

intellect: consciousness in relationship of ethics to, 34; and Platonic Idea, 107; as restricted to phenomena, 18; as sole determinant of action, 16–17; vs. will, 18, 20, 21–22, 25–26, 60. See also thought; will and intellect

intention vs. will, 60

"Internal Connections of Kantian Philosophy to Judaism" (Cohen), 102, 130–49

international law, as foundation for natural law, 58

intuited presentiment, 106–8, 115

Is and Ought: as basis for the value of Idea, 23; content of Being in relations to what is, 12–14, 22, 24–25, 33; importance of difference between, 16, 39, 40–41; law of the human being as residing in what Ought to be, 15; and logic as determiner of truth-value, 22; as moving beyond the reductionism of psychology, 21; pantheism's lack of distinction between, 16, 39; and role of ethics in reason, 20; subjectivity issue, 68

Israelite prophets, 46. See also Jewish prophets

I-Thou relation, and correlation, 253

Jacoby, Johann, 197

Jerusalem (Mendelssohn), 132

Jesus Christ, 27–29, 92, 153, 165, 166, 229

Jewish prophets: avoidance of mysticism by, 110; in Cohen's rejection of Zionism, 237; Cohen's religious adoption of, 101, 227–28; on development vs. Plato, 124–25; idea of human being as central to morality, 146; internal correspondence with Kant, 148; and messianic idea, 161–63; morality as condition of social ideal, 105, 109–14, 116–17, 118, 122–24, 125–26, 127–28; nature of truth for, 109; political role of, 131–32; Protestantism's relationship to, 148–49, 159, 228; against sacrifice, 153–54; social idealism of, xvii–xviii, 110, 146–47; on the state, 123–25; on war and warriors, 118–19

Jews. See German Jewry

Joachim of Fiore, 29n25

Job, Book of, 113, 142

Judah Halevi, 142

Judaism: atonement as universal, 153–55; challenge to the idea of God vs. God of religion, xvi; Cohen's dedication to, xvii, 201–4, 214–15; Cohen's integration into philosophy, 206, 212–13; faith and

Judaism *(continued)*

knowledge, 155–56; focus on morality and human being, 170–71; focus on world that is and not world beyond, 158–59, 161–62; as forerunner of modern rationalism, 102; freedom and morality, 159–61, 169; as ground for universalistic ethics and politics, 102, 150–66; idealization of human being in, 172–73; and Kantian philosophy, xviii, 102–3, 130–49, 167–73, 230; law vs. doctrine in, 155–57; liberal, 204, 216; Mendelssohn on, 131; monotheism vs. Christianity, 252; moral idealism of, 151–53, 154, 155–56, 159–61, 164–65; myth vs. religion, 163; as natural religion, 131; pantheism, as threat to idea of God, 153; peace as social ideal, 146–47; as preserver of culture and civilization, 151, 157, 209; progress in, 150–51, 165–66; purity in, 239; reason as basis for ethics in, 133–34; ritual law in, 132, 134–35, 156–58, 227–28; ritual worship in, 49, 170–71; Sabbath, 102, 146, 156–57, 159, 197, 198–99, 226; sacrifice as religious institution in, 153–54, 173; salvation in, 154; socialism as legacy of, 197; Spinoza on, 130–31; unique Being of the one God, 151–53, 248, 251, 260–62; unity of the heart in, 136–37, 240.

See also *entries beginning with* messiah

judgment of origin, 55, 244

juridical (moral) person, 65

jurisprudence: actions as realm of, 54–55, 61–62; and ethics, 1, 53–55, 59–67; as ground for unity of juridical person, 68; historical school of, 58–59; as methodological analogy, 1, 53–55; as theory of the state, 60

justification by faith, 155

Kant, Immanuel: Cohen on his judgment on Judaism, 102, 130–49, 230; vs. Cohen on "pure" cognition, 190–91;

Cohen's adoption of God of ethics from, 199; concept of experience, 189–90; cosmopolitanism of, xviii, 146; dreaming Idealism, 79, 82; ethics and Enlightenment rational religion, xv; on freedom and causality, 168–69; on God, 138, 206; on Idea as limited to practical reason, 23; impersonal nature of theology, 139; on Judaism, xviii, 131–32; on natural law, 58; on primacy of practical reason, 21; rehabilitation of teleology, 246; relationship to his Jewish students, 130, 147–48; role in German philosophical dominance of 19th century, 187; role in revival of Protestantism, 20; social idealist aim for history, 146; vs. Spinoza, 15; as teacher (Rosenzweig's view), 187; on Trinity, 140; on what Is and what Ought to be, 12–14

Kant and the Epigones (Liebmann), xiii

Kantian philosophy: and Christianity, 131, 133, 144; Cohen's reconciliation of religion to, xi, xiv, 195–96, 199–201, 211–12, 215–36; ethics of, xv, xviii, 23, 57, 137–42, 199; eudaimonism, opposition to, 135–37; freedom of the will, xv, 143–45; on God, 137–43, 199, 206; history vs. philosophy of religion, 130–33, 148–49; Idea and thing-in-itself, 23–25; and Judaism, xviii, 102–3, 143–45, 147–48, 167–73, 230; messianism and social idealism, 146–47; origin of moral reason vs. Judaism, 137–38; reason and revelation, 133–35; and Spinoza, 130–31; as system of culture, 190; theory of knowledge, xiv; what Is and what Ought to be, 21; will and universal law, 137–38

Kant's Grounding of Ethics (Cohen), xv, 180

Kant's Theory of Experience (Cohen), xii–xiii, xiii, 189

Kaufmann, David, 102

Keller, Gottfried, 219–20

Kimchi, David, 195

knowledge: art's relationship to, 18–19; as cognition, 42; deriving solely from consciousness, 180n6; drive or desire's relationship to, 169; ethics as form of, 26, 41, 105; of ethics as promised to all human beings by idea of God, 117; facts of nature as objects of, 50; vs. faith, 2, 41–42, 90–91, 155–56; fundamental law of truth as harmony of natural and ethical knowledge, 87; of God through Idealism, 128; as grounded in fundamental principles, 133; vs. Idea, 23; Kantian theory of, xiv; vs. moral ideas, 32; religion as a kind of, 44, 51, 109–10; scientific-systematic pursuit of, 105–10, 113, 114–16, 117–25, 126–27, 128–29; transcendental Idealism as key to validity of, xiii; virtue as, 16, 42, 168. *See also* cognition

Lange, Friedrich Albert, xii–xiii, 188, 199–200
law: action as expression of, 60; and consciousness, 27; divine, 58; vs. doctrine in Judaism, 155–57; and ethics, 56, 57, 59, 89; historical perspective, 57–58; international law as foundation for natural law, 58; Jewish ritual law, 132, 134–35, 156–58, 227–28; as methodology to seek totality of multiple states, 51; natural law, 23–24, 57–59, 80–82, 95; positive law and positive state, 57, 73–75; power of, 27; as presupposing unity of action, 61; as reflecting necessarily true claims about the world, xiii; ritual law in Judaism, 132, 134–35, 156–58, 227–28; and science, 26–27; unity of legal object, 61; and the will, 16–17, 60, 137–38. *See also* constitutional law; jurisprudence
Lazarus, Moritz, 103, 193, 203, 212–13
legal associations, as path from plurality to totality, 64–65
legal person, 64n48

Leibniz, Gottfried Wilhelm, 16, 28, 83, 85, 95
Lessing, Gotthold Ephraim, 28, 74, 239
liberal Judaism, 204, 216
logic: and the absolute, 70; as basis of nature itself, 83; as characteristic of correlation, 244; as determiner of truth-value, 22; ethical implication of perception leading to, 10; and ethics as only preconditions of pure feeling, 219; ethics' relationship to, 1, 2, 10, 20, 26, 33–34, 38, 39, 55, 61, 69, 72, 79, 83, 133, 219; God as logical concept, 2, 78; Idealist, 69n1, 72; mathematics' relationship to, 55, 56, 79; as necessary for creation, 140, 249; as not in itself ethics, 33; and psychology, 10; religion's relationship to, 248–50, 258; role in purity, 82–83; as trajectory of consciousness, xxiv, 242; and unity, 61
Logic (Kant), 23, 55, 80–81
logic of origin, 181, 246, 248, 249
Logic of Pure Cognition (Cohen), 1, 6, 23, 55, 80–81, 209, 244–46
Logos, 107, 133, 230, 231
love, aesthetic vs. religious concepts of, 255
love and justice as attributes of God, 47.
    See also correlation
"Love and Justice in the Concepts of God and Man" (Cohen), 212
love and knowledge, xvii, 109–10
love for idea, and love for God, 258

Maimon, Salomon, 147, 148, 229
Maimonides, Moses, xvii, 47n39, 89, 139–40, 141, 145, 170, 209–10, 229
Malebranche, Nicolas, 11n8, 28
Manichaeism, 88
Marburg Home for Students and Apprentices, 211
Marburg University, 188, 199–215, 220–21
Marx, Karl, 32n26, 197
material causation, 81
materialism: historical, 32; vs. idealism, xiii, 1, 12–13, 34

mathematical constructions, human beings as, 15

mathematical Ideas, as concealed behind appearance, 24

mathematical vs. moral certainty, 82

mathematics: jurisprudence as corollary method for ethics, 55; logic's relationship to, 55, 56, 79; as necessary for creation, 140, 249

Mendelssohn, Moses, xii, 131–32

messianic idea, 88, 161–65, 172, 202, 208n73

messianic socialism, 197, 198–99

messianism, 112, 113, 126, 146–47, 149, 210, 233, 238

metaphysics: Cohen's exclusion from concept of correlation, 250; and consequence of denying logic's role as determiner of truth-value, 22; and development, 38–39; dreaming metaphysics, 85; entrusting of truth-value to will, 25; ethics' relationship to, 15, 16, 95; and God as unique being, 262; grounding all problems of reason in identity of consciousness and being, 71; and human as absolute individual, 262; vs. Idealism, 69; and Idealist form of pantheism, 92; monotheism of, 71; and moral Being, 25; mythology and mythological religion, 40–53; and naturalism, 69; psychology as subservient to, 18–20; and speculation on time before or after nature, 80; Spinoza's, 15, 94; and spiritualism, 69–70; transcendence as challenge to, 71–72

methodological concepts: connection between logic and ethics, 79, 82, 83, 84, 99; experiment in ethics, 56–57; vs. foundation laying, 224, 244–45; fundamental law of truth in connection between ethics and logic, 79, 82, 83, 84, 99; and idea of God, 83–85; individual in sociological methodology, 37;

jurisprudence's relationship to ethics, 1, 53–55; law's role in seeking totality of multiple states, 51; naturalism's danger for ethics, 12–15; pantheism's underlying defects, 140–42; psychology's lack of criterion for concept of human being, 17; pure cognition to derive knowledge from consciousness, 180n6; thing-in-itself as, xiv, 2, 24

milieu theory (in social ethics), 171n13

militaristic principles in Plato's ideal state, 122–25

modus (in Spinoza), 94

Mommsen, Theodor, 201

monotheism: Cohen's profession of, 202; and correlation between human being and God, 221, 227, 229; of the idea, 139; Judaism vs. Christianity on, 252; of metaphysics, 71; vs. pantheism, 198; vs. polytheism, 111–12, 158, 180, 221; unique Being of the one God, 151–53, 248, 251, 260–62. See also idea of God

moral Being, 25, 66, 67, 85, 89n22

moral community, 63–64, 172

moral idealism, Judaism as tending towards, 151–53, 154, 155–56, 159–61, 164–65

moral ideas, distinguished from theoretical concepts, 34

morality: as based in autonomous self-legislation, xv, 103; Christian contribution to moral autonomy, 202–3, 229; Christian vs. Jewish focus on life vs. afterlife, 158; cognition as agreement of nature and morality in fundamental law of truth, 82, 83, 84; as condition of social ideal, 101, 105, 109–14, 116–17, 118, 122–24, 125–26, 127–28; created world as necessary for realization of, 248; culture and civilization as requiring moral ideal, 45–46, 86; in eternity of the Ideal, 78–79, 82–83, 85, 87; God as foundation of, xvi, 46–47, 72–73, 82, 86, 111, 152,

156, 252; harmonization of nature and, 96–97, 98, 99–100, 136–37; human being as central to, 43, 105, 145–46, 170–71; human being's moral weakness and relationship to God, 111; idea of God as within scope of, xvi, 82, 86; individual, plurality and totality as stages of moral involvement, xxv; as inhering in legality, 56; Jewish prophets as architects of political morality, 146; Kantian origin of moral reason vs. Judaism, 137–38; Kant's creative, 13; knowledge vs. moral ideas, 32; pantheism vs. moral freedom, 145; power relations and moral ideas, 31–32, 33; preservation of nature for carrying out moral life, 81–84; psychology's narrowing of, 20; and reason as foundation of religion, 135, 262; religion's relationship to, 47, 53, 150–51, 166, 168; as self-evident, prejudice of, 43; social and economic milieu as determinant of individual moral character, 34n27; state as context for, 30, 43–44, 53, 93–94; unity of moral individual, 65

moral reason, Kant vs. Judaism on origin of, 137–38

music vs. philosophy, 18–19

mutual relation between human being and God. *See* correlation

mysticism: Cohen's critique of, 84, 142, 152, 153, 220, 257–58; death and afterlife, 111, 142–43; and problem of suffering, 111; prophets' avoidance of, 110; and rejection of evil, 88n21

mythology and mythological religion: and ethical culture movement, 42–44; ethics as independent of, 40–41, 72, 152; faith vs. knowledge, 41–42; fate as problem for ethics, 40–41, 44; God as idea of truth vs. mythological person, 79–80, 89–90, 98, 163; and moral Being as illusion, 25; pantheism's relationship to, 97; Plato's critique of, 127; power of evil as myth,

88; as problem for value of religion, 163; relationship of ethics to religion, 45–48; and religion's entanglement in art, 48–50. *See also* religion

nationality, 236

Natorp, Paul, 214, 220, 259

naturalism: biological reductionism as source for morality, 80–82; Cohen's critique of, 1; of dialectical development, 39; and eternity challenge to ethics, 77–78; ideal of the wise man, 27; individual focus of history, 27; and loss of concept of the human being, 15–16; and metaphysics, 69; methodological danger for ethics from, 12–15; and pantheism, 39, 97; and psychology, 12; Spinoza's, 94

natural law, 23–24, 57–59, 80–82, 95

natural religion, Judaism as, 131

natural sciences, relationship to ethics, xiii, 33–34, 56–57, 61, 77–78, 87, 115

nature: All as, 96; consciousness as precursor to, 76–77; as creation, 109, 248; in eternity of the Ideal, 78–79, 87; ethics' relationship to, 13, 69–100; facts of nature as objects of knowledge, 50; as generated entity, 224–25, 227; God's relationship to, 84, 85, 87, 98–99, 109, 140, 225, 248–49; harmonization with morality, 96–97, 98, 99–100, 136–37; Idea as power of, 39; logic as basis of, 83; preservation of nature for carrying out moral life, 81–84; as right, 27; transcendence in independent content vs. in nature, 97–99; truth's relationship to, 82, 83, 84; will of human being vs. will of nature, 19. *See also* pantheism

neo-Kantian philosophy, xi–xii; Cohen as leading exponent of, xii–xiii, 188–89; existentialism's challenge to, xx; and rise of natural science, xiii. *See also* Cohen, Hermann

Nicholas of Cusa, 84, 89, 140, 222
Nobel, Nehemiah Anton, 237
Noeldeke, Theodor, 212
nonfoundation of being, 70
nonmediate, Aristotelian, 70
nous (mind), 71

obligation: and religion, xviii, 132; and will, 1, 60, 61
On Eternal Peace (Kant), 146
Origen, 168
original sin, 144–45, 160
origin and generation. *See* generation and origin
Orphic theology, 114, 126
Ought and Is. *See* Is and Ought
overman (Übermensch), 25, 34

pantheism: Cassirer on, 180; Cohen's challenge to, 2, 15–16, 39, 192, 232; and correlation, 256; as lacking unity of consciousness, 260; vs. moral freedom, 145; Rosenzweig on Cohen's understanding of, 198; as threat to idea of God, 153; underlying methodological defects, 140–42
Parmenides, 106
particularity: community as congregation and, 63–64; culture and civilization as, 66; individual and wise man ideal, 27; as inherent in the concept of religion, 51; and the state, 30, 51; vs. totality, 59
partnerships, and problem of unified legal subject, 62
Paulinism, 132, 134
peace: as Jewish social ideal, 146–47; as progress in ethical concept of the state, 74
people, concept of: family vs. juridical person, 65; individual's relationship to, 30; as plurality rather than unity, 66
perception. *See* sense perception
pessimism, existential, 86

Philippson, Ludwig, 213
Philo, 230–31
philosophy: cognition as, 42; Cohen on importance of history of, 181; culture and civilization as counter to, 42–43; ethics as center of, 3–4, 20; vs. music, 18–19; of the a priori, 55–56; psychology's dependent role in, 223–24; reliance upon scientific knowledge, 55; Rosenzweig on Germany's 19th-century dominance of, 185–87. *See also* Kantian philosophy; neo-Kantian philosophy; Plato and Platonism
philosophy of race, 63
philosophy of religion: Cohen's development of his, 212–13, 217–18, 220; correlation in, 242–62; and German Jewry, 193–94; vs. history, 130–33, 148–49; idea of God in, 89–90; Kant's Christian, 131, 133, 144
physiology: biological reductionism, 80–82; in concept of human being, 9–10, 35–36, 45. *See also* naturalism; psychology
pious, equating the poor with the, 113–14
Plato and Platonism: appearances, xiii, 23–24, 101, 181n7; concept of the absolute, 70; ethical perspective, 3, 10, 17, 101, 105, 106, 108, 115–16, 167; Idea, 23, 106, 107–8; idealism of, 14, 189; and idea of God, 71; Idea of the Good, 24, 48, 71, 113, 116, 167; limitations on understanding the human being, 113, 119–20; purity, 26; role in Wissenschaft, xvii–xviii; scientific-systematic pursuit of knowledge as condition of social ideal, xvii, 105–8, 110, 113, 114–16, 117–25, 126–27, 128–29; on the soul, 10, 11, 120–21; on soul of the state, 7–8, 65–66, 120–21, 122; unity as unification (*henosis*), 96; on what Is and what Ought to be, 14, 23; will as child of ethics, 17. *See also* Socrates
pleasure principle, Kantian and Jewish repudiation of, 136
Plotinus, 95, 168

plurality, xxv–xxvi; and concept of the human being, 5–6; in correlation between human being and God, 6–7, 9–16, 62–63, 253; as enduring within totality, 8; ethics as focused on plurality over individual, 63, 65; individual as member of, 9; legal associations as path from plurality to totality, 64–65; moral community, 63–64, 172; part of self-evident morality controlled by culture, 43; as stage of moral development, xxv, 1; unity's relationship to, 5–6, 66

polis, Plato's, 118

politics: Cohen's, xviii, 128, 197–99, 200, 201–4; ethics' relationship to, 32, 35, 50, 53–68, 128, 209; Jewish prophets as architects of political morality, 146; Judaism as ground for universalistic, 102, 150–66; Kant on Judaism as statutory laws, 131–32; and Plato's social ideal, 117–20, 122–25; religion and, 50–51. *See also* constitutional law; state, the

polytheism vs. monotheism, 111–12, 158, 180, 221

positive law and positive state, 57, 73–75

positivism, 75

potencies (Schelling), 38

power relations and moral ideas, 31–32, 33

power (social or political), as drive of human consciousness, 50

practical Christianity, 158–59

practical reason, xv, 1, 21, 23, 41, 141, 168–69. *See also* ethics

prayer, 136, 257

predicates of God, 140

preservation of nature for moral life, 81–84

progress: eternity of the ideal as moral progress, 85; Judaism's role in, 150–51, 165–66; messianic idea and, 163; natural sciences as alone in generating, 87; peace as progress for state, 74

prophetism, 46–47, 109. *See also* Jewish prophets

Protestantism: Kant's role in revival of, 20; Reformation, 155, 158, 202–3; renewed respect for Jewish prophets, 159, 228; Rosenzweig on Jews as Protestants, 203; value of ethical teaching from prophets for, 149

providence, 86

Psalms, Book of, 233–34, 256

psychology: and actions, 60–61; and aesthetics, 49; Altmann on correlation and, 258–62; and concept of the human being, 17, 20, 21; of cultural consciousness, 191, 223; dependent role in philosophy, 223–24; and drive to act externally, 50; and ethics, 9–26, 43, 45, 62; on the individual, 9–16; vs. logic as component of religion, 258; Plato as founder of, 10; as precondition of ethics, 1, 9–26; as subservient to metaphysics, 18–20; and unity of cultural consciousness, 223; will and thought, 16–26

pure cognition, 82, 84, 180n6, 190–91. *See also* logic of pure cognition

pure consciousness, 49, 154–55

pure feeling, 219

pure will, 41, 67–68, 73, 74, 75–76, 136, 178

purity: with both logic and ethics, 82–83; before God as freedom of human being, 173; nature and history as presuppositions for, 76; Platonic, 26; of soul vs. original sin, 144–45, 160; sources in Judaism, 239

purpose, and correlation, 244, 245–46, 249–50

Pythagoras, 83, 106

race, problem of, 63, 203–4

radical evil, 144

rationalism, xix, 69–70, 89, 102. *See also* reason

reality: vs. actuality, 23; of God, 220;

on German dominance of philosophy and literary arts, 185–87

Rousseauian philosophy, 13

Saadia ben Joseph Al-Fayyumi (Saadia Gaon), 133, 134, 139, 140, 145

Sabbath, 102, 146, 156–57, 159, 197, 198–99, 226

sacrifice, religious institution of, 153–54, 173

salvation, Jewish, 154

Savigny, Friedrich Carl von, 58n46

Schelling, Friedrich Wilhelm Joseph von, 15, 16, 38, 93, 96, 186

Schiller, Friedrich, 180, 186, 214

Schleiermacher, Friedrich, 2, 15, 16, 256

Scholasticism, 21. 170, 84, 140

Scholem, Gershom, xvii, 88n21

Schopenhauer, Arthur, 18, 83, 86, 187, 188

science and scientific knowledge: art's relationship to, 18–19; concept of development in, 36–37; ethics' relationship to, xiii, 33–34, 56–57, 61, 77–78, 87, 115; facts about real world, xiii, 70; and law, 26–27; of legislation, 59; philosophy's reliance upon, 55; Plato's scientific cognition, 105–8; pursuit of, 105–10, 113, 114–16, 117–25, 126–27, 128–29; role in generating progress, 87

scientific method, 107

self-consciousness, ethical, 73–74, 85, 89

self-determination, God as person as threat to, 90

self-idealization through freedom, 172

self-perfection, ideal of, 88, 90, 145, 170

sense perception: autonomy as grounded in consciousness rather than, 181; and consciousness, 69; God as beyond, 109–10; as leading to logic being implied by ethics, 10; vs. pure reason, 133; pure thought in opposition to, 76; and sovereignty of reason, 135–37

"The Significance of Judaism for the Progress of Religion" (Cohen), 102, 150–66

sin, 111, 154, 161, 228

skepticism vs. compassion, 112

slavery, Plato vs. prophets on, 125–26

social and economic milieu, and individual moral character, 34n27

social consciousness, 110, 111

social idea and reformation of states, 64

"The Social Ideal in Plato and the Prophets" (Cohen), 101–29

social idealism: Christian return to social ideal, 158–59; Jewish prophets and morality as condition of social ideal, 101, 105, 109–14, 116–17, 118, 122–24, 125–26, 127–28; and messianism, 146–47; Pentateuch as foundational text for, 146; Plato and scientific-systematic pursuit of knowledge as condition of social ideal, xvii, 101, 105–8, 110, 113, 114–16, 117–25, 126–27, 128–29; social classes, 118–20

social institutions, evolution of, 35–36

socialism, xviii, 32–33, 112, 197, 198

society: cosmopolitanism, xv, xviii, 112, 146, 197; as moral educator, 64, 66; spiritual vs. secular forms for, 52. See also culture and civilization

Society for Ethical Culture, 42n35

Society for the Advancement of the Academic Study of Judaism, 211

sociology, 1, 35–39, 43. See also culture and civilization

sociology of religion, 212

Socrates: on concept of human being, 5, 7; on ethics as the doctrine of human being, 3–4; as originator of the Idea, 106; on purpose, 245–46; on virtue as knowledge, 16, 42

Sophism, 42, 43, 57

soul, human: in domain of totality, 8, 122; as extension of individual self, 10; Plato on, 10, 11; purity of, 144–45, 160; Rosenzweig on Cohen's advocacy for, 192; and yearning for God, 257

soul of the state, 7–8, 65–66, 120–21, 122

sovereignty of reason, 135–36

space and time, epistemological roles of, xiii, 74, 80, 123–24, 209

Spinoza, Benedict de, xvii, 11n8, 14–16, 94–95, 96–97, 130–31, 140, 169–70, 232–33

spirit: compassion as surrogate for, 112; and ethics, 34, 89–90; holy spirit as human spirit, 230, 232

spiritualism and metaphysics, 69–70

spirituality. See God; religion

spiritual peculiarity, ethics problem as emerging from, 80

Stadler, August, 205n68

The Star of Redemption (Rosenzweig), 175

state, the: vs. church, 52–53, 208–9; ethics' relationship to, 32, 35, 50, 53–68, 73–75, 128, 208–9; and humanity, 68, 74, 208; and law, 51, 57, 73–75; militaristic principles in Plato's ideal state, 122–25; as moral actor, 30; morality as residing in, 43–44, 53, 93–94; nationality, 236; Plato vs. prophets on, 118–20, 123–25; and reality, 73–74; soul of, 7–8, 65–66, 120–21, 122; as totality, 51, 65, 66, 67, 208; as work of art, 50

state of the ideal, appearance in reality, 74

Steinheim, Ludwig, 193, 205n62

Steinthal, Heymann, 195

Stöcker, Adolf, 201

Stoicism, 14–15, 27, 29, 57, 94

Strauss, Leo, xiv–xv, xx

sublation of object into philosophical idea, Cohen's avoidance of, 207

substance and identity, 97

suffering: in Cohen's focus later work, 222; and compassion, 112–14; guilt and problem of, 86, 113; human being and, 111, 252; Jewish historic suffering as leading to religious progress, 165; Messiah as representative of, 113; need for knowledge to address, 114–15

synthetic principle, 23

systematic pursuit of knowledge: as

condition of Platonic social ideal, xvii, 101, 105–8, 110, 113, 114–16, 117–25, 126–27, 128–29; conflict with religion as not permitted, 259; defined, xxiii

teleology: in Darwinism, 80–81; and natural law, 95; rehabilitation by Kant for ethics, 246; and unity of human race, 68. *See also* correlation

telos (end-in-itself), 145–46

theocracy, 52, 102, 130–31, 157–58

theodicy, 87, 252

Theological-Political Treatise (Spinoza), 232–33

theology and ethics, 4, 20, 73, 139

theoretical and practical reason, distinction between. *See* Is and Ought

theoretical knowledge. *See* knowledge

thing-in-itself, xiii–xiv, 2, 18, 19, 23–25

thinker within the soul, 219

thought. *See* will and intellect

"Thoughts on Reading for Youth" (Cohen), 229

Tillich, Paul, 261

time, epistemological role of, 74, 80, 123–24, 209

Tönnies, Ferdinand, 64n48

totality: church vs. state in ethics based on, 53; correlation of individual, plurality, and totality, xxv–xxvi, 6–7, 9–16, 62–63; as goal of classical Greek idealism, 14; as highest form of unity, 65; history and the state, 31; importance of applying ethics in, 43; individual as individual in, 250; and juridical persons, 65; legal associations, as path from plurality to totality, 64–65; as necessary to build concept of human being, 8; vs. particularity, 59; people as, 30; Plato as working against, 127–28; plurality within, 8; pure feeling and love for humanity, 219; soul as articulated in, 8, 122; soul as lying in domain of, 8, 122; as stage of moral involvement, xxv, 1; state as, 51,

65, 66, 67, 208; unity of humanity from messianic idea, 162–63. *See also* unity

tragedy, and Greek perspective on suffering, 111

transcendence: as challenge for metaphysics, 71–72; cognition as foundation of, 261; of God, xvi, 47, 71, 100, 101, 141–42, 171, 251; in independent content vs. nature, 97–99; as originating in Idea of the Good, 108

transcendental Idealism: anthropocentricity of Kant's, xiii; Cohen's application to ethics, xv, xvii, 181; and dreaming idealism, 79–80n12; and Plato and Platonism, 189; validity of knowledge through, xiii

Treatise on Perpetual Peace (Kant). See *On Eternal Peace* (Kant)

Treitschke, Heinrich von, xiv, 192n15, 193, 201–2, 203–4

Trinity, Kant on, 140

Troeltsch, Ernst, 231

truth: God as idea of, 79–80, 89–90, 98, 163; God's relationship to, 179; idea of God as, 87–88, 91; for Jewish prophets, 109; and logic, 22, 80; nature's relationship to, 82, 83, 84. *See also* fundamental law of truth

truth-value, will vs. intellect, 21–22, 25

"Two Proposals for Securing our Future" (Cohen), 211, 238

unified humanity in future, as goal of prophets, 126

unique Being of the one God, 151–53, 248, 251, 260–62

unity, xxv–xxvi; of action, 61, 67, 136–37; as completion and beginning in cycle, 9; of consciousness, 223, 258, 260; and freedom of will, 172; God's role in revealing, 47, 136; of the heart in Judaism, 136–37, 240; of the human being, 8, 53, 66, 67, 191; humanity as central to, 180;

of individual morality, 65; of legal object, 61; of legal subject, 61, 62, 64–65; in natural vs. ethical cognition, 82; of the people as idea of political morality, 30; plurality's relationship to, 5–6, 66; and psychology, 12, 61; reason as necessary for, 116, 189–90; in society, 36; of soul, 122; of the state, 65, 66, 73; and totality, 65, 162–63; truth as unity of the different, 82–83; of will and intellect, 86–87, 137, 178–79

universal Idealism, and pantheism, 91–92

universalism, xviii, 51

universalistic ethics and politics, 102, 150–66

universal law, Kantian philosophy, 137–38

University of Jena, 185, 186–87

unwritten laws, 57

virtue, knowledge as, 16, 42, 168

Völkerpsychologie (folk psychology), xii

war and warriors, Plato vs. prophets on, 118–19

Weisse, Christian Hermann, 93

what Is and what Ought to be. *See* Is and Ought

will: autonomy of, 18–20, 180; consciousness as encompassing, 69; and desire, 25, 169; ethics as determiner of, 25, 26; of human being vs. nature, 19; vs. intellect, 18, 20, 21–22, 25–26, 60; vs. intention, 60; and the law, 16–17, 60, 137–38; as motive of pantheism, 91–92; and obligation, 1, 60, 61; Platonic will as affect, 121–22; pure will, 41, 67–68, 73, 74, 75–76, 136, 178; as realized in time, 209; of the state, 67; and truth-value, 21–22, 25; as will of freedom to act morally or not, 160. *See also* freedom of the will

will and intellect: in Christianity, 16, 84; ethics' relationship to, 33–34, 41; in Jewish worship, 170–71; knowledge and

will and intellect *(continued)*
 drive or desire, 169; material power
 relations and ideas, 31; and psychology,
 16–26; search for ground of being
 independent of, 70; Spinoza vs. Cohen,
 94–95; unity of, 86–87, 137, 178–79; will
 not reducible to intellect, 60
willing, as guarantor of morality, 86–97
Wissenschaft. *See* systematic pursuit of
 knowledge
"Witch's Multiplication Table" (Goethe's
 Faust), 18

World Congress for Religious Progress
 (Cohen's essay), 102, 150–66
world that is and not world beyond, 158–59,
 161–62
Wundt, Wilhelm, 11n9

yearning, spiritual, 256–57, 258
Yohanan ben Zakkai, 154

Zionism, xi, xv, xviii, 194, 203, 236–38
Zoroastrianism, 88
Zunz, Leopold, 148, 193, 195–96